THE RESPONSIBILITY TO PROTECT AND THE FAILURES OF THE UNITED NATIONS SECURITY COUNCIL

What can be done if the United Nations Security Council fails to protect people from mass atrocities? At a time of inaction and political paralysis at the United Nations, this book explains the legality of alternative action beyond the Security Council.

This book takes a fresh look at the responsibility to protect and offers new and compelling insights into the powers and limits of the UN Security Council. It argues that the Security Council's responsibility to maintain international peace and security, and its responsibility to protect, do not die with its own failures. Other actors can and must take up responsibility to save those in need. In a persuasive and detailed examination of the legal framework, this research identifies options for coercive measures to be taken beyond the Council that could be used to break the deadlock, including through the General Assembly and regional organisations.

It provides a must-have resource for students, academics, and researchers on key principles of international law. It also offers insight for governments, policy-makers, and other international actors on how they can uphold their legal responsibilities, maintain peace and security, and prevent their failures from undermining the very existence of the UN itself.

Volume 75 in the series Studies in International Law

Studies in International Law

Recent titles in this series

Complicity and its Limits in the Law of International Responsibility
Vladyslav Lanovoy

Complicity in International Criminal Law
Marina Aksenova

Arctic Law and Governance: The Role of China and Finland
Edited by Timo Koivurova, Qin Tianbao, Tapio Nykänen and Sébastien Duyck

States, the Law and Access to Refugee Protection: Fortresses and Fairness
Edited by Maria O'Sullivan and Dallal Stevens

Revisiting the Concept of Defence in the Jus ad Bellum: The Dual Face of Defence
Johanna Friman

The International Legal Protection of Persons in Humanitarian Crises
Dug Cubie

The International Committee of the Red Cross and its Mandate to Protect and Assist: Law and Practice
Christy Shucksmith

The Impact of Investment Treaty Law on Host States: Enabling Good Governance
Mavluda Sattorova

Allocating International Responsibility Between Member States and International Organisations
Nikolaos Voulgaris

Predictability and Flexibility in the Law of Maritime Delimitation, 2nd edition
Yoshifumi Tanaka

Feminist Engagement with International Criminal Law: Norm Transfer, Complementarity, Rape and Consent
Eithne Dowds

Asylum Control and Access to Protection: Admission, Readmission and Human Rights
Mariagiulia Giuffré

Intertemporal Linguistics in International Law: Beyond Contemporaneous and Evolutionary Treaty Interpretation
Julian Wyatt

For a complete list of titles in this series, see www.bloomsburyprofessional.com/uk/series/studies-in-international-law

The Responsibility to Protect and the Failures of the United Nations Security Council

P M Butchard

• H A R T •
OXFORD • LONDON • NEW YORK • NEW DELHI • SYDNEY

HART PUBLISHING

Bloomsbury Publishing Plc

Kemp House, Chawley Park, Cumnor Hill, Oxford, OX2 9PH, UK

1385 Broadway, New York, NY 10018, USA

HART PUBLISHING, the Hart/Stag logo, BLOOMSBURY and the Diana logo are trademarks of Bloomsbury Publishing Plc

First published in Great Britain 2020

A catalogue record for this book is available from the British Library.

Library of Congress Cataloging-in-Publication data

Names: Butchard, Patrick M., author.

Title: The responsibility to protect and the failures of the United Nations Security Council / P M Butchard.

Description: Oxford ; New York : Hart, 2020. | Series: Studies in international law; 75 | Based on author's thesis (doctoral - Unviersity of Liverpool, 2017) under title: The responsibility to protect when the UN Security Council fails to act : is there room for a tertiary responsibility? | Includes bibliographical references and index.

Identifiers: LCCN 2019050076 (print) | LCCN 2019050077 (ebook) | ISBN 9781509930807 (hardcover) | ISBN 9781509930814 (Epub)

Subjects: LCSH: United Nations—Peacekeeping forces. | United Nations. Security Council. | Responsibility to protect (International law)

Classification: LCC KZ6376 .B88 2020 (print) | LCC KZ6376 (ebook) | DDC 341.6/7—dc23

LC record available at https://lccn.loc.gov/2019050076

LC ebook record available at https://lccn.loc.gov/2019050077

ISBN: HB: 978-1-50993-080-7
ePDF: 978-1-50993-082-1
ePub: 978-1-50993-081-4

Typeset by Compuscript Ltd, Shannon

For
Harrison and Theodore

Acknowledgements

Researching mass atrocity crimes certainly takes its toll, but not just on the researcher – on those who have supported me every step of the way. Since 2013, when I embarked on my PhD project, and then turned that PhD into the current book, I have had a consistent pillar of support from my wife, Jo. Through six years of sacrifices, challenges and the arrival of our two brilliant little boys, Jo has been my support, my adviser, my encouragement, and often my therapist – but above all, my friend.

I would also like to thank my PhD supervisor, Professor Christian Henderson, and all the colleagues who offered their support and comments throughout the course of this research: Michelle Farrell, Greg Messenger, Rob Knox and Ben Murphy. Many thanks also to Professor Nigel White for his insightful comments and interrogation of this research.

Contents

Abbreviations

AC	Appeals Cases
ASEAN	Association of Southeast Asian Nations
ASIL Proc	American Society of International Law Proceedings
AU	African Union
CFSP	European Union Common Foreign and Security Policy
CoI	Commission of Inquiry
DARIO	Draft Articles on the Responsibility of International Organisations, ILC Report (2011) UN Doc A/66/10, 54
DARIO Commentary	Commentary to the Draft Articles on the Responsibility of International Organisation, ILC Report (2011), UN Doc A/66/10, 69
EC Bull	Bulletin of the European Community
ECOMOG	Economic Community of West African States Monitoring Group
ECOWAS	Economic Community of West African States
ECtHR	European Court of Human Rights
FCO	UK Foreign and Commonwealth Office
G77	Group of 77
GA	United Nations General Assembly
GATS	General Agreement on Trade in Services (15 April 1994), 1869 UNTS 183
GATT	General Agreement on Tariffs and Trade 1947 (GATT 1947) (30 October 1947) 55 UNTS 187; General Agreement on Tariffs and Trade 1994 (GATT 1994) (15 April 1994) 1867 UNTS 187
HRC	United Nations Human Rights Council
ICC	International Criminal Court

ICJ	International Court of Justice
ICTY	International Criminal Tribunal for the Former Yugoslavia
ICTR	International Criminal Tribunal for Rwanda
ILC	International Law Commission
KFOR	Kosovo Force
LNTS	League of Nations Treaty Series
MNF	Multi-National Force (in Iraq)
NATO	North Atlantic Treaty Organization
OAS	Organization of American States
OAU	Organization of African Unity
OHCHR	United Nations Office of the High Commissioner for Human Rights
QIL	Questions of International Law
Res	Resolution
RIAA	United Nations Reports of International Arbitral Awards
SC	United Nations Security Council
TEU	Treaty on European Union
TFEU	Treaty on the Functioning of the European Union
UNAMIR	United Nations Assistance Mission in Rwanda
UNCIO	Documents of the United Nations Conference on International Organisation (Multi-volume, New York, United Nations 1945)
UNCTAD	United Nations Conference on Trade and Development
UNEF	United Nations Emergency Force
UNSMIS	United Nations Supervision Mission in Syria
UNTS	United Nations Treaty Series
VCLT	Vienna Convention on the Law of Treaties (23 May 1969) 1155 UNTS 331
WTO	World Trade Organization

Table of Cases

International Court of Justice

International Criminal Tribunal for the Former Yugoslavia

International Criminal Court

European Court of Justice/Court of Justice of the European Union

European Court of Human Rights

Arbitration

UK Courts

I

A Warning to Humanity

IT IS A very quiet and eerie place, the camp at Birkenau. Also known as Auschwitz II, the second camp, it remains a vast open space speckled with the remnants of the small buildings where men, women and children, mainly Jews from various countries of Europe, witnessed the darkest doings of man. Unlike the original Auschwitz camp, which had previously been an army barracks, Birkenau was purpose-built for atrocity by the Nazis. There can be no mistake that the camp was intended to imprison and intimidate. Even today, the ghosts of the empty guard towers surrounding the site still have a very real influence on the general mood for those who choose to visit.

Following the distinctive railway track from the famous main entrance building, walking on uneven ground through the centre of the camp, it is a 1-km march between deep trenches and dominant barbed-wire fences. At the end of this track lie the untouched ruins of two brutal structures – gas chambers – destroyed by the Nazis themselves near the end of the war. The rubble lies, exposed to the elements, undisturbed. The tracks of the railway unite and cease in the middle of these two broken structures, where there lies a memorial to the estimated one and a half million people who were murdered at Auschwitz between 1940 and 1945. Eternally imprinted onto the memorial, repeated in many European languages, is a powerful message:

FOR EVER LET THIS PLACE BE
A CRY OF DESPAIR
AND A WARNING TO HUMANITY

To the current author, the camps at Auschwitz–Birkenau are not just a warning to humanity about the existence or use of death camps – they are a warning about the atrocities of genocide, war crimes, crimes against humanity and ethnic cleansing in general, no matter what method is used to commit them. Unfortunately, this warning did not prevent a repetition of atrocities, and Birkenau still cries out in despair.

1. THE SCOPE AND AIM OF THIS BOOK

1.1. Background and Motivation

The horrors of the two world wars are referenced in the preamble of the Charter of the United Nations.[1] Saving future generations from the 'scourge of war', which twice 'brought untold sorrow to mankind', is written as a primary motivation for establishing this system of collective security. With this, States had a vision for the United Nations to be the world's protector – via Article 24(1) of this Charter, States conferred primary responsibility for the maintenance of international peace and security onto this organisation. In particular, onto the UN Security Council.

With this great responsibility came great powers of enforcement.[2] The Security Council became the exclusive authority for ordering military force or using mandatory coercive measures, where appropriate, to maintain or restore international peace and security. Within this organ, the five 'great powers'[3] at the end of the Second World War were bestowed the right of a veto[4] – the ability to block a course of action, based upon the 'heavy burden' they would entail as the main actors in fulfilling the Council's decisions.[5]

But when it comes to protecting the peoples of the world from atrocity crimes, unfortunately the United Nations, or the international community in general, does not have a legacy of which to be proud. The Security Council has a history of inaction, including when it comes to purely humanitarian crises, and especially where there is a competing interest between the Permanent Five – or, perhaps, a mutual disinterest on the part of the international community in general.[6]

At the 2005 World Summit, in response to increasing inaction, and competing arguments in favour of dubious legal rights to intervene in crises,[7] the international community unanimously accepted that they had a responsibility to protect their populations from genocide, war crimes, crimes against humanity, and ethnic cleansing.[8] This was a spark of hope that a new strategy for preventing and halting these atrocity crimes might find a more general consensus.

[1] Charter of the United Nations (adopted 26 June 1945, entered into force 24 October 1945, as amended) 1 UNTS XVI ('UN Charter').

[2] UN Charter, Chapter VII.

[3] The so-called 'permanent five' Members of the UN Security Council: the United States, the United Kingdom, China, France and the USSR (now Russia); see Art 23(1) UN Charter.

[4] See Art 27(3) UN Charter.

[5] See, in the preparatory documents to the Charter, *Statement by the Delegations of the Four Sponsoring Governments on the Voting Procedure in the Security Council*, attached to *Statement by My John Sofianopoulos, Chairman of Technical Committee III/I on the Structure and Procedures of the Security Council* (8 June 1945) Doc III/1/37 (1), 11 UNCIO 710, Annexed to Doc 1050 III/1/58, [9].

[6] See section 2.3 below.

[7] See section 2 below.

[8] See Chapter II generally.

The international community accepted that they had a *primary* responsibility to protect their own populations from these atrocities. Furthermore, they accepted that the international community in general also had a responsibility to assist and encourage States in their primary responsibility to protect. This author will refer to this more general responsibility as the 'secondary' responsibility to protect. This secondary responsibility also entails 'timely and decisive' collective action, through the United Nations, to use a range of peaceful and coercive measures, where appropriate, to step in and protect the populations of a State where it is 'manifestly failing' to protect. This 'timely and decisive' action is to be taken through the Security Council.[9]

However, if both the State (with a primary responsibility) and the Security Council (with a secondary responsibility) fail to act in response to said mass atrocities, it may be difficult, if not impossible, for the international community to take appropriate action – especially if the use of military force or other coercive measures is required. Even since 2005, and after accepting this responsibility to protect, the Security Council has been deadlocked in the face of humanitarian crisis. The situation in Syria is the clearest and most recent example of this problem,[10] where the Council has been blocked time and time again by the veto of a permanent member. This is especially concerning because measures considered by the Council would have gone ahead if not for this veto, and indeed in the face of a majority of States in the General Assembly calling for such action.[11]

Such deadlock does not observe the warnings of the past. Therefore, this author sought to investigate the responsibility to protect, and whether there is room for it to *continue* beyond the UN Security Council. The responsibility to protect is not, yet, a legal doctrine in and of itself.[12] It does not yet have the weight of a specific legal obligation. This book does not dispute that. The responsibility to protect, in its current form, is a mechanism of guidelines and tools which help States to identify how and when it is possible or legal to act responsibly, without prescribing a definite course of action for any particular scenario. On the other hand, what the responsibility to protect does prescribe, in terms of its underlying moral obligation, is that *something* must be done, and that inaction is not an option.

With this in mind, this book outlines the reasons why the responsibility to protect is capable of prevailing over the inaction of the Security Council, by investigating the legality of alternative action beyond the Council. By investigating whether there are any alternative tools available for other competent actors to utilise in these circumstances, the book argues that the responsibility to protect is capable of therefore continuing beyond Security Council deadlock. Again, it must be stressed that it is not the purpose of this book, or the responsibility

[9] See Chapter II, section 3.
[10] See Chapter II, section 3.2.2.
[11] See Chapter II, section 3.2.2.
[12] See Chapter III, section 1.3.

to protect, to determine which specific measures or methods the international community should use to react in response to the threat or commission of mass atrocity crimes – instead, it identifies the means and methods available to the actors who must make a choice as to how to implement their responsibilities. By seeking to clarify the availability of alternative measures beyond the UN Security Council, this book intends to demonstrate that there is, at the very least, the legal space for this responsibility to continue. By demonstrating this, it will also establish that there exists a space in which the responsibility could grow, and determine the criteria and guidance that is to be applied to the use of such alternative measures.

As well as finding the legal space for action beyond the UN Security Council, the book's findings raise an important question about the relationship between the responsibility to protect and the responsibility for the maintenance of international peace and security.[13] By finding alternative routes to fulfil the responsibility to protect, the research also, by extension, finds alternative routes for the fulfilment of the responsibility for the maintenance of international peace and security – particularly where atrocity crimes threaten or breach this peace and security. Based on this overlap, this author argues that the responsibility to protect, when a situation crosses the threshold to become a concern for the responsibility to maintain peace and security, could then become a *legal* responsibility. This is based upon analysis of the responsibility to maintain peace and security as a legal obligation, found within the UN Charter, conferred by States on the UN Security Council, and thus also reverting onto the international community following the Council's failure.[14]

This author calls this space for development the 'tertiary' responsibility to protect. This is the concept of responsibilities on States and regional groups *beyond* the remit of the Security Council. It is an acknowledgement that the responsibility to protect remains with the international community when the Security Council fails to do so, and therefore should continue beyond this point. In other words, if it is possible for the responsibility to protect to continue because there are legally permissible avenues to do so, there is no reason why it *should not* continue.

To investigate the availability of options beyond the Security Council, the book concentrates on the legality of forcible and coercive measures such as military force and 'sanctions', rather than more peaceful measures such as diplomacy. This scope is based upon three considerations. Firstly, most peaceful, non-coercive measures rarely conflict with other obligations or principles of international law, and so the question of their use beyond the Security Council within the responsibility-to-protect framework relies heavily on their suitability and hypothetical application to any given crisis – a matter not at issue here.

[13] See generally, Chapter III.
[14] See Chapter III, section 4.

Secondly, the use of coercive and forcible measures beyond the UN is one of the most heavily debated issues that goes to the very heart and purpose of the collective security system, and this debate alone arguably adds to the increased uncertainty of the legality and appropriateness of such action. By clarifying the legality of such methods in the specific context of UN Security Council failure, and in the face of mass atrocity crimes, this study can demonstrate the existence of a largely unused reserve of measures that are available to implement the general responsibility to protect, and therefore argues for its continuation beyond the UN Security Council.

Thirdly, the responsibility to protect itself acknowledges that action through the UN Security Council may be necessary where peaceful means have proved to be inadequate. The point where the UN Security Council can objectively be said to have *failed* in its responsibilities necessarily implies that political or diplomatic means of resolving a crisis are no longer enough to prevent or halt atrocities from occurring. Therefore, much more robust action might be required, and we must explore which actors are left to take such action when the Security Council has failed to step in.

1.2. Structure of the Study

To demonstrate the viability of these assertions, the book investigates measures beyond the Security Council by undertaking a thorough investigation of the main international law principles governing their use – the prohibition of force, and the principle of non-intervention. It begins in section 2 of this chapter by firstly debunking the myth of 'humanitarian intervention'. Unilateral forcible measures such as this are not what this study is about – they are illegal, and this section details why this is the case despite arguments to the contrary.

Chapter II will then outline the role of the responsibility to protect and introduce the problem of the Security Council's failures, and how this impedes the protection of populations from the worst crimes anyone could commit. This chapter outlines how the Council may be paralysed by an unreasonable use of the veto power by a permanent member (as was the case with the Syrian crisis), and also how the Council may simply remain inactive (as the world has recently seen following the atrocities committed in Myanmar).

Chapter III argues that the failures of the Security Council are a breach of a legal responsibility to maintain international peace and security, and this responsibility endures beyond the Security Council and is assumed by actors with residual responsibility. For the responsibility to protect, this continuation becomes the 'tertiary responsibility to protect'.

Chapters IV and V investigate whether the prohibition of force and the principle of non-intervention, respectively, leave room for the tertiary responsibility to protect to be implemented beyond the Security Council. In Chapter IV, the author addresses the legality of forcible measures, revisiting the prohibition of force in international law, as recognised in Article 2(4) of the UN Charter, and undertakes a thorough assessment of its scope. While rejecting the legality of all unilateral measures, the author argues that there exists a more nuanced interpretation of the prohibition of force based upon the original intentions of the drafters of the UN Charter, which could allow forcible action to be taken by the UN General Assembly if it had the competence to do so.[15]

Secondly, Chapter V addresses whether the principle of non-intervention, and the doctrine of countermeasures, leave room for the tertiary responsibility to protect to be implemented using non-forcible coercive measures such as 'sanctions'[16] beyond the Security Council. It finds that the law of countermeasures, generally, allows certain international obligations to be 'violated' in response to a prior breach of an obligation by another party, subject to other applicable criteria. The chapter highlights research into the question of whether countermeasures can be used by States not directly injured by a breach of an obligation, especially where that prior breach is of an obligation *erga omnes* – owed to the international community as a whole.

After investigating possible legal avenues relating to the prohibition of force and the principle of non-intervention (and the doctrine of countermeasures therein), in order to determine whether the tertiary responsibility exists, these avenues must actually be capable of being implemented by actors who have the competence to do so. Therefore, once the scope of these principles has been outlined, Chapter VI investigates the implementation of this tertiary responsibility in two situations: (i) within the United Nations, addressing the competence and ability of the General Assembly in this regard; and (ii), beyond the United Nations, investigating the legal restrictions on the ability of regional organisations or, failing that, individual States, to act.

It must also be noted at this stage that this author recognises that the responsibility to protect is not *just* about the use of force or coercive measures. A considerable proportion of this emerging doctrine concentrates – quite rightly – on the tools and guidance for *preventing* atrocity crimes and their causes. This book does not dismiss this. However, the scope of the research is understandably much narrower in its focus, and is concerned with the responsibility in the very specific light of Security Council failure. It is only because of this scope of investigation that so much attention is paid to forcible and coercive measures, and there is no aim for the responsibility to protect to be used duplicitously as an excuse for expanding the range of coercive measures available unilaterally, which would be prone to abuse. It is for this reason that the book uses the responsibility to protect as a framework to *restrict* the use of such measures to the very narrow scenario at hand, rather than to seek general authority to use such measures even where the Security Council is able and willing to live up to

[15] The competence of the UN General Assembly is addressed in Chapter VI.
[16] Including asset freezes, trade restrictions and embargoes.

its responsibilities itself. It is also for this reason that the book seeks to suggest a framework for the institutional use of alternative routes beyond the UN Security Council, with unilateral measures only being very rarely recommended as a last resort once all other alternatives have been tried. Importantly, the book finds that these alternative measures do come with very clear legal safeguards to prevent their misuse, and prevent the unilateral abuse of powers by States with their own political interests unlinked to the prevention of mass atrocity crimes.

2. THE MYTH OF HUMANITARIAN INTERVENTION

Before embarking on the core issues of this book, it is necessary to address the contentious issue of the so-called 'right' of humanitarian intervention. This theory is an idea that is often conflated and erroneously merged with the Responsibility to Protect, especially in the context that this book seeks to address. From the outset, the author wishes to make clear that this book – although investigating forcible and coercive measures beyond the UN Security Council – does not advocate for or support the proposition that States have a legal right to intervene unilaterally in other States, even in the case of mass atrocity crimes. This theory is categorically rejected, for the reasons that follow.

The term 'humanitarian intervention' is an enigmatic shape-shifter in the realms of international law commentary. Some refer to humanitarian intervention as a phrase encompassing any coercive intervention on humanitarian grounds, without the consent of the State concerned, and with the aim of preventing widespread death or suffering – *including* action authorised by the Security Council.[17] Others use the term to describe less-coercive action that does not necessarily involve the use of force, and not necessarily without the consent of the State concerned, encompassing a wide range of action that can even include the work of humanitarian relief agencies and charities.[18]

But the form of 'humanitarian intervention' that has undermined discussion of the responsibility to protect is that which describes forcible coercive action taken *unilaterally* (ie without the authorisation of the Security Council), without the consent of the target State, in response to a humanitarian catastrophe and with the primary aim of alleviating and further preventing such suffering.[19]

[17] This is the definition adopted by Weiss: TG Weiss, *Humanitarian Intervention: Ideas in Action*, 2nd edn (Cambridge, Polity Press, 2012) 6. See also WM Reisman, 'Hollow Victory: Humanitarian Intervention and Protection of Minorities' (1997) 91 *ASIL Proc* 431.

[18] See eg A Roberts, 'The So-Called "Right" of Humanitarian Intervention' (2000) 3 *Yearbook of International Humanitarian Law* 3, 5; see also A Roberts, 'Humanitarian War: Military Intervention and Human Rights' (1993) 69 *International Affairs* 429, 445.

[19] For example, this is the definition adopted by Chesterman: S Chesterman, *Just War or Just Peace: Humanitarian Intervention and International Law* (Oxford, Oxford University Press, 2001) Introduction, 5; see also NJ Wheeler, *Saving Strangers: Humanitarian Intervention in International Society* (Oxford, Oxford University Press, 2000) 8, who uses 'humanitarian intervention' as a label to cover both UN-authorised intervention and unilateral intervention, but does distinguish between the

The distinguishing feature of this form of humanitarian intervention is the unilateral nature of the intervention.[20] This reflects the so-called 'doctrine' of humanitarian intervention, which purportedly allows for unilateral military action as an exceptional necessity beyond the remit of the Security Council when certain criteria are met. This is also often referred to as a 'right' of humanitarian intervention, allegedly found in customary international law.

This section will briefly set out some key examples of State practice to demonstrate how the political train of thought in the international community has evolved, from the Cold War era through to more recent examples of interventions that come coupled with justifications based on humanitarian values. This is useful to understand at a general level whether the international community continued to believe that it had a responsibility to prevent atrocities like those of the Second World War, and how the collective conscience of States developed through to the acceptance of the responsibility they recognise today. The international opinions through this time reveal important nuances about the general trend of interventionism in international law, and thus provide context for the eventual recognition of the responsibility to protect.

2.1. The Fundamental Legal Barriers

Barriers to any intervention within a State can be attributed to the long-standing legal principles of State sovereignty, non-intervention and the prohibition of the use of force.[21] These principles are essential to maintaining a stable system of international law that can provide States with the freedom and ability to exist, trade and prosper in a peaceful and secure world.

Starting with State sovereignty and non-intervention, a principle that has long-established roots from the Peace of Westphalia treaties of 1648,[22] the UN Charter recognises in Article 2(7) that:

> Nothing contained in the present Charter shall authorize the United Nations to intervene in matters which are essentially within the domestic jurisdiction of any state or shall require the Members to submit such matters to settlement under the present Charter; but this principle shall not prejudice the application of enforcement measures under Chapter VII.

two (at footnote 23, 8); see also the definition used in M Brenfors and M M Petersen, 'The Legality of Unilateral Humanitarian Intervention – A Defence' (2000) 69(4) *Nordic Journal of International Law* 449, 450.

[20] See Wheeler, ibid; also, Brenfors and Petersen, ibid.

[21] These principles will be further evaluated and analysed in detail: see Chapters IV and V generally.

[22] For a discussion of sovereignty in the context of the responsibility to protect, see L Glanville, *Sovereignty and the Responsibility to Protect: A New History* (Chicago, University of Chicago Press, 2013) 49–59 and Chapter 3.

Equally, the Charter affirms under Article 2(1) that '[t]he Organisation is based upon the principle of the sovereign equality of all its Members'. Note here that these provisions refer to obligations upon the UN or principles of 'the Organisation'. However, there does seem to be a wide consensus that the general principles of sovereignty and non-intervention also apply to States individually, being recognised as having the status of customary international law.[23]

These principles were expanded upon in the *Declaration on Friendly Relations* from the General Assembly in 1970,[24] where it was emphasised that the territorial integrity and political independence of any State are inviolable and that 'no State or group of States has the right to intervene, directly or indirectly, for any reason whatever, in the internal or external affairs of any other State'.[25] The vital nature of this principle as a bedrock of international law is clear, so much so that the International Court of Justice (ICJ) confirmed the status of these provisions of the Declaration as declaratory of customary international law.[26]

Secondly, the prohibition of the threat or use of force is provided by Article 2(4) of the Charter:

> All Members shall refrain in their international relations from the threat or use of force against the territorial integrity or political independence of any state, or in any other manner inconsistent with the Purposes of the United Nations.

This provision has been fiercely debated over many years, and for many different purposes. For some, there are questions as to how far this provision prohibits the use of force, and whether it allows for action in particular circumstances by using interpretations that may or may not stretch the wording of it beyond recognition.[27] Others recognise it as a watertight prohibition, where the only exceptions are Security Council authorisation under Chapter VII, or a State's inherent right of self-defence as recognised by Article 51 of the Charter.[28]

Taken together, the principle of non-intervention coupled with the prohibition of the use of force provide the general starting position when addressing any question of intervention. But, of course, these principles *are* limited to some extent. The Charter, and indeed the *Declaration on Friendly Relations*, recognise that these principles do not prejudice the application of measures relating to the maintenance of international peace and security – in particular, enforcement measures under Chapter VII of the Charter that are authorised by

[23] See eg *Case Concerning Military and Paramilitary Activities in and against Nicaragua (Nicaragua v USA)* (Merits) [1986] ICJ Rep 14 (*Nicaragua* case), 106–07, [202].

[24] UNGA Res 2625(XXV), *Declaration on Principles of International Law concerning Friendly Relations and Co-operation among States in accordance with the Charter of the United Nations*, Annex.

[25] ibid.

[26] *Case Concerning Armed Activities on the Territory of the Congo (Democratic Republic of the Congo v Uganda)*, Judgment of 19 December 2005, (2005) ICJ Reports 168, [162].

[27] See below, Chapter IV.

[28] See below, Chapter IV.

the Security Council.[29] For humanitarian intervention to be legally permissible, it must either somehow conform to these principles, or at the very least create an exception in customary international law in a way that is compatible with the fact that the prohibition of force is recognised as a non-derogable principle of *jus cogens*.[30]

2.2. Requirements of Customary International Law

The most authoritative 'definition' of custom is found in Article 38 of the Statute of the International Court of Justice, where the sources of law that the Court should apply are listed. Article 38(1)(b) requires that the Court shall apply international custom, as evidence of a general practice accepted as law.

Cassese notes that this reflects the widely held view that custom is made up of two elements: (i) a general practice of States; and (ii) a belief on behalf of a State that this practice is accepted as law (also known as *opinio juris*) or is required by social, economic or political exigencies (*opinio necessitates*).[31] Cassese clarifies that practice by States in response to economic, political, or military demands is regarded as *opinio necessitatis*, and if this practice does not encounter strong and consistent opposition from other States, but is consistently accepted or acquiesced, then this practice gradually crystallises into a customary rule dictated by international law (*opinio juris*).[32] The point from this example is that any customary rule must emerge from 'settled practice'.

More fundamentally, this is reflected in several judgments of the ICJ. Firstly, in the *North Sea Continental Shelf* cases,[33] the Court expanded on custom, stating that:

> [T]wo conditions must be fulfilled. Not only must the acts concerned amount to a settled practice, but they must also be such, or be carried out in such a way, as to be evidence of a belief that this practice is rendered obligatory by the existence of a rule of law requiring it. The need for such a belief, ie, the existence of a subjective element, is implicit in the very notion of the *opinio juris sive necessitatis*. The States concerned must therefore feel that they are conforming to what amounts to a legal obligation. The frequency, or even habitual character of the acts is not in itself enough.[34]

This was confirmed in the *Nicaragua* case,[35] where the court further made clear that, for a rule to be established as one of custom, the corresponding practice

[29] Article 2(7) UN Charter; and *Declaration on Friendly Relations* (n 24).

[30] For further discussion of the prohibition of force and Article 2(4)'s jus cogens status, see Chapter IV below.

[31] A Cassese, *International Law*, 2nd edn (Oxford, Oxford University Press, 2005) 156.

[32] ibid, 157.

[33] *North Sea Continental Shelf Cases* (Judgment) (*Federal Republic of Germany/Denmark; Federal Republic of Germany/Netherlands*), Judgment of 20 February 1969, [1969] ICJ Reports 3.

[34] ibid, [77].

[35] *Case Concerning Military and Paramilitary Activities in and against Nicaragua (Nicaragua v USA)* (Merits), Judgment of 27 June 1986, [1986] ICJ Rep 14, [185].

need not be 'in absolutely rigorous conformity' with the rule.[36] Instances of inconsistent conduct by a State should generally be treated as breaches of that rule, and not as indications of the existence or recognition of a new rule.[37]

With these fundamental principles in mind, we may now assess whether the doctrine of humanitarian intervention exists in customary international law by reference to State practice and *opinio juris*.

2.3. Relevant History and Practice of Intervention

This section aims to highlight the evolution of thought in the international community regarding human rights violations and mass atrocities as a basis for the interference in a sovereign State, and therefore the lack of support for a customary right to humanitarian intervention. The purpose of this section is not to analyse or evaluate the legal arguments in detail,[38] but to demonstrate the lack of practice and *opinio juris* for humanitarian intervention.

2.3.1. Relevant Interventions in the Cold War Era

During the Cold War, there were three main instances of State practice that have been highlighted by commentators as the primary examples of intervention that carry with them a 'humanitarian' character. India's intervention in East Pakistan in 1971, Vietnam's invasion of Cambodia in 1978, and Tanzania's use of force in Uganda in 1979 most effectively highlight the majority of views within the international community of such intervention during this time. In these cases, the 'humanitarian' character of the States' interventions were mainly cited as a *political* justification for their actions, rather than a strictly legal one, with the use of force being justified mainly on grounds of self-defence.

2.3.1.1. India's Intervention in East Pakistan – 1971

When Pakistan was formed of West Pakistan and East Pakistan,[39] West Pakistan dominated the Eastern region in an imbalance of power, politics and the economy.[40] These circumstances accelerated a call for more autonomy in East Pakistan, with the Awami League representing this popular opinion within that region.[41]

[36] ibid, [186].

[37] ibid.

[38] Although some of the legal arguments relating to humanitarian intervention and the prohibition of force will be addressed in Chapter IV.

[39] See eg International Commission of Jurists, *The Events in East Pakistan* (Geneva, International Commission of Jurists Secretariat, 1972) 7–11, available at www.icj.org/the-events-in-east-pakistan-1971-a-legal-study/ (accessed 31 July 2019).

[40] ibid, 10.

[41] For excellent detail on this situation, see NJ Wheeler, *Saving Strangers: Humanitarian Intervention in International Society* (Oxford, Oxford University Press, 2000) ch 2 generally.

Thus, in the 1970 general election, the Awami League won a landslide majority of seats within East Pakistan, making it the biggest single party in Pakistan's National Assembly.[42] As talks and negotiations about constitutional reform between President Yahya Khan and Sheik Mujibur Rahman, the leader of the Awami League, collapsed, the President suspended the National Assembly indefinitely.[43] Eventually, negotiations deteriorated further and, following a 'Declaration of Emancipation' from the Awami League, the Pakistan Army moved into the region on 25 March 1971, unleashing a brutal and violent crackdown within Dacca.[44]

Conflict followed, with estimates that over a nine-month period one million people were killed and as many as ten million refugees fled into India.[45] Harrowingly, Kuper[46] suggests that this ruthless action included the use of torture and extermination camps.[47] In addition to the influx of refugees, clashes on the border with India escalated a deteriorating relationship between India and Pakistan – with India threatening to take action in response.[48]

Eventually, India invaded both East and West Pakistan in response to an airstrike against Indian airfields by Pakistani military forces. This sparked a war that lasted less than two weeks, with Pakistan's army surrendering on 16 December 1971, and India recognising East Pakistan as the new independent State of Bangladesh.[49] Primarily, India's justification for this intervention implied that it acted in self-defence in light of 'aggression' from Pakistan.[50] The Indian representative at the Security Council also suggested that part of India's motives was the aim to 'rescue the people of East Bengal from what they [were] suffering.'[51]

Evans[52] suggests that, while India may well have had a strategic interest in intervening within the region, the humanitarian objective was strong.[53] Yet, the international community's reaction to this crisis was less than supportive. As Wheeler notes, the strongest reaction from the international community was to affirm Pakistan's right to sovereignty and the principle of non-intervention.[54]

[42] See Wheeler (n 41) 56; International Commission of Jurists (n 39) 12; see also S Chesterman, *Just War or Just Peace: Humanitarian Intervention and International Law* (Oxford, Oxford University Press, 2001) 72.

[43] International Commission of Jurists (n 39) 14.

[44] ibid, 27.

[45] See Chesterman (n 42) 72–73; International Commission of Jurists (n 39) 24–26; Wheeler (n 41) 58–59.

[46] L Kuper, *The Prevention of Genocide* (New Haven, CT, Yale University Press, 1985).

[47] ibid, 47; see also Wheeler (n 41) 57.

[48] Wheeler (n 41) 59–60.

[49] International Commission of Jurists (n 39) 42–44.

[50] See eg UNSC Verbatim Record, 1606th Meeting (4 December 1971) UN Doc S/PV.1606(OR), [155].

[51] ibid, [185].

[52] G Evans, *The Responsibility to Protect: Ending Mass Atrocity Crimes Once and for All* (Washington, DC, Brookings Institution Press, 2008).

[53] ibid, 23–24.

[54] Wheeler (n 41) 58–59, 65–71.

Others were more explicit in suggesting that the events in East Pakistan could not justify India's actions against the territorial integrity and political independence of Pakistan.[55]

With no progress made in the Security Council, the issue was taken to the General Assembly.[56] Eventually, the Assembly passed Resolution 2793 (XXVI)[57] calling for both sides to initiate an immediate ceasefire and a withdrawal of forces from the other's territory. Most notably, Wheeler highlights that the discussion by States in the General Assembly revealed little or no support for any kind of intervention on humanitarian grounds.[58]

2.3.1.2. Vietnam's Intervention in Cambodia – 1978

In 1975, the Khmer Rouge came to power in Cambodia (then known as Kampuchea) – a rise of power that would scar the Cambodian people. A broad and systematic violation of human rights followed, with Amnesty International estimating that hundreds of thousands of people were murdered by the government while deaths from malnutrition or disease amounted to unconscionable figures that ranged between one and two million.[59] At the same time, the government launched cross-border attacks against Vietnam, on some occasions destroying Vietnamese villages along the disputed border and massacring civilians.[60]

In response, and after failed attempts at peaceful dialogue, Vietnam invaded Cambodia on Christmas Day, 1978.[61] In terms of Vietnam's justifications for its intervention, it was argued (quite unconvincingly) that a distinction should be drawn between the 'border war' fought between the two States and the 'revolutionary war' between the people and their government – maintaining at the Security Council that it acted in self-defence, in response to the attacks on its territory by the Khmer Rouge.[62] In fact, Vietnam did not actually formally acknowledge any such presence of Vietnamese troops within Cambodia.[63]

[55] See eg US Representative, UNSC Verbatim Record, 1611th Meeting (12 December 1971) UN Doc S/PV.1611(OR), [19].

[56] Chesterman (n 42) 74; see also UNSC Res 303 (1971).

[57] UNGA Res 2793 (XXVI) *Question considered by the Security Council at its 1606th, 1607th and 1608th meetings on 4, 5 and 6 December 1971.*

[58] Wheeler (n 41) 68.

[59] See Amnesty International, *Political Killings by Governments* (London, Amnesty International, 1983) 38–44; for a brief account of this situation, see International Commission on Intervention and State Sovereignty (ICISS), *The Responsibility to Protect: Research, Bibliography, Background* (Ottawa, International Development Research Centre, 2001) 57–61; for a more in-depth analysis, see Wheeler (n 41) ch 3 generally; see also G Klintworth, *Vietnam's Intervention in Cambodia in International Law* (Canberra, Australian Government Publishing Service, 1989).

[60] Wheeler (n 41) 79–81; Klintworth (n 59) 20.

[61] ibid, 83–85.

[62] UNSC Verbatim Record, 2108th Meeting (11 January 1979) UN Doc S/PV.2108(OR), [115] and [126]–[127]; For an assessment of Vietnam's self-defence argument, see: Wheeler (n 42) 86–89; Klintworth (n 59) 27.

[63] ICISS (n 59) 58.

The international response to the situation was similar to that of India's intervention in Pakistan in the sense that the deplorable human rights record of Khmer Rouge was acknowledged, but nevertheless the principle of non-intervention and State sovereignty toppled this.[64]

Widespread condemnation of the invasion followed. For example, the United Kingdom stated:

> Whatever is said about human rights in Kampuchea, it cannot excuse Viet Nam, whose own human rights record is deplorable, for violating the territorial integrity of Democratic Kampuchea, an independent State Member of the United Nations.[65]

France also expressed its concerns about any justifications for intervention based upon a humanitarian crisis:

> The notion that because a régime is detestable foreign intervention is justified and forcible overthrow is legitimate is extremely dangerous. That could ultimately jeopardize the very maintenance of international law and order and make the continued existence of various regimes dependent on the judgement of their neighbours.[66]

Moreover, the Soviet Union's support for Vietnam – coming from the other side of the Cold War divide – endorsed the 'two wars' argument, yet did not go as far as to validate any humanitarian basis for intervention.[67] Instead, the Soviet Union used the atrocities as a background to support the argument that the Pol Pot regime was overthrown by his own people[68] – a contradiction in the Soviet human rights position that was later pointed out by the United Kingdom.[69]

Thus, when the Soviet Union once again vetoed Resolutions within the Council, the issue went to the General Assembly, where, in contrast to the arguably 'softer' approach that was taken in the India/East Pakistan situation, Vietnam's intervention was condemned.[70] Most crucially, the General Assembly maintained the general position of the international community as emphasising the sovereignty, territorial integrity and independence of States.[71] As is evident, similarly to the situation between India and Pakistan, the interests of the State and sovereignty seemed to take precedence.

2.3.1.3. Tanzania's Intervention in Uganda – 1979

The President of Uganda, Idi Amin, is said to have been responsible for the murder of between 100,000 and 500,000 people during his reign of power – violations

[64] Chesterman (n 42) 79–81.
[65] UNSC Verbatim Record, 2110th Meeting (13 January 1979) UN Doc S/PV.2110(OR), [65].
[66] UNSC Verbatim Record, 2109th Meeting (12 January 1979) UN Doc S/PV.2109(OR), [36].
[67] UNSC 2108th Meeting (n 62) [35], [41], [146].
[68] UNSC 2108th Meeting (n 62) [148]–[149].
[69] UNSC 2110th Meeting (n 65) [64]; see also Wheeler's discussion (n 41) 96–97.
[70] UNGA Res 34/22 (1979) *The Situation in Kampuchea – 'Deeply Regretting the Armed Intervention by Outside Forces in the Internal Affairs of Kampuchea'*.
[71] ibid, preamble and [9].

of human rights that attracted a widespread condemnation through the international community.[72] In October 1978, during a period of tense relations with neighbouring Tanzania, Amin occupied and annexed a small region of north-west Tanzania.[73] Countering this 'act of war', Tanzanian troops forced Ugandan forces back onto their home territory, only to be invaded a second time by Amin's command.[74] Met with this further attack, Tanzania countered Uganda's attacks, and responded with an invasion of its own to destroy a number of Ugandan army bases with the aim of preventing any further attacks.[75]

As Uganda called upon the help of Libya, this dispute escalated until Tanzania made the decision to topple Idi Amin's regime.[76] Justifying Tanzania's actions, President Nyerere, without explicitly adopting the language of self-defence, made a 'two-wars' argument similar to that made by Vietnam, stating: 'First there are Ugandans fighting to remove the Fascist dictator. Then there are Tanzanians fighting to maintain national security.'[77]

Tanzania did not invoke any humanitarian ground for its intervention, despite the gross record of human rights violations by the Amin regime. Unlike in the Vietnam situation, the international community's response to this intervention was surprisingly muted.[78] While Uganda had requested a meeting at the Security Council, this was later withdrawn, and the issue did not receive attention in either the Security Council or the General Assembly.[79] Commentators such as Tesón[80] suggest that this reaction by the international community legitimised Tanzania's intervention,[81] but Chesterman warns that it may be an exaggeration to see this as the international community accepting Tanzania's actions as *lawful* – rather than just simply legitimate, but nevertheless still illegal.[82]

But, we may ask, why was the international community's reaction to the Tanzanian intervention so 'indifferent' compared to the popular condemnation of Vietnam's actions in Cambodia – even though the justifications put by the intervening parties were relatively similar? It has been suggested that the lack of condemnation in the Tanzanian case was due to the fact that Tanzania was not seen as having any 'hegemonic' intentions in invading Uganda, whereas this

[72] Amnesty International (n 59) 44; for a background to this situation, see: ICISS (n 59) 61–63; Wheeler (n 41) ch 4 generally; and Amnesty International, *Human Rights in Uganda* (London, Amnesty International, 1978).

[73] ICISS (n 59) 61–63.

[74] ibid.

[75] ibid.

[76] ibid.

[77] As quoted by Wheeler (n 41) 118–19.

[78] ICISS (n 59) 62.

[79] ibid.

[80] FR Tesón, *Humanitarian Intervention: An Inquiry into Law and Morality*, 2nd edn (Dobbs Ferry, NY, Transnational Publishers, 1997).

[81] ibid, 187, 191.

[82] Chesterman (n 42) 78.

was a popular opinion regarding Vietnam[83] – with China even suggesting that Vietnam's invasion was part of a wider hidden agenda by the Soviet Union.[84]

Frank[85] suggests that the international community's acquiescence in the face of the Tanzanian invasion may be explained by the political feelings at the time.[86] He explains that Idi Amin was universally notorious, while the Tanzanian President, Julius Nyerere, was widely respected, and that despite this clear support for being rid of such a brutal dictator as Amin, Tanzania's actions were not justified as humanitarian intervention based on fears that such action would set a precedent legitimating a general right of States to engage in humanitarian intervention.[87] If this is true, and such fears did exist within the international community, then the silence of the world seems nothing more than a compromise between two competing positions – one that saw a legal basis for the action in humanitarian intervention; and another that accepted the outcome of the Tanzanian intervention, but did not want to create such a legal precedent. If this is the case, then the international community cannot correctly be described as accepting the legality of humanitarian intervention as law.

2.3.2. Conclusions on Cold War Interventions

By identifying these three cases of intervention during the Cold War, we can see that the pattern of thought within the international community followed a trend of non-intervention based upon State sovereignty, independence and territorial integrity. The majority opinion of that time was that violations of human rights and mass atrocities – no matter how severe they had been reported to be – could not *in themselves* form the basis of any interference or action against a sovereign State. The States undertaking interventions even stayed clear of such arguments, basing their interventions on claims of self-defence (whether expressly or impliedly), and only utilising the arguments of human rights violations as a political background to support the outcome of their actions.

Indeed, the majority of arguments at that time in favour of a humanitarian basis for intervention came from commentators rather than States, and even then that led to a divide within the academic community.[88] Evans pins this era under the title of 'cynicism and self-interest',[89] but whether that may or may not be the case, it is certainly evident that there was very little support for any intervention

[83] See generally ICISS (n 59) 63; and in more depth Wheeler (n 41) 122–32.

[84] See China, UNSC 2108th Meeting (n 62) [97]–[104].

[85] TM Frank, 'Interpretation and Change in the Law of Humanitarian Intervention' in JL Holzgrefe and RO Keohane (eds), *Humanitarian Intervention: Ethical, Legal and Political Dilemmas* (Cambridge, Cambridge University Press, 2003).

[86] Frank (n 85) 219.

[87] ibid.

[88] eg Chesterman (n 42) 75; see also the positions of writers in RB Lillich (ed), *Humanitarian Intervention and the United Nations* (Charlottesville, University Press of Virginia, 1973).

[89] Evans (n 52) 19.

into an independent State being based upon the fact of a humanitarian crisis alone – never mind any kind of *doctrine* of 'humanitarian intervention'.

2.3.3. Situations in the Post-Cold War Era

In the 1990s, the international community became more cooperative in their international relations following the end of the Cold War. We shall look now to examples of humanitarian crises during this post-Cold War era, prior to the adoption of the responsibility to protect, and evaluate whether there was a shift in the international community's collective conscience when faced with these dire situations. As we shall see, there was a distinctive shift towards UN-based operations. However, a lack of political will to take more coercive measures, and an unconscionable failing in response to the situation in Rwanda in 1994, reveal that there is still a strong reluctance among some States to violate or encroach upon the principles of State sovereignty and non-intervention, demonstrating further evidence that a right of humanitarian intervention is not widely accepted.

2.3.3.1. The Situation in Iraq – 1990–1993

When Iraq invaded and annexed Kuwait in August 1990, the international community struck back at this illegal use of force with both condemnation and a robust response. The Security Council convened to condemn the aggressive action within hours of the invasion, recognising the situation as a breach of international peace and security and calling for Iraq to withdraw its forces from Kuwait immediately.[90] Eventually, when economic sanctions proved ineffective,[91] the Security Council authorised States to use 'all necessary measures' under Chapter VII of the Charter, in cooperation with Kuwait, allowing a coalition of State forces to intervene militarily and restore international peace and security.[92]

Once the operation to remove Iraqi forces from Kuwait was over, this series of events was followed by a vicious repression of Kurdish civilians in northern Iraq, and Shiites in the south.[93] When the Security Council's ceasefire resolution relating to the Kuwait situation was passed, it made no mention of the deteriorating situation relating to civilians in Iraq.[94] But after a short hesitation, the Council passed Resolution 688,[95] calling for an end to the repression of civilians within Iraq, insisting upon immediate access for international humanitarian

[90] UNSC Res 660 (1990) (2 August 1990) UN Doc S/RES/660(1990).
[91] UNSC Res 661 (1990) (6 August 1990) UN Doc S/RES/661(1990).
[92] UNSC Res 678 (1990).
[93] See ICISS (59) 84–89; Wheeler (n 41) ch 5 generally.
[94] UNSC Res 678 (1990) (29 November 1990) UN Doc S/RES/678(1990).
[95] UNSC Res 688 (1991) (5 April 1991) UN Doc S/RES/688(1991). This resolution was passed by 10 votes in favour, 3 against (Yemen, Zimbabwe and Cuba), and 2 abstentions (China and India).

organisations, and appealing to Member States to contribute to these humanitarian relief efforts.[96]

But as the suffering and tragedy of the Kurdish people was broadcast on television into the homes of millions of Western States, political pressure mounted in what has been dubbed the 'CNN Effect' or the 'BBC Effect'.[97] Initially reluctant to intervene, the US found support from France and the UK in establishing 'safe havens' to protect the Kurdish people.[98] These 'safe havens' were then protected by no-fly zones established by the coalition forces, and the threat of ground troops within the region.[99]

These 'safe havens' and the no-fly zones had not been expressly authorised by the Security Council, leading to claims from the coalition parties that their actions were justified 'in support' of Resolution 688, and through an 'implied authorisation' from the Security Council.[100] In later clashes between Iraqi forces and US/UK forces from 1992 1999 the use of force was justified in self-defence and pre-emptive action against Iraqi missile locations.[101]

During this time, the UK altered its position in favour of a 'doctrine' of humanitarian intervention, suggesting that humanitarian crises as a basis for the interference in a State's affairs was in fact a legal possibility.[102] The Legal Counsellor of the UK Foreign and Commonwealth Office (FCO) explicitly said:

> Resolution 688 … was not made under Chapter VII. Resolution 688 recognised that there was a severe human rights and humanitarian situation in Iraq and, in particular, northern Iraq; but the intervention in northern Iraq 'Provide Comfort' was in fact, not specifically mandated by the United Nations, but the states taking action in northern Iraq did so in exercise of the customary international law principle of humanitarian intervention.[103]

Division persisted between the permanent members of the Security Council over the legality of the military action right through to 1999, when clashes between the coalition forces and Iraqi forces intensified,[104] and France eventually dropped its support for the coalition.[105]

[96] ibid.

[97] eg ICISS (n 59) 87; Wheeler (n 41) 148–49.

[98] See C Gray, *International Law and the Use of Force*, 3rd edn (Oxford, Oxford University Press, 2008) 35–39; Wheeler (n 41) 147–52. France later left the coalition, criticising the US for exceeding its mandate (ICISS (n 59) 89).

[99] Wheeler (n 41) 147–52.

[100] For an in-depth discussion on the legal arguments and implied authorisation, see C Gray, 'From Unity to Polarization: International Law and the Use of Force against Iraq' (2001) 13(1) *European Journal of International Law* 1, 8–16; Gray (n 98) 36–39, 348–68.

[101] Gray (n 98) 36–39, 348–68.

[102] See Gray (n 98) 37.

[103] Oral Evidence of Mr A Aust to the Foreign Affairs Committee, available in 'United Kingdom Materials on International Law' (1992) 63 *British Yearbook of International Law* 615, 827.

[104] See discussion in UNSC Verbatim Record, 4008th Meeting (21 May 1999) UN Doc S/PV.4008.

[105] Gray (n 98) 36–39.

2.3.3.2. The Failure to Respond to the Genocide in Rwanda – 1994

The Rwandan genocide of 1994 is possibly the most important example of the quandary that is at the centre of this book. While approximately 800,000 people were killed in a systematic slaughter that lasted almost 100 days, the UN system failed to prevent, or halt, this colossal atrocity.[106] As the UN Secretary-General called for the peacekeeping force UNAMIR (UN Assistance Mission in Rwanda), whose resources were scarce, to be reinforced with the aim of coercing a ceasefire,[107] the Security Council instead reduced the numbers of the force and withdrew a majority of its troops and civilian workers from the country.[108] The genocide of those 800,000 people followed in April to July.

An independent inquiry found that part of the reason for this failure was a persistent lack of political will that hampered the ability of the Security Council to make any effective decisions that would have an impact on the situation.[109] The report made 14 key recommendations to the UN, including in particular: initiating an Action Plan to prevent genocide;[110] a greater preparedness on the part of the Security Council and others to act to prevent genocide and gross violations of human rights, emphasising that the political will to act should not be subject to different standards;[111] and improving the protection of civilians in conflict situations.[112]

The main theme of these recommendations is clear: inaction is inexcusable when faced with atrocities such as genocide. There can be no doubt that the moral conscience of the world collectively compels a response to these dire situations.[113] But it is the question of *how* the world should respond that faces the greatest of challenges. One might think that the ability of the Security Council to act beyond the barriers of State sovereignty and the non-use of force would be enough to stop or halt mass atrocities when the time comes. One might also expect that the Security Council would act at the right time, in the right way, authorising the necessary measures to stop mass death. That would be the case in an ideal world. However, the case of the Rwandan Genocide of 1994 reveals that just because the Security Council *can* act does not always mean that it *will*. Furthermore, the lack of any intervention, or argument in favour of humanitarian intervention in response to this genocide, indicates further the lack of belief in the legality of such a doctrine.

[106] *Report of the Independent Inquiry into the Actions of the United Nations during the 1994 Genocide in Rwanda* (15 December 1999) UN Doc S/1999/1257.

[107] Report of the Secretary-General, *Special Report of the Secretary-General on the United Nations Assistance Mission for Rwanda* (20 April 1994) UN Doc S/1994/470.

[108] UNSC Res 912 (1994) (21 April 1994) UN Doc S/RES/912(1994).

[109] *Report of the Independent Inquiry* (n 106) 1, 43–49.

[110] ibid, Recommendation 1, 53.

[111] ibid, Recommendation 3.

[112] ibid, Recommendation 5.

[113] If there is doubt, then it can only derive from perpetrators, instigators and those complaisant or indifferent.

2.3.3.3. NATO's Intervention in Kosovo – 1999

When the threat of mass atrocities came over the horizon in the late 1990s, reluctance on the part of some veto-holding permanent members of the Security Council to act encouraged a few States to take it upon themselves to act.

This was in support of NATO's intervention in Kosovo in 1999. Operation Allied Force was NATO's response to the crisis in (what was at the time) Yugoslavia. Kosovar Albanians were the target of the use of excessive force against peaceful protests by Serbian authorities that eventually escalated into a repressive internal conflict by forces under President Milošević.[114] As the situation descended towards humanitarian catastrophe, with an increasing number of civilians being targeted in the bloodshed, the UN Security Council passed Resolution 1199.[115] Under this Resolution, the Security Council acted under Chapter VII of the Charter to demand 'the withdrawal of security units used for civilian repression'.[116]

While many attempts at diplomatic settlement were made, the crisis eventually descended into a conflict where war crimes and mass human rights abuses took place.[117] Then, in March 1999, NATO aircraft started an aerial bombing campaign against Yugoslavia, primarily in the Kosovo region – a campaign that would last 78 days, with no prior express Security Council approval.[118]

Many different political and moral arguments were put forward by NATO spokespersons and the NATO Secretary-General, mainly focusing on the need to prevent a further humanitarian catastrophe,[119] but the *legal* justifications from NATO members ranged considerably. For example, during an emergency meeting called after NATO started its intervention, there were several responses from NATO members to Russia's condemnation of the organisation's use of force.[120] The US stressed that the NATO action was taken with the greatest reluctance, but was necessary and justified to stop the violence and prevent an even greater humanitarian disaster because Belgrade had been undermining and thwarting all other diplomatic efforts.[121]

Only a minority of States concerned explicitly relied upon the humanitarian crisis as a *legal* justification for their actions, rather than a solely political one. When Yugoslavia started legal action (later continued by Serbia

[114] For full details and facts, see Independent International Commission on Kosovo, *The Kosovo Report: Conflict, International Response, Lessons Learned*, (Oxford, Oxford University Press, 2000) ch 2.

[115] UNSC Res 1199 (1998) (23 September 1998) UN Doc S/RES/1199(1998).

[116] ibid, [4].

[117] *The Kosovo Report* (n 114) 81–84.

[118] *The Kosovo Report* (n 114) 85–87. Note again here the connotations relating to the idea of an 'implied authorisation' by the Security Council (see n 100).

[119] See eg C Gray, *International Law and the Use of Force*, 3rd edn (Oxford, Oxford University Press, 2008) 39–42.

[120] UNSC Verbatim Record, 3988th Meeting (24 March 1999) UN Doc S/PV.3988.

[121] ibid (US Representative) 4–5.

and Montenegro) in the ICJ against 10 NATO Member States, it was alleged that those who undertook military action breached the prohibition of the use of force and, by assisting military forces within the State, also breached the principle of non-intervention.[122] During proceedings, Belgium made some notable arguments.[123] When arguing that the intervention had an 'unchallengeable basis' in the Security Council resolutions relating to the situation in the region, the representative of Belgium suggested that 'we need to go further and develop the idea of armed humanitarian intervention'.[124]

Belgium also made the argument that the intervention was 'a case of a lawful armed humanitarian intervention for which there is a compelling necessity'.[125] Ultimately, although it had the potential to shed light upon the legal validity of humanitarian intervention, a chance to clarify the position was lost following the events in Kosovo when the ICJ found that it did not have jurisdiction in these cases.[126]

Similar to Belgium, the UK argued:

> The action being taken is legal. It is justified as an exceptional measure to prevent an overwhelming humanitarian catastrophe. Under present circumstances in Kosovo, there is convincing evidence that *such a catastrophe is imminent*. …
>
> Every means short of force has been tried to avert this situation. In these circumstances, and as an exceptional measure on grounds of overwhelming humanitarian necessity, military intervention is legally justifiable. The force now proposed is directed exclusively to averting a humanitarian catastrophe, and is the minimum judged necessary for that purpose.[127]

Notwithstanding these arguments, the Independent International Commission on Kosovo found that NATO's intervention was *legitimate*, but not *legal*.[128] Such a decision raises a fundamental quandary when it comes to the choice between illegality and inaction. However, the Commission did seem to put a limit on this when it said:

> Such a conclusion is related to the controversial idea that a 'right' of humanitarian intervention is not consistent with the UN Charter if conceived as a legal text, but that it may, depending on context, nevertheless, reflect the spirit of the Charter

[122] See eg *Legality of Use of Force* (Application) (*Yugoslavia v United States of America*), Application of 29 April 1999, available at: www.icj-cij.org/files/case-related/114/7173.pdf (accessed 31 July 2019). Cases were brought by 10 States in total, including Belgium, Canada, France, Germany, Italy, Netherlands, Portugal, Spain, the UK, and the US.

[123] *Legality of Use of Force* (Provisional Measures, Oral Proceedings) (*Yugoslavia v Belgium*), Verbatim Record of 10 May 1999, ICJ Document CR 99/15, available at: www.icj-cij.org/files/case-related/105/105-19990510-ORA-02-00-BI.pdf (accessed 31 July 2019).

[124] ibid, 11, [16].

[125] *Legality of the Use of Force* (Oral Proceedings) (n 123) 12–13, [17]–[18].

[126] See eg *Legality of Use of Force* (Preliminary Objections) (*Serbia and Montenegro v United Kingdom*), Judgment of 15 December 2004, (2004) ICJ Reports 1307.

[127] UNSC 3988th Meeting (n 120) (UK Representative) 12 (emphasis added).

[128] Independent International Commission on Kosovo, *The Kosovo Report: Conflict, International Response, Lessons Learned* (Oxford, Oxford University Press, 2000) 186, 289.

as it relates to the overall protection of people against gross abuse. Humanitarian intervention may also thus be legitimately authorized by the UN, but will often be challenged legally from the perspective of Charter obligations to respect the sovereignty of states.[129]

2.3.4. *The United Kingdom's 'Norm-Entrepreneurship' and the International Reaction*

The UK has been, by far, the strongest advocate of 'humanitarian intervention' in the post-Cold War era. As well as using it as the argument for NATO's intervention in Kosovo, the UK has put forward its position on the doctrine on many other occasions. On 22 April 1999, then-Secretary of State for Defence George Robertson made a policy statement in support of a legal use of military action in exceptional circumstances to avoid a humanitarian catastrophe.[130] In 2000, this position developed into a more principled approach to build humanitarian intervention into more of a 'doctrine', and ideas were put to the UK Parliament and the UN Secretary-General, suggesting a range of criteria that should be adhered to for the use of force in pursuit of humanitarian intervention.[131]

Whilst supporting the limited use of force unilaterally, but nevertheless calling for the possibility of acting should the situation arise, the UK government reasserted these principles in a set of Policy Guidelines in 2001.[132] But even more recently, the UK renewed its support for humanitarian intervention in the context of the Syrian crisis in 2013. When considering limited military airstrikes against the Syrian regime in response to chemical weapons attacks on its own population, the UK set out its legal justification if it were to carry out such strikes, specifically addressing the issue of *unilateral* action in the following terms:

> If action in the Security Council is blocked, the UK would still be permitted under international law to take exceptional measures in order to alleviate the scale of the overwhelming humanitarian catastrophe in Syria by deterring and disrupting the further use of chemical weapons by the Syrian regime. Such a legal basis is available, under the doctrine of humanitarian intervention, provided three conditions are met.[133]

[129] ibid, 186. The Commission went on to set out a principled approach to developing a legal framework for humanitarian intervention – a framework that would rely on the support of the international community to make it a reality: see 185–99.

[130] Statement by Mr George Robertson, 22 April 1999, in 'United Kingdom Materials on International Law' (1999) 70 *British Yearbook of International Law* 586.

[131] House of Commons Debs, vol 343, cols 459–60W: 31 January 2000, also available in 'United Kingdom Materials on International Law' (2000) 71 *British Yearbook of International Law* 517, 644. Unfortunately, it is not the place or purpose of this book to assess these criteria in detail.

[132] Foreign and Commonwealth Office, *UK Paper on International Action in Response to Humanitarian Crises*. 2001, reprinted in 'United Kingdom Materials on International Law' (2001) 72 *British Yearbook of International Law* 551, 695–96.

[133] UK Prime Minister's Office, *Chemical Weapon Use by Syrian Regime: UK Government Legal Position* (29 August 2013) [4], available at www.gov.uk/government/publications/chemical-weapon-use-by-syrian-regime-uk-government-legal-position/chemical-weapon-use-by-syrian-regime-uk-government-legal-position-html-version (accessed 31 July 2019).

What is striking about this statement by the UK government is the explicit reference to the fact that it would be willing to act even if the Security Council is blocked. This is striking because, through the years of arguing for this right to intervene, there has been no indication as to how it would fit within the UN Charter's existing international peace and security system. Furthermore, there has been little by way of addressing fears as to whether this would have any effect upon the system's integrity and effectiveness. In 1999, UN Secretary-General Kofi Annan aired these concerns when he asked: '[I]s there not a danger of such interventions undermining the imperfect, yet resilient, security system created after the second world war, and of setting dangerous precedents for future interventions without a clear criterion to decide who might invoke these precedents and in what circumstances?'[134]

This concern was echoed by the UK's House of Commons Foreign Affairs Select Committee, which asked the government to clarify its position on the legality of acting without the authorisation of the UN Security Council. These questions were outlined and answered in Written Evidence to the Committee by Hugh Robertson MP, a minister in the FCO.[135] Specifically, the Committee highlighted the Independent International Commission on Kosovo's conclusion that the NATO intervention in the 1990s was *illegal* but *legitimate*. In response to this, Robertson stated that:

> The Government's position has not changed in light of the report of the Independent International Commission on Kosovo. It did not agree with the Commission's view that NATO's action in Kosovo in 1999 was illegal. The Government does not consider the Commission, while made up of experts, to be authoritative. Its views are not binding in any way, but represent the views of its independent members.[136]

Therefore, even in the face of experts, the UK clearly believes that humanitarian intervention has always been legal. In fact, Robertson's evidence suggests that the UK relied on the doctrine of humanitarian intervention on three occasions, those being: (i) in protecting the Kurds in Northern Iraq in 1991; (ii) in maintaining the no-fly zones in northern and southern Iraq from 1991; and (iii) in using force against the Federal Republic of Yugoslavia in relation to Kosovo in 1999.[137]

[134] UN Secretary-General, *Address to UN General Assembly*, UN Press Release GA/9596, 20 September 1999, www.un.org/News/Press/docs/1999/19990920.sgsm7136.html (accessed 31 July 2019); see also UNGA Verbatim Record, 4th Plenary Meeting, 54th Session (20 September 1999) UN Doc A/54/PV.4.

[135] UK Foreign and Commonwealth Office Further Supplementary Submission, *Further Supplementary Written Evidence from the Rt Hon Hugh Robertson MP, Minister of State, Foreign and Commonwealth Office: Humanitarian Intervention and the Responsibility to Protect (USA 19)*, 14 January 2014, Foreign Affairs Select Committee, available at http://data.parliament.uk/writtenevidence/committeeevidence.svc/evidencedocument/foreign-affairs-committee/government-foreign-policy-towards-the-united-states/written/5367.pdf (accessed 31 July 2019).

[136] ibid, 4.

[137] ibid, 3.

On the specific issue of acting without Security Council authorisation, the Foreign Affairs Select Committee asked for an assessment of the implications of such action. Again, the government's position was reiterated:

> The position of the Government is that intervention may be permitted under international law in exceptional circumstances where the UN Security Council is *unwilling or unable* to act in order to avert a humanitarian catastrophe subject to the three conditions set out above. The Government does not consider that this has adverse implications for the UN.[138]

In April 2014, the House of Commons Defence Select Committee produced a report on the very topic of intervention,[139] and expressed concern that 'it is unclear to what degree the UK Government's interpretation of the legal position is accepted by either the international community or the general public in the UK'.[140] It called upon the government, in its next National Security Strategy, to set out in detail the principles of its legal position, including its relationship with the UN Charter, international law and (as shall be discussed in the following chapter) the concept of the responsibility to protect.[141] In the government's response to the report,[142] it noted its recommendation and then directed the Defence Select Committee back to Hugh Robertson's evidence to the Foreign Affairs Select Committee detailing the government's legal position, and so the discussion came full circle.[143]

Indeed, it is telling that the UK is often alone in purporting the legality of humanitarian intervention. For example, when the US conducted airstrikes against a Syrian military airbase in April 2017, in response to chemical weapons attacks against civilians, the US did not offer any *legal* basis for its actions – only moral and political justifications.[144] While some states did support the action itself, they did not offer any support for any legal basis for the action,

[138] ibid, 5 (emphasis added).

[139] UK House of Commons Defence Committee, *Intervention: Why, When and How? Fourteenth Report of Session 2013–14*, vol I, 28 April 2014, available at: www.publications.parliament.uk/pa/cm201314/cmselect/cmdfence/952/952.pdf (accessed 31 July 2019).

[140] ibid, 26, [38] and 29, [49]. See also UK House of Commons Defence Committee, *Intervention: Why, When and How? Fourteenth Report of Session 2013–14*, vol II (Written Evidence), 28 April 2014, available at: www.publications.parliament.uk/pa/cm201314/cmselect/cmdfence/952/952vw.pdf (accessed 31 July 2019).

[141] House of Commons Defence Committee (n 139) 29, [49].

[142] UK House of Commons Defence Committee, *Intervention: Why, When and How? Government Response to the Committee's Fourteenth Report of Session 2013–14, Fourth Special Report of Session 2014–15*, 29 July 2014, available at: www.publications.parliament.uk/pa/cm201415/cmselect/cmdfence/581/581.pdf (accessed 31 July 2019).

[143] ibid, 5.

[144] For a detailed overview of the US airstrikes against the Syrian military airbase, see T Ruys, L Ferro and C Vander Maelen, 'Digest of State Practice: 1 January–30 June 2017' (2017) 4(2) *Journal on the Use of Force and International Law* 371, 396ff; see also P Butchard, 'Donald Trump's Syria Strike Is Illegal' *Liverpool News* (10 April 2017) https://news.liverpool.ac.uk/2017/04/10/donald-trumps-syria-strike-illegal/.

or indicate any relevant opinio juris in this regard.[145] States who did mention the strikes' compatibility with international law were clear in their opinion that such unilateral action was not compatible with international law or the prohibition of force, with some States accusing the US of aggression.[146]

One year later, in April 2018, another chemical weapons attack took place in the city of Douma near Damascus.[147] The US, the UK and France accused the Syrian regime of being behind the attack,[148] but the Security Council failed to agree on establishing an independent and impartial investigation into the incident.[149] Subsequently, these States conducted military strikes against three targets within Syria which were allegedly linked to a Syrian chemical weapons programme.[150]

The UK's legal justification was the same as that before the proposed airstrikes in 2013, arguing that unilateral humanitarian intervention is 'permitted under international law, on an exceptional basis, to take measures in order to alleviate overwhelming humanitarian suffering'.[151] France and the US, on the other hand, did not speak of humanitarian intervention, or offer any explicit legal justification for their interventions in international law, once again simply focusing on political arguments about the need to deter the use of chemical weapons.[152] France dismissed arguments that the actions could be contrary to the UN Charter by arguing 'the Charter was not designed to protect criminals'[153] and that their action

> is fully in line with the objectives and values proclaimed from the outset by the Charter of the United Nations. … This action was indeed necessary in order to address the repeated violations by the Syrian regime of its obligations.[154]

Of course, France was right that the UN Charter was not designed to protect criminals – just like it was fundamentally designed not to allow unilateral uses

145 Ruys et al (n 144) 399–400.

146 ibid, 400–02.

147 For a complete overview of this, and the international reaction, see: T Ruys, C Vander Maelen and S Van Severen, 'Digest of State Practice: 1 January–30 June 2018' (2018) 5(2) *Journal on the Use of Force and International Law* 324, 352–68.

148 See UNSC Verbatim Record, 8225th Meeting (9 April 2018) UN Doc S/PV.8225, 10–11 (United States), 11–13 (France), and 13 (United Kingdom).

149 UNSC Verbatim Record, 8228th Meeting (10 April 2018) UN Doc S/PV.8228 and S/PV.8228(Resumption 1).

150 Ruys et al (n 147) 355.

151 UK, Prime Minister's Office, 'Policy Paper: Syria Action – UK Government Legal Position' (14 April 2018) www.gov.uk/government/publications/syria-action-uk-government-legal-position/syria-action-ukgovernment-legal-position; see also comments of the UK representative in, UNSC Verbatim Record, 8233rd Meeting (14 April 2018) UN Doc S/PV.8233, 6–7.

152 See Ruys et al (n 147) 357–59. Although the US did produce a legal opinion only on the *domestic* constitutionality of the use of force, rather than the legality of the action in international law international law (359).

153 UN Doc S/PV.8233 (n 151) 8–9.

154 ibid.

of force too.[155] Once again, this political rhetoric purposely did not address the glaring legal issue with these military strikes. It is almost as if France was aware that their actions were illegal but went ahead with them anyway.

Even the supportive international reactions to these strikes were careful to express such support in purely political, rather than legal, terms.[156] States were clearly understanding of the need for some sort of action to be taken, but they very noticeably stopped short of endorsing any legal doctrine allowing unilateral action.[157] Furthermore, the UK's legal argument was met with heavy criticism from legal academics.[158] Dapo Akande, for example, provided his legal opinion for the deputy leader of the opposition Labour Party, persuasively rejecting the UK government's legal position and the suggestion that humanitarian intervention exists as a doctrine in customary international law.[159]

In September 2018, the UK Parliament's House of Commons Foreign Affairs Select Committee released its report following its inquiry into the responsibility to protect and humanitarian intervention.[160] The inquiry was to consider the legal basis to intervene militarily in other states for humanitarian purposes, and the role of the concept of the 'responsibility to protect' to protect civilian populations, specifically assessing the legal basis for the UK's role in conducting the above-mentioned airstrikes in Syria.[161] In its written evidence to the Committee, the FCO reiterated its support for unilateral humanitarian intervention as a right consistent with international law:

> It is the UK's view that humanitarian intervention – that is the use of strictly necessary and proportionate force undertaken in the absence of host state consent to avert an overwhelming and large scale humanitarian emergency – is consistent with international law.
>
> The UK's strikes against Syrian chemical weapons facilities in April 2018 were carried out under the legal basis of humanitarian intervention. The action we took was necessary and proportionate, and designed to alleviate human suffering by degrading the chemical weapons capability of the Syrian regime and deterring the future use of

[155] See further Chapter IV.

[156] See the very detailed coverage of the international responses in Ruys et al (n 147) 362–68.

[157] ibid.

[158] See eg M Milanovic, 'The Syria Strikes: Still Clearly Illegal' *EJIL: Talk!* (15 April 2018) www.ejiltalk.org/the-syria-strikes-still-clearly-illegal/, and the debates within the comments therein; see also in the context of recent events, R Barber, 'Uniting for Peace Not Aggression: Responding to Chemical Weapons in Syria Without Breaking the Law' (2019) 24(1) *Journal of Conflict and Security Law* 71, 80–81, 84–87, 96–98.

[159] Opinion of Professor D Akande, 'The Legality of the UK's Air Strikes on the Assad Government in Syria', (16 April 2018) available at: www.tom-watson.com/legal_advice_on_uk_air_strikes_on_syria (accessed 1 June 2019).

[160] UK, House of Commons Foreign Affairs Committee, 'Global Britain: The Responsibility to Protect and Humanitarian Intervention', HC 1005 (10 September 2018) https://publications.parliament.uk/pa/cm201719/cmselect/cmfaff/1005/1005.pdf.

[161] See generally UK House of Commons Foreign Affairs Committee, 'Responsibility to Protect and Humanitarian Intervention Inquiry' (10 September 2018) www.parliament.uk/business/committees/committees-a-z/commons-select/foreign-affairs-committee/inquiries1/parliament-2017/inquiry8/.

> chemical weapons. The government has published its legal position setting this out in more detail. Many nations have confirmed that our actions under this legal basis have been necessary and legitimate.[162]

The Committee noted the opinions of several commentators and other written evidence opposing the legality of humanitarian intervention.[163] However, the Committee also suggested that there was a 'degree of consensus' about the legitimacy of the airstrikes in the international reaction to them.[164] The Committee concluded:

> Whilst noting the divisions in legal opinion around the concept of humanitarian intervention, we agree that it seems unlikely the creators of the UN Charter would have expected that the prohibition on the use of force would be applied in a way that prevented states from protecting civilian populations and stopping mass atrocities. We therefore believe that under specific circumstances, proportionate and necessary force should be available to be used as a last resort to alleviate extreme humanitarian distress on a large scale. The absence of humanitarian intervention as a final recourse could result in the paralysis of the international system and a failure to act, resulting in grave consequences for civilian populations.[165]

The potential paralysis of the international system is certainly a warning to the international community to find a path that avoids inaction. But this itself does not make an unlawful act become legally permissible. Unfortunately, this report also pays very little attention to the fundamental omission of the UK government's argument – and that is the very clear lack of international support or *opinio juris* in favour of the existence of a 'right' of humanitarian intervention.

Most notably, the Group of 77 have outright rejected the existence of a 'right' to humanitarian intervention, stressing that it had 'no legal basis in the United Nations Charter or in the general principles of international law'.[166] This has also been the long-standing position of the Non-Aligned Movement, as declared in 2004 for example:

> The Ministers reaffirmed the Movement's commitment to enhance international cooperation to resolve international problems of a humanitarian character in full compliance with the Charter of the United Nations, and, in this regard, they reiterated the rejection by the Non-Aligned Movement of the so-called 'right' of humanitarian intervention, which has no basis either in the Charter of the United Nations or in international law.[167]

[162] UK, Foreign and Commonwealth Office, 'Written Evidence from the Foreign and Commonwealth Office (RTP0016)' (3 July 2018) http://data.parliament.uk/writtenevidence/committeeevidence.svc/evidencedocument/foreign-affairs-committee/responsibility-to-protect-rtp-and-humanitarian-intervention/written/84214.pdf, [15]–[16].

[163] Foreign Affairs Committee Report (n 160) [15].

[164] ibid, [17].

[165] ibid, [18].

[166] Group of 77, *Declaration of the South Summit* (10–14 April 2000, Havana, Cuba) [54], available at www.g77.org/summit/Declaration_G77Summit.htm (accessed 31 July 2019).

[167] Non-Aligned Movement, 'Final Outcome Document: XIV Ministerial Conference of the Non-Aligned Movement (Midterm Review)' (17–19 August 2004) (on file with the author), [8] and [295].

This outright rejection of a right to humanitarian intervention has been repeated on several occasions by the Non-Aligned Movement.[168] In this light, the UK's assertions seem quite lonely in a world that, in political terms, is much larger than when the UN Charter came into existence. The need to protect a nation's sovereignty in the international forum remained central to those States involved in the Group of 77 or the Non-Aligned Movement, and so a vaguely defined 'right' of humanitarian intervention, with an unclear position in international law, was unlikely to gain any sort of widespread recognition.

2.4. Conclusions on Humanitarian Intervention

The above discussion highlights the very tense and controversial divide between the understandable call to intervene in the face of horrific atrocities and the fundamental need to uphold the law. Although humanitarian intervention has grown to incorporate a principled approach, with important criteria added to the 'doctrine', this is clearly not enough – the doctrine has not gained the requisite support either in practice or in the *opinio juris* of States to create such a right in customary international law.[169]

3. BETWEEN ILLEGALITY AND INACTION

A new era of international cooperation may have come about in the 1990s, but the post-Cold War attitudes towards intervention on humanitarian grounds remained split. States still found it difficult to balance the cries for help from innocent civilians – suffering from unconscionable atrocities – with the principles of non-intervention, State sovereignty and the prohibition of the use of force.

[168] See, for example: Non-Aligned Movement, 'Final Document of the 12th Conference of Heads of State or Government of Non-Aligned Countries' (29 August–3 September 1998, Durban, South Africa) Annexed to UN Doc A/53/667–S/1998/1071, [8]; Non-Aligned Movement, 'Final Outcome Document: 13th Summit Conference of Heads of State or Government of the Non-Aligned Movement' (24–25 February 2003, Kuala Lumpur, Malaysia), Annexed to UN Doc A/57/759–S/2003/332, [16], [354]; Non-Aligned Movement, 'Final Outcome Document: 14th Summit Conference of Heads of State or Government of the Nonaligned Movement' (11–16 September 2006, Havana, Cuba) Doc NAM 2006/Doc.1/Rev.3, [249]; Non-Aligned Movement, 'Final Outcome Document: XV Summit of Heads of State and Government of the Non-Aligned Movement' (16 July 2009) Doc NAM2009/FD/Doc.1, [440]; Non-Aligned Movement, 'Final Outcome Document: 16th Summit of Heads of State or Government of the Non-Aligned Movement' (26–31 August 2012, Tehran, Iran) Doc NAM 2012/Doc.1/Rev.2, [598]; Non-Aligned Movement, 'Final Outcome Document: 17th Summit of Heads of State and Government of the Non-Aligned Movement' (17–18 September 2016, Island of Margarita, Venezuela) Doc NAM 2016/CoB/Doc.1. Corr.1, [777].

[169] See further, for example, I Brownlie, 'International Law and the Use of Force by States Revisited' (2000) 21 *Australian Yearbook of International Law* 21; M Kohen, 'The Principle of Non-Intervention 25 Years after the Nicaragua Judgment' (2012) 25 *Leiden Journal of International Law* 157, 162; A Sarvarian, 'Humanitarian Intervention After Syria' (2016) 36(1) *Legal Studies* 20, 30.

Even when humanitarian motives were presented, there are questions as to whether the noble goal to protect was in fact their *primary* goal to protect. The international community is therefore faced with a very serious problem: how to respond to a threat or crises of mass atrocities in a way that is both appropriate and legal, particularly when the only body with the power and authority to do so – the UN Security Council – fails to act, or is paralysed by an abuse of the veto power.[170]

As is evident from the previous historical examples, noting Kosovo and Rwanda in particular, such difficulties arise from the temperamental relationship between morality and legality, coupled with the fundamental and important need to uphold the rule of law in all circumstances. Although there is this moral obligation that calls upon the world to respond to mass atrocities, it would undermine the very foundations of our legal principles and systems to respond in such a way that is in itself illegal. In his Millennium Report as Secretary-General, Kofi Annan addressed this critical issue, and asked a very significant question:

> I … accept that the principles of sovereignty and non-interference offer vital protection to small and weak States. But to the critics I would pose this question: if humanitarian intervention is, indeed, an unacceptable assault on sovereignty, how *should* we respond to a Rwanda, to a Srebrenica – to gross and systematic violations of human rights that offend every precept of our common humanity?[171]

Canada responded to the Secretary-General's call, and sponsored the establishment of the International Commission on Intervention and State Sovereignty (ICISS) – a Commission tasked with addressing the legal and practical issues of intervention. The resulting report was titled 'The Responsibility to Protect',[172] to which we shall now turn.

[170] For a further discussion of the paralysis of the Security Council, and the role of the veto power in this regard, see Chapter II, section 3.2.2.

[171] Report of the Secretary-General, *We the Peoples: The Role of the United Nations in the Twenty-First Century*, (27 March 2000) UN Doc A/54/2000, [217].

[172] International Commission on Intervention and State Sovereignty, *The Responsibility to Protect* (Ottawa, International Development Research Centre, 2001).

II

The Responsibility to Protect

In an attempt to address the tense relationship between intervention and State sovereignty, the government of Canada founded the International Commission on Intervention and State Sovereignty (ICISS). In the wake of the Kosovo intervention, the Commission produced a report which proposed an innovative approach to both sovereignty and intervention, namely the responsibility to protect.[1] This chapter will outline the Commission's proposed responsibility, and will assess the international community's adoption of this at the 2005 World Summit, outlining the primary responsibilities of the State and the secondary responsibility of the international community. The subsequent implementation of the responsibility will be demonstrated by comparing a number of cases – including the military intervention by the international community in Libya, compared to the inaction and deadlock in response to the crisis in Syria. These cases are raised to introduce the core problem that this book seeks to address – the inaction or paralysis of the UN Security Council.

1. THE ICISS REPORT

1.1. Changing the Debate

The first major contribution of the Commission was to shift the language of the debate from 'humanitarian intervention' to 'the responsibility to protect'. The ICISS recognised that the language of a 'right to intervene' was unpopular with less powerful States, including the Global South, and that even humanitarian aid agencies had taken issue with the use of the word 'humanitarian' in a way that was essentially 'militarising' or aggressive.[2] But their decision to avoid this language was not just one of semantics or political sensitivity, but an important move in reconceptualising the issue of intervention and its relationship with State sovereignty.[3]

One of the most pressing tasks for the ICISS was to attempt to balance the relationship between the moral duty to prevent or halt atrocities with the *legal*

[1] International Commission on Intervention and State Sovereignty (ICISS), *The Responsibility to Protect* (Ottawa: International Development Research Centre, 2001).

[2] ibid, [1.40].

[3] ibid, [1.41].

principle granting a State its sovereignty. As the UN Secretary-General had said, 'surely no legal principle – not even sovereignty – can ever shield crimes against humanity'.[4] But the Commission made a ground-breaking decision to address this issue by redefining sovereignty *as responsibility* – as opposed to the traditional notion of sovereignty as power, as noted by the Commission itself.[5] Not only did this help to alter the language into something less confrontational, it also evolved the general approach to humanitarian crises towards something significantly more proactive.

This idea of 'sovereignty as responsibility' in this context can be attributed to the work of Francis Deng.[6] The Commission utilised this idea to shift the concentration of the debate to a duty to protect, focusing upon the broader issues involved with situations of humanitarian catastrophes rather than just the interveners and the intervention itself.[7] It was suggested that the responsibility to protect 'resides first and foremost with the State whose people are directly affected' by the crisis in question.[8] This, the Commission said, reflects not only position of international law, but also the practical realities of who is best placed to make a positive difference.[9] Rather than focus just on intervention, the responsibility to protect seeks to put the onus on the domestic authorities who may be better placed to take action at a much earlier stage to prevent domestic issues from turning into conflicts or other situations that might increase the risk of atrocities from taking place.

Noting that this position might not always offer a solution in all circumstances, the Commission suggested that a residual responsibility also lies with the broader international community.[10] It was put forward that:

> This fallback responsibility is activated when a particular state is clearly either *unwilling or unable* to fulfil its responsibility to protect or is itself the actual perpetrator of crimes or atrocities; or where people living outside a particular state are directly threatened by actions taking place there. This responsibility also requires that in some circumstances action must be taken by the broader community of states to support populations that are in jeopardy or under serious threat.[11]

These positions later became the 'primary' and 'secondary' responsibilities that were accepted by the international community.[12] The Commission can be praised for taking this approach. Not only does it seem logically sound, but

[4] Report of the Secretary-General, *We the Peoples: The Role of the United Nations in the Twenty-First Century* (27 March 2000) UN Doc A/54/2000, [219].

[5] ICISS Report (n 1) ch 2, [2.4].

[6] FM Deng et al, *Sovereignty as Responsibility: Conflict Management in Africa* (Washington DC, Brookings Institution Press, 1996).

[7] ICISS Report (n 1) [2.29].

[8] ibid, [2.30].

[9] ibid.

[10] ibid, [2.31].

[11] ibid (emphasis added).

[12] See section 2.2.

this approach ensures that the most appropriate action is taken by the most appropriate actors – and it comes with a significantly lesser threat (inherent in a doctrine of humanitarian intervention) that the sovereignty of a State, or even the underpinnings of the UN Charter, would be wrongly disregarded.

The ICISS anticipated that this new approach would incorporate a responsibility to protect: human rights, generally;[13] human security;[14] in response to civil war, or circumstances of a failed State;[15] and, in response to natural disasters or environmental catastrophe.[16] It should be noted, however, that this scope is also significantly wider than what was eventually accepted by the international community, where only atrocity crimes such as genocide, war crimes, crimes against humanity and ethnic cleansing were adopted as part of the responsibility to protect.[17]

1.2. A Focus on Peace

Most importantly, the ICISS looked beyond intervention and stressed a continuum of responsibilities that focused on the prevention of mass atrocities and humanitarian disasters. It established: (i) a 'responsibility to prevent', addressing root and direct causes of both internal conflict and other crises that put populations at risk;[18] (ii) a 'responsibility to react', responding to situations with the necessary and appropriate measures including, in extreme cases, military intervention;[19] and (iii) a 'responsibility to rebuild', providing full assistance with the necessary reconstruction, recovery and reconciliation to further prevent such crises from reoccurring.[20]

In terms of the 'responsibility to prevent', the Commission stressed that the focus on preventing atrocities should come well before the point of simply reacting early to a crisis. In this sense, the responsibility to prevent addresses risk factors ranging from an outbreak of unrest to the 'root causes' of tensions that may include the lack of respect and protection of human rights.[21] Therefore, this part of the responsibility concentrates on actions available well *before* the manifestation of a humanitarian crisis – very different to the position of a 'right' to intervene.

[13] ICISS Report (n 1) [2.16]–[2.20].
[14] ibid, [2.21]–[2.23].
[15] ibid, [4.40].
[16] ibid.
[17] See TG Weiss, 'R2P after 9/11 and the World Summit,' (2006) 24 *Wisconsin International Law Journal* 741, 750, who labels the World Summit Outcome as 'R2P-Lite'.
[18] ibid, ch 3.
[19] ibid, ch 4.
[20] ibid, ch 5.
[21] ibid, ch 3 generally, and [3.1]–[3.3].

The guidance from the Commission in this respect was very comprehensive. Taking note of the UN's growing commitment to conflict prevention,[22] and the (then) recent steps taken in this field,[23] the ICISS called for an incorporation of the responsibility to protect in peaceful methods of prevention. A number of methods of support were suggested, reflecting what could be described as 'preventive diplomacy' – a range of peaceful political processes overseen by the UN's Department of Political Affairs.[24] This, essentially, encompasses an enhanced capacity-building role for the international community, aimed at: increasing respect and protection of human rights and the rule of law; addressing the 'root causes' of potential conflict; providing support for advancing good governance; or establishing 'good offices' missions and mediation efforts to promote peaceful dialogue or reconciliation.[25]

Additionally, the ICISS said that the responsibility to prevent calls for a better 'early warning' capacity, bearing in mind particular risk factors connected with the responsibility to protect.[26] In terms of more *direct* measures of prevention, the Commission also made suggestions that included: positive or negative economic inducements;[27] political and diplomatic deployments;[28] the involvement of the International Criminal Court (ICC);[29] and, a *limited* role for military action for prevention in the form of preventive deployment.[30]

The 'responsibility to rebuild' is very similar in the tools that it utilises. Under this part of the responsibility to protect, the ICISS emphasised the importance of the work that *follows* an intervention. In this sense, 'there should be a genuine commitment to helping to build a durable peace, and promoting good governance and sustainable development'.[31] The Commission acknowledged that this part of the responsibility may call for years of work, even if the mass atrocities have been completely averted.[32] Working for durable peace therefore requires a number of tasks including: diplomatic peacebuilding; peacekeeping for the maintenance of security; the disarmament, demobilisation and reintegration of militia or armed forces; and, above all, justice and reconciliation for the victims of atrocity crimes.[33]

It is clear from all of these examples that the ICISS foresaw a much greater involvement for peaceful processes and diplomatic solutions than was

[22] ibid, [3.5]–[3.9].

[23] See eg Report of the Secretary-General, *Prevention of Armed Conflict* (7 June 2001) UN Doc A/55/985–S/2001/574.

[24] UN Department of Political Affairs, http://www.un.org/undpa/en (accessed 31 July 2019).

[25] ICISS Report (n 1) [3.3].

[26] ibid, [3.10]–[3.17].

[27] ibid, [3.27].

[28] ibid, [3.26].

[29] ibid, [3.28]–[3.30].

[30] ibid, [3.32].

[31] ibid, [5.1].

[32] ibid, [5.2].

[33] ibid, ch 5 generally.

acknowledged by the debate on humanitarian intervention. Of course, humanitarian intervention was always said to be an option of 'last resort', but it is a particular strength of the ICISS report that it acknowledges the alternatives and puts forward such guidance on peaceful measures, instead of simply concentrating on the 'intervention' aspect of responding to atrocities.

1.3. Intervening with Caution

Of course, the Commission's push for focus on the more peaceful measures in preventing and halting mass atrocities is welcomed and applauded. The focus of this book, however, is on the highly debated legal position of intervention against a State's sovereignty, independence, and territorial integrity – either using forcible or non-forcible means. In this regard, the ICISS did make some notable remarks about the 'responsibility to react' that are important for our discussion.

The ICISS emphasised the need to take every action short of coercive measures or military force before any such intervention is taken.[34] When this becomes difficult, the Commission stated:

> When preventive measures fail to resolve or contain the situation and when a state is unable or unwilling to redress the situation, then interventionary measures by other members of the broader community of states may be required. These coercive measures may include political, economic or judicial measures, and in extreme cases – but only extreme cases – they may also include military action. As a matter of first principles, in the case of reaction just as with prevention, less intrusive and coercive measures should always be considered before more coercive and intrusive ones are applied.[35]

What is interesting about the ICISS position is that it outlines measures *short of force* that would be preferable – measures, such as sanctions and embargos, that could still impose upon a State's sovereignty and independence.[36] Such measures are still coercive in nature, but do not come with the risks of military action, and so they are certainly to be considered before any intervention of a military kind.

However, the Commission did warn that 'these non-military measures can be blunt and often indiscriminate weapons and must be used with extreme care to avoid doing more harm than good – especially to civilian populations'.[37] In the more extreme cases, if the need and necessity does arise to resort to force,

[34] ibid [4.3].
[35] ibid, [4.1].
[36] ibid, [4.6]–[4.9].
[37] ibid, [4.5].

the ICISS suggested six criteria to be undertaken before such action is taken.[38] Those criteria called for: (i) intervention to be authorised by the *right authority*; (ii) a *just cause* for intervention; (iii) those who intervene do so with the *right intention*; (iv) any military action to be of a *last resort*; (v) *proportional means* so that the intervention is the minimum necessary to secure the humanitarian objective in question; and (vi) the intervention must have *reasonable prospects* of succeeding.

It is not the aim of this book to assess this legitimacy criteria. Instead, this study concentrates largely on the general *legality* of the measures being proposed. For now, it is worthwhile to note what the Commission said about the 'right authority' criterion. Considering that the bedrock principles of the non-use of force and non-intervention are recognised by the UN Charter, the Commission noted the *primary* role of the UN Security Council as the 'right authority' for authorising interventions.[39] However, the Commission also noted the problems that have been aired about the Security Council. Firstly, the Commission considered the issue of the veto, while highlighting the current unrepresentative make-up of the Council, and deplored the unconscionable possibility of one veto-holding State 'overriding the rest of humanity on matters of grave humanitarian concern'.[40] Related to this, the political will of the Security Council was underlined as another potential block to the necessary decisions being made, as was the case in 1994 regarding Rwanda.

Considering this, the Commission warned that any inaction by the Security Council would undermine not only the Council itself, but the UN security system as a whole.[41] The Commission therefore asked: what alternative authorities are there when the Security Council fails to act? This is the question that is at the heart of this book, and the fact that the ICISS considered it in their seminal report on the responsibility to protect binds this issue to the emerging concept in such a way that makes it one of the most important questions surrounding the Security Council today.

The Commission considered two possible alternatives – each of which will be examined, analysed and tested in light of wider questions of international law in later chapters. One possibility noted by the Commission was for the international community to take action through the General Assembly.[42] More specifically, it suggested that a recommendation to intervene could be made through the 'Uniting for Peace' procedure[43] following an Emergency Special Session, which would provide a high degree of legitimacy if supported by

[38] ibid, [4.10]–[4.16].
[39] ibid, [6.2]–[6.6].
[40] ibid, [6.20].
[41] ibid, [6.22]–[6.27], [6.36]–[6.40].
[42] ibid, [6.29]–[6.30].
[43] UNGA Res 366 (V), *Uniting for Peace* (3 November 1950) UN Doc A/RES/377(V).

Member States – although, in the view of the Commission, this may not provide any *legal* authority for intervention.[44]

Another possibility considered was collective action by regional organisations under Chapter VIII of the Charter. The Commission raised the question as to whether regional organisations could act within or against their own Member States, and whether approval from the Security Council could be granted *after* action had been taken.[45] This particular issue will be addressed in Chapter VI alongside an assessment of the role of regional organisations in implementing the responsibility to protect beyond the Security Council.

Thirdly, the Commission gave a warning as to the implications of the Security Council's inaction. Most crucially, the Commission warned:

> [I]f the Security Council fails to discharge its responsibility in conscience-shocking situations crying out for action, then it is unrealistic to expect that concerned states will rule out other means and forms of action to meet the gravity and urgency of these situations.[46]

2. RESPONSE TO THE ICISS REPORT

2.1. Calls for Recognition

The first notable response to the ICISS report came from the Secretary-General's High-Level Panel on Threats, Challenges and Change. This Panel produced a report in 2004 that recognised the emergence of a 'responsibility to protect'.[47] In particular, the Panel stated:

> We endorse the emerging norm that there is a collective international responsibility to protect, exercisable by the Security Council authorizing military intervention as a last resort, in the event of genocide and other large-scale killing, ethnic cleansing or serious violations of international humanitarian law which sovereign Governments have proved powerless or unwilling to prevent.[48]

As Chhabra and Zucker note,[49] the High-Level Panel seems to have omitted mass starvation, civil war and natural disasters from the atrocities covered by the ICISS's version of the responsibility to protect.[50] But what is most notable

[44] ICISS Report (n 1) [6.29]–[6.30], [6.7]. This book delves into this question of level authority and the General Assembly's powers under the UN Charter in Chapter VI.

[45] ibid, [6.31]–[6.35].

[46] ibid, [6.39].

[47] High-Level Panel on Threats, Challenges and Change, *A More Secure World: Our Shared Responsibility* (New York, UN Publications, 2004).

[48] ibid, [203].

[49] T Chhabra and JB Zucker, 'Defining the Crimes' in J Genser et al (eds), *The Responsibility to Protect: The Promise of Stopping Mass Atrocities in Our Time* (Oxford, Oxford University Press, 2011).

[50] ibid, 40.

about the Panel's position is that it refers to the responsibility to protect as an 'emerging norm', suggesting that it might become a rule of customary international law in the future, and therefore a legally binding duty.[51]

The Panel also put forward a set of legitimacy criteria, similar to those put forward by the ICISS, recommending that the Security Council should *always* address them when considering an intervention.[52] Interestingly, these criteria did not address the ICISS's 'right authority' criterion, but the Panel did recommend that individual States should also subscribe to their legitimacy criteria, while stopping short of addressing the issue of Security Council inaction.[53] The Security Council has not adopted any of these, or any other similar criteria.

Secretary-General Kofi Annan produced his own report,[54] pushing for more momentum within the international community on the endorsement of the responsibility to protect, also describing it as an 'emerging norm'.[55] Equally, he repeated the call for the Security Council to adopt a resolution setting out legitimacy principles that it should use as guidance when deciding whether to authorise a use of force or intervention.[56] These calls were the final push for the international community to adopt the responsibility to protect, with the Secretary-General aiming for the 2005 World Summit as the perfect opportunity to do so.

2.2. The 2005 World Summit – Recognising the Responsibility to Protect

In the run up to the 2005 World Summit, the international conversation on the concept of a responsibility to protect intensified. At first, some groups were hesitant to accept the concept, especially those who had previously rejected a 'right' to humanitarian intervention. For example, the Non-Aligned Movement expressed concern that the responsibility to protect had similarities with 'humanitarian intervention', and it was suggested that any development of the concept should concentrate on its relationship with the principles of non-intervention and State sovereignty.[57] On the other hand, States such as Canada sought to quell such fears when addressing the General Assembly debate, reiterating that the aim *was not* to 'argu[e] for a unilateral right to intervene in one country whenever another country feels like it', emphasising that the responsibility to

[51] The legal nature of the responsibility to protect is considered below in Chapter III.

[52] High-Level Panel on Threats, Challenges and Change (n 47) [207].

[53] ibid, [209].

[54] Report of the Secretary-General, *In Larger Freedom: Towards Development, Security and Human Rights for All* (21 March 2005) UN Doc A/59/2005.

[55] ibid, [135].

[56] ibid, [126].

[57] Statement by Ambassador Radzi Rahman (Malaysia) on behalf of the Non-Aligned Movement, *Informal Meeting of the Plenary of the General Assembly Concerning the Draft Outcome Document*, 21 June 2005, [4(g)(i)].

protect is not a license for intervention but 'an international guarantor of international accountability'.[58]

Eventually, the international community united unanimously and accepted its own version of the responsibility to protect at the 2005 World Summit. The text of this ground-breaking recognition is worth reciting in full:

> 138. Each individual State has the responsibility to protect its populations from genocide, war crimes, ethnic cleansing and crimes against humanity. This responsibility entails the prevention of such crimes, including their incitement, through appropriate and necessary means. We accept that responsibility and will act in accordance with it. The international community should, as appropriate, encourage and help States to exercise this responsibility and support the United Nations in establishing an early warning capability.
>
> 139. The international community, through the United Nations, also has the responsibility to use appropriate diplomatic, humanitarian and other peaceful means, in accordance with Chapters VI and VIII of the Charter, to help protect populations from genocide, war crimes, ethnic cleansing and crimes against humanity. In this context, we are prepared to take collective action, in a timely and decisive manner, through the Security Council, in accordance with the Charter, including Chapter VII, on a case-by-case basis and in cooperation with relevant regional organizations as appropriate, should peaceful means be inadequate and national authorities are manifestly failing to protect their populations from genocide, war crimes, ethnic cleansing and crimes against humanity. We stress the need for the General Assembly to continue consideration of the responsibility to protect populations from genocide, war crimes, ethnic cleansing and crimes against humanity and its implications, bearing in mind the principles of the Charter and international law. We also intend to commit ourselves, as necessary and appropriate, to helping States build capacity to protect their populations from genocide, war crimes, ethnic cleansing and crimes against humanity and to assisting those which are under stress before crises and conflicts break out.[59]

The first noticeable difference between the international community's acceptance of the responsibility to protect and the original version promoted by the ICISS is that it has a defined scope encompassing 'genocide, war crimes, crimes against humanity, and ethnic cleansing'. The ICISS approach was significantly wider in that it also sought to apply the responsibility to other humanitarian situations such as: gross violations of human rights; response to civil war; circumstances of a failed State; and in response to natural disasters or environmental catastrophe.

The structure of the responsibilities themselves, however, remained intact. As the Outcome Document states, each individual State has the responsibility

[58] Prime Minister Paul Martin (Canada), UNGA Verbatim Record, 5th Plenary Meeting, 59th Session (22 September 2004) UN Doc A/59/PV.5, 31.

[59] 2005 World Summit Outcome Document, in UNGA Res 60/1 (15 September 2005) UN Doc A/RES/60/1, [138]–[139].

to protect its populations – this is the *primary responsibility* of the domestic State. The States of the world then agreed that the international community should 'encourage and help States' to exercise this responsibility. More crucially, however, the Outcome goes on to state that the international community also has the responsibility to use appropriate diplomatic, humanitarian and other peaceful means to help protect populations – this forms the first part of the *secondary responsibility* on the international community. The second part of this *secondary responsibility* comes when peaceful measures prove to be inadequate and the national authorities are 'manifestly failing' in their primary responsibility to protect. Here, the 'manifestly failing' threshold seems to replace the ICISS's threshold of states being 'unwilling or unable', and the question remains as to whether this has any effect on the 'activation' of this part of the international community's secondary responsibility. Importantly, as the Outcome states, action in response to such a manifest failure would be taken through the Security Council.

3. IMPLEMENTATION OF THE WORLD SUMMIT OUTCOME

3.1. The Secretary-General's Reports

One of the most notable contributions to the development of the responsibility to protect is arguably that of the UN Secretary-General's annual reports on the matter.[60] From 2009, the Secretary-General released annual reports on different aspects of the responsibility to protect, often forming the basis for consideration in informal interactive dialogues of the General Assembly.[61]

In his first report,[62] the Secretary-General introduced a 'Three-Pillar' approach to implementing the responsibility to protect. Pillar I of this approach reflects the protection responsibilities of the State – ie the State's primary responsibility to protect its own populations.[63] Pillar II is the international community's responsibility to give assistance to States in their primary responsibilities, and to build their capacities in being able to do so.[64] Finally, Pillar III is the 'timely and decisive response' required by the international community to respond collectively when a State is manifestly failing to protect in accordance with Pillar I.[65] This approach highlights the broad scope of the responsibility,

[60] Subsequently continued by the most recent UN Secretary General, António Guterres.

[61] Although there are no detailed official UN Records for these meetings, see a collection of official statements compiled at: Global Centre for the Responsibility to Protect, 'Summaries of UN General Assembly Interactive Dialogues on R2P' *Global Centre for the Responsibility to Protect* (September 2017) available at: www.globalr2p.org/resources/897 (accessed 31 July 2019).

[62] Report of the Secretary-General, *Implementing the Responsibility to Protect* (12 January 2009) UN Doc A/63/677.

[63] ibid, [11] and section II.

[64] ibid, [11] and section III.

[65] ibid, [11] and section IV.

and therefore the equality of each Pillar, demonstrating that the responsibility to protect is not just another way of framing or expanding a 'right' to intervention. The ICISS's sequential method, on the other hand – utilising a framework of the responsibility to *prevent, react* and *rebuild* – can be more illustrative in how the tools and methods of each Pillar overlap. Nevertheless, while the focus of this study, by its concentration on coercive and forceful methods of intervention, is more concerned with the responsibility to *react* – and thus by implication 'Pillar III' of the Secretary-General's framework – comparisons are still made to the methods of *prevention* where necessary. This is not an attempt to make any of these Pillars of 'unequal length' – ie the study does not consider Pillar III any more important than Pillars I and II. As the Secretary General argues:

> If the three supporting pillars were of unequal length, the edifice of the responsibility to protect could become unstable, leaning precariously in one direction or another. Similarly, unless all three pillars are strong the edifice could implode and collapse. All three must be ready to be utilized at any point, as there is no set sequence for moving from one to another, especially in a strategy of early and flexible response.[66]

Subsequent reports of the Secretary-General have often concentrated on the prevention of atrocity crimes, often looking at long-term international capacity-building in this respect.[67] When the Secretary-General did discuss methods that might be utilised to implement Pillar III more generally,[68] these were largely discussed as methods that may be utilised 'through the Security Council', as provided for in the World Summit Outcome itself.[69] In fact, these reports have often cautiously excluded discussing what measures can be taken after the Security Council has failed to step in – after a situation has deteriorated so far that preventing atrocities becomes a mission of stopping ongoing crimes from causing further harm to a population. However, in his first report, the Secretary-General did acknowledge the ability of the General Assembly to take 'collective measures',[70] but this was subsequently contradicted in his 2016

[66] ibid, [12].

[67] See Report of the Secretary-General, *Early Warning, Assessment, and the Responsibility to Protect* (14 July 2010) UN Doc A/64/864; Report of the Secretary-General, *Responsibility to Protect: State Responsibility and Prevention* (9 July 2013) UN Doc A/67/929–S/2013/399; Report of the Secretary-General, *Fulfilling Our Collective Responsibility: International Assistance and the Responsibility to Protect* (11 July 2014) UN Doc A/68/947–S/2014/449; Report of the Secretary-General, *Implementing the Responsibility to Protect: Accountability for Prevention* (10 August 2017) UN Doc A/71/1016–S/2017/556; Report of the Secretary-General, *Responsibility to Protect: From Early Warning to Early Action* (1 June 2018) UN Doc A/72/884–S/2018/525; Report of the Secretary-General, *Responsibility to Protect: Lessons Learned for Prevention* (10 June 2019) UN Doc A/73/898–S/2019/463.

[68] See eg Report of the Secretary-General, *Responsibility to Protect: Timely and Decisive Response* (25 July 2012) UN Doc A/66/874–S/2012/578; Report of the Secretary-General, *The Role of Regional and Sub-Regional Arrangements in Implementing the Responsibility to Protect* (18 June 2011) UN Doc A/65/877–S/2011/393.

[69] World Summit Outcome (n 59) [139].

[70] *Implementing the Responsibility to Protect* (n 67) [56], also acknowledging its ability to recommend 'sanctions' at [57]–[58].

Report[71] where he stated: 'While only the Security Council has the authority to mandate coercive means, deadlock in that body should never be used as an excuse for general inaction.'[72]

When taking stock of 10 years of the international community's recognition of the responsibility to protect in 2015, the Secretary-General made two important points.[73] Firstly, addressing common perceptions that Pillar III was solely concerned with the use of force, he stated:

> This perception needs to be countered. First, the choice is not between inaction and the use of force. Non-military tools have made a tangible difference in responding to the commission of atrocity crimes and preventing their escalation. Second, even in intractable situations characterized by continuing violence, international actors have attempted to fulfil their responsibility to protect through political, diplomatic and humanitarian means. These efforts may at times have fallen short of delivering a long-term protective environment, but they have succeeded in saving lives. Finally, in some circumstances it may not be judged possible to employ force for protection purposes without potentially causing more harm than good.[74]

The Secretary-General also made a very important acknowledgement when he confirmed that: 'The Security Council has too often failed to live up to its global responsibility, allowing narrower strategic interests to impede consensus and preclude a robust collective response.'[75] It is in this context that this book discusses the responsibility to protect beyond the UN Security Council – acknowledging that the framework does not only provide for the use of force, but also non-coercive measures.

3.2. Implementation by the Security Council

3.2.1. Recognition and Implementation in Libya

According to the Global Centre for the Responsibility to Protect, as of June 2019, the responsibility to protect had been invoked by the UN Security Council in 81 resolutions.[76] In one of its first Resolutions citing the responsibility to protect, the Council 'reaffirms the provisions of paragraphs 138 and 139 of the

[71] Report of the Secretary-General, *Mobilizing Collective Action: The Next Decade of the Responsibility to Protect* (22 July 2016) UN Doc A/70/999–S/2016/620.

[72] ibid, [46].

[73] Report of the Secretary-General, *A Vital and Enduring Commitment: Implementing the Responsibility to Protect* (13 July 2015) UN Doc A/69/981–S/2015/500.

[74] ibid, [38].

[75] ibid, [44]; for consideration of instances where the Security Council has failed in its responsibility to protect, see Chapter III generally.

[76] Global Centre for the Responsibility to Protect, 'R2P References in United Nations Security Council Resolutions and Presidential Statements' (Global Centre for the Responsibility to Protect, June 2019) available at: www.globalr2p.org/resources/335 (accessed 31 July 2019). This webpage provides the most up-to-date collection of these resolutions.

2005 World Summit Outcome Document'.[77] This was repeated in several other thematic Resolutions.[78]

The Security Council often also reaffirms a State's primary responsibility to protect when addressing situations. The most notable example of this is the Council's response to Colonel Muammar Gaddafi's threat of committing atrocity crimes in Libya in 2011. Gaddafi responded to an increase in popular protests against his leadership by cracking down on those who supported his removal from power, labelling these protestors 'cockroaches', and publicly vowing to track them down 'house by house' and kill them.[79] The Security Council responded to this crackdown by expressing 'deep concern at the deaths of civilians, and rejecting unequivocally the incitement to hostility and violence against the civilian population made from the highest level of the Libyan government'.[80]

The Council recalled Libya's responsibility to protect its population,[81] referred the situation to the ICC, and adopted a selection of coercive measures including travel bans, arms embargos and asset freezes.[82] Subsequently, when the violence continued, the Security Council authorised Member States, under Chapter VII, to take *all necessary measures* (excluding a foreign occupation force) to protect civilians and civilian populated areas under threat of attack, as well as all necessary measures to enforce a no-fly zone.[83]

This response to the threat of mass atrocities has been hailed by Zifcak[84] as the first coercive intervention authorised by the Security Council and undertaken pursuant to the responsibility to protect.[85] Similarly, the Secretary-General believed this Resolution 'affirms, clearly and unequivocally, the international community's determination to fulfil its responsibility to protect civilians from violence perpetrated upon them by their own government'.[86]

[77] UNSC Res 1674 (2006) (28 April 2006) UN Doc S/RES/1674(2006), [4].

[78] See eg: UNSC Res 1894 (2009) (11 November 2009) UN Doc S/RES/1894(2009) preamble [7]; UNSC Res 2117 (2013) (5 December 2013) UN Doc S/RES/2117(2013), preamble [17]; UNSC Res 2150 (2012) (16 April 2014) UN Doc S/RES/2150 (2014), [1]; UNSC Res 2170 (2014) (15 August 2014) UN Doc S/RES/2170(2014) preamble [15]; UNSC Res 2171 (2014) (21 August 2014) UN Doc S/RES/2171(2014) preamble [7] and operative [16]; UNSC Res 2185 (2014) (20 November 2014) UN Doc S/RES/2185(2014) preamble [23]; UNSC Res 2220 (2015) (22 May 2015) UN Doc S/RES/2220(2015) preamble [11]; UNSC Res 2250 (2015) (9 December 2015) UN Doc S/RES/2250(2015) [8]; UNSC Res 2286 (2016) (3 May 2016) UN Doc S/RES/2286(2016) preamble [20]; UNSC Res 2349 (2017) (31 March 2017) UN Doc S/RES/2349(2017) [12].

[79] See K Fahim and DD Kirkpatrick, 'Qaddafi's Grip on the Capital Tightens as Revolt Grows' *New York Times* (22 February 2011) www.nytimes.com/2011/02/23/world/africa/23libya.html?pagewanted=all (accessed 31 July 2019).

[80] UNSC Res 1970 (2011) (26 February 2011) UN Doc S/RES/1970(2011) preamble [2].

[81] ibid, preamble [9].

[82] ibid.

[83] UNSC Res 1973 (2011) (17 March 2011) UN Doc S/RES/1973(2011), [4] and [8].

[84] S Zifcak, 'The Responsibility to Protect after Libya and Syria' (2012) 13 *Melbourne Journal of International Law* 59.

[85] ibid, 61.

[86] UNSG Press Release, 'Secretary-General Says Security Council Action on Libya Affirms International Community's Determination to Protect Civilians from Own Government's Violence'

Unfortunately, when NATO's bombing campaign to protect civilians morphed into one of regime change, this raised the question as to whether NATO went beyond the Security Council's authorisation.[87] Russia and China, in particular, warned against any arbitrary interpretation of the Resolution and any actions going beyond those mandated by the Council – highlighting also the consequences of civilian deaths that arose from NATO's targeting of certain facilities.[88] On the other hand, Thakur reasoned that if the Resolution's restrictions had been respected, then the civil war and the international intervention could well have been longer and more lives could have been lost in the long run.[89]

While NATO's operation might be seen as implementing the responsibility to *react* to atrocity crimes, it became apparent that the subsequent, and equally important, responsibility to *rebuild* was not sufficiently implemented. In 2013, the Secretary-General noted that because of the lack of operational capability in Libya's defence and police forces, revolutionary brigades continued to play a key role in providing security.[90] Moreover, 'a considerable number of revolutionary fighters are not willing to surrender their weapons to State authorities and be absorbed into official State security structures or resume civilian life'.[91] Furthermore, a 2016 investigation by the Office of the UN High Commissioner for Human Rights found that widespread violations of international human rights law and international humanitarian law were still ongoing.[92]

These failures, and the arguments against NATO's conduct in Libya, have also enhanced strong divides over the crisis in Syria.

3.2.2. The Problem of Security Council Paralysis – The Situation in Syria

The most fundamental flaw with relying solely on the Security Council for any robust response to a crisis is demonstrated by its inability to act in the Syrian crisis since 2011.[93] From simple protests, followed by a crackdown on civilians,

(18 March 2011) Press Release SG/SM/13454-SC/10201-AFR/2144, available at www.un.org/press/en/2011/sgsm13454.doc.htm (accessed 31 July 2019).

[87] Zifcak (n 84) 66.

[88] UNSC Verbatim Record, 6528th Meeting (4 May 2011) UN Doc S/PV.6528, 9–10; see also on this point, Report of the Secretary-General, *Responsibility to Protect: Timely and Decisive Response* (25 July 2012) UN Doc A/66/874–S/2012/578, [54]–[55]; and generally, Human Rights Council, *Report of the International Commission of Inquiry on Libya* (28 January 2014) UN Doc A/HRC/19/68.

[89] R Thakur, 'R2P after Libya and Syria: Engaging Emerging Powers' (2013) 31(2) *Washington Quarterly* 61, 70.

[90] Report of the Secretary-General, *On the United Nations Support Mission in Libya* (21 February 2013) UN Doc S/2013/104, [43].

[91] ibid.

[92] Human Rights Council, *Investigation by the Office of the United Nations High Commissioner for Human Rights on Libya* (15 February 2016) UN Doc A/HRC/31/47, [60]–[65].

[93] This is by no means the only example of inaction, but has been selected here due to its topical relevance to the main issue at the heart of this book – the paralysis and inaction of the UN Security Council. For discussion on other situations where it has been suggested the Security Council has

to an all-out civil war, the situation in Syria has deteriorated from the beginning of the crisis in March 2011.[94] Human Rights Watch has reported that the death toll from the Syrian crisis reached 470,000 in February 2016,[95] and 511,000 by March 2018.[96] In that time, the Human Rights Council's Independent Commission of Inquiry on Syria (CoI) reported on allegations of war crimes, genocide, crimes against humanity, and the use of chemical weapons against civilians, committed by both the Syrian regime, and some rebel factions, including the terrorist group ISIL (or Da'esh) that utilised the crisis to build a stronghold in Syria.[97] As early as 2012, the Inquiry determined:

> The Government has manifestly failed in its responsibility to protect the population; its forces have committed widespread, systematic and gross human rights violations, amounting to crimes against humanity, with the apparent knowledge and consent of the highest levels of the State. Anti-Government armed groups have also committed abuses, although not comparable in scale and organization with those carried out by the State.[98]

The most recent report by the Commission of Inquiry noted that: 'Violence throughout the Syrian Arab Republic continues to be waged in blatant violation of basic international humanitarian and human rights law principles, primarily affecting civilians countrywide.'[99]

The Security Council's response to this crisis has been abysmal – it has been unable to take any robust action, or to follow up on its demands with any sort of coercive measure, having been paralysed by the veto of Syria's ally, Russia. For example, a draft resolution in October 2011 would have condemned the

not fully lived up to its responsibilities, see for example: A de Waal, 'Darfur and the Failure of the Responsibility to Protect' (2007) 83(2) *International Affairs* 1039; and L Glanville, 'Darfur and the Responsibilities of Sovereignty' (2011) 15(3) *The International Journal of Human Rights* 462.

[94] See, generally, *BBC News*, 'Syria: the Story of the Conflict' (11 March 2016) www.bbc.co.uk/news/world-middle-east-26116868 (accessed 31 July 2019); for the beginning of the crisis, see Human Rights Council, *Report of the Independent International Commission of Inquiry on the Syrian Arab Republic* (23 November 2011) UN Doc A/HRC/S-17/2/Add.1; and for the most recent assessment of the situation at the time of writing, see Human Rights Council, *Report of the Independent International Commission of Inquiry on the Syrian Arab Republic* (9 August 2019) UN Doc A/HRC/39/65.

[95] Human Rights Watch, *World Report 2017: Events of 2016* (HRW, 2017) 571, available at: www.hrw.org/sites/default/files/world_report_download/wr2017-web.pdf (accessed 31 July 2019).

[96] Human Rights Watch, *World Report 2019: Events of 2018* (HRW, 2018) 554, available at: www.hrw.org/sites/default/files/world_report_download/hrw_world_report_2019.pdf (accessed 31 July 2019).

[97] See, generally, the *Reports of the Independent International Commission of Inquiry on the Syrian Arab Republic*: A/HRC/S-17/2/Add.1 (23 November 2011); A/HRC/19/69 (22 February 2012); A/HRC/21/50 (15 August 2012); A/HRC/22/59 (5 February 2013); A/HRC/23/58 (4 June 2013); A/HRC/24/46 (11 September 2013); A/HRC/25/65 (12 February 2014); A/HRC/27/60 (13 August 2014); A/HRC/28/69 (5 February 2015); A/HRC/30/48 (13 August 2015); A/HRC/31/68 (11 February 2016); A/HRC/33/55 (6 September 2016); A/HRC/34/64 (1 March 2017) (Special Inquiry into the Events in Aleppo); A/HRC/36/55 (8 August 2017).

[98] Human Rights Council, *Report of the Independent International Commission of Inquiry on the Syrian Arab Republic* (22 February 2012) UN Doc A/HRC/19/69, [126].

[99] *Report of Commission of Inquiry on Syria* (n 94) 1.

'grave and systematic human rights violations and the use of force against civilians by the Syrian authorities', and also threatened the use of sanctions.[100] Russia and China vetoed this based upon, among other things, NATO's over-interpretation of the authorisation granted in response to the Libyan crisis.[101] In particular, Russia argued that: 'The international community is alarmed by statements that compliance with Security Council resolutions on Libya in the NATO interpretation is a model for the future actions of NATO in implementing the responsibility to protect.'[102] The US representative responded strongly against Russia's arguments: 'Let there be no doubt: this is not about military intervention; this is not about Libya. That is a cheap ruse by those who would rather sell arms to the Syrian regime than stand with the Syrian people.'[103]

This bickering between the Permanent Five continued on most occasions that the situation in Syria was discussed in the Security Council, as did the pattern of Russia (sometimes backed up by China) vetoing any robust Resolution that either cited Chapter VII, or made demands to the Syrian authorities. Up until the time of writing, Russia had vetoed 12 draft resolutions.[104] These included attempts to, for example: refer the situation to the ICC;[105] condemn and demand an end to human rights violations;[106] demand humanitarian access and a cessation of aerial bombing in certain areas;[107] to mandate humanitarian ceasefires;[108] and to adopt sanctions following an investigation into the use of chemical weapons.[109] These all took place in the face of evidence and allegations of crimes against humanity, and widespread human rights violations by the Syrian regime and by certain opposition forces.[110]

The Council did unite on some occasions, for example to establish a small UN Supervision Mission in Syria (UNSMIS) with an envoy led by former

[100] UNSC Draft Resolution of 4 October 2011, UN Doc S/2011/612, [1] and [11].

[101] UNSC Verbatim Record, 6627th Meeting (4 October 2011) UN Doc S/PV.6627, 4–5.

[102] ibid.

[103] ibid, 8.

[104] See UNSC Draft Resolutions, and corresponding UNSC Verbatim Records detailing the veto and debate therein: Draft Resolution S/2012/77, Meeting S/PV.6711 (4 February 2012); Draft Resolution S/2012/538, Meeting S/PV.6810 (19 July 2012); Draft Resolution S/2014/348, Meeting S/PV.7180 (22 May 2014); Draft Resolution S/2016/846, Meeting S/PV.7785 (8 October 2016); Draft Resolution S/2016/1026, Meeting S/PV.7825 (5 December 2016); Draft Resolution S/2017/172, Meeting S/PV.7893 (28 February 2017); Draft Resolution S/2017/315, Meeting S/PV.7922 (12 April 2017); Draft Resolution S/2017/884, Meeting S/PV.8073 (24 October 2017); Draft Resolution S/2017/962, Meeting S/PV.8105 (16 November 2017); Draft Resolution S/2017/970, Meeting S/PV.8107 (17 November 2017); Draft Resolution S/2018/321, Meeting S/PV.8228 (10 April 2018).

[105] ibid, Draft Resolution S/2014/348.

[106] ibid, Draft Resolution S/2012/77.

[107] ibid, Draft Resolution S/2016/846.

[108] ibid, Draft Resolution S/2016/1026.

[109] ibid, Draft Resolution S/2017/172.

[110] See V Nanda, 'The Future under International Law of the Responsibility to Protect after Libya and Syria' (2013) 21(1) *Michigan State University College of Law International Law Review* 1; see also *Reports of the Commission of Inquiry on Syria*, above.

Secretary-General Kofi Annan to help implement a Six-Point Plan[111] to achieve a ceasefire and the path to peace.[112] Unfortunately, severe hostilities and the lack of adherence to the proposed ceasefire meant that UNSMIS had to withdraw from Syria before the peacemaking plan could be implemented.[113] Equally, other Resolutions adopted by the Council[114] were left either unheeded or unimplemented.[115]

Because of this lack of unanimity of its permanent members, the Security Council has largely been paralysed and incapable of implementing its responsibility to protect in the face of the manifest failures of Syria during its civil war and the unconscionable atrocities that have taken place there. Much of Russia and China's blocking of the Council goes against the very will of the international community, as evidenced through Resolutions of the General Assembly, where the Assembly itself has *deplored* 'the failure of the Security Council to agree on measures to ensure compliance of Syrian authorities with its decisions'.[116] Noting the repeated encouragement by the Secretary-General and the High Commissioner for Human Rights for the Security Council to refer the situation to the ICC, the Assembly finally established its own 'International, Impartial and Independent Mechanism to Assist in the Investigation and Prosecution of Persons Responsible for the Most Serious Crimes under International Law Committed in the Syrian Arab Republic since March 2011'.[117]

Therefore, the situation in Syria highlights a very serious problem with the implementation of the responsibility to protect when the interests of permanent members of the Security Council may be involved. It is not necessary to understand why the Security Council is deadlocked – the point is it is failing in its responsibility to protect by failing to respond appropriately and allowing a crisis to spiral out of control. In these situations, we must understand whether the responsibility to protect continues beyond this paralysis, or whether it ceases with the Council's inaction.

[111] Annexed to UNSC Res 2042 (2012) (14 April 2012) UN Doc S/RES/2042(2012).

[112] UNSC Res 2043 (2012) (21 April 2012) UN Doc S/RES/2043(2012); This mission was authorised with 300 *unarmed* military observers, and overseen by the UN's Department of Peacekeeping Operations (DPKO): DPKO, 'UNSMIS: Mission Profile', https://peacekeeping.un.org/sites/default/files/past/unsmis/index.shtml (accessed 31 July 2019).

[113] See UNSC Verbatim Record, 6826th Meeting (30 August 2012) UN Doc S/PV.6826.

[114] See eg the authorisation of passage of humanitarian aid in UNSC Res 2258 (2015) (22 December 2015) UN Doc S/RES/2258(2015).

[115] See eg *Report of the Commission of Inquiry on Syria* (A/HRC/31/68), [148].

[116] UNGA Res 66/253 B, *The Situation in the Syrian Arab Republic* (7 August 2012) UN Doc A/RES/66/253 B, preamble [16].

[117] UNGA Res 71/248, *International, Impartial and Independent Mechanism to Assist in the Investigation and Prosecution of Persons Responsible for the Most Serious Crimes under International Law Committed in the Syrian Arab Republic since March 2011* (11 January 2017) UN Doc A/RES/71/248.

3.2.3. *The Problem of Security Council Inaction – Recent Developments in Myanmar*

The crisis in Syria is clearly a situation where competing geopolitical interests in the region have meant that the Security Council has been unable to act in any meaningful way. But when atrocity crimes started to occur in Myanmar (Burma), this geopolitical divide caused the Council to go from failing in *meaningful* action, to failing in *any* action whatsoever. In what an internal UN review labelled 'a systematic failure of the United Nations', [118] the entire UN system stood by while the Myanmar military undertook so-called 'clearance operations' against ethnic Rohingya in Rakhine State, reportedly committing some of the most serious atrocities against the civilian population.[119]

Rakhine State, and the minority Rohingya Muslims who live there, have had a difficult history of persecution and segregation within Myanmar for many decades.[120] Rohingyas had already previously fled Myanmar to Bangladesh in the late 1970s following a nationwide crackdown on 'illegal immigration'.[121] While many returned, in 1982 Myanmar passed a 'Citizenship Law' which did not recognise the Rohingya as one of the State's 135 'national races'.[122] Various other restrictions on the rights of Rohingya occurred from this point, leading to the further internal and external displacement of Rohingyas in 1991–1992 following human rights violations by Myanmar security forces,[123] and again in 2001 following anti-Muslim riots across Myanmar.[124] Spouts of widespread violence also occurred between Muslim and Buddhist groups in 2012 across Rakhine State, leading to the restricted movement of Muslim communities and curfews for up to two years.[125] The Rohingya were also prohibited from self-identifying in the 2014 national census – the country's first since 1983.[126]

[118] Gert Rosenthal, *A Brief and Independent Inquiry into the Involvement of the United Nations in Myanmar From 2010 to 2018* (29 May 2019) available at: www.un.org/sg/sites/www.un.org.sg/files/atoms/files/Myanmar%20Report%20-%20May%202019.pdf (accessed 31 July 2019); also reported at *UN News*, 'UN Chief Accepts Independent Report on Myanmar, Highlighting "Systemic" Failure Surrounding Rohingya Crisis' (17 June 2019) https://news.un.org/en/story/2019/06/1040681.

[119] See Amnesty International, *'We Will Destroy Everything': Military Responsibility For Crimes Against Humanity in Rakhine State, Myanmar* (London, Amnesty International, 2018) available at: www.amnesty.org/en/documents/asa16/8630/2018/en/ (accessed 31 July 2019).

[120] For a detailed overview of the background to the Rohingya/Rakhine State crisis, see Amnesty International, *'Caged Without A Roof': Apartheid in Myanmar's Rakhine State* (London, Amnesty International, 2017) available at: www.amnesty.org.uk/files/CagedwithoutaRoof-ApartheidMyanmar-AIreport.pdf (accessed 31 July 2019); see also Amnesty International (n 119) 20–24.

[121] Amnesty International (n 120) 20.

[122] ibid; see also S Adams, *'If Not Now, When?': The Responsibility to Protect, the Fate of the Rohingya and the Future of Human Rights* (Global Centre for the Responsibility to Protect, 2019) available at: www.globalr2p.org/media/files/adamsrohingya_opaper_final.pdf, at 6.

[123] Amnesty International (n 120) 20; see also Amnesty International, *Union of Myanmar (Burma): Human Rights Abuses against Muslims in the Rakhine (Arakan) State* (Amnesty International, May 1992) available at: www.amnesty.org/en/documents/ASA16/006/1992/en/ (accessed 31 July 2019).

[124] Amnesty International (n 120) 20.

[125] ibid, 22.

[126] ibid, 8 and 19; see also Adams (n 122) 7.

In 2015, the election of Nobel Peace Prize winner Aung San Suu Kyi brought hope of a transition from military rule to a functioning democracy in Myanmar. Aung San Suu Kyi seemed to take a step in the right direction by setting up an Advisory Commission on Rakhine State, chaired by former UN Secretary-General Kofi Annan.[127] But this hope was relatively short-lived when Rakhine State was engulfed by a dark cloud of violence that would ultimately overshadow both her domestic political influence and her international reputation.

An armed group known as the Arakan Rohingya Salvation Army (ARSA) attacked police posts in October 2016, leading to a four-month military operation within Rakhine State which was once again stained by accusations of widespread human rights violations.[128] Particularly harrowing evidence emerged of the unlawful killings of families and the possible commission of crimes against humanity.[129] Up to 87,000 people fled Myanmar into Bangladesh.[130] In March 2017, the UN Human Rights Council adopted Resolution 34/22,[131] establishing an Independent International Fact-Finding Mission on Myanmar 'to establish the facts and circumstances of the alleged recent human rights violations by military and security forces, and abuses, in Myanmar, in particular in Rakhine State'.[132] The Myanmar government did not engage with or allow the Mission access to Rakhine State.[133]

Then, in August 2017, the Advisory Commission on Rakhine State released its report,[134] which made detailed recommendations on many issues, including the closure of displacement camps and access to citizenship. The Myanmar government welcomed the report and undertook to give the recommendations 'full consideration with a view to carrying out the recommendations to the

[127] Amnesty International (n 120) 25; see also Myanmar, Office of the State Counsellor, 'Establishment of the Advisory Commission on Rakhine State' (23 August 2016) available at: www.statecounsellor.gov.mm/en/node/228 (accessed 31 July 2019).

[128] Amnesty International (n 120) 22; see also Adams (n 122) 7.

[129] Amnesty International (n 120) 23; Amnesty International, *'We Are At Breaking Point' – Rohingya: Persecuted in Myanmar, Neglected in Bangladesh* (London, Amnesty International, December 2016) available at: www.amnesty.org/en/documents/asa16/5362/2016/en/ (accessed 31 July 2019); UN Office of the High Commissioner for Human Rights (OHCHR), 'Flash Report: Report of OHCHR Mission to Bangladesh, Interviews with Rohingyas Fleeing from Myanmar since 9 October 2016' (3 February 2017), www.ohchr.org/Documents/Countries/MM/FlashReport3Feb2017.pdf (accessed 31 July 2019).

[130] Amnesty International (n 120) 23.

[131] UN HRC Res 34/22 (24 March 2017) UN Doc A/HRC/RES/34/22.

[132] ibid, [11].

[133] See Human Rights Council, *Report of the Independent International Fact-Finding Mission on Myanmar* (12 September 2018) UN Doc A/HRC/39/64.

[134] Advisory Commission on Rakhine State, *Towards a Peaceful, Fair and Prosperous Future for the People of Rakhine: Final Report of the Advisory Commission on Rakhine State* (August 2017) available at: www.rakhinecommission.org/app/uploads/2017/08/FinalReport_Eng.pdf (accessed 31 July 2019).

fullest extent, and within the shortest timeframe possible, in line with the situation on the ground'.[135]

Yet again this step towards resolution was short-lived. Only hours later, ARSA launched a coordinated attack against around 30 police posts in Rakhine State.[136] In response, the military launched a brutal retaliation against the Rohingya community.[137] As the military undertook so-called 'clearance operations', evidence emerged that Rohingya villages had been burned and destroyed.[138] Hundreds of thousands fled Myanmar into Bangladesh, where survivors told harrowing stories of atrocities committed by military personnel as the world watched the crisis unfold on 24-hour news cycles and social media. In one account that will stay with this author for life, a survivor told journalists how attackers took babies and toddlers from their parents and grandparents and threw them into the fires of their burning village.[139] According to Médecins Sans Frontières, at least 6,700 Rohingya were killed in Rakhine State between 25 August and 24 September 2017, 730 of which were children below the age of five.[140]

The UN Security Council was briefed by the Secretary-General on 28 September 2017 on the serious human rights violations,[141] and Adams argues that there was no question that, 'given the multiple sources of intelligence available to them, the entire Council was aware of the scale and intensity of the atrocities underway in Rakhine State'.[142] On 12 December 2017, the Security Council was briefed by the Secretary-General's Special Representative on Sexual Violence in Conflict, who indicated that 'a pattern of widespread and systematic sexual violence has been used as a tool of dehumanization and collective punishment'.[143] Most aptly, the Special Representative warned the Council that 'inaction is not an option'.[144]

[135] Myanmar, Office of the State Counsellor, 'Statement by the Office of the State Counsellor on the Final Report of the Advisory Commission on Rakhine State' (24 August 2017) available at: www.statecounsellor.gov.mm/en/node/998 (accessed 31 July 2019).

[136] Amnesty International (n 120) 24; Amnesty International (n 119) 38–41.

[137] See, in detail, Amnesty International (n 119) s 4.

[138] Human Rights Watch, 'Burma: 40 Rohingya Villages Burned Since October', *HRW* (17 December 2017), available at: www.hrw.org/news/2017/12/17/burma-40-rohingya-villages-burned-october (accessed 31 July 2019).

[139] This account was told by contributors to the Channel 4 *Dispatches* documentary 'Myanmar's Killing Fields', available at: www.channel4.com/programmes/dispatches/on-demand/67615-001 – also linked to: *PBS Frontline*, 'FRONTLINE Uncovers New Accounts of Atrocities Against Myanmar's Rohingya Minority' (PBS, 3 May 2018) available at: www.pbs.org/wgbh/frontline/announcement/frontline-uncovers-new-accounts-of-atrocities-against-myanmars-rohingya-minority/.

[140] Médecins Sans Frontières, 'MSF Surveys Estimate that at Least 6,700 Rohingya Were Killed During the Attacks in Myanmar' (12 December 2017) available at: www.msf.org/myanmarbangladesh-msf-surveys-estimate-least-6700-rohingya-were-killed-during-attacks-myanmar (accessed 31 July 2019).

[141] See UNSC Verbatim Record, 8060th Meeting (28 September 2017) UN Doc S/PV.8060.

[142] Adams (n 122) 8.

[143] UNSC Verbatim Record, 8133rd Meeting (12 December 2017) UN Doc S/PV.8133, 4.

[144] ibid, 6.

Unfortunately, as Adams argues, 'Their response was tepid at best.'[145] This 'tepid' response was a Presidential Statement issued by the Council on 6 November 2017, over 10 weeks after the military crackdown began,[146] which condemned 'the widespread violence that has taken place in Rakhine State' and expressed 'grave concern' over

> reports of human rights violations and abuses in Rakhine State, including by the Myanmar security forces ... including those involving the systematic use of force and intimidation, killing of men, women, and children, sexual violence, and including the destruction and burning of homes and property.[147]

Some sources allege that the reason for a simple Presidential Statement, and not any further action or binding Resolution from the Security Council, was because of diplomatic pressure in private from China – a key ally to Myanmar.[148] Adams suggested:

> In their intransigent backroom diplomatic defense of Myanmar, Chinese diplomats exposed the enduring problem of a UN Security Council that is immobilized and unable to function when a permanent member threatens to use its veto power to protect the interests of a state that is committing atrocities.[149]

It is certainly clear that key members of the Council, including Russia and China, opposed the Council being briefed by the chair of the Human Right's Council's Fact Finding Mission to Myanmar, arguing that it would set a bad precedent for the Council 'to invite a special mechanism on a country-specific issue of the Human Rights Council', and 'will also erode the mandate of the General Assembly and the Human Rights Council and duplicate the work of other United Nations bodies'.[150] States supporting the briefing argued that the situation 'clearly endangers international peace and security' and therefore it is 'absolutely without doubt the Security Council's responsibility to hear the allegations concerning the gravest crimes under international law related to the situation and to deliberate on how to proceed'.[151]

Ultimately, the Fact Finding Mission was able to brief the Security Council on its report,[152] which included a 444-page supplement of detailed evidence

[145] ibid.
[146] UNSC Presidential Statement (6 November 2017) UN Doc S/PRST/2017/22.
[147] ibid.
[148] Adams (n 122) 8–9.
[149] ibid, 9.
[150] Letter dated 18 October 2018 from the Permanent Representatives of Bolivia (Plurinational State of), China, Equatorial Guinea and the Russian Federation to the United Nations addressed to the President of the Security Council, (22 October 2018) UN Doc S/2018/938; these States also failed in their attempt to block the briefing through a procedural vote: see UNSC Verbatim Record, 8381st Meeting (24 October 2018) UN Doc S/PV.8381 and S/PV.8381 (Resumption 1).
[151] S/PV.8381 (n 150), 3 (UK, speaking also on behalf of Côte d'Ivoire, France, Kuwait, the Netherlands, Peru, Poland, Sweden and the US).
[152] Human Rights Council, *Report of the Independent International Fact-Finding Mission on Myanmar* (12 September 2018) UN Doc A/HRC/39/64.

and findings.[153] On 24 October 2018, the Security Council heard from the Mission's chair, Marzuki Darusman, that the Mission had found sufficient information to warrant the investigation and prosecution of senior officials in the Tatmadaw (Myanmar Armed Forces) on charges of genocide – indicating that genocidal intent to destroy the Rohingya in whole or in part could be reasonably inferred.[154] With this stark finding, Darusman warned the Security Council:

> The international community must be gravely concerned. Myanmar presents precisely the kind of threat to peace and security that the United Nations – particularly the Council – was created to address. We urge the Council to take action.[155]

The report was met by with hostility some permanent members of the Council. For example, Russia called the Mission's report 'underprepared and one-sided'.[156] China went further, arguing that because the Mission did not enter Myanmar, its results are 'based on biased, incomplete information'.[157] China argued, 'They are neither objective nor impartial, and therefore not credible. Its conclusions, suggestions and recommendations constitute wilful interference in Myanmar's internal affairs and are an affront to its sovereignty.'[158] On the other hand, China supported Myanmar's efforts to establish its own Commission of Enquiry into the situation in Rakhine State,[159] which was announced in May 2018,[160] and established in July 2018.[161] Unfortunately, this Commission was also met with accusations of bias and a lack of independence by Human Rights Watch[162] and the International Commission of Jurists.[163]

The findings of the Fact-Finding Mission, and the lack of response by the Security Council, led the Human Rights Council to establish its own Independent Investigative Mechanism for Myanmar,[164] with a mandate to 'collect,

[153] Human Rights Council, *Report of the Detailed Findings of the Independent International Fact-Finding Mission on Myanmar* (17 September 2018) UN Doc A/HRC/39/CRP.2.

[154] S/PV.8381 (n 150) 5.

[155] ibid 6.

[156] ibid 2 (Russia).

[157] ibid 22 (China).

[158] ibid.

[159] ibid, 22 (China).

[160] Myanmar, Office of the President, 'Republic of the Union of Myanmar Office of the President Announcement 3/2018', Press Release 3/2018 (31 May 2018) available at: www.president-office.gov.mm/en/?q=briefing-room/announcements/2018/06/04/id-8827 (accessed 31 July 2019).

[161] Myanmar, Office of the President, 'Government of the Republic of the Union of Myanmar Establishes the Independent Commission of Enquiry', Press Release 8/2018 (30 July 2018), available at: www.president-office.gov.mm/en/?q=briefing-room/statements-and-releases/2018/07/30/id-8914 (accessed 31 July 2019).

[162] Human Rights Watch, 'Myanmar: Disband Panel on Crimes Against Rohingya' *HRW* (19 December 2018), available at: www.hrw.org/news/2018/12/19/myanmar-disband-panel-crimes-against-rohingya (accessed 31 July 2019).

[163] International Commission of Jurists, *Myanmar: New Commission Of Inquiry Cannot Deliver Justice Or Accountability, International Response Required* (ICJ, 7 September 2018) available at: www.icj.org/wp-content/uploads/2018/09/Myanmar-COI-cannot-deliver-justice-or-accountability-Advocacy-Analysis-brief-2018-ENG.pdf (accessed 31 July 2019).

[164] UN HRC Res 39/2 (3 October 2018) UN Doc A/HRC/RES/39/2.

consolidate, preserve and analyse evidence of the most serious international crimes and violations of international law committed in Myanmar since 2011' with a view to providing evidence and resources for future trials or tribunals that may prosecute any crimes that have taken place.[165] This Mechanism was still in the process of being set up at the time of writing.

Unfortunately, by mid-2019, the crisis and violence in Rakhine State was still far from over, with Amnesty International reporting further possible atrocity crimes being committed by military forces and the so-called Arakan Army in the wake of intensified fighting between the military and the terrorist group.[166]

The internal review of the UN's failures pointed to the collective responsibility of the UN system, highlighting problems in communication, politics and a lack of an overall collective strategy in the UN Secretariat.[167] But it must be recalled that it is the UN Security Council – not the Secretariat – that has primary responsibility for the maintenance of international peace and Security under the Charter.[168] It cannot be said that the Security Council did not know about these atrocities being committed – the world knew; we watched it unfold. And still, whether it was unable or unwilling, the Security Council did nothing. The Security Council failed.

4. CONCLUSIONS

The responsibility to protect has great potential in providing a framework of tools and guidance that may be used to identify the actors responsible for protecting populations from atrocities, and the means they may utilise to implement their responsibilities. Unfortunately, inaction remains a very clear limitation of this framework. We can see from the crises in Syria and Myanmar that, whether the Security Council is formally blocked by a permanent member or fails to act completely because of back-room political pressure, crises may be left to spiral into a pattern of unconscionable suffering.

While it might be argued that the Security Council itself has not stopped operating completely, these instances do reveal a stark problem with its ability to function and uphold its responsibility to protect where global political interests conflict. In these circumstances, where atrocity crimes are imminent or ongoing, and the Council has not upheld its promise to the world, but action beyond simple diplomacy and politics is necessary – is the international community able to do more?

[165] ibid, [22]–[23].

[166] Amnesty International, *'No One Can Protect Us': War Crimes and Abuses in Myanmar's Rakhine State*, (London, Amnesty International, 2019) available at: www.amnesty.org/download/Documents/ASA1604172019ENGLISH.PDF (accessed 31 July 2019).

[167] Rosenthal (n 118) 14–16.

[168] The scope and nature of this responsibility is considered in detail in Chapter III.

Even in these situations, the responsibility to protect itself does not provide any further guidance as to who is responsible for moving forward and finding a solution to the crises. The secondary responsibility of the international community to take peaceful measures is indeed a continuing part of the responsibility to protect, but this is only relevant insofar as those peaceful means remain adequate.

In this grey area between the utopia of a centralised Security Council maintaining international peace and security as it should, and the chaos of unsanctioned unilateral military or coercive action by States or pacts, is there any legal and legitimate room for the responsibility to protect to operate? For the reasons that follow, this book argues that, yes, there is – and there is not just legal leeway available to act, but there is also a legal *duty* for the international community to uphold and protect those populations in need.

III

The Legal Responsibilities of the United Nations Security Council

THIS CHAPTER ADDRESSES the responsibility to protect in situations where the UN Security Council fails to act. To do so, this chapter aims to give greater clarity to the legal nature of the responsibilities of the UN Security Council, and the consequences for the Council's failure to uphold them. The Security Council has primary responsibility for the maintenance of international peace and security under Article 24 of the UN Charter. The 'triggers' for this responsibility are inherently linked to the thresholds at which the Security Council may utilise its coercive powers under Chapter VII of the Charter, namely: 'threats to the peace', 'breaches of the peace' or 'acts of aggression' as outlined in Article 39.

This chapter argues that Article 39 of the UN Charter is the embodiment of the Council's primary responsibility for the maintenance of international peace and security where these triggers emerge. In other words, Article 39 was put into the Charter to detail explicitly the role of the Security Council in these situations. It stipulates the general and procedural duties of the Council in situations that move beyond the threshold of being 'likely to endanger international peace and security'.[1] When this happens, the author argues that the Council is under an obligation to investigate a situation, and if it determines that the threat, breach or act of aggression exists, then the Council must either make the recommendations it deems appropriate or decide upon measures to take in accordance with Articles 41 and 42.

Indeed, the precise legal nature of the Security Council's responsibility to maintain international peace and security and, by extension, its responsibility to protect, has been left relatively unexplored in the academic literature. Here, the author establishes that there is a connected relationship between the responsibility to protect and the responsibility for the maintenance of international peace and security. Where a humanitarian crisis involving the threat or commission

[1] See Arts 33, 34 and 37 of Chapter VI of the Charter, dealing with the settlement of international disputes 'likely to endanger international peace and security' before they become 'threats' to international peace and security and therefore fall within the scope of Art 39 and Chapter VII of the Charter instead.

of atrocity crimes constitutes a threat to international peace and security, the responsibility to maintain international peace and security is engaged. By assessing the legal nature of this responsibility, in order to determine whether the Security Council is under an obligation to act in response to such threats to the peace, the chapter sheds light on what a 'failure' of the Security Council's responsibilities might look like, and therefore whether there are any legal consequences to inaction.

In its analysis of Article 39 of the UN Charter, this chapter argues that the responsibility of the Security Council includes a legal obligation on the Council, at the very least, not to ignore situations that fall within the maintenance of peace and security. Where the Security Council fails to act in these situations, the responsibility for the maintenance of peace reverts to the actors with residual responsibility in this regard. Therefore, in situations where the responsibility to protect and the responsibility for the maintenance of international peace and security overlap, the responsibility to protect could merge with this legal responsibility and continue beyond the Security Council in the event of failure. This possibility is introduced as the 'tertiary' responsibility to protect. However, this would only be possible if other actors with residual responsibility have the legal competences and powers to implement such a responsibility, as will be determined in subsequent chapters.

1. THE SECURITY COUNCIL'S RESPONSIBILITY TO PROTECT

1.1. The Security Council's Role in the World Summit Outcome

We have seen in the previous chapter that the responsibility to protect involves a *primary* responsibility on the State and a *secondary* responsibility on the international community to assist with this or, where the State with primary responsibility is manifestly failing to protect, to respond to the threat or existence of mass atrocities directly. The key provision of the World Summit Outcome,[2] paragraph 139, details this *secondary* responsibility, dealing with the Secretary-General's Pillars II (international assistance and capacity building) and III (the need for a timely and decisive response) when the requisite criteria that necessitate such action are met.[3] Since the provision makes reference to Chapters VI, VII and VIII of the Charter, it is clear that the Security Council has a central role in both Pillars II and III of the responsibility to protect.

[2] 2005 World Summit Outcome Document, in UNGA Res 60/1 (15 September 2005) UN Doc A/RES/60/1, [138]–[139].

[3] See Report of the Secretary-General, *Implementing the Responsibility to Protect* (12 January 2009) UN Doc A/63/677, 8–9 and s IV.

This is because the powers contained in those Chapters can be utilised in scenarios beyond just enforcement action under Chapter VII. For example, the powers of the Security Council under Chapter VI in particular relate to the peaceful settlement of disputes – methods of diplomacy, mediation and even adjudication that can form the basis of important strategies both before and after a crisis, ie in the *prevention* of a crisis, or *rebuilding* of a society after a crisis.

However, the focus of this chapter will be the powers and responsibilities of the Council of a coercive or forcible nature, which are required by the responsibility to protect if peaceful means are inadequate. As has been explained earlier, such coercive or forcible methods, for the purpose of this book, involve methods and powers that would otherwise infringe upon the principles of non-intervention and the prohibition the use of force had they not been utilised without the proper legal authority.

1.2. Overlap with the Council's Primary Responsibility to Maintain International Peace and Security

Humanitarian crises, falling within the scope of the responsibility to protect, may also reach a threshold whereby they become a concern for the maintenance of international peace and security, engaging the Council's responsibility under Article 24(1). The 'triggers' for the latter responsibility may be considered those that determine whether the Security Council has jurisdiction to utilise its coercive powers under Chapter VII of the Charter, those of 'threats to the peace', 'breaches of the peace' or 'acts of aggression' as outlined in Article 39. Therefore, if humanitarian crises leading to or involving the commission of atrocity crimes reach at least the threshold of a 'threat to the peace', then the responsibility to protect overlaps with the responsibility for the maintenance of international peace and security.

Numerous determinations by the Security Council clearly reveal that situations involving atrocities relevant to the responsibility to protect constitute threats to international peace and security. Following Iraq's invasion of Kuwait, the UN Security Council became concerned with Iraq's repression of its own civilian population. In Resolution 688 (1991),[4] the Council was 'gravely concerned by the repression of the Iraqi civilian population',[5] condemning this repression and determining that 'the consequences of which threaten international peace and security in the region'.[6] The Council also demanded that Iraq end its repression, and hoped that dialogue could be opened to ensure that

[4] UNSC Res 688 (1991) (5 April 1991) UN Doc S/RES/688(1991).
[5] ibid, preamble [2].
[6] ibid, operative [1].

these citizens' human and political rights were respected, 'as a contribution to removing the threat to international peace and security in the region'.[7] Here, the Council clearly recognised that the repression of civilians and human rights could *contribute* to a threat to international peace and security.

However, when the situation in the former Yugoslavia continued to deteriorate, the Council adopted Resolution 808 (1993)[8] and expressed alarm at reports of 'widespread violations of international humanitarian law' and the practice of 'ethnic cleansing'.[9] It accordingly determined that this situation constituted a threat to international peace and security.[10] Similarly, when the situation in Rwanda spiralled towards genocide, the Security Council was initially 'disturbed by the magnitude of human suffering', and was 'concerned that the continuation of the situation in Rwanda constitutes a threat to peace and security in the region'.[11] In June 1994, the Council determined that 'the magnitude of the humanitarian crisis in Rwanda constitutes a threat to peace and security in the region'.[12] When establishing the International Criminal Tribunal for Rwanda, the Council reiterated its concern at the reports of genocide 'and other systematic, widespread and flagrant violations of international humanitarian law have been committed in Rwanda',[13] and determined that this situation continued to constitute a threat to international peace and security.[14]

Furthermore, in 1996, the Security Council made clear its concern 'at the continued deterioration in the security and humanitarian situation in Burundi that has been characterized in the last years by killings, massacres, torture and arbitrary detention, and at the threat that this poses to the peace and security of the Great Lakes Region as a whole'.[15]

In its more general and thematic resolutions, the Security Council has also determined general types of crises that can constitute threats to international peace and security. For example, in Resolution 1314 (2000),[16] concerning children and armed conflict, the Council noted that:

> [T]he deliberate targeting of civilian populations or other protected persons, including children, and the committing of systematic, flagrant and widespread violations of international humanitarian and human rights law, including that relating to children, in situations of armed conflict may constitute a threat to international peace and security.[17]

[7] ibid, operative [2].
[8] UNSC Res 808 (1993) (22 February 1993) UN Doc S/RES/808(1993).
[9] ibid, preamble [6].
[10] ibid, preamble [7]; see also UNSC Res 827 (1993) (25 May 1993) UN Doc S/RES/827(1993), establishing the International Criminal Tribunal for the former Yugoslavia (ICTY), preamble [3]–[4].
[11] UNSC Res 918 (1994) (17 May 1994) UN Doc S/RES/918(1994), preamble [18].
[12] UNSC Res 929 (1994) (22 June 1994) UN Doc S/RES/292(1994), preamble [10].
[13] UNSC Res 955 (1995) (8 November 1994) UN Doc S/RES/955(1994), preamble [4].
[14] ibid, preamble [5].
[15] UNSC Res 1072 (1996) (30 August 1996) UN Doc S/RES/1072(1996), preamble [3].
[16] UNSC Res 1314 (2000) (11 August 2000) UN Doc S/RES/1314(2000).
[17] ibid, [9].

The Security Council repeated this determination in the context of its general debate on civilians in armed conflict.[18]

Subsequent to the adoption of the responsibility to protect at the 2005 World Summit, the Security Council responded to the threat of atrocities in Libya in 2011, initially '[d]eploring the gross and systematic violation of human rights, including the repression of peaceful demonstrators',[19] and considering that the attacks against civilians could amount to crimes against humanity.[20] In Resolution 1973 (2011),[21] the Council reiterated the responsibility of Libya to protect its population,[22] and determined this situation in Libya 'continues to constitute a threat to international peace and security'.[23] Concerning crimes against humanity, although not explicitly referenced as a specific threat to international peace and security, there was a general consensus among States to regard these atrocities as such during a Security Council debate on the issue of peace and justice in October 2013.[24]

More recently, in response to the situation in Syria, the Security Council has determined that the use of chemical weapons anywhere constitutes a threat to international peace and security.[25] In 2014, the Council, while reaffirming the responsibility of Syria to protect its populations,[26] determined that the deteriorating humanitarian situation in Syria constitutes a threat to international peace and security.[27] Regarding the acts of the so-called Islamic State in Iraq and the Levant (ISIL, also known as Da'esh), the Security Council also made an unprecedented determination in this regard in Resolution 2249 (2015).[28]

These determinations by the Security Council clearly reveal that situations involving atrocities relevant to the responsibility to protect, including genocide, war crimes, crimes against humanity and ethnic cleansing, constitute threats to international peace and security. Moreover, it is also clear that gross and systematic violations of human rights and international humanitarian law may, in certain circumstances, constitute such a threat. Therefore, in these situations,

[18] UNSC Res 1296 (2000) (19 April 2000) UN Doc S/RES/1296(2000), [5]; see also UNSC Res 1894 (2009) (11 November 2009) S/RES/1894(2009), [3].

[19] UNSC Res 1970 (2011) (26 February 2011) UN Doc S/RES/1970(2011), preamble [2].

[20] ibid, preamble [6]. Note that the Security Council took action under Chapter VII in this resolution but did not determine any new threat to the peace, or recall any such subsequent determination, within the meaning of Art 39 of the Charter.

[21] UNSC Res 1973 (2011) (17 March 2011) UN Doc S/RES/1973(2011).

[22] ibid, preamble [4].

[23] ibid, preamble para [21].

[24] See generally the views of States in UNSC Verbatim Record, 6849th Meeting (17 October 2012) UN Doc S/PV.6849, and see also UN Doc S/PV.6849 (Resumption 1).

[25] UNSC Res 2118 (2013) (27 September 2013) UN Doc S/RES/2118(2013), preamble [3], [13], and operative [1].

[26] UNSC Res 2165 (2014) (14 July 2014) UN Doc S/RES/2165(2014), preamble [12].

[27] ibid, preamble [18]. See also UNSC Res 2191 (2014) (17 December 2014) UN Doc S/RES/2191(2014), preamble [19].

[28] UNSC Res 2249 (2015) (20 November 2015) UN Doc S/RES/2249(2015), preamble [5].

the responsibility to protect also engages the responsibility for the maintenance of international peace and security.

1.3. The Legal Status of the Responsibility to Protect

The reason why we must determine that situations concerning the responsibility to protect overlap with the responsibility to maintain international peace and security is because the responsibility to protect currently has no settled legal force. The legal nature of the responsibility to protect is subject to a wide divergence of opinion. This author adopts the position that the responsibility to protect itself is a *moral* and *political* undertaking, and a useful conceptual framework for implementing existing international obligations. It has the potential to develop into a rule of customary international law in future, but only if States implement the responsibility through practice, and accept it as a legal principle through the requisite *opinio juris*.[29]

In his first report on the responsibility to protect, the UN Secretary-General suggested that the responsibility to protect is based upon pre-existing principles of international law.[30] In particular, he stressed that

> the provisions of paragraphs 138 and 139 of the Summit Outcome are firmly anchored in well-established principles of international law. Under conventional and customary international law, States have obligations to prevent and punish genocide, war crimes and crimes against humanity. … It should also be emphasized that actions under paragraphs 138 and 139 of the Summit Outcome are to be undertaken only in conformity with the provisions, purposes and principles of the Charter of the United Nations. In that regard, the responsibility to protect does not alter, indeed it reinforces, the legal obligations of Member States to refrain from the use of force except in conformity with the Charter.[31]

The Secretary-General also suggested in a later report that: 'The responsibility to protect is a concept based on fundamental principles of international law as set out, in particular, in international humanitarian, refugee and human rights law.'[32] While it is clear that the obligations to prevent and publish certain crimes, such as genocide, clearly exist in international law,[33] it is not clear whether the

[29] For a similar discussion, see M-E Loiselle, 'The Normative Status of the Responsibility to Protect after Libya', (2013) 5 *Global Responsibility to Protect* 317.

[30] Report of the Secretary-General, *Implementing the Responsibility to Protect* (12 January 2009) UN Doc A/63/677, [2].

[31] ibid, [3]; see also [11(a)], [13].

[32] Report of the Secretary-General, *Responsibility to Protect: Timely and Decisive Response* (25 July 2012) UN Doc A/66/874–S/2012/578, [9]; see also most recently, Report of the Secretary-General, *Implementing the Responsibility to Protect: Accountability for Prevention* (10 August 2017) UN Doc A/71/1016–S/2017/556, [9]–[17].

[33] See Convention on the Prevention and Punishment of the Crime of Genocide 1948 (adopted 9 December 1948, entered into force 12 January 1951) 78 UNTS 277; see also a detailed discussion in Chapter V, section 2.3.

Secretary-General believes there exists a general obligation to *protect*, or to act in the face of such atrocities. In other words, it is not clear whether he also considers the elements of the responsibility to take timely and decisive action as originating from pre-existing international obligations. On the other hand, this idea may have traction regarding the responsibility to maintain international peace and security, as will be addressed below.

Ultimately, the responsibility to protect *in and of itself* currently falls short of having the status of a binding legal doctrine, and there are several factors that indicate such a conclusion. The Summit Outcome document was adopted as a General Assembly Resolution, a non-binding instrument forming a 'recommendation' according to Article 10 and Article 13 of the Charter.[34] As mentioned above, prior to the World Summit Outcome, the responsibility to protect had been described by the High-Level Panel, and Secretary-General Kofi Annan, as an 'emerging norm'.[35] Some States, Russia for example, disagreed with this position, arguing that it presupposes that there is wide support within the international community for such a norm.[36]

Even so, the significance of the World Summit Outcome – a unanimous declaration from the international community on the existence of the responsibility to protect – should not be dismissed altogether. The ICJ has previously recognised that General Assembly Resolutions, although not legally binding in themselves, may provide evidence of an existing *opinio juris*.[37] It could well be argued, therefore, that the World Summit Outcome provides evidence of an existing *opinio*, or acceptance, by the international community of the concept of the responsibility to protect as a legal obligation.[38] However, the second criterion for customary international law, a general State practice, is still required for a law of custom to exist. In the case of the responsibility to protect, there is much disagreement as to whether such practice exists.[39]

Of course, the responsibility to protect was later endorsed by the Security Council in Resolution 1674 (2006).[40] Here, the Council 'reaffirmed' the

[34] This is in contrast to the legally binding nature of Security Council 'decisions' under Art 25.

[35] High-Level Panel on Threats, Challenges and Change, *A More Secure World: Our Shared Responsibility* (New York, UN Publications, 2004) [203]; Report of the Secretary-General, *In Larger Freedom: Towards Development, Security and Human Rights for All* (21 March 2005) UN Doc A/59/2005, [135].

[36] UNGA Verbatim Record, 87th Plenary Meeting, 59th Session (7 April 2005) UN Doc A/59/PV.87, 6 (Russian Federation).

[37] See *Legality of the Threat or Use of Nuclear Weapons* (Advisory Opinion of 8 July 1996) [1996] ICJ Reports 226, [70].

[38] See eg WW Burke-White, 'Adoption of the Responsibility to Protect' in J Genser et al (eds), *The Responsibility to Protect: The Promise of Stopping Mass Atrocities in Our Time* (Oxford, Oxford University Press, 2011) 22–24. However, whether the World Summit Outcome itself is enough to evidence acceptance of a *legal* responsibility to protect may also be up for debate.

[39] ibid. See also AJ Bellamy and R Reike, 'The Responsibility to Protect and International Law' (2010) 2 *Global Responsibility to Protect* 267; C Stahn, 'Responsibility to Protect: Political Rhetoric or Emerging Legal Norm?' (2007) 101 *American Journal of International Law* 99.

[40] UNSC Res 1674 (2006) (28 April 2006) UN Doc S/RES/1674.

commitments to the responsibility to protect.[41] This may be a significant step forward, even if it is simply a mere 'reaffirmation' of the concept, as Burke-White notes:

> While the Council's language in Resolution 1674 falls short of a formal decision requiring that member states implement the Responsibility to Protect, it is *part of an ongoing process of legalization*. At the very least, the Council's reaffirmation of the Responsibility to Protect strengthens the claim that member states have legal duties to advance the political commitment contained in paragraphs 138 and 139 of the Outcome Document.[42]

In light of the above, it seems that the responsibility to protect is a notion that could rightfully be described as an 'emerging norm', but perhaps not in the sense that it has legally binding force. The use of that phrase is not to guarantee that it *will* become a norm of international law one day, but is an acknowledgement of the fact that it *might*, and it is certainly capable of becoming such should the international community demonstrate a general practice required for customary international law. This reiterates the importance of the concept, and the significance in the ICISS's efforts to change the terms of the debate about responding to humanitarian crises. The responsibility to protect has, even at this stage, come closer to being more widely accepted than the so-called 'doctrine' or 'right' of humanitarian intervention ever did. And so, even though it will have no bearing on the legal findings of this book, it is worth noting the future possibilities that the responsibility to protect has in store for shifting a 'lack of political will' into a *duty* to do the right thing.[43]

2. THE RESPONSIBILITY TO MAINTAIN INTERNATIONAL PEACE AND SECURITY

2.1. The Legal Nature of Article 24(1)

The UN Charter places *primary* responsibility upon the Security Council for the maintenance of international peace and security, as provided by Article 24(1):

> In order to ensure prompt and effective action by the United Nations, its Members confer on the Security Council primary responsibility for the maintenance of international peace and security, and agree that in carrying out its duties under this responsibility the Security Council acts on their behalf.

To this author's knowledge, the legal nature of this responsibility has not been thoroughly determined. There has been no definitive study, nor any clear

[41] ibid, [4].

[42] Burke-White (n 38) 30–31 (emphasis added).

[43] On this possibility, see A Peters, 'The Security Council's Responsibility to Protect' (2011) 8 *International Organizations Law Review* 15.

opinio juris from States, on whether this specific responsibility is, quite simply, a legal obligation. But even Article 24(1) itself refers to the Security Council 'carrying out its *duties* under this responsibility'.

In 1950, Hans Kelsen[44] offered an interpretation of this provision,[45] suggesting that it 'means nothing else but that the Charter confers upon the Security Council primary responsibility for the achievement of the general purpose of the United Nations'.[46] When defining this 'responsibility', Kelsen viewed the provision as conferring a legal *competence* on the Security Council, rather than imposing a legal *duty*.[47] To Kelsen, the use of the word 'duties' in the provision is incorrect, and should instead be interpreted to mean that the Charter grants 'functions' to the Council.[48]

These assertions are based upon Kelsen's general theory that there cannot exist a legal obligation without a corresponding sanction,[49] and he accordingly argued:

> Since there is no provision for a sanction which might be executed against the Security Council – or any other organ of the United Nations – the Charter does not impose 'duties' upon these organs but confers functions or powers upon them.[50]

Kelsen further reasons that the heading under which Article 24 is presented is titled 'Functions and Powers', not 'Duties'.[51]

This author does not find Kelsen's argument convincing, for two reasons. First, the word 'duty' has a much more specific meaning to 'function', and Kelsen stretches the ordinary meaning of the phrase too far. Secondly, it does not take such a stretch of ordinary meanings to accept the possibility that a 'function' of the Security Council could include implementing a legal duty to maintain international peace and security.

Apart from Kelsen, other authors have argued that Member States have 'conferred' or 'delegated' *powers* to the Security Council through Article 24(1).[52] For example, Sarooshi argues that Member States have 'conferred' (or, in his view, 'delegated' via the Charter) powers onto the Security Council through

[44] H Kelsen, *The Law of the United Nations: A Critical Analysis of Its Fundamental Problems* (New York, Fredrick A Praeger 1950).

[45] For his general discussion, see ibid, 279–95.

[46] ibid, 283.

[47] ibid, 285.

[48] ibid.

[49] See ibid, 154, where Kelsen argues that 'the function determined by the legal order is the content of a legal obligation only if the legal order provides a sanction for the non-performance of the function'. He further suggests that 'it makes no legal difference whether the Charter stipulates that an organ 'may' or that an organ 'shall' perform a definite function'. This is incompatible with the intentions of the drafters of the Charter, as discussed below.

[50] ibid.

[51] ibid, and see also 288–89.

[52] See eg D Sarooshi, *The United Nations and the Development of Collective Security: The Delegation by the UN Security Council of its Chapter VII Powers* (Oxford, Oxford University Press, 1999) 26–31.

Article 24(1).[53] In doing so, Sarooshi also suggests that this is a 'delegation' of a discretionary power, arguing:

> The ability of States to act in the area of maintaining international peace and security is a right and not an obligation. Thus, the Security Council has clearly inherited a discretionary right to act to restore international peace and security, but not an obligation to act.[54]

Similarly, Abass[55] interprets Article 24(1) as transferring 'power' to the Security Council.[56] However, Abass reads this as being conditional upon the Council abiding by obligations also imposed by the provision itself.[57]

In other commentary, Delbrück[58] considers the phrase 'primary responsibility' to be a problematic one,[59] and simply dismisses the references in the provision to 'duties' under the responsibility as an 'unfortunate choice' of words.[60] Delbrück cites Kelsen in support of the argument that the Charter is 'an order of competences', not duties,[61] and argues that the final phrase in Article 24(1), according to which the Member States 'agree that in carrying out its duties under this responsibility the Security Council acts on their behalf', is legally erroneous and superfluous.[62]

These arguments are also not convincing. To suggest that a phrase in a legally binding Charter is 'erroneous and superfluous' undermines and dismisses out of hand the detailed discussions had at the drafting conference in San Francisco over many of the words and phrases throughout the Charter.[63] Equally, to suggest the use of the word 'duties' is incorrect without any indication from the preparatory works that the resulting interpretation was not intended undermines the very basic principles of treaty interpretation.[64]

Indeed, the French version of Article 24, which has equal legal weight,[65] sheds further light on this issue. In English, the last phrase of Article 24(1) reads 'and agree that in carrying out its duties under this responsibility the Security

[53] ibid, 26–31.
[54] ibid, n 113.
[55] A Abass, *Regional Organisations and the Development of Collective Security: Beyond Chapter VIII of the UN Charter* (Oxford, Hart Publishing, 2004).
[56] ibid, 131–39; see similarly, N White, 'The Legality of Bombing in the Name of Humanity' (2000) 5(1) *Journal of Conflict and Security* Law 27, 29.
[57] ibid, 136.
[58] KJ Delbrück, 'Article 24' in B Simma (ed), *The Charter of the United Nations: A Commentary*, 2nd edn (Oxford, 2002).
[59] ibid, 445.
[60] ibid, 448, n 27.
[61] ibid.
[62] ibid, 449.
[63] This author has previously made a similar point about other provisions of the UN Charter: see PM Butchard, 'Back to San Francisco: Explaining the Inherent Contradictions of Article 2(4) of the UN Charter' (2018) 23(2) *Journal of Conflict and Security Law* 229.
[64] See Vienna Convention on the Law of Treaties (VCLT), 1155 UNTS 331 (adopted 23 May 1969, entered into force 27 January 1980) Arts 31 and 32.
[65] ibid, Art 33.

Council acts on their behalf'. The French version reads 'et reconnaissent qu'en s'acquittant des devoirs que lui impose cette responsabilité le Conseil de sécurité agit en leur nom'. While the English text refers to 'duties under this responsibility', the French version literally translates to 'duties *imposed* by this responsibility'.[66] This provides some very convincing evidence that the wording of the provision was intended to have a mandatory character, and the responsibility to maintain international peace and security *imposes duties* upon the Security Council. To further investigate this possibility, and identify what 'duties' this responsibility might involve, this chapter will now explore the obligations of the Security Council under Article 39 of the Charter.

2.2. Obligations of the Security Council under Article 39 of the Charter

To demonstrate this legal nature of the responsibility for the maintenance of international peace and security, this section will argue that the Charter imposes specific obligations on the Security Council. By identifying such obligations, and how the Council may fail in them, we can also determine the legal consequences of inaction. As will be discussed below, many authors, and indeed States themselves, have opined that the Security Council is not under any obligation to act in a particular way, but has a wide discretion to use its powers as it sees fit. However, before the Council can utilise its coercive and enforcement powers under Chapter VII of the Charter, it must make a determination under Article 39. The importance of Article 39 should not be underestimated in this regard. Article 39 is not only a gateway to Chapter VII enforcement measures, but it is also a conduit for the implementation of the Security Council's primary responsibility under Article 24.

Article 39 provides:

> The Security Council shall determine the existence of any threat to the peace, breach of the peace, or act of aggression and shall make recommendations, or decide what measures shall be taken in accordance with Articles 41 and 42, to maintain or restore international peace and security.

Clearly, there are two tasks for the Council under this provision: (i) determining the nature of a situation, and (ii) making recommendations or decisions. The opening words of the provision clearly stipulate that the Security Council 'shall determine' the existence of a threat to peace etc. This is a clear use of mandatory language, therefore imposing an obligation on the Security Council to determine such a threat. But does this mean that the Security Council *must* make a determination where a threat to the peace actually exists as an objective fact? Or does this leave the Council full discretion as to the existence of such a threat, making

[66] Author's own translation, emphasis added.

the obligation to determine simply a requirement to make a declaration of this before it acts?

2.2.1. *Article 39 – The Scope of Security Council Discretion*

It is not the purpose of this book to revisit the debate over the scope and limitations of the Security Council's discretion under Article 39. However, it is important to outline the position of this author that the Council's discretion under this provision is subject to at least one important restriction. That is, the Security Council does have some discretion to determine when a situation matches one of those listed in Article 39, but it must remain within the ordinary meanings of those phrases.

During the discussion of the Spanish Question in 1946, the Security Council established a subcommittee to determine the scope of Article 39 and whether the situation in Spain at the time could fall under that provision.[67] In its report,[68] the subcommittee determined:

> Although the activities of the Franco regime do not, at present, constitute an existing threat to the peace within the meaning of Article 39 of the Charter *and therefore the Security Council has no jurisdiction to direct or to authorize enforcement measures under Article 40 or 42*, nevertheless such activities do constitute a situation which is a potential menace to international peace and security and which therefore is a situation 'likely to endanger the maintenance of international peace and security' within the meaning of Article 34 of the Charter.[69]

The subcommittee seems very clear in its report that the Security Council does not have absolute discretion to determine that there exists a threat to the peace where such a threat does not objectively exist. Nevertheless, some authors have argued that in the actual making of a determination, the Security Council has discretion in deciding what constitutes a threat to the peace, breach of the peace or act of aggression.[70] Indeed, even during the debates surrounding the Spanish question, Poland had argued that the Security Council 'is free within the purposes and principles of the Organisation to determine whether a situation'

[67] UN Department of Political Affairs, UNSC Repertoire 1946–1951, Chapter XI, *Consideration of Articles 39–40* (New York, United Nations, 1954) 423–27, available at: www.un.org/en/sc/repertoire/46-51/46-51_11.pdf#page=5 (accessed 31 July 2019) emphasis added.

[68] UNSC, 'Report of the Subcommittee on the Spanish Question appointed by the Security Council on 29 April 1946' (1 June 1946) UN Doc S/75.

[69] ibid, 14, [30], see also [18], where it states: 'Before direct action under Article 41 or 42 can be ordered, the Charter requires that the Security Council mast determine under Article 39 the existence of a threat to the peace or a breach of the peace, or an act of aggression.'

[70] See eg JA Frowein and N Krisch, 'Article 39' in B Simma (ed), *The Charter of the United Nations: A Commentary*, 2nd edn (Oxford, Oxford University Press, 2002) vol I, 719–20 and 726–27; see also GH Oosthuizen, 'Playing the Devil's Advocate: the United Nations Security Council Is Unbound by Law', (1999) 12 *Leiden Journal of International Law* 549, who makes the suggestion that such a discretion could be absolute.

falls within Article 39.[71] Discussing the subcommittee's report, France agreed that the Charter allowed for action in response to *potential* threats, but noted that the real question was on the Council's reliance on either Article 39 or Article 34, 'according to whether the threat is more or less remote, or more or less imminent'.[72] Australia even went as far as to say that there was no disagreement with Poland's legal interpretation of Article 39 – rather, the disagreement was based upon the evidence and the facts of that particular case.[73]

But, ultimately, any discretion the Council has cannot be unlimited, for the reasons that follow. Firstly, Article 24(2) requires the Council to act in accordance with the purposes and principles of the Charter, implying some limits on the Council's discretion.[74] Secondly, as highlighted by De Wet,[75] the use of vague terms such as 'threat to the peace' in Article 39 cannot remove them from the ambit of legal interpretation, which logically implies that the discretion cannot be unlimited.[76] De Wet suggests that if an unbound discretion had been intended, a distinction between the three situations in Article 39 would have been obsolete.[77]

Further, Martenczuk[78] suggests that an unlimited discretion under Article 39 would put at risk the 'carefully crafted balance of competences in the Charter'.[79] In this sense, Martenczuk argues that the powers in Chapter VI and VII of the Charter are distinct and would become obsolete if the Council were free at any given time to declare the provisions of Chapter VII applicable.[80] More extremely, another argument suggests that if the Council's discretion was limitless in determining the existence of a situation under Article 39, then its involvement in the affairs of Member States could be unfettered.[81] In this regard, Martenczuk states:

> Clearly, neither had the Member States intended the Council to constitute a sort of world government, nor would the Council be equipped to fulfil such a role. The view that the Council enjoys an unlimited discretion under Article 39 could lead to patently dysfunctional results.[82]

[71] UNSC (n 68), Reservations, 19–20.

[72] UNSC Verbatim Record, 44th Meeting (6 June 1946) UN Doc S/PV.44 (OR) 322.

[73] UNSC Verbatim Record, 47th Meeting (18 June 1946) UN Doc S/PV.47 (OR) 375–76.

[74] See the International Criminal Tribunal for the former Yugoslavia (ICTY) *Prosecutor v Tadić* (Jurisdiction) Case IT-94-1AR72 (2 October 1995) [29]; and see D Schweigman, *Authority of the Security Council under Chapter VII of the UN Charter: Legal Limits and the Role of the International Court of Justice* (Dordrecht, Kluwer Law International, 2001) 186–89.

[75] Erika De Wet, *The Chapter VII Powers of the United Nations Security Council* (Oxford, Hart Publishing, 2004).

[76] ibid, 136.

[77] ibid, 137.

[78] B Martenczuk, 'The Security Council, the International Court and Judicial Review: What Lessons from Lockerbie?' (1999) 10(3) *European Journal of International Law* 517.

[79] ibid, 542.

[80] ibid, 542.

[81] De Wet (n 75) 137, 176–77; Martenczuk (n 78) 542.

[82] Martenczuk (n 78) 542.

Although such a situation is unlikely to transpire, both politically and realistically, and especially in light of the veto power and voting procedures of the Council, this argument makes a very important point – the Council's powers are so extreme by their own nature that the discretion to use them *must* have come with legal limitations. If the Council could be said to enjoy an unlimited discretion in making a determination under Article 39, then it seems contradictory for the Council to be under an obligation to make such a determination *prior* to using its powers in the first place, as seems to be the common interpretation of Article 39. Frowein and Krisch do concede this point, suggesting that there must be some meaning to the terms 'threat to the peace', 'breach of the peace' and 'act of aggression'.[83]

This author submits that the Council's discretionary threshold must, at a minimum, stay within the object and purpose of the UN Charter, and the ordinary meanings of the terms in Article 39, as required by the Vienna Convention on the Law of Treaties (VCLT).[84] As Tzanakopoulos argues:

> [T]he Council cannot term anything and everything a 'threat to the peace', subject only to reaching political consensus, otherwise the prerequisite of such a determination in Article 39 would be devoid of any meaning. As such, the Council has discretionary power to select any of the possible alternative meanings of the term 'threat to peace', as long as these *remain*, but do not *exceed*, the interpretative radius of the provision.[85]

Based on these arguments, this author submits that the Security Council has an *objective minimum threshold* to adhere to when exercising its discretion, based upon the 'ordinary meaning' of the terms in accordance with Article 31(1) of the VCLT. As with the practice cited above concerning humanitarian crises, over time this objective minimum threshold may change to accommodate the wider range of threats that the world has witnessed emerging over the years. What was not a foreseeable threat in 1945 may now be a more apparent threat in today's world. This change over time is also in line with the VCLT, since Article 31(3)(b) calls for subsequent practice to be taken into account in the interpretation of a treaty where that practice establishes the agreement of the parties regarding its interpretation.

But then we have the question as to what happens when a threat to the peace, breach of the peace or act of aggression *does* exist and can be objectively determined to be so. Considering the 'ordinary meaning' of those terms, and the 'object and purpose' of the UN Charter, is the Security Council under an obligation to determine a situation to be one that falls under Article 39 in such

[83] Frowein and Krisch (n 70) 719–20.

[84] VCLT, Art 31(1); for a similar argument, see A Tzanakopoulos, *Disobeying the Security Council: Countermeasures against Wrongful Sanctions* (Oxford, Oxford University Press, 2011) 61–62; see also Schweigman (n 74) 266.

[85] Tzanakopoulos (n 84) 61–62.

circumstances, and what would such an obligation involve? With this in mind, we shall address the mandatory character of Article 39 of the Charter.

2.2.2. Article 39 – Mandatory Language

During the drafting of the UN Charter,[86] some States argued that action by the Council under Article 39 should be automatic. In a subcommittee tasked to clarify the meaning of 'determine' in Article 39, Uruguay urged that it should be made clear that the Council would, *automatically*, 'determine the existence of any threat to the peace' and not do so *solely at the urging of an interested party*.[87] In other words, Uruguay was calling for a determination to be made by the Council where a situation actually existed and was objectively identifiable. Similarly, several States called for a definition of aggression, and even a list of actions that would entail Council action automatically.[88]

However, these recommendations were abandoned, mainly because the opposing States said that it would be impossible to list all situations that would constitute aggression, and also because they favoured a Security Council discretion to decide when an act of aggression had been performed.[89] States argued that any attempt to make Council action automatic would be dangerous, and could mean premature applications of enforcement measures.[90] Ultimately, the drafting committee decided 'to adhere to the text drawn up at Dumbarton Oaks and leave to the Council the *entire discretion* as to what constitutes a threat to the peace, a breach of the peace, or an act of aggression'.[91]

The existence of this discretion is undeniable. But, since the drafting of the Charter, it must be asked whether the Council's discretion is affected by its previous determinations under Article 39. Indeed, some of these phrases now have legally recognised meanings, such as the Definition of Aggression,[92] which has been recognised by the ICJ as forming part of customary international law.[93]

[86] *Documents of the United Nations Conference on International Organisation* (multivolume, New York, United Nations, 1945) (hereinafter *UNCIO*).

[87] *Report of Eighth Meeting of Committee III/3* (18 May 1945) Doc.391 III/3/19, 12 *UNCIO* 334, 335. The Subcommittee eventually produced a draft document in *Draft by Subcommittee of Proposals for Amending Paragraphs 1 and 2 of Chapter VIII, B* (21 May 1945) Doc 478, III/3/B/1, 12 *UNCIO* 657, but a Chinese amendment was later favoured instead (see below).

[88] *Report of Ninth Meeting of Committee III/3* (19 May 1945) Doc 442, III/3/20, 12 *UNCIO* 341. A Bolivian proposal to insert a definition of aggression was defeated at the *Tenth Meeting of Committee III/3* (23 May 1945) Doc 502, III/3/22, 12 *UNCIO* 348–49.

[89] 12 *UNCIO* 341, 342.

[90] 12 *UNCIO* 341, 342.

[91] *Report of Mr Paul-Boncour* (10 June 1945) Doc 881, III/3/46, 12 *UNCIO* 502, 505 (emphasis added).

[92] UNGA Res 2214(XXIX), *Definition of Aggression* (14 December 1974) UN Doc A/RES/3314(XXIX).

[93] *Case Concerning Military and Paramilitary Activities in and against Nicaragua (Nicaragua v USA)* (Merits), Judgment of 27 June 1986, [1986] ICJ Rep 14 [*Nicaragua* case], [195].

There is no clear rule of precedent in the Security Council – the Council is not bound by its own previous practice *directly*. But it is arguable that the Council must acknowledge current customary international law relevant to the interpretation of the terms in Article 39, and such developments in the law may of course originate from the Council's own determinations.

However, Frowein and Krisch suggest that the Security Council 'is under no obligation to make a determination under Art 39, even if it considers that a threat to or breach of the peace exists – Art 39 empowers, but does not oblige the [Security Council] to act'.[94] This argument results in the contradictory interpretation that the Council is bound to make such a determination where it wishes to act, but is not bound to make a determination where it does not wish to act and a situation such as a threat to the peace actually does exist.[95] In this regard, Gill[96] argues that:

> [T]he wide margin of discretion the Council enjoys in carrying out its responsibilities and the practice of the Security Council over nearly half a century make it clear that the Council is not under any *legal* obligation to decide whether a given situation falls within the terms of Article 39.[97]

These arguments are less convincing when we consider why Article 39 uses mandatory language such as 'shall' when referring to *both* the act of 'determining' and the decision to make recommendations or take measures under Articles 41 and 42. During the drafting of the Charter, a Chinese amendment was adopted that reflects what became Article 39.[98] The proposed amendment stated that '[t]he Security Council *should* determine … and *should* make recommendations or decide upon …' actions to be taken.[99]

The use of the word 'may' in another paragraph of the amendment (which became Article 40 of the Charter) was explained as leaving 'to the discretion of the Council whether to take provisional measures or whether to proceed immediately to final action'.[100] This explanation accepts the use of the word 'may' as indicating discretionary language. It is also telling that the amendment therefore did not use the same word 'may', but rather 'should', in the context of the Council's role in making determinations or taking action.

The Coordination Committee, tasked with ensuring that there was a consistent use of language throughout the Charter, substituted the words 'should' in the Chinese amendment, with the word 'shall' – reflecting the final version of

[94] Frowein and Krisch (n 70) 719.
[95] ibid, 726–27.
[96] TD Gill, 'Legal and Some Political Limitations on the Power of the UN Security Council to Exercise its Enforcement Powers under Chapter VII of the Charter' (1995) 26 *Netherlands Yearbook of International Law* 33.
[97] ibid, 40 (emphasis in original).
[98] *Report of Fourteenth Meeting of Committee III/3* (26 May 1945) Doc 628, III/3/33, 12 *UNCIO* 379, quoting Doc WD 36.
[99] ibid (emphasis added).
[100] 12 *UNCIO* 379, 380.

Article 39. This decision to use 'shall' is not expressly addressed in relation to Article 39 directly,[101] but the Coordination Committee discussed elsewhere the significance of the word 'shall' in the Charter as a whole. Discussions of the Committee indicated numerous times that 'shall' was to indicate mandatory language or an obligation, whereas 'may' indicated discretion.[102] More specifically, the Coordination Committee expressly discussed the reasons behind changing 'should' to 'shall' in the context of other Charter provisions when it was said: '[T]he introductory phrase of the article established an obligation and that therefore the Technical Committee's word 'should' would be better translated by "shall" than by "may".'[103] Therefore, the final wording of Article 39 uses mandatory language, indicating the presence of one or more obligations.

The existence of obligations in Article 39 has also been noted by Hans Corell, former Under-Secretary-General for Legal Affairs and Legal Counsel of the United Nations. During an address in 2001, Corell interpreted Article 39 in the following light, stating:

> Of particular importance is Article 39 of the Charter. Under this provision, the Security Council *shall* decide what measures shall be taken in accordance with the Charter (Articles 41 and 42), to maintain or restore international peace and security. This means that the Council has a right out *obligation* to act. The question is whether the Council can find a common position when the need arises.[104]

Specifically, on the subject of humanitarian crises and mass atrocities, Corell has also argued:

> In such situations, under Article 39 of the Charter, the Security Council has an obligation to determine what measures should be taken in accordance with the Charter to maintain or restore international peace and security. If the members of the Council bow in unity to this obligation, they will also in unity realize that it is more effective to take measures at an early stage in order to prevent that the situation deteriorates and necessitates intervention by coercive means.[105]

[101] See *Report of Thirteenth Meeting of Coordination Committee* (10th June 1945), WD 256, CO/107, 17 *UNCIO* 69–71, on the Coordination Committee discussing what became Art 39.

[102] See eg discussions in: *Report of the Fifteenth Meeting of Coordination Committee* (13 June 1945) WD 289, CO/117, 17 *UNCIO* 89, 92; *Report of Twenty-Sixth Meeting of Coordination Committee* (25 July 1945) WD 426, CO/190, 17 *UNCIO* 180, 182; see also, *Report of Twenty-Ninth Meeting of Coordination Committee* (21 August 1945) WD 429, CO/193, 17 *UNCIO* 212.

[103] *Report of Fourteenth Meeting of Coordination Committee* (13 June 1945) WD 288, CO/116, 17 *UNCIO* 77, 78.

[104] H Corell, 'To Intervene or Not: The Dilemma that Will Not Go Away' (Conference on the Future of Humanitarian Intervention, Duke University, Durham, NC, 19 April 2001) 4, available at: http://legal.un.org/ola/media/info_from_lc/duke01.pdf (accessed 31 July 2019) emphasis in original. See also H Corell, 'Reflections on the Responsibility to Protect' (International Network of Universities, Workshop on Humanitarian Intervention Malmö University, Malmö, 4 March 2010) available at: www.havc.se/res/SelectedMaterial/20100304responsibilitytoprotect.pdf, (accessed 31 July 2019).

[105] H Corell, 'From Territorial Sovereignty to Human Security' (Canadian Council of International Law, 1999 Annual Conference, Ottawa, 29 October 1999) available at: www.un.org/law/counsel/ottawa.htm (accessed 31 July 2019).

Of course, Corell was speaking in a personal capacity in both instances. Nevertheless, the arguments are illuminating further still when Corell acknowledged the existence of the Security Council's discretion in its determinations *alongside* the obligatory nature of Article 39.[106]

States have often stated the view that a determination under Article 39 *must* be made *prior* to the Council using its enforcement powers under Chapter VII – as if a determination is the gateway to unlock the Council's Chapter VII enforcement powers – and this is now a seemingly settled interpretation.[107] But the requirement that the Council 'shall determine the existence of' a threat to the peace makes no explicit qualification that this should be done as a prerequisite to using its Chapter VII powers. This author submits that this prevalent 'gateway' interpretation of Article 39 is simply the logical by-product of two obligations that come under Article 39. The obligation 'to determine' is joined by a mandatory 'and shall' to the obligation to 'make recommendations, or decide' upon enforcement measures. The two obligations on the Council are separate, but nevertheless dependent on the other being carried out – ie if a determination is made by the Council, then recommendations or decisions must also be made. Conversely, if the Council wishes to make a recommendation or decision within the meaning of Article 39, then the Council must also determine the existence of a threat to the peace, breach of the peace or act of aggression.

2.2.3. *The Obligation to Determine – An Obligation to Investigate*

Where a threat to the peace, breach of the peace or act of aggression exists as an objective fact, this author submits that the Council must determine the existence of that situation to be so. Regarding the responsibility to protect, this could indicate an obligation to determine whether the threat or commission of atrocity crimes constitutes a 'threat to the peace'.

Much discussion of this issue refers to the concept of 'a determination', ie a *noun* describing the action of either declaring or deciding that a situation meets a certain threshold. This may be compared to the 'legal' definition of the word 'determination', where a 'determination' is a decision or judgement akin to that

[106] Corell (2001) (n 104) 10.

[107] See eg: UN Office of Legal Affairs, *Repertory of Practice of United Nations Organs* (1945–54) vol II, 366–76 (hereinafter, *Repertory*); *Repertory*, Supplement No 3 (1959–66) vol II, 228–31; UNSC Verbatim Record, 35th Meeting (18 April 1946) UN Doc S/PV.35 (Official Record) 184–85 (UK); UNSC Verbatim Record, 1129th Meeting (10 June 1964) UN Doc S/PV.1129(OR) [21] (Indonesia); UNSC Verbatim Record, 1131st Meeting (15 June 1964) UN Doc. S/PV.1131(OR) [89] (UK); UNSC Verbatim Record, 1264th Meeting (19 November 1965) UN Doc S/PV.1264(OR) [13] (Jordan); UNSC Verbatim Record, 1340th Meeting (16 December 1966) UN Doc S/PV.1340(OR) [32]–[33] (Uruguay) [11] (Jordan) (calling for such a determination to be explicit, not merely by reference to Art 39 alone); UNSC Verbatim Record, 3453rd Meeting (8 November 1994) UN Doc S/PV.3453, 3 (France); UNSC Verbatim Record, 5474th Meeting (22 June 2006) UN Doc S/PV.5474, 17 (Russia), and 30 (Mexico); UNSC Verbatim Record, 5500th Meeting (31 July 2006) UN Doc S/PV.5500, 3 (US).

of a court or other authority.[108] This is different to the factual definition of 'determine', which involves the establishment or discovery of a certain set of facts.[109]

The latter definition could indicate that the Council is under an obligation to investigate, or establish, whether a situation is a threat to international peace and security or otherwise. In the author's view, this would compel the Council to continuously determine the nature of situations that may threaten international peace and security. Under such a continuous obligation, the 'determination' would not be a 'declaration' at all, but the act of continuously assessing facts, constantly monitoring threats and establishing the true nature of a situation.

Alexander Orakhelashvili[110] comes close to advocating for a duty to investigate when he discusses the requirements of exercising discretion in law. In particular, he argues: 'Discretion must be exercised lawfully, that is in regular form and procedure, free of an error of law or fact or a misuse of authority, and by taking all essential facts into consideration.'[111] Orakhelashvili goes on to suggest that there is also a requirement of 'genuineness' when making a determination under Article 39,[112] and suggests that to identify the 'genuineness' of a threat to international peace and security, the Council must use tools at its disposal such as fact-finding.[113] This idea is reflected in the General Assembly's *Declaration on Fact-Finding*,[114] which declares in particular: 'The Security Council should consider the possibility of undertaking fact-finding to discharge effectively its primary responsibility for the maintenance of international peace and security in accordance with the Charter.'[115]

The language of this Declaration rightly suggests that fact-finding may not always be necessary – especially with regard to situations that may be highly publicised and well monitored, and thus the facts are well known and substantiated. However, this language does seem to suggest that fact-finding is closely linked to the Council's primary responsibility for the maintenance of international peace and security, and thus, by extension, Article 39. It is not controversial, therefore, to suggest that investigations and fact-finding play a significant role in the Council's obligation to determine, and in certain circumstances may be *required* to establish the true nature of a situation and whether or not there exists a threat to international peace and security.

[108] *Oxford Dictionary* definition, http://www.oxforddictionaries.com/definition/english/determine (accessed 31 July 2019); see also *Oxford Advanced Learner's Dictionary*, http://www.oxforddictionaries.com/definition/learner/determine (accessed 31 July 2019).

[109] ibid.

[110] A Orakhelashvili, *Collective Security* (Oxford, Oxford University Press, 2011).

[111] ibid, 154.

[112] ibid, 155–64.

[113] ibid, 155–64.

[114] UNGA Res 46/59 (1991) *Declaration on Fact-finding by the United Nations in the Field of the Maintenance of International Peace and Security* (9 December 1991) UN Doc A/RES/46/59.

[115] Ibid, Annex, [8].

Dinstein[116] accuses Orakhelashvili and other commentators of 'conjuring up' such mandatory criteria for Article 39,[117] suggesting that it is intended to limit the Council's broad-spectrum of discretion when acting under Article 39. It is interesting to note, therefore, that Dinstein himself has acknowledged the mandatory nature of Article 39, and has explicitly highlighted the obligatory effect of the mandatory 'shall' within the provision.[118]

But Dinstein's more recent concerns are worth addressing. The current author believes that Article 39 does impose important obligations on the Council. But this does not necessarily mean that the Council's discretion is limited, and nor is its authority undermined. And this can be demonstrated by utilising the following hypothetical examples.

If the Council, in light of the findings of an investigation that it authorised, decided that the situation was *not* a threat to the peace, then logically it would be unlikely that such a situation would *actually be* a threat to the peace. So long as the investigations are properly undertaken (which is a different matter), those investigations would indicate whether there exists a situation within the meaning of Article 39. Such investigations may even constitute a 'determination' in themselves within the meaning of Article 39, depending on the mandate granted by the Security Council. In such a case, whether the Security Council accepts the findings of an investigation mandated to investigate a situation is irrelevant. The Security Council, by default, has fulfilled its obligation to 'determine the existence' of a situation under Article 39, and the findings of the investigation are authoritative evidence in that regard. Even if the Security Council ignored the findings of its own investigation, it is arguable that the Council has already met its obligation to 'determine the existence' of a situation under Article 39.[119]

On the other hand, if the Council heard the findings another UN investigation – on behalf of the Human Rights Council or the General Assembly, for example[120] – there would still be an obligation on the Council under Article 39 to make its own determinations. It may choose to accept the outcome of a UN investigation and endorse that organ's own findings, thus meeting its obligations to 'determine'. However, it may also choose *not* to accept, on the basis of such investigations and the facts presented therein, that a situation is a threat to the peace, or otherwise under Article 39, provided that it votes as a

[116] Y Dinstein, *War, Aggression and Self-Defence*, 5th edn (Cambridge, Cambridge University Press, 2012).

[117] ibid, 309, [821]; see also Y Dinstein, *War, Aggression and Self-Defence*, 6th edn (Cambridge, Cambridge University Press, 2017) 334, [876].

[118] See Y Dinstein, *War, Aggression and Self-Defence*, 3rd edn (Cambridge, Cambridge University Press, 2001) 255; see also more recently Dinstein (2017) (n 117) 341, [895].

[119] Of course, it would be highly unlikely that the Security Council would disregard the outcome of one of its own investigations.

[120] This situation was largely unprecedented until the Security Council was briefed by the Human Rights Council's International Fact-Finding Mission for Myanmar, as discussed in detail in Chapter II, section 3.2.3.

Council to do so.[121] The opinion of the Security Council that a situation does not meet the threshold of Article 39, even where another body such as the General Assembly has determined otherwise, should not automatically be considered as violating Article 39. The Security Council is the organ most suitably placed and specialised to make such determinations, and its decisions therein should be assumed to be correct and within its authority. Questions of procedural integrity can of course rebut this presumption, such as the internal principles of the UN designed to ensure independence and integrity. As put forward in the *Declaration on Fact-Finding*, for example:

> 3. Fact-finding should be comprehensive, objective, impartial and timely.
>
> …
>
> 25. Fact-finding missions have an obligation to act in strict conformity with their mandate and perform their task in an impartial way. Their members have an obligation not to seek or receive instructions from any Government or from any authority other than the competent United Nations organ. They should keep the information acquired in discharging their mandate confidential even after the mission has fulfilled its task.
>
> …
>
> 27. Whenever fact-finding includes hearings, appropriate rules of procedure should ensure their fairness.[122]

If such standards are not met, then the authority of the Security Council's determinations may be undermined. Unfortunately, such questions are beyond the scope of this book. If the Council's procedures and investigations meet the highest standards of integrity and other general principles, the substantive outcomes of its determinations should be given their proper weight as those from the body with the primary responsibility for the maintenance of international peace and security.

In circumstances where the Security Council is *unable* to agree with the opinion of another organ, due to the veto of a permanent member, and thus the paralysis of the Council generally, then there also may be room to argue that the Council is thus unable to fulfil its primary responsibilities.

Considering these arguments, this author submits that the obligation on the Council, in light of an objectively identifiable threat, is to establish whether this threat exists.[123] This could include such a duty to investigate, for example,

[121] The action or inaction of the Council in response to such investigations may also be relevant to the second part of Art 39 which requires recommendations or decisions to take measures, as shall be discussed below. Regarding the Fact-Finding Mission for Myanmar, as detailed above (and up until the time of writing) the Council did not vote on or take any further action after being briefed by the Mission.

[122] *Declaration on Fact-Finding* (n 114) Annex, [3], [25], [27].

[123] See further, M Selkirk, 'Judge, Jury and Executioner – Analysing the Nature of the Security Council's Authority Under Article 39 of the UN Charter' (2000–03) 9 *Auckland University Law Review* 1101, 1107ff.

utilising fact-finding missions to determine whether the facts match the threshold of a threat to the peace.[124] Alternatively, it could imply a duty to hear the evidence of other UN investigations relating to a situation. Of course, one would not go further than advocating the possibility of a 'duty to investigate', simply because these are the only duties that seem logically connected to the wording of Article 39, and the purposes advocated by the drafters of the Charter.

2.2.4. The Obligation to 'Make Recommendations, or Decide …' – An Obligation to Act?

The second obligation requires the Security Council to 'make recommendations, or decide what measures shall be taken in accordance with Articles 41 and 42, to maintain or restore international peace and security'. This is not an obligation to take specific action. As discussed above, the drafters of the Charter were cautious to impose any restrictions on how the Council should act, out of fear that the imposition of sanctions may be premature and inappropriate, instead calling for the Council to have some discretion in its decisions to act.

It is widely considered that the Security Council is not under any obligation to act in a particular way, but has a wide discretion to use its powers as it sees fit.[125] But it is important to distinguish between discretion in deciding the *type* of action it decides to take, and discretion in deciding *whether to act* at all.

Article 41 provides that '[t]he Security Council *may* decide' on non-forcible measures.[126] The word 'may' has been specifically inserted to give the Council the option to impose sanctions, or not, as it determines appropriate.

Similarly, Article 42 states:

> Should the Security Council consider that measures provided for in Article 41 would be inadequate or have proved to be inadequate, it *may* take such action by air, sea, or land forces as may be necessary to maintain or restore international peace and security. Such action may include demonstrations, blockade, and other operations by air, sea, or land forces of Members of the United Nations.[127]

Like Article 41, this provision also utilises the word 'may' in giving the Security Council the discretionary power to utilise military measures. Therefore, a decision 'as to what measures shall be taken in accordance with Articles 41 and 42', as required by Article 39, gives the Council a choice between these two provisions. In other words, the Council cannot be compelled to use force or impose sanctions.

However, this author believes that the discretion of the Council cannot extend to a decision to not take any action whatsoever. Article 39 requires the Security

[124] ibid.
[125] See below section 2.2.4.1.
[126] Emphasis added.
[127] Emphasis added.

Council to choose to *make recommendations* or *take action* under Article 41 or 42, as it sees fit. Or, if the Council deems necessary, it may do both. In other words, if the Security Council has determined that international peace and security requires maintenance or restoration, the Council must decide between: (i) making recommendations for its maintenance or restoration; (ii) acting as it sees fit under Article 41 or 42; or (iii) both. It cannot, and must not, do nothing. Inaction, or a failure to decide upon these choices, results in a breach of the Council's legal duties under its responsibility to maintain international peace and security.

2.2.4.1. An Obligation to Act in Security Council Practice

Although explicit acceptance of this interpretation has not been widespread, is has nevertheless found occasional support throughout the lifetime of the Security Council. Statements during the situation in Southern Rhodesia showed support for the primary obligations of the Security Council under Article 39. In particular, Argentina declared:

> We believe that, when action in the content of Chapter VII of the Charter is involved, the Security Council's primary obligation under Article 39 is to determine 'the existence of any threat to the peace, breach of the peace, or act of aggression' and then to decide on whatever measures it considers appropriate.[128]

Although this statement was made in support of an argument to reference Article 39 clearly and expressly when making a determination, what is notable is the suggestion that 'to decide on whatever measures it considers appropriate' is part of the Security Council's primary obligation under Article 39. This was supported by Japan, who made this interpretation much clearer when it was said:

> [M]y delegation fully shares the view of the representative of Argentina [1332nd meeting] that it is the primary obligation of the Council, under Chapter VII, Article 39 of the Charter, to determine 'the existence of any threat to the peace, breach of the peace, or act of aggression', *and then* to decide on whatever measures are appropriate.[129]

Finally, during the same situation, France, although arguing against making a determination under Article 39 in this situation, when referring to the legal obligations on the Council, noted that 'the Council, once this threat has been established, would, on the basis of Chapter VII of the Charter, *have to adopt*

[128] UNSC Verbatim Record, 1332nd Meeting (9 December 1966) UN Doc S/PV.1332(OR), [55] (Argentina).

[129] UNSC Verbatim Record, 1333rd Meeting (12 December 1996) UN Doc S/PV.1333(OR), [47] (Japan), emphasis added.

various measures, which Governments … would be requested to apply'.[130] Although these statements made during the situation in Southern Rhodesia do not support an obligation to undertake specific measures, they do suggest that the Security Council must at least *do something* in light of Article 39.

This idea that the Security Council has *duties*, and thus must not *do nothing*, is generally supported by statements made during the very early practices of the Security Council. During the Council's deliberations regarding the Palestine question in early 1948, there was some debate as to whether a breach of the peace within Palestine would be the same as a 'breach of the peace' in Article 39.[131] The UK argued that Article 39 referred only to a threat to or breach of *international* peace, and that since Palestine had no international status, the situation could not therefore fall within the meaning of Article 39.[132] However, the US disagreed with this, and highlighted that the word 'any' in the context of 'any threat to the peace, breach of the peace' includes 'international' and all other kinds of threats to the peace, breaches of the peace or acts of aggression.[133]

In explaining that interpretation of Article 39, the US representative said the following:

> I would claim that that word was substituted with great care and with full understanding of its importance, so that the Security Council, having found 'any threat to the peace', might be able to proceed to the inquiry with respect to the application of remedies, or a prevention of that further step of extension of the conflagration into a breach of international peace, for this Article further says 'and shall make recommendations …'; then we strike something astonishing – the distinctive 'or' – "or decide what measure shall be taken in accordance with Articles 41 and 42, to maintain or restore international peace and security".
>
> This is a great responsibility. This is where a change occurs in the Charter. From being a quasi-judicial body, the Security Council becomes political and executive. The Council is no longer limited to recommendations, but can announce decisions and order their implementation.[134]

In support of this, the US representative made some very important constitutional statements that highlight the fundamental nature of Article 39. First, the US declared the general nature of the obligation:

> First of all, the Security Council has a *duty* that is laid down in Chapter VII, and which we claim it cannot evade or avoid. The facts being perfectly clear, graphically described as a condition of warfare, how can the Security Council avoid this duty proscribed by Article 39 of the Charter?[135]

[130] UNSC Verbatim Record, 1277th Meeting (9 April 1966) UN Doc S/PV.1277(OR), [90] (France) (emphasis added).

[131] See, generally, discussions in UNSC Verbatim Record, 296th Meeting (18/19 May 1948) UN Doc S/PV.296 (Official Records).

[132] ibid, 2–4 (UK).

[133] ibid, 6–10 (US).

[134] ibid, 7 (US).

[135] ibid, 6 (US).

Secondly, the US further supported this by expanding upon the nature of the 'obligation to determine', arguing:

> We do not have to determine, as suggested by the representative of the United Kingdom, who is the aggressor, who is at fault, if both parties are at fault, or which one is more at fault than the other. But as the guardians of the peace of the world, *it is our primary duty to find out*, under Article 39, whether there exists any threat to the peace. That is the limit, the boundary, of the duty which the resolution offered by the United States delegation asks the Security Council to perform.[136]

The final notable statement during this situation was made by France, but this time regarding the obligation to determine rather than the obligation to act. The representative of France made a point of highlighting the particular language used in the Articles of Chapter VII detailing the Council's powers compared to the language of Article 39 – notably highlighting the mandatory language in Article 39 compared to the permissive or discretionary language in the other provisions.[137] The French representative put forward his interpretation, stating:

> [U]nder the provisions of the Charter, the Council has no power of appraisal at the time when the existence of a threat to the peace is determined. ... [I]n my opinion, since a certain state of affairs has to be recorded if the facts are established, the recording must take place.
>
> ...
>
> But as regards the determination of the existence of a threat to the peace, I personally consider that, if the threat is certain – and this is a case where, in my opinion, it is certain, where no one can doubt that it exists – it is the duty of the Security Council to declare it.[138]

This interpretation is in line with the idea that the Council, when faced with undeniable and established facts that a situation is, *objectively*, a threat to the peace or otherwise, must make such a determination. The caveat in this interpretation is that the facts must be established and, as discussed above, this may well be done through the Council's own investigations, thus already meeting its obligation to 'determine' whether a situation under Article 39 exists.

More recently, when the discussion of the responsibility to protect was on the minds of States, more important statements were made with regard to this idea that the Council is compelled to act in certain situations. For example, in 'the Boston Letter', the United States wrote to the United Nations when the relevant paragraphs of the World Summit Outcome were being drafted, to highlight that the Council has never been under an obligation to act in a certain way. The letter said:

> [W]e note that the Charter has never been interpreted as creating a legal obligation for Security Council members to support enforcement action in various cases involving

[136] ibid, 9 (US) (emphasis added).
[137] UNSC Verbatim Record, 310th Meeting (29 May 1948) UN Doc S/PV.310 (Official Records) 33–34 (France).
[138] ibid.

serious breaches of international peace. Accordingly, we believe just as strongly that a determination as to what particular measures to adopt in specific cases cannot be predetermined in the abstract but should remain a decision within the purview of the Security Council.[139]

This statement helps us to identify the limits to any interpretation of an obligation under Article 39. Like it was discussed during the drafting of the Charter that the Council was not under an obligation to take specific enforcement action, this letter from the US rightly highlights that the decision on *what type of* action to take is for the Security Council itself to determine. And therein lies the outer limits of the Security Council's obligation to act. It must *at the very least* make recommendations, or decide on measures under Articles 41 or 42.

At the same time, there is also no widespread support for the contrary argument – that the Council *may* ignore situations that threaten international peace. The maintenance of international peace and security is a fundamental purpose of the United Nations, and the purpose of taking 'effective collective measures' to protect this has even been highlighted in Article 1 of the Charter itself. To argue that there is scope for the Security Council to do *nothing* in response to such a situation would go against the very fabric of the Charter and the organisation in which it belongs. Indeed, even the Council itself has been *conscious* of its duty to act. In Resolution 294 (1971), the Council was explicitly '[c]onscious of its duty to take effective collective measures for the prevention and removal of threats to international peace and security and for the suppression of acts of aggression'.[140]

Therefore, when faced with any situation of a threat to the peace, breach of the peace or acts of aggression, the Security Council must take what action it sees fit, but it is not enough for it to simply remain indecisive or silent.

3. THE FAILURES OF THE SECURITY COUNCIL

3.1. Identifying Failure

The main revelation from the above is that the Council is not free to remain silent or accept inaction. It has a duty to do something. But what about the much-debated veto of the permanent five members of the Security Council, and the paralysis this may cause?[141] Although the use of the veto alone would not

[139] Letter from Ambassador Bolton to UN Member States Conveying US Amendments to the Draft Outcome Document Being Prepared for the High Level Event on Responsibility to Protect (30 August 2005) available at www.responsibilitytoprotect.org/files/US_Boltonletter_R2P_30Aug05%5b1%5d.pdf, 1 (hereinafter 'the Bolton Letter').

[140] UNSC Res 294 (1971) (15 July 1971) UN Doc S/RES/294(1971) preamblular [5].

[141] The veto power is provided for in Art 27(3) of the UN Charter, where all *decisions* of the Council require the 'concurring vote' of each of the permanent five members: Russia, China, the US, the UK, and France.

likely amount to such a failure, the systematic abuse of this veto which causes the paralysis of the Council, especially in the face of a situation that can be objectively determined to engage its responsibilities, can indeed cause the Council to fail in its obligations under Article 39, and therefore its responsibilities under the Charter. The question at this point therefore becomes: how do we authoritatively determine that the Security Council has failed in its responsibilities? This author makes two suggestions at this point.

First, it is within the competences of another organ of the United Nations – namely the General Assembly – to establish a fact-finding mission or an inquiry into whether the Security Council is failing in its responsibilities.[142] Such an investigation would arguably be an authoritative determination of the failures of the Security Council, provided they adhere to the key principles protecting the integrity of inquiries.[143]

During the drafting of the UN Charter, there were indications that UN-established inquiries could have a role in achieving accountability of the five permanent members. When discussing the limitations of the veto power, New Zealand and the UK had a very in-depth exchange about the possibility of a permanent member being held to account if it should commit aggression and endanger international peace and security. The UK proposed that, while the permanent five members could not be subject to enforcement measures under Chapter VII of the Charter due to the veto, the establishment of an investigation or inquiry under Article 34 was not subject to this veto in some circumstances.[144] This would be the case where the permanent member blocking action may be considered a 'party to a dispute' under Article 27(3) and must abstain from voting.

In such circumstances, it would be possible for the Security Council itself, blocked from *acting* by an abuse of the veto power, to launch an inquiry under Chapter VI without being subject to that member's veto into whether the actions of that member are causing it to fail in its legal responsibilities.

3.2. Legal Consequences of Failure

Article 24(1) confers 'primary' responsibility on the Security Council. When it can be objectively determined that the Council has failed in its responsibilities, these responsibilities may then be assumed by the actor determined to have 'secondary' responsibility in this regard.

[142] See generally, *Declaration on Fact-Finding* (n 114) Annex.

[143] See further, ibid, Annex, [3], [25], [27]; Orakhelashvili (n 110) 151–56.

[144] See *Statements of Questions by the Delegate of New Zealand and Replies by the Delegate of the United Kingdom at Ninth Meeting*, Committee III/1, Doc WD3 (17 May 1945) 11 *UNCIO* 317, 7–9.

It has been recognised by the ICJ in *Certain Expenses*[145] that this responsibility may be 'primary', but it is not 'exclusive'.[146] In comparison, the Court's opinion in the *Construction of a Wall* case suggested that Article 24 referred to a primary, but not exclusive, *competence* in the maintenance of international peace and security.[147] Therefore, both the *responsibility* to maintain peace and security, and the legal *competence* to do so, do not lie solely with the Security Council.

Nevertheless, there is a delicate balance to be met when considering when these 'residual' responsibilities and competencies can and should be engaged. Indeed, the ICJ highlighted that, under Article 24, the Security Council was conferred responsibility 'in order to ensure prompt and effective action' and stressed that:'It is only the Security Council which can require enforcement by coercive action against an aggressor.'[148]

Similarly, the General Assembly's *Uniting for Peace* Resolution[149] was:

> *Conscious* that failure of the Security Council to discharge its responsibilities on behalf of all the Member States ... does not relieve Member States of their obligations or the United Nations of its responsibility under the Charter to maintain international peace and security.[150]

The Resolution then went on to recognise that 'such a failure does not deprive the General Assembly of its rights or relieve it of its responsibility under the Charter in regard to the maintenance of international peace and security'.[151]

It is therefore possible that this responsibility 'reverts' to States as a collective, or the international community. This conforms to the idea that States 'delegated' or 'conferred' responsibility onto the Security Council via Article 24(1).[152] Much of the hesitation and rejection of this is based upon the (seemingly correct) assumption that the international community as a whole does not possess a collective 'police power'.[153] In this regard, White argues that it is the Assembly and the ICJ that would have 'subsidiary competence in the field of international peace and security, not states acting unilaterally or multilaterally'.[154] Indeed, White highlights the flaw in the argument when he notes 'the idea of rights reverting back to states in the event of Security Council inaction assumes that

[145] *Certain Expenses of the United Nations (Article 17, paragraph 2 of the Charter)* (Advisory Opinion of 20 July 1962) [1962] ICJ Rep 151 (hereinafter '*Certain Expenses*').

[146] ibid, 163.

[147] *Legal Consequences of the Construction of a Wall in the Occupied Palestinian Territory* (Advisory Opinion of 9 July 2004) [2004] ICJ Rep 136 (hereinafter *Construction of a Wall*) [26].

[148] *Certain Expenses* (n 147) 163.

[149] UNGA Res 377(V), *Uniting for Peace* (3 November 1950) UN Doc A/RES/377(V).

[150] ibid, Resolution A, preamble [7].

[151] ibid, Resolution A, preamble [8].

[152] Sarooshi (n 52) 28–31; Abass (n 55) 135–36.

[153] Although see Sarooshi (n 52) 28–31, n 108; see also Abass (n 55) 136, arguing the *use* of these police powers can only be used on a *collective* basis.

[154] White (n 56) 29.

they possessed such rights before 1945, and that they could claim them back based on a perception of Security Council inadequacy'.[155]

However, by accepting that responsibility in this context means 'duty', rather than 'power', these concerns are very much alleviated. The reverting of responsibility *back* onto the international community would be reverting a *duty* to maintain international peace and security. This does not in any way involve the transfer of legal powers to the international community as a whole – powers that they do not have.

By extension, this means that the international community would assume a responsibility to maintain international peace and security *in a way that they are legally able to do so*. The question of what institutions or actors have competence to implement this responsibility is important in determining the legal powers that are available to implement this residual responsibility. While this resumption of responsibility necessitates that the legal duty to act continues in this residual responsibility, this does not mean that the legal powers of the Security Council also move with it. The powers of the Security Council to act are recognised as separate from the responsibility for the maintenance of peace and security itself, as indicated in Article 24(2), which specifically establishes that: 'The specific *powers* granted to the Security Council for the discharge of *these duties* are laid down in Chapters VI, VII, VIII, and XII.'[156]

No matter what powers States possessed before the UN Charter, it is now very clear that the unilateral use of force beyond the United Nations is prohibited by both custom and Article 2(4) of the UN Charter.[157] Therefore, any implementation of the responsibilities assumed by the international community must remain in accordance with the UN Charter, and any legal powers they already possess.

Importantly, this resumption of responsibility also indicates that in situations where the responsibility to protect overlaps with the responsibility to maintain international peace and security, there is a convincing possibility of the responsibility to protect 'piggybacking' this continuation of the legal duty and therefore existing and applying beyond the failures of the Security Council to implement its own responsibilities.

4. THE TERTIARY RESPONSIBILITY TO PROTECT – A CONTINUUM OF RESPONSIBILITY

In the event of a failure of a primary responsibility to maintain international peace and security, this responsibility may be fully assumed by the actors who are accepted to have a residual responsibility in this regard. Accordingly, there

[155] ibid.
[156] Emphasis added.
[157] See further Butchard (n 63), and Chapter IV below.

is a continuum of responsibility whereby a failure does not result in the responsibility ceasing to exist, but instead continues to be assumed by the next actor with residual responsibility.

The inherent link between the responsibility to protect and the responsibility to maintain international peace and security necessitates that the responsibility to protect must also exist on a 'residual' basis like the responsibility to maintain peace and security. This is especially true in situations where the two overlap, where there is at least a threat to international peace and security that engages these two responsibilities. This creates a 'continuum' of responsibility whereby the responsibility to protect endures beyond the inaction of the Security Council. This author labels this continuation of responsibility as the 'tertiary responsibility to protect'.

The challenge with investigating residual responsibilities is identifying the actor who assumes responsibility following a failure. In the context of the responsibility to protect, it is the *international community's* responsibility to protect when it acts *through* the UN Security Council. This is confirmed by the World Summit Outcome itself, where States declared: '[*W*]*e are prepared* to take collective action, in a timely and decisive manner, through the Security Council, in accordance with the Charter.'[158]

The Secretary-General has noted that Pillar II of the responsibility to assist and build capacity of States 'is an ongoing responsibility to use peaceful means to protect populations'.[159] Accordingly, where the Security Council fails, the international community still maintain its secondary responsibility to assist and build capacity. However, responsibility to take a timely and decisive response in accordance with Pillar III must also continue beyond the Security Council's inaction. As the Secretary-General pointed out: 'Faced with imminent or ongoing atrocity crimes, we must never ask "whether" to respond or expect others to shoulder the burden for us; instead, we must ask "how" we can assist in a collective response.'[160]

In this regard, the Secretary-General was of the opinion that peaceful tools are available to protect populations, including 'fact-finding, monitoring, reporting and verification; commissions of inquiry; public advocacy; quiet diplomacy; arbitration, conciliation and mediation; community engagement; humanitarian assistance and protection; the protection of refugees and displaced persons; civilian and technical assistance; and consent-based peacekeeping.'[161] However, the World Summit Outcome clearly speaks of taking action through the Security Council 'should peaceful means be inadequate and national authorities are manifestly failing to protect their populations from genocide, war crimes,

[158] World Summit Outcome (n 2) [139] (emphasis added).

[159] Report of the Secretary-General, *Mobilizing Collective Action: The Next Decade of the Responsibility to Protect* (22 July 2016) UN Doc A/70/999–S/2016/620, [45].

[160] ibid, [46].

[161] ibid, [47]; see also *Timely and Decisive Response*, (n 32) [22] and [27].

ethnic cleansing and crimes against humanity'.[162] Therefore, the continuation of the international community's responsibility to take *peaceful* measures does not address the continuation of the Pillar III responsibility to take timely and decisive action when peaceful means are inadequate, and in situations that necessarily *require* such coercive measures to prevent or halt mass atrocities.[163]

In light of this, the World Summit Outcome clearly identifies a residual responsibility to protect for the international community.[164] This implies that the international community should assume this responsibility when the Security Council fails to act. However, where the responsibility to maintain international peace and security is engaged, this responsibility may not always automatically revert to the international community. As the ICJ noted, the General Assembly also has a residual responsibility to maintain international peace and security.[165] Therefore, there may be an extra step before the responsibility to maintain peace and security 'leaves the United Nations' and falls onto the wider international community. While the responsibility to protect is automatically assumed by the international community upon failure of the Security Council, the responsibility for maintaining peace and security does not necessarily do the same, unless it can also be demonstrated that the General Assembly also remains inactive and does not assume its residual responsibilities.[166]

Therefore, to establish that the tertiary responsibility to protect exists and continues beyond the action of the Security Council, it is necessary to establish that the relevant actor has a legal competence to implement it. This could include a competence relating to the maintenance of international peace and security. This actor must also be capable of acting where the body with primary responsibility (often with more legal powers) has failed in its responsibilities. In the end, there would be no legal value to a tertiary responsibility to protect where this is not legally capable of being implemented.

5. CONCLUSIONS

This chapter has sought to establish that the Security Council, contrary to popular belief, does have a legal obligation to maintain international peace and security and, by extension, to protect populations from genocide, crimes against humanity, war crimes and ethnic cleansing within the framework of the responsibility to protect. At its very fundamental level, its legal obligations are to *do*

[162] World Summit Outcome (n 158) [139].
[163] See also *Timely and Decisive Response* (n 32) [31]; Report of the Secretary-General, *A Vital and Enduring Commitment: Implementing the Responsibility to Protect* (13 July 2015) A/69/981–S/2015/500, t [62].
[164] World Summit Outcome (n 2) [139].
[165] *Certain Expenses* (n 145) 163.
[166] See Chapter VI, section 1.4.

something, and it is a failure of the Council's responsibilities to remain inactive or paralysed.

The formulation of Article 39 suggests that the provision is more than just a procedural requirement of a determination, but an obligation to investigate, substantiate and decide whether a situation requires appropriate action under Chapter VII. It empowers, but also obliges, the Security Council to fulfil its primary responsibility for international peace and security and gives it clear instructions on how to go about that. The obligation to 'determine' requires the analysis of facts, evidence and the legal thresholds of threats to the peace, breaches of the peace and acts of aggression. It is, ultimately, so much more than a simple requirement to acknowledge that a situation fits within the Council's jurisdiction – Article 39 is, quite simply, an obligation to take such situations seriously and act accordingly.

This fundamental legal position, of course, is not a solution. It is, however, a new starting point. A starting point from which we can identify the failures of the Security Council as breaches of its legal duties. This not only strengthens the call for action, but also provides us with legal consequences to such failures. The most fundamental of those consequences, it has been argued, is the fact that these responsibilities to not die with the Security Council's failures. When the Council fails to adhere to these obligations, its primary responsibility may be assumed by the actor with residual responsibility. This residual responsibility is assumed by that actor where they have the legal powers and competences to implement it, but the responsibility itself does not create or grant those powers. In the first instance, residual responsibility lies with the General Assembly according to the competences outlined in the UN Charter, followed by the international community should the General Assembly also remain inactive.

Therefore, to investigate whether the responsibility to protect continues in a tertiary form in these circumstances, the subsequent Chapters will firstly investigate whether there is *room* in the fundamental principles of non-intervention and the prohibition of force for action to be taken beyond the Security Council. If there are legal avenues within these principles, it must then be determined whether the actor with residual responsibility is *capable*, within its legal competences, of implementing this tertiary responsibility to protect. By establishing whether these legal avenues exist, we establish the legal space available for the tertiary responsibility to protect to fill.

IV

The Tertiary Responsibility and Forcible Measures

THE USE OF force to implement the responsibility to protect is arguably the most controversial aspect of the responsibility. It is a tiny part in a vast framework of measures to prevent and supress atrocity crimes, yet it seems to receive the most attention, and this may well have the potential to undermine the success of the responsibility to protect in the long term. Nevertheless, the focus of this book is on the use of forcible and coercive measures as part of the responsibility to protect beyond the deadlock of the Security Council, and so it is necessary to delve into this controversial debate.

This chapter will address the prohibition of force, as outlined in Article 2(4) of the UN Charter, in the specific context of humanitarian crises.[1] As will be shown, there are many authors who seek to dilute this fundamental principle in favour of finding undesirable loopholes in the rule, such as the so-called right of humanitarian intervention.[2] With the aim of investigating whether there is room for a tertiary responsibility to protect beyond the Security Council, this investigation naturally led to the question as to whether force itself can be used beyond the Council. Since the authorisation of the Security Council has long been considered the only 'exception' to the prohibition of force, alongside the right of self-defence, the answer seemed to be clear from the outset. However, there were still questions surrounding the use of force by the UN General Assembly, and indeed by regional organisations, without the direct participation of the Security Council.

During the research for this chapter, this author looked back to the original intentions of the drafters of the UN Charter, and has uncovered revealing intentions and nuances in the debates therein that can clarify the doctrinal operation of the prohibition of force. In particular, instead of interpreting Article 2(4) as prohibiting *all* uses of force, with the powers of the Security Council and the right of self-defence as 'exceptions' to this, it is argued that the prohibition was only ever one outlawing *unilateral* uses of force, and the so-called 'exceptions'

[1] This chapter draws upon the findings and research published by the author in PM Butchard, 'Back to San Francisco: Explaining the Inherent Contradictions of Article 2(4) of the UN Charter' (2018) 23(2) *Journal of Conflict and Security Law* 229.

[2] The myth of a 'doctrine' of humanitarian intervention was debunked in Chapter I, section 2.

are in fact circumstances that were never precluded by the prohibition in the first place. This may seem a semantic distinction, but the effects of this original interpretation are more substantive, and may indicate a number of legitimate avenues for the use of military action through the UN General Assembly which will be addressed in Chapter VI.

By further clarifying the legality and role of measures beyond the Security Council, this chapter continues to shed light on the viability of a tertiary responsibility to protect.

1. THE PROHIBITION OF FORCE

1.1. Sources of the Prohibition

Article 2 of the UN Charter provides that: 'The Organization and its Members, in pursuit of the Purposes stated in Article 1, shall act in accordance with the following Principles.' Article 2(4) states:

> All Members shall refrain in their international relations from the threat or use of force against the territorial integrity or political independence of any state, or in any other manner inconsistent with the Purposes of the United Nations.

Some academic commentators have explored the meaning of 'force' and the types of coercive action that may be included in its definition.[3] Others have considered the meaning of 'international relations' and how far this restricts the scope of the prohibition of the use of force between states, compared to using force to intervene in internal matters such as civil wars, or against non-state actors.[4] The focus of this chapter, however, is on the scope of the prohibition between States in general and its relationship with the circumstances where force is lawful, in order to reveal the legal space in which a tertiary responsibility to protect might operate.

The prohibition of force is also a recognised rule of customary international law, as discussed by the ICJ in the *Nicaragua* case.[5] In this case, the Court explained the interplay between the prohibition as a treaty-based rule, and as a customary rule. The Court reasoned that although these principles would

[3] See eg: T Ruys, 'The Meaning of "Force" and the Boundaries of *Jus ad* Bellum: Are "Minimal" Uses of Force Excluded from UN Charter Article 2(4)?' (2014) 108(2) *American Journal of International Law* 159; B Asrat, *The Prohibition of Force under the UN Charter: A Study of Art 2(4)* (Iustus Förlag, 1991) 39–41, 94–138; A Randelzhofer, 'Article 2(4)' in B Simma (ed), *The Charter of the United Nations: A Commentary* (Oxford, Oxford University Press, 2002) 117–21; O Corten, *The Law Against War: The Prohibition on the Use of Force in Contemporary International Law* (Oxford, Hart Publishing, 2012) ch 2.

[4] See eg Randelzhofer (n 3) 121–23; Corten (n 3) 127–35.

[5] *Case Concerning Military and Paramilitary Activities in and against Nicaragua (Nicaragua v USA)* (Merits), Judgment of 27 June 1986, [1986] ICJ Rep 14 (hereinafter '*Nicaragua* case').

certainly overlap, they maintained a *separate existence*.[6] Importantly, the idea that these rules were identical was rejected by the Court:

> The Court has not accepted this extreme contention, having found that on a number of points the areas governed by the two sources of law do not exactly overlap, and the substantive rules in which they are framed are not identical in content.[7]

In fact, the Court noted that there are some areas where the scope of the two prohibitions diverge, such as in the realm of self-defence where Article 51 of the Charter requires acts of self-defence to be reported to the UN Security Council, potentially rendering a use of force that does not comply with this rule unlawful, whereas there is no such comparable rule in custom.[8] The reason for maintaining a separate existence between customary law and treaty law is largely practical – different rules may be *applied* in different contexts, and may even be subject to different institutional tools by which they can be given effect or enforced.[9]

The ICJ also looked to several declarations of the UN General Assembly for evidence of *opinio juris*, and to shed light on the content of the customary principle of the prohibition of force.[10] For example, the Court looked to the *Friendly Relations Declaration*[11] as evidence of *opinio juris* establishing customary international law relating to the prohibition of force.[12] In this declaration, States proclaimed and expanded upon many principles of international law. Most relevantly, the declaration proclaimed:

> The principle that States shall refrain in their international relations from the threat or use of force against the territorial integrity or political independence of any State, or in any other manner inconsistent with the purposes of the United Nations.[13]

This is almost a word-for-word duplication of the principle that exists in Article 2(4). We may assume, therefore, that the pronouncements that followed this principle in the declaration might also aid the interpretation of the prohibition in the Charter, notwithstanding the application of specific mechanics of the Charter regime. This follows the rules of the VCLT,[14] which is now also considered to reflect customary international law,[15] where any subsequent agreement

[6] *Nicaragua* case (n 5) [174]–[176]; see also Yoram Dinstein, *War, Aggression and Self-Defence*, 5th edn (Cambridge, Cambridge University Press, 2012) 94, [252] ff.

[7] *Nicaragua* case (n 5) [181].

[8] *Nicaragua* case (n 5) [175]–[176]; see also [181].

[9] *Nicaragua* case (n 5) [178]. The Court did, however, emphasis that the two rules did flow from a common point.

[10] *Nicaragua* case (n 5) [184], [188]–[195].

[11] UNGA Res 2625(XXV), *Declaration on Principles of International Law concerning Friendly Relations and Co-operation among States in accordance with the Charter of the United Nations* (24 October 1970) UN Doc A/RES/2625(XXV) Annex.

[12] *Nicaragua* case (n 5) [191].

[13] *Friendly Relations Declaration* (n 11) Annex, Principle 1.

[14] Vienna Convention on the Law of Treaties (adopted 23 May 1969, entered into force 27 January 1980)) 1155 *UNTS* 331.

[15] See eg *Territorial Dispute (Libyan Arab Jamahiriya/Chad)*, Judgment of 3 February 1994, [1994] ICJ Reports 6, [41]; see also *Maritime Delimitation and Territorial Questions between Qatar and*

or practice of States can be taken into account in the interpretation of a treaty provision.[16]

Some of the particular duties that the *Friendly Relations Declaration* considered as falling within this general principle of the prohibition of force include, for example: the violation of existing international borders by force; the organisation of irregular forces for incursion into the territory of a State; and the prohibition of illegal occupation, acquisition or recognition of territory seized by force.[17] These examples, while not conclusively determined to be customary international law individually,[18] provide some evidence as to what States believe to be prohibited by the customary prohibition of force. This regime of declarations is much more specific than the basic language of Article 2(4). Yet, what the declarations do not explain is *how* they fall within the specific language of the prohibition itself. For example, is the use of force to violate international boundaries illegal because it is against the territorial integrity of a State; because it is against the political independence of a State; or, because it is inconsistent with the purposes of the United Nations? Of course, violating international boundaries through force might be rendered illegal because they constitute more than one of these forms of prohibited violence. What it is important to recognise is that these declarations do not give us any specific answers as to how the prohibition itself functions.

1.2. Common Interpretations of Article 2(4)

There are two main competing interpretations of Article 2(4).[19] The first approach reads the prohibition in its widest possible sense, treating it as a 'general prohibition' of the threat or use of force in international relations. In other words, it is said to apply to all but 'internal' uses of force – a blanket ban – leaving no room or flexibility for new exceptions to arise through State practice or custom.[20] According to this view, all uses of force outside of self-defence are a violation of Article 2(4), unless specifically authorised by the Security Council. This position relies on the same reading of Article 2(4) as a 'general prohibition

Bahrain (Jurisdiction and Admissibility) (*Qatar v Bahrain*), Judgment of 15 February 1995, [1995] ICJ Reports 6, [33].

[16] VCLT (n 14), Art 31(3)(a)–(b).

[17] *Friendly Relations Declaration* (n 11) Annex, Principle 1.

[18] The ICJ has declared some provisions of the Declaration as reflecting custom, but it is unclear whether it considers *all* of the provisions to be such: see *Armed Activities on the Territory of the Congo (Democratic Republic of Congo v Uganda)*, Judgment of 19 December 2005, [2005] ICJ Reports 168, paras [162] and [300].

[19] For an overview of these competing approaches, see eg: Corten (n 3) 4–27; C Gray, *International Law and the Use of Force*, 2nd edn (Oxford, Oxford University Press, 2008) 30–31; L Moir, *Reappraising the Resort to Force: International Law,* Jus ad Bellum, *and the War on Terror* (Oxford, Hart Publishing, 2010) 5–9.

[20] Corten highlights this in the context of an overall restrictive approach to interpreting customary international law: see Corten (n 3) 5, 15–27.

of force', where the powers of the Security Council in Chapter VII of the Charter are 'exceptions' to this general rule. Accordingly, the use of force by or on behalf of the Security Council would be covered in principle by the primary rule in Article 2(4), but excluded by an exception in a secondary rule elsewhere in the Charter.

The second approach interprets Article 2(4) much more narrowly. According to this view, the prohibition is open to further exceptions beyond the commonly accepted instances of self-defence and the powers of the Security Council – and is said to include the so-called right of unilateral humanitarian intervention. This position relies on the suggestion that the use of force is lawful if: (i) it does not violate the territorial integrity of the State; (ii) it does not jeopardise the political independence of the State; and (iii) the use of force itself is conducted in a manner consistent with the purposes of the UN Charter. Advocates for this position argue, for example, that the use of force could be legal where it does not result in a 'territorial conquest or political subjugation' and thus does not violate the territorial integrity or political independence of the target State,[21] so long as it is also in pursuit of, or consistent with, the purposes of the UN under Article 1 of the Charter. Such a purpose, some argue, may include the protection of human rights.[22]

Therefore, there are two extremes in interpreting Article 2(4) – an all-encompassing prohibition (the 'wide interpretation') or a prohibition that is qualified and leaves room for lawful uses of force (the 'narrow interpretation').[23]

1.3. Legal Problems of Article 2(4)

1.3.1. Article 2(4) and the Powers of the Security Council

The UN Charter undoubtedly allows the Security Council to use force. Article 42 of the Charter, for example, grants the Council following power:

> Should the Security Council consider that measures provided for in Article 41 would be inadequate or have proved to be inadequate, it may take such action by air, sea, or land forces as may be necessary to maintain or restore international peace and security. Such action may include demonstrations, blockade, and other operations by air, sea, or land forces of Members of the United Nations.

[21] FR Tesón, *Humanitarian Intervention: An Inquiry into Law and Morality*, 2nd edn (New York, Transnational Publishers, 1997) 151.

[22] ibid, 152–57.

[23] Dinstein refers to the first all-encompassing interpretation as 'the non-restrictive scope of the prohibition' – Dinstein (n 6) 89–91, [240]–[244]; however, this is not to be confused with the methodology of interpreting customary international law that Corten refers to as the 'restrictive approach' – Corten, (n 3). Confusingly, the phrase 'restrictive interpretation' is sometimes used to describe interpretations of Art 2(4) that attempt to specifically restrict the scope of that provision, and thus have the opposite effect to the all-encompassing interpretation: see eg S Chesterman, *Just War or Just Peace: Humanitarian Intervention and International Law* (Oxford, Oxford University Press, 2001) 48–51.

Because of the ability of the Security Council to use force, supporters of the 'wide interpretation' of Article 2(4) arrive at the simple conclusion that this power is an *exception* to the prohibition.[24] However, although these provisions refer to the use of force, they do not provide any *explicit* exception that limits the application of Article 2(4).[25]

The Security Council is bound by Article 24(2) to 'act in accordance with the Purposes and Principles' of the Charter when exercising its powers. The 'Principles'[26] include the prohibition of force, and respect for the principle of *sovereign equality*,[27] which includes respect for territorial integrity and political independence – according to discussion during the drafting of the Charter,[28] and the *Friendly Relations Declaration*.[29] This provision, this author argues, creates a contradiction in the wide interpretation of the prohibition of force. If Article 2(4) really was a blanket ban on force, it would mean that the Charter would require the Council, when using its powers, to act in accordance with a Principle that essentially excludes the type of force foreseen in those very powers.

But some arguments seek to explain this contradiction. Carswell, for example, offers a solution based upon an interpretation of Article 2(4) itself, while maintaining a wide interpretation of the prohibition.[30] He suggests that the prohibition only applies to *Members* of the UN, rather than the Organisation or the Security Council itself.[31] This is based upon the fact that Article 2(4) refers to 'all Members …' refraining from the threat or use of force. In this regard, Carswell also goes on to suggest that a consequence of the Security Council delegating powers to Member States for enforcement action is that those States are acting on behalf of the UN Organisation and thus are not captured by Article 2(4).[32] He therefore stresses that 'as long as the actions of UN States can be ascribed to the Security Council, they are the actions of the UN Organization as such and are not captured by Article 2(4)'.[33]

There are some fundamental problems with this interpretation. First, it ignores the effect of Article 48 of the Charter. Article 48 requires:

> 1. The action required to carry out the decisions of the Security Council for the maintenance of international peace and security *shall be taken by all the Members of the United Nations* or by some of them, as the Security Council may determine.

[24] See n 19.
[25] Unlike, for example, Art 2(7) on non-intervention which does provide for an explicit exception referring to Chapter VII of the Charter.
[26] Art 2, UN Charter.
[27] Art 2(1), UN Charter.
[28] See below, section 2.
[29] *Friendly Relations Declaration* (n 11) Annex, Principle 6.
[30] AJ Carswell, 'Unblocking the UN Security Council: The *Uniting for Peace Resolution*' (2013) 18(3) *Journal of Conflict and Security Law* 453.
[31] ibid, 461–462.
[32] ibid.
[33] ibid, 461.

2. Such decisions shall be carried out by the Members of the United Nations *directly* and *through their action* in the appropriate international agencies of which they are members.[34]

The intention of Article 48 is not to stipulate the actor to which the use of force should be attributable when undertaking enforcement action. But, by requiring Member States to *directly* undertake this action, or to do so through their membership of other international organisations, it clearly indicates who must undertake the use of force to carry out binding Council decisions.[35] While Article 48 may have been inserted with the intention of utilising the armed forces that were originally to be provided to the UN under special agreements in accordance with Article 43, since such agreements never transpired, Article 48 as a standalone provision certainly leaves room for States to use force without necessarily being under the formal command of the Security Council. In other words, Article 48 remains compatible with the Council's recent practice of *authorising* Member States to use force, rather than *commanding* them to do so.[36]

Carswell's argument also disregards the fact that when the Security Council *authorises* (rather than commands) Members to use force, the Member States concerned do not have to be under any chain of command linking the conduct of a State's national forces to the United Nations. According to the International Law Commission's (ILC) commentaries to the Draft Articles on the Responsibility of International Organisations:[37]

> [The] conduct of military forces of States or international organizations is not attributable to the United Nations when the Security Council authorizes States or international organizations to take necessary measures outside a chain of command linking those forces to the United Nations.[38]

Carswell's argument that the Council's powers are 'delegated' when authorisations are made, and therefore their actions are attributable *only* to the Security Council,[39] is unconvincing in light of the ILC's commentary because

[34] Emphasis added.

[35] Such 'decisions' are binding by virtue of Art 25 of the Charter, where Members agree to 'accept' and 'carry out' these decisions.

[36] For an interesting overview of this practice, see N Blokker, 'Is the Authorisation Authorized? Powers and Practice of the UN Security Council to Authorize the Use of Force by "Coalitions of the Able and Willing"' (2000) 11(3) *European Journal of International Law* 541; see also Gray (n 19) 254, 327–69; J Frowein and N Krisch, 'Article 42' in Simma (n 3) 754–59.

[37] ILC, 'Draft Articles on the Responsibility of International Organisations, with Commentaries', http://legal.un.org/ilc/texts/instruments/english/commentaries/9_11_2011.pdf (accessed 31 July 2019); also included in ILC, 'Report of the International Law Commission on the Work of its Sixty-Third Session' (26 April–3 June and 4 July–12 August 2011) UN Doc A/66/10, from 69; see also UNGA Res 66/100, *Responsibility of International Organisations* (9 December 2011) UN Doc A/RES/66/100, Annex.

[38] ILC Commentaries (n 37) 16.

[39] Carswell (n 30) 10–11; for an overview of this position, see also D Sarooshi, *The United Nations and the Development of Collective Security: The Delegation by the UN Security Council of its Chapter VII Powers* (Oxford, Oxford University Press, 1999) chs 1 and 4, and 164–65.

the Commission specifically excluded attribution to the UN in cases of authorisations.[40] In addition, while it is not the intention of this chapter to go into the debate surrounding the attribution of *conduct* for UN-controlled forces such as those utilised for peacekeeping,[41] the current author argues that it is a legal fiction to suggest that a Member State would not be 'using force' for the purposes of Article 2(4) simply because those actions might be attributable to the UN for the purposes of determining legal *responsibility* for other internationally wrongful acts.[42]

In all cases of forcible action by the Council, Members will always be the actors 'using' such force. In light of this fact, the question remains as to how such conduct, even though authorised or ordered by the Council, can be rendered consistent with the Members' obligations under Article 2(4). But this issue goes further. The Security Council, as well as being obliged itself to act in accordance with the Principles in Article 2, may also be under an indirect obligation on the Council not to order Members to do something that likewise would not be in accordance with those Principles.[43] After all, could it be said that the Council was acting 'in accordance' with such Principles if it allowed or encouraged Members to violate or ignore them?[44]

In light of these issues, the wide interpretation of Article 2(4) cannot explain why Members using force on behalf of the Council is consistent with the prohibition. There is merit in Carswell's general logic that Article 2(4) simply does not include the powers of the Security Council within its scope. As we shall discuss below, this was the original intention of the drafters of the Charter – the legal framework of Article 2(4) just operates very differently to how Carswell interpreted the provision.

1.3.2. Jus Cogens *and the 'Exceptions' to Article 2(4)*

A second problem with the wide interpretation of Article 2(4) arises from the provision's status as a *jus cogens* norm. It is widely accepted that Article 2(4) is also a norm of *jus cogens* – a peremptory norm of general international law.[45]

[40] ILC Commentaries (n 37) 16.

[41] The ILC Commentary succinctly outlines this debate: ILC Commentaries (n 37) 19–26.

[42] See ILC Draft Articles on Responsibility of International Organisations (n 37) Art 7; ILC Commentaries (n 37) 22–25, where it is suggested that attribution of conduct for joint operations should be based upon a factual criterion.

[43] States have also suggested that *all* the principles in Art 2 must be respected by both Members and the Organisation: see UNGA, 'Report of the Special Committee on Principles of International Law concerning Friendly Relations and Co-operation among States' (16 November 1964) UN Doc A/5746, [218].

[44] Such an authorisation might be considered a 'derogation' from a jus cogens norm, if Art 2(4) really was an all-encompassing prohibition: see below.

[45] See eg *Nicaragua* case (n 5) [190]; Corten gives a very detailed overview of the state practice and opinio juris to this effect; Corten (n 3) 200–13; see also Asrat (n 3) 51–52; Gray (n 19) 30; Dinstein (n 6) 105–07.

Although this has been questioned,[46] it is not the purpose of this Chapter to investigate this, so we will proceed on the assumption that the prohibition is *jus cogens*.

Article 53 of the VCLT states:

> A treaty is void if, at the time of its conclusion, it conflicts with a peremptory norm of general international law. For the purposes of the present Convention, a peremptory norm of general international law is a norm accepted and recognized by the international community of States as a whole as a norm from which no derogation is permitted and which can be modified only by a subsequent norm of general international law having the same character.

This provision reveals the key characteristics of *jus cogens*.[47] For our purposes, the fact that 'no derogation is permitted' by a *jus cogens* norm is important. According to the *Oxford English Dictionary*, a 'derogation' is the 'partial abrogation or repeal of a law, contract, treaty, legal right, etc',[48] and the *Oxford Advanced Learner's Dictionary* defines a 'derogation' as 'an occasion when a rule or law is allowed to be ignored'.[49]

On the other hand, an 'exception' is defined as: 'Something that is excepted; a particular case which comes within the terms of a rule, but to which the rule is not applicable; a person or thing that does not conform to the general rule affecting other individuals of the same class.'[50] This definition suggests that an exception must first come within the terms of a rule – ie a lawful use of force must first be one that is generally covered by the prohibition in question (the primary rule), but is excluded from the scope of that prohibition by another corresponding rule (a secondary rule).

To explain, Helmersen uses the following definition of 'exception': 'a special situation excluded from the coverage of an otherwise applicable rule'.[51] Helmersen also argues that 'exceptions' are not the same as 'derogations' for the purposes of *jus cogens*:

> Exceptions limit the scope of rules. This means that an apparent derogation that is covered by an exception is not a derogation, since it regulates something that is outside the scope of the rule. For example, rule A prohibits X, Y and Z, but has an exception in rule B that says it does not cover Y. If two states conclude a treaty that

[46] See eg J Green, 'Questioning the Peremptory Status of the Prohibition of the Use of Force' (2011) 32 *Michigan Journal of International Law* 215.

[47] While a norm of *jus cogens* is found in 'general international law', the fact that the prohibition of force is also found in Art 2(4) is enough for us to address its interpretation in light of its corresponding *jus cogens* status. After all, Art 2(4) is the most authoritative manifestation of the rule purported to be *jus cogens*.

[48] *Oxford English Dictionary* definition, www.oed.com/view/Entry/50657 (accessed 31 July 2019).

[49] *Oxford Advanced Learner's Dictionary*, www.oxfordlearnersdictionaries.com/definition/english/derogation (accessed 31 July 2019).

[50] *Oxford English Dictionary* definition, www.oed.com/view/Entry/65724 (accessed 31 July 2019).

[51] ST Helmersen, 'The Prohibition of Force as *Jus Cogens: Explaining Apparent Derogations*' 61(2) *Netherlands International Law Review* 167, 175.

> allows Y between them, the treaty is not a derogation from rule A. Nor is the treaty a derogation if rule A by its scope covers only X and Z.[52]

Following Helmersen's logic, the 'exceptions' to the prohibition of force might be found in separate rules that limit the scope of the prohibition itself. Therefore, Article 51 of the Charter might be a separate rule allowing for self-defence, and likewise with the powers of the Security Council in Chapter VII. But there are problems with these mechanics. While 'exceptions' are not always the same as 'derogations', any treaty provision which provides for a power or right which could allow a generally applicable *jus cogens* rule to be ignored could be considered a 'derogation', especially if that treaty-based rule does not also have a corresponding status of *jus cogens*.[53]

In other words, the 'exceptions' to Article 2(4) – if it was an all-inclusive prohibition – must also have the status of *jus cogens* so that they are not derogations from that *jus cogens* rule. This is based upon the fact that, when the prohibition of force became *jus cogens*, it attained a 'separate' status within 'general international law'. From that point on, according to Article 64 of the VCLT, any existing treaty provision which is in conflict with a newly established norm of *jus cogens* becomes void and terminates. How, then, can the provisions of the UN Charter allowing for the use of force be reconciled with the fact that Article 2(4) has attained such a status? Linderfalk[54] argues that this indicates why that the *jus cogens* version of Article 2(4) must be different to Article 2(4) itself:

> [T]he relevant *jus cogens* norm cannot possibly be identical with the principle of non-use of force as such. If it were, this would imply that whenever a State exercises a right of self-defence, it would in fact be unlawfully derogating from a norm of *jus cogens*.[55]

Green[56] and Linderfalk try to explain this phenomenon by suggesting that the *jus cogens* version of the prohibition of force must also contain the exceptions

[52] ibid, 176.

[53] Helmersen seems to suggest that having a corresponding rule in customary law is enough: ibid, 176–77, 180. However, this would suggest that a simple loophole of *jus cogens* would be for a group of states to establish a customary rule between them so as to avoid a 'treaty-based derogation', and cannot be reconciled with the fact that ad-hoc consent to an act prohibited by a *jus cogens* rule is also considered a derogation: see ILC, 'Draft Articles on Responsibility of States for Internationally Wrongful Acts, with Commentaries', http://legal.un.org/ilc/texts/instruments/english/commentaries/9_6_2001.pdf (accessed 31 July 2019); also included in ILC, 'Report of the International Law Commission on the Work of its Fifty-Third Session' (23 April–1 June and 2 July–10 August 2001) UN Doc A/56/10, Art 26, and [6]; reproduced in [2001] (Vol II, Part Two) *Yearbook of the International Law Commission* 31. Thus, it seems more logical to argue that any exception to a *jus cogens* rule must also have the status of *jus cogens*.

[54] U Linderfalk, 'The Effect of *Jus Cogens* Norms: Whoever Opened Pandora's Box, Did You Ever Think About the Consequences?' (2007) 18(5) *European Journal of International Law* 853.

[55] ibid, 860.

[56] Green (n 46).

of the Charter built into the *jus cogens* rule itself.[57] To support this, they both construct possible versions of the prohibition that might reflect the norm in *jus cogens* by broadly defining the rule to encompass the exceptions to the prohibition.[58] For example, Green suggests the *jus cogens* version of the prohibition might say:

> The use of armed force directed against the territorial integrity or political independence of any state or which is in any other manner inconsistent with the purposes of the UN is prohibited other than when it is employed in a necessary and proportional manner in response to an armed attack by another state against a member of the UN or when authorized by the Security Council under Article 42 of the UN Charter, following a threat to the peace and breach of the peace or an act of aggression as determined by the Security Council.[59]

Both Green and Linderfalk concede the impracticalities and unattractiveness of this approach.[60] Nevertheless, these suggestions are in line with the idea that the prohibition of force *includes* the relevant 'exceptions' within its scope, so as to ensure that any treaty-based provision reflecting those exceptions are not derogating from an all-inclusive prohibition of force. Linderfalk and Green are essentially creating their own qualified version of Article 2(4), and this could work so long as those qualifications (ie the powers of the Security Council, the right of self-defence) are capable of having the status of *jus cogens* too.[61]

Orakhelashvili takes a much more extreme step, suggesting *jus ad bellum* as a whole is *jus cogens*, arguing: '[I]f the very prohibition of the use of force is peremptory, then every principle specifying the limits on the entitlement of States to use force is also peremptory.'[62] Green disagrees with this argument, even if we were to envisage a '*jus cogens* network' of norms relevant to *jus ad bellum*, because for many of the rules within the *jus ad bellum* it might be difficult to make a case for their peremptory status.[63]

Unfortunately, neither Orakhelashvili's argument nor Green and Linderfalk's approaches are very convincing, because they require us to accept the assertion that the powers of the Security Council also have the status of *jus cogens*, as we shall now discuss.

[57] Linderfalk (n 54) 860; Green (n 46) 229–30; see also a discussion of this issue in A de Hoogh, '*Jus Cogens* and the Use of Armed Force' in M Weller (ed), *The Oxford Handbook of the Use of Force in International Law* (Oxford: Oxford University Press, 2015).

[58] Green (n 46) 232–33, especially n 82; Linderfalk (n 54) 860–67.

[59] Green (n 46) 234. Linderfalk (n 54) 867, see also 860 and 865, also suggests similarly unattractive alternatives.

[60] ibid.

[61] See below on why this author believes this is not possible.

[62] A Orakhelashvili, *Peremptory Norms in International Law* (Oxford, Oxford University Press, 2008) 50–51.

[63] Green (n 46) 231; see also de Hoogh (n 57) 1172.

1.3.2.1. The Security Council Powers are not *Jus Cogens*

The powers of the Security Council in Chapter VII of the Charter must also at least form part of customary international law to achieve *jus cogens* status.[64] For non-Member States in particular, this would be inherently difficult given that they are not subject to the jurisdiction or powers of the Security Council.

A similar conclusion is reached by Helmersen, where he suggests:

> An exception reflecting Article 42 would have to be created by state practice and *opinio juris*. With the existence of the UN Charter, UN member states using force on the basis of the Charter would simply be obeying the Charter, and not simultaneously generating state practice in favour of the existence of a concurrent customary rule. State practice would have to be generated by non-members.[65]

If non-Member States cannot be bound by the jurisdiction of the Security Council, no 'exception' to the *jus cogens* prohibition of force allowing for such powers can exist as part of any construction of the *jus cogens* rule itself, because that 'exception' is not capable of binding States as a whole. In customary international law, it is unlikely that there exists any comparable rule binding *all* States to the powers of the Security Council, especially in the scenario where a State has not signed up to the UN Charter.[66]

In the General Assembly declarations recognising the prohibition of force, lawful uses of force are given effect by statements such as: 'Nothing in the foregoing paragraphs shall be construed as enlarging or diminishing in any way the scope of the provisions of the Charter concerning cases in which the use of force is lawful.'[67] These limitations in the declarations stipulate that the relevant provisions in the Charter remain unaffected – *not* that they are also exceptions for States who have not signed the Charter. There is no obvious customary exception explicitly allowing the Security Council to use force as a standalone customary power.

Indeed, evidence to the contrary suggests non-Members are in fact *not* bound by the Security Council's decisions. The ICJ's Advisory Opinion on the *Continued Presence of South Africa in Namibia*[68] acknowledged that non-Members of the UN are not bound by Articles 24 or 25 of the Charter – the key provisions granting the Security Council its powers, and requiring States to accept and act

[64] Linderfalk (n 54) 863–64.

[65] Helmersen (n 51) 183–84. Indeed, Helmersen rightly highlights that this also explains why the reporting requirement of self-defence does not exist in customary international law: see Helmersen (n 51) 184; also *Nicaragua case* (n 5) [200].

[66] See eg VCLT Art 34, on treaties creating obligations for third states.

[67] *Friendly Relations Declaration* (n 11) Annex, Principle 1, [13], see also operative [2], 'General Part'; compare also UNGA Res 2131(XX), *Declaration on the Inadmissibility of Intervention in the Domestic Affairs of States and the Protection of Their Independence and Sovereignty* (21 December 1965) UN Doc A/RES/2131(XX) [8].

[68] *Legal Consequences for States of the Continued Presence of South Africa in Namibia (South West Africa) notwithstanding Security Council Resolution 276 (1970)* (Advisory Opinion), Opinion of 21 June 1971, [1971] ICJ Reports 16.

in accordance with its decisions.[69] Furthermore, as Vitzthum[70] highlights, before Switzerland became a Member of the UN it decided *autonomously* whether or not to participate in measures adopted by the Security Council.[71] Similarly, the Federal Republic of Germany, whilst a non-Member during the situation concerning Southern Rhodesia, voluntarily participated in sanctions as called for by resolutions such as Resolution 232 (1966)[72] – but still maintained that it was participating in these sanctions 'in spite of the fact that the Federal Republic of Germany is not a Member of the United Nations'.[73]

1.3.2.2. Self-Defence is not *Jus Cogens*

Self-defence is recognised by Article 51 of the Charter. According to the wording of the provision, it is not an explicit exception to Article 2(4) itself. The opening words of the provision state that: 'Nothing in the present Charter shall impair …'. This indicates that Article 51 is a 'limited' exception to the whole Charter system. It is a limited exclusion of the Charter's scope due to the fact that the provision itself still maintains the jurisdiction of the Security Council over the maintenance of international peace and security, and goes further still to require that any '[m]easures taken by Members in the exercise of this right of self-defence shall be immediately reported to the Security Council'.

Furthermore, Article 51 refers to a State's 'inherent' right of self-defence. This has been determined by the ICJ to indicate the existence of the right to self-defence in international customary law.[74] The Charter therefore gives effect to a customary law rule, whilst creating a limitation upon the Members' use of that customary right by maintaining the jurisdiction of the Security Council.

By its existence in customary international law, one could certainly infer that the right of self-defence is *capable* of achieving the status of *jus cogens*. Consequently, the right could also theoretically form part of any general construction of the *jus cogens* rule and not necessarily a derogation that would render the rule unlawful. But, whether self-defence can be said to have *jus cogens* status is far from clear, with commentators offering opposing views on this matter, particularly in light of the absence of any declaration by States.[75]

[69] ibid, [126].

[70] WG Vitzthum, 'Article 2(6)' in Simma (n 3).

[71] ibid, 143–44 and the positions cited therein; see also Helmersen (n 51) 184.

[72] UNSC Res 232 (1966) (16 December 1966) UN Doc S/RES/232(1966) [6], Compare this with para [7] of the same Resolution which only requires *Members* of the UN to carry out the decision in accordance with Art 25.

[73] See Note by the Secretary General, transmitting Note Verbale dated 17th February 1967 from the Acting Permanent Observer of the Federal Republic of Germany (20 February 1967) UN Doc S/7776, 3; see also Vitzthum (n 70) 143.

[74] *Nicaragua case* (n 5) [193].

[75] Dinstein suggests that it is unclear whether self-defence has *jus cogens* status: Dinstein (n 6) 192–93, [509]; Kahgan, on the other hand, argues that it does: C Kahgan, '*Jus Cogens* and the

Furthermore, if the right of self-defence had *jus cogens* status, and therefore could not be derogated from, the limitation imposed in Article 51 of the UN Charter that self-defence only applies *until* the Security Council steps in to take necessary measures to maintain or restore peace and security requires explanation.[76] This is clearly a restriction of the right of self-defence for Members of the UN, and we therefore run into the same problem regarding the powers of the Security Council being unable to obtain *jus cogens* status, as discussed above.

1.3.2.3. Other Attempts to Explain the *Jus Cogens* Legal Problem

One way to explain the *jus cogens* problem is to suggest that *jus cogens* does not require a rule to be recognised as such by *all* States – but simply a vast majority of States. This argument has been made by some authors notwithstanding the fact that Article 53 of the VCLT refers to *jus cogens* being *accepted* by States 'as a whole'.[77] In support of this position, Kahgan makes the following argument:

> Obviously, no norm could realistically be considered a principle of general international law if it did not, at a minimum, meet the criteria of acceptance and adherence required for customary international law. However, whether a norm has been denominated or identified as customary international law should not frustrate, eliminate, or immunize its categorization and recognition as a norm of an even more profound nature, such as *jus cogens*. That inquiry requires assessment of the extent of recognition and acceptance such as would cause its *elevation* to the status of general international law, whereby it would bind even nonconsenting states.[78]

The current author does not accept Kahgan's argument here. There is a fundamental difference between: (i) a State accepting that a norm they are already bound by constitutes *jus cogens*; and (ii) a State not consenting to be bound by that rule altogether. This is especially true for a written treaty provision. The fact that a State may not have signed up to the UN Charter, and thus not yet consented to the jurisdiction of the Security Council, is crucial to this point. Article 53 of the VCLT specifically states that *jus cogens* 'is a norm *accepted* and *recognized* by the international community of States as a whole *as a norm from which* no derogation is permitted … etc'.[79] No matter what the threshold or legal test for 'elevating' a norm into one of *jus cogens* and being *recognised* as such by the international community as a whole, the current author argues

Inherent Right to Self-Defence', (1997) 3 *ILSA Journal of International & Comparative Law* 767, 791 (see n 105), see also 824–27.

[76] On this point, see de Hoogh (n 57) 1173.

[77] See eg Kahgan (n 75) 775–76.

[78] Kahgan (n 75) 776 (emphasis in original).

[79] Emphasis added.

that a rule must actually *bind* all of that international community in the first place.[80]

The only alternative to explain the reach of the Security Council's powers would be to argue that the UN Charter is some form of 'world constitution' – a supranational authority that transcends the sovereignty of States with the ability to bind non-Members.[81] However, this is not a viable solution either. It is more widely accepted that the UN has no such status, and there has not been any authoritative indication of this being the case by the international community.[82]

Finally, another alternative explanation might be to suggest that the *jus cogens* version of the prohibition is one which prohibits only the use of force *not* authorised by the Security Council, or *not* in self-defence in response to an armed attack.[83] This position certainly alleviates the problems outlined, and is very closely linked to the interpretation preferred by this chapter's findings, as outlined below. However, when States have accepted the *jus cogens* nature of the prohibition, they do not refer to such a precise formulation – the preference, as outlined by Corten, is to treat Article 2(4) itself as the *jus cogens* principle, or at least the formulation found within that provision.[84] Any alternative formulation also creates a distinction between Article 2(4) and the *jus cogens* version of the norm – a distinction that has never been recognised by States, and is not compatible with the practice that accepts Article 2(4) as having *jus cogens* status.[85]

In light of these arguments, there are two possibilities. Either the prohibition of force is not a blanket ban on force at all and allows for the Security Council's powers and self-defence within the rule itself, or Article 2(4) is not a norm of *jus cogens*. Based upon the wide acceptance of the status of the prohibition as *jus cogens*, the answer certainly does not seem to be the latter.

[80] Unfortunately, this is a question about *jus cogens* that remains a topic of debate, and it is beyond the scope of this book to address it here. For further discussion of this issue, see eg: M Byers, 'Conceptualising the Relationship Between *Jus Cogens* and *Erga Omnes* Rules' (1997) 66 *Nordic Journal of International Law* 211, 220–29; U Linderfalk, 'The Creation of *Jus Cogens* – Making Sense of Article 53 of the Vienna Convention' (2011) 71 *ZaöRV* 359, www.zaoerv.de/71_2011/71_2011_2_a_359_378.pdf (accessed 31 July 2019); D Dubois, 'The Authority of Peremptory Norms in International Law: State Consent or Natural Law?' (2009) 78 *Nordic Journal of International Law* 133; MW Janis, 'The Nature of *Jus Cogens*' (1988–87) 3 *Connecticut Journal of International Law* 359.

[81] Linderfalk (n 54) 863–64.

[82] See eg J Frowein and N Krisch, 'Action with Respect to Threats to the Peace, Breaches of the Peace and Acts of Aggression' in Simma (n 3) 715; see also Vitzthum (n 70) 146–48. On the other hand, see: B Fassbender, 'The United Nations Charter As Constitution of the International Community' (1998) 36 *Columbia Journal of Transnational Law* 529; H Kelsen, *The Law of the United Nations: A Critical Analysis of Its Fundamental Problems* (New York, Fredrick A Praeger 1950) 107–10.

[83] Similar arguments suggest that the *jus cogens* version of the prohibition only covers *illegal* uses of force or aggression: see eg de Hoogh (n 57) 1173–75; see also Helmersen (n 51) 185–86.

[84] See Corten (n 3) 200–13.

[85] ibid.

As we shall now explore, the very wording of Article 2(4) is sufficient to provide for these 'exceptions' built within the rule itself.

2. THE ORIGINAL INTERPRETATION OF ARTICLE 2(4)

2.1. Recourse to the Preparatory Works of the Charter

Because of the problems outlined above, this author believes that there was a need to revisit the preparatory works of the Charter to either confirm the two common interpretations of Article 2(4), or to determine its meaning. Article 32 of the VCLT allows recourse to the preparatory works of a treaty as a supplementary means of interpretation either to confirm an interpretation based on Article 31 or to determine the true meaning when the 'ordinary meaning' of the terms (i) leaves the meaning ambiguous or obscure; or (ii) leads to a result that is manifestly absurd or unreasonable.

The ordinary meaning of the terms in Article 2(4), especially 'territorial integrity' and 'political independence', have never been thoroughly deciphered. As will be outlined below, if some of the interpretations of those terms were to be accepted, especially when they result in the wide interpretation of Article 2(4), they may well lead to manifestly absurd results such as the inherent contradictions just outlined. For these reasons, it is important to revisit the drafting of the Charter to understand what the drafters had in mind when formulating the prohibition of force.

2.2. Explaining the Construction of Article 2(4): The Drafters' View

The 'Dumbarton Oaks Proposal' was the proposal put forward as a basis for a new international organisation by the original inviting parties at the United Nations Conference on International Organisation[86] at San Francisco in 1945. The Article 2(4) equivalent, before the Proposals were debated and amended, read very simply:

> All members of the Organization shall refrain in their international relations from the threat or use of force in any manner inconsistent with the purposes of the Organization.[87]

The construction of this original proposal is quite clear in maintaining the possibility of States using force on behalf of the Security Council, as per the Charter,

[86] *Documents of the United Nations Conference on International Organisation* (multi-volume, New York, United Nations 1945) cited hereinafter as *UNCIO*.

[87] *Dumbarton Oaks Proposals for a General International Organisation*, Doc 1, G/1, 3 *UNCIO* 1, 3 (Chapter II, para 4).

and in self-defence, assuming that these types of force are 'consistent' with the purposes of the Organisation. Rather than outlawing simply the threat or use of force, the original proposal sought to outlaw only force that was 'inconsistent with the purposes of the Organisation'.

If the prohibition of force was designed to preclude all threats and uses of force in international relations, the drafters of the provision could have simply required all members 'to refrain from the threat or use of force in their international relations against any State'. But, as Simon[88] points out, the drafters went on to specify that it was force against 'territorial integrity', 'political independence', and in a manner 'inconsistent with the Purposes of the UN' that were specifically prohibited. Similarly, Schachter argues that such additions to the original proposal *must* logically qualify the prohibition of force, or else they are redundant.[89]

The only qualification in the original proposal for Article 2(4) was the phrase precluding force 'inconsistent with the Purposes of the UN'. By extension, this suggests that the original proposal allowed for force *consistent* with the Purposes of the UN. It was meant to allow for lawful uses of force in the way that it was constructed, and this was explicitly noted by some States during the drafting of the Charter.[90] There seems to be no obvious reason why this would change when further terms were added to strengthen the prohibition itself, especially when no explicit exception was inserted to counteract the effect of such terms.[91]

One of the most-cited debates during the drafting of the Charter comes from the Eleventh Meeting of Committee I/1, on 4 June 1945.[92] In this meeting, there was extensive discussion of the possibility of the provision being interpreted as allowing some forms of unilateral force beyond self-defence, especially if argued that such force was 'consistent with the purposes of the organisation'.[93] The delegate of Norway felt that the language of the provision, which at the time reflected essentially the final version of Article 2(4) bar some minor amendments, did not reflect satisfactorily its intentions. Norway called for it to be made very clear that the prohibition 'did not contemplate any use of force, outside of action by the Organization, going beyond individual or collective self-defense'.[94] To suggest that the provision's intentions did not contemplate such force, while maintaining the possibility of action by the UN and in self-defence, necessarily and logically suggests that Norway certainly considered

[88] SG Simon, 'The Contemporary Legality of Unilateral Humanitarian Intervention' (1993–94) 24 *California Western International Law Journal* 117, 131.

[89] O Schachter, 'International Law in Theory and Practice: A General Course in International Law' (1982) 178 *Recueil des cours de l'Académie de droit international* 9, 140.

[90] See eg *Verbatim Minutes of the Second Meeting of Commission I* (20 June 1945) Doc 1123, I/8, 6 *UNCIO* 65, 68–69 (Peru).

[91] See above, n 25, and accompanying text.

[92] *Eleventh Meeting of Committee I/1* (5 June 1945) Doc 784, I/1/27, 6 *UNCIO* 331.

[93] ibid, 334–35.

[94] ibid, 334.

those *lawful* uses of force as being recognised by Article 2(4) itself. In fact, the Norwegian representative even went as far as to suggest the *removal* of the terms 'territorial integrity' and 'political independence' to make this purpose clear, considering that these principles could already be said to be protected elsewhere in the Charter and under international law generally.[95]

In reply, the delegate of the United Kingdom agreed with the reasoning of the Norwegian delegate, but insisted that 'the wording of the text had been carefully considered so as to preclude interference with the enforcement clauses of [Chapter VII] of the Charter'.[96] The UK explained the addition of 'territorial integrity' and 'political independence' through an Australian amendment as using 'most intelligible, forceful and economical language'.[97]

This author submits that this is evidence of an interpretation, at least on the part of Norway and the UK, that Article 2(4) itself allows for the use of force as provided for in the Charter, and in self-defence. The significance of the UK's explanation seems to have been overshadowed in academic commentary by a focus on what the US delegate also said at the same meeting. The United States is widely and famously cited as arguing that 'the intention of the authors of the original text was to state in the broadest terms an absolute all-inclusive prohibition; the phrase 'in any other manner' was designed to insure that there should be no loopholes'.[98] It is this key phrase that is often cited by commentators to support the wide interpretation of Article 2(4), and thus the view that it is an absolute blanket ban on force.[99]

At first glance, this seems to reveal an apparent divergence between the positions of the UK and the US in this meeting. However, considering the fact that these States were both a leading part of the drafting of the original Dumbarton Oaks Proposal, and the US is clearly referring to language that was already within that original proposal, it seems unlikely that their statements on this issue would be fundamentally incompatible. Logically, it cannot be possible for the prohibition to be all-encompassing with no loopholes, while at the same time allowing for the use of force by the Security Council through its 'consistency' with the Purposes of the UN. As highlighted above, the original proposal could not have been absolute either.[100]

Instead, it seems more plausible that the US was referring to 'no loopholes' in the 'absolute all-inclusive prohibition' of force in any manner *inconsistent* with the Purposes of the Charter, while clearly leaving room for the requisite in-built 'loopholes' of self-defence and the powers of the Security Council. It is in this context that this statement of the United States should be understood.

[95] 6 *UNCIO* 331 (n 92) 334–35.
[96] ibid, 335.
[97] ibid.
[98] ibid.
[99] See eg Chesterman (n 23) 49–50.
[100] See text at n 89 and surrounding discussion.

This reading is supported by the subsequent report of the Rapporteur to the same committee.[101] This report made an explicit and special note in relation to Article 2(4), to alleviate Norway's concerns, stating:

> The Committee likes it to be stated in view of the Norwegian amendment to the same paragraph that the *unilateral use of force* or similar coercive measures is not authorized or admitted. The use of arms in legitimate self-defense *remains admitted and unimpaired*. The use of force, therefore, *remains legitimate only to back up the decisions of the Organization* at the start of a controversy or during its solution in the way that the Organization itself ordains. The intention of the Norwegian amendment is thus covered by the present text.[102]

There could be no clearer or more authoritative statement that it was the intentions of the drafters of this very provision that Article 2(4) *itself*: (i) outlawed the use of *unilateral* force; but (ii) maintained the possibility of using force in self-defence, and as per the powers of the UN Security Council.

This interpretation is also referred to elsewhere during the drafting. When discussing an amendment by New Zealand to add another 'Principle' to the Charter which would have required active resistance by States to acts of aggression, which was ultimately rejected, Australia noted that Article 2(4) 'was not entirely negative but implied the positive use of force'.[103]

It is submitted on this basis that Article 2(4) was carefully constructed in a way so as to acknowledge the lawful uses of force recognised under the Charter, whilst also maintaining a wide prohibition in instances of unilateral action beyond the Organisation. This undermines any argument for the extreme narrow interpretation, but also indicates the prohibition is not as far-reaching as the wide interpretation.

Yet, since the drafting of the Charter, we have seen that this interpretation of Article 2(4) has not been *explicitly* acknowledged, or at least not investigated in full.[104] Unfortunately, the result is a very complicated and complex working of the provision, due to the competing balance between protecting States from unilateral force as far as possible, while still maintaining the possibility of Security Council enforcement action. This was once described by Peru during

[101] *Report of Rapporteur of Committee 1, Commission I* (9 June 1945) Doc 885, I/1/34, 6 *UNCIO* 387.

[102] ibid, 400 (emphasis added).

[103] *Twelfth Meeting of Committee 1, Commission I* (6 June 1945) Doc 810, I/1/30, 6 *UNCIO* 342, 346.

[104] However, Perkins interprets Art 2(4) as prohibiting only unilateral uses of force, but of course does not further investigate the wider implications of this beyond his arguments surrounding 'counterintervention'. See JA Perkins, 'The Right of Counterintervention' (1987) 17 *Georgia Journal of International & Comparative Law* 171, 198–99 (in particular n 90); see also Brownlie (n 108) 268, where Brownlie suggests that the final part of the prohibition requiring 'inconsistency with the Purposes of the UN' might well explain the legality of the actions of the Security Council under Chapter VII of the Charter, but does not further investigate this possibility.

the drafting of the Charter as 'an awkward, unhappy, equivocal wording'.[105] Peru also noted that the delegate of Norway described it as illogical, 'because it comprises two negations'.[106] But the delegates nevertheless still emphasised the original purpose of the provision in still leaving room for UN-sanctioned force.[107]

2.2.1. *The Drafters' View of Territorial Integrity and Political Independence*

Article 2(4) refers specifically to 'territorial integrity' and 'political independence'. Referring to the preparatory works of the Charter, Brownlie argued that 'territorial integrity' and 'political independence' were inserted at the insistence of smaller States to offer very specific guarantees or protections under the prohibition, and not to restrict the prohibition of force.[108] Notwithstanding such 'specific guarantees', Brownlie argues that the terms do not *qualify* the prohibition of force.[109] Respectfully, this author disagrees in part with Brownlie's interpretation of the preparatory debates, for the following reasons.

Firstly, there was a clear intention for the Security Council *itself* to be bound by these principles, suggesting that they are not as far-reaching and restrictive as Brownlie believed. Particularly revealing is a debate concerning a Czechoslovakian proposal which explicitly considered the Security Council to be bound to respect 'territorial integrity' and 'political independence'.[110] The proposal was suggested in the context of what became Article 24, where the Council is required to act in accordance with the Principles of the Charter. The Czechoslovakian proposal clearly considered the Council to be bound by such principles, and suggested that there should be a provision for a situation to be referred to the General Assembly if measures were required that would infringe upon those principles. In full, the proposal stated:

> Should the Security Council come to the conclusion that international peace and security can be maintained only by measures not in conformity with these fundamental principles (*respect for the territorial integrity and political independence of States-members*), and especially by territorial changes, the matter should be laid before the Assembly. At the request of any party to the dispute, the question shall also be laid before the Assembly. In these cases the Assembly should decide by a two-thirds majority vote.[111]

[105] *Verbatim Minutes of the Second Meeting of Commission I* (20 June 1945) Doc 1123, I/8, 6 *UNCIO* 65, 68–69 (Peru).

[106] ibid.

[107] ibid, 68.

[108] Ian Brownlie, *International Law and the Use of Force by States* (Oxford, Oxford University Press, 1963) 266–67.

[109] ibid, 267.

[110] See *Document Table on Chapter VI Sections B, C, and D* (15 May 1945) Doc 360, III/1/16, 11 UNCIO 766, 770 (citing Doc 2 G/14(b) 2).

[111] ibid, emphasis added.

However, the proposal was withdrawn, and the Czechoslovakian representative suggested that it was merely an 'observation' that the Security Council was bound to respect territorial integrity and political independence elsewhere in the Charter.[112]

This very issue arose for discussion following a Norwegian amendment to the Charter that would have required the Council to abide by certain principles when settling a dispute.[113] The proposal required that 'no solution should be imposed upon a state of a nature to impair its confidence in its future security or welfare'.[114] Norway expanded upon this proposal, referring to the Czechoslovakian proposal for support, and sought assurances relating to the powers of the Security Council that States' territorial integrity and political independence should be protected, *particularly in the application of coercive actions and sanctions*.[115] Norway made clear that its proposal was made with a view to establishing rules of conduct for the Security Council.[116]

Rejecting Norway's proposal, States pointed out that the Security Council was already bound by the purposes and principles of the Charter. The United Kingdom said that its purpose was already served by the purposes in Article 1 of the Charter, where it is required that the Organisation was to 'bring about by peaceful means, and *in conformity with the principles of justice and international law,* adjustment or settlement of international disputes'.[117] In other words, the UK was suggesting that, when *settling* an international dispute – especially following the use of enforcement measures to restore or maintain peace and security – the Council must act in accordance with justice and international law.

Norway replied that it was not concerned with Council's *pacific* settlement of disputes, but with its coercive action, where the Council has at its disposal 'overwhelming powers'.[118] In response, the United States attempted to reassure Norway by arguing that the purposes and principles of the Charter 'constituted the highest rules of conduct', and assured that Article 24 of the Charter just simply was not the right place to put Norway's amendment.[119] The US argued: 'Furthermore, the Charter had to be considered in its entirety and if the Security Council violated its principles and purposes it would be acting *ultra vires*.'[120]

[112] *Continuation of the Report of the Activities of Committee III/1 Concerning Sections A, B, C, and D of Chapter VI of the Dumbarton Oaks Proposals* (14 June 1945) Doc WD 313, III/1/51, 11 UNCIO 555, t 557; see also *Summary Report of Thirteenth Meeting of Committee III/1* (24 May 1945) Doc 555, III/1/27, 11 UNCIO 375, 378.

[113] See proposal at n 110, 11 *UNCIO* 766, 770 (citing Doc 2 G/7(n)(1) 4).

[114] ibid.

[115] *Thirteenth Meeting of Committee III/1* (n 112) 11 *UNCIO* 375, 378–79.

[116] ibid, 378.

[117] ibid, emphasis added.

[118] ibid.

[119] ibid, 379.

[120] ibid.

Finally, the Australian delegate noted the importance of Norway's amendment, but insisted that its proper place was 'in another part of the Charter to which Australia had proposed an amendment that all nations should refrain from threat or use of force against one another'. He argued: 'This idea, as well as the Czechoslovak desire for guarantees of independence and territorial integrity, was concerned with the same basic question as the Norwegian amendment, but belonged in an earlier section of the Charter.'[121]

This is fundamentally important. Australia's statement suggests that Norway's aim for the Security Council to respect the purposes and principles of the UN is achieved through its own amendment to Article 2(4) – an amendment which added the terms 'territorial integrity' and 'political independence' to the prohibition of force.[122]

If this does not convince others that the Security Council is obligated to act in accordance with Article 2(4), there can be no doubt that it must act in accordance with Article 2(1) – which provides for the principle of sovereign equality, on which the Organisation itself is based. During the drafting of this provision, it was made very clear that the principle of sovereign equality includes respect for political independence and territorial integrity.[123] By being required to act in accordance with this principle in Article 24, the Security Council is bound to respect the territorial integrity and political independence of all States – *especially* when undertaking or authorising enforcement action. Because the powers of the Security Council are very clearly accepted within the Charter itself, there seems to be no alternative but to accept that territorial integrity and political independence can, in *some way*, leave room for enforcement measures.

In light of this, there are three possibilities: (i) the meanings of 'territorial integrity' and 'political independence' are much more narrow than assumed; (ii) the scope of these principles is very wide and, thus, the Security Council's powers are much more limited than assumed; or (iii) 'territorial integrity' and 'political independence' are much more dynamic principles than first thought, containing inherent qualifications based upon the consent of States and other rules of customary international law.

The current author submits that the latter possibility is the most convincing. This will be demonstrated as the next section highlights the key consequences of the original intentions of the drafters on the legal and doctrinal mechanics of Article 2(4).

[121] ibid.

[122] See eg *Amendments to the Dumbarton Oaks Proposals Submitted on Behalf of Australia* (5 May 1945) Doc 2, G/14(1), 3 *UNCIO* 543.

[123] See eg *Report of Rapporteur of Committee 1 to Commission I* (9 June 1945) Doc 885, I/1/34, 6 *UNCIO* 387, 397–98; See also *Friendly Relations Declaration* (n 11) Annex, Principle 6.

3. THE MECHANICS OF ARTICLE 2(4)

This section will explain the mechanics of Article 2(4) in light of the original intentions of the drafters of the Charter, as just outlined. It is important to understand exactly how Article 2(4) operates in order to answer our overall question that is the focus of this chapter – ie whether there is legal space for the tertiary responsibility to protect to be implemented using *forcible* measures beyond the Security Council. As this section will reveal, the principles of 'territorial integrity' and 'political independence' operate in such a way so as to provide for, and perhaps even limit, the powers of the Security Council.[124] This is because they are subject to one general caveat – and that is the inherent restriction of the scope of those principles as provided for through a State's consent to the powers contained within the UN Charter. This nuanced limitation will now be explained.

3.1. Inherent Qualifications of Territorial Integrity

There are two main competing interpretations of 'territorial integrity'. There is the narrow interpretation, which says that territorial integrity prohibits the annexation of territory, or the use of force for territorial conquest. In essence, it relates only to the changing of borders or boundaries, and may also prohibit the illegal occupation of territory.

This view is supported by authors such as D'Amato[125] and Tesón,[126] who primarily advocate for a right of unilateral humanitarian intervention. Brenfors and Petersen[127] submit that the intention of Article 2(4) was to abolish this 'classic' form of the use of force, which they argue is not the type of force used for a 'true' humanitarian intervention.[128] Brenfors and Petersen believe that 'Article 2(4) was to be understood as covering only acts of invasions, subsequent border changes or abrogation of independence'.[129] According to this school of thought, such invasions and annexations are legally distinct from forcible interventions to protect populations from impending or ongoing atrocities, and accordingly do not infringe upon the principle of territorial integrity.

[124] Further detail on *how* the powers of the Security Council and self-defence are compatible with Art 2(4) is provided in Butchard (n 1) 262–65.

[125] A D'Amato, *International Law: Process and Prospect*, 2nd edn (New York, Transnational Publishers, 1995) ch 3 generally; see also A D'Amato, 'The Invasion of Panama Was a Lawful Response to Tyranny' (1990) 84 *American Journal of International Law* 516, 520.

[126] FR Tesón, *Humanitarian Intervention: An Inquiry into Law and Morality*, 2nd edn (New York, Transnational Publishers, 1997) 146–57 generally.

[127] M Brenfors and MM Petersen, 'The Legality of Unilateral Humanitarian Intervention – A Defence' (2000) 69(4) *Nordic Journal of International Law* 449–99, 466.

[128] ibid, 470–71; see also Tesón (n 126) 151.

[129] Brenfors and Petersen (n 127) 471.

On the other hand, there is a wide interpretation of 'territorial integrity' that conflates 'integrity' with territorial 'inviolability' – ie the notion that borders are inviolable, and therefore *any* interference within a State itself would violate the territorial integrity of that State. This is supported by commentators such as Chesterman,[130] Brownlie[131] and Elden.[132]

Elden highlights two alternatives for the meaning of 'integrity': first, the notion of being 'whole' versus being 'fractured'; and secondly the more personality-based notions of respect, honour and pride.[133] These notions are closely related to the dictionary definitions of 'integrity', which include: (i) a soundness of moral principle or the character of uncorrupted virtue; or (ii) the something undivided or an integral whole.[134] The latter notion is also further defined as: the condition of having no part or element taken away or wanting; or an undivided or unbroken state.[135]

Of course, it is not possible for territory itself to 'be honest' or 'have strong moral principles', and so it is unlikely that the principle of territorial integrity refers to this 'unimpaired moral state' or 'freedom from moral corruption'.[136] It is more likely that the legal use of the term refers to the wholeness of a State's territory, and its borders remaining fixed and unalterable through force.

Yet, the much wider view of 'territorial integrity' suggests that this 'integrity' of territory extends to the complete *inviolability* of borders or boundaries. Lauterpacht is widely cited as suggesting that 'territorial integrity, especially where coupled with political independence, is synonymous with territorial inviolability'.[137] Lauterpacht, in fact, goes on to argue:

> Thus a state would be acting in breach of its obligations under the Charter if it were to invade or commit an act of force within the territory of another state, in anticipation of an alleged impending attack or in order to obtain redress, without the intention of interfering permanently with the territorial integrity of that state.[138]

Lauterpacht seems to suggest that the intention of a State, and how it directs its use of force, is irrelevant to the protection of territorial integrity. But if territorial integrity was synonymous with territorial inviolability, and did prohibit *any* act of force within territory or *any* incursion into territory regardless of the intention, then even the use of force for the maintenance of international peace

[130] S Chesterman, *Just War or Just Peace: Humanitarian Intervention and International Law* (Oxford, Oxford University Press, 2001).
[131] Brownlie (n 108).
[132] S Elden, *Terror and Territory: The Spatial Extent of Sovereignty* (Minneapolis, University of Minnesota Press, 2009).
[133] ibid, 142–45.
[134] *Oxford English Dictionary* definition, www.oed.com/view/Entry/97366 (accessed 31 July 2019).
[135] ibid.
[136] ibid.
[137] L Oppenheim, *International Law*, ed Hersch Lauterpacht, 7th edn (London, Longmans, 1952) vol II, 154 (as cited in Chesterman (n 130) 50, and Bowett (n 144) 152).
[138] ibid.

and security on behalf of the UN would be included within this definition. This would also require accepting that Article 2(4) really was an 'absolute' prohibition of force, because *any* force foreseen by the UN Charter would be captured by this phrase 'territorial inviolability' – and, as just highlighted above, this is inconsistent with the original intentions of the drafters.

Similarly, Chesterman dismisses any restrictive interpretation of Article 2(4), suggesting that a narrow view of territorial integrity would demand an 'Orwellian' construction of those terms.[139] It is not entirely clear what Chesterman means by this, but his argument is based upon a similar assertion previously put by Schachter,[140] who states:

> The idea that wars waged in a good cause such as democracy and human rights would not involve a violation of territorial integrity or political independence demands an Orwellian construction of those terms. It is no wonder that the argument has not found any significant support.[141]

When arguing this point, Schachter briefly defines territorial integrity as 'the right of a state to control access to its territory'.[142] However, Schachter himself seems to support the possibility of a limited intervention to save lives, which he terms as a 'limited rescue mission', but maintains that 'it is difficult to extend that argument to justify an armed invasion to topple a repressive regime'.[143] It seems that even with the more restrictive interpretations of Article 2(4), there are more nuanced understandings of territorial integrity that should be investigated. Indeed, we must be careful not to stretch or abuse the meaning of these terms to justify uses of force on potentially duplicitous grounds. But this does not mean that we should ignore the effect of those terms altogether.

Rejecting overly wide interpretations, and the link to territorial inviolability, Bowett insists on giving 'territorial integrity' its plain meaning, arguing that: 'The rights of territorial integrity and political independence have never been absolute, but always relative to similar rights in other States, so that "integrity" has always been a more accurate term than "inviolability".'[144] Bowett's argument certainly calls for a more doctrinal and nuanced investigation into these terms.

The very possibility of the Council being bound itself by territorial integrity and political independence, whether through Article 2(4), or through the principle of sovereign equality in Article 2(1) of the Charter, leads the current

[139] Chesterman (n 130) 51–52.
[140] O Schachter, "The Legality of Pro-Democratic Invasion" (1984) 78 *American Journal of International Law* 645, 649.
[141] ibid.
[142] ibid.
[143] ibid.
[144] DW Bowett, *Self-Defence in International Law* (Manchester, Manchester University Press, 1958) 152.

author to consider the possibility of these terms having inherent qualifications.[145] This argument submits that the principles themselves are limited in scope by a voluntary relinquishment of sovereignty by the State, or by reason of existing rights of other States. In other words, when a State consents to circumstances normally affecting territorial integrity or political independence, it limits the application of those principles. Accordingly, it is submitted that enforcement measures in the Charter find their compatibility with the principles of territorial integrity and political independence by inherently qualifying those principles, rather than through overly narrow interpretations of situations that might usually fall within their scope.

This explanation becomes particularly fitting in circumstances involving the use of military occupation by the Security Council. Territorial integrity clearly prohibits the unlawful military occupation of a States' territory.[146] However, is it possible to occupy territory *lawfully*, thus rendering such an occupation outside of the scope of territorial integrity? For example, if an agreement between State A and State B, for State A to have a military base on the territory of State B, could we consider this consent as a voluntary limitation of State B's right of territorial integrity in those particular circumstances? A similar theory might be applied to UN peacekeeping, where States consent to the presence, and sometimes occupation, of peacekeepers within its territory.[147] Equally, where the Security Council may authorise an enforcement mission, that mission may in some circumstances occupy areas of a State in which they operate in order to maintain or restore international peace and security. Such an occupation seemingly does not violate 'territorial integrity' and render the operation unlawful. Therefore, the very nature of the mission – that it is based upon a mandate granted by powers under the UN Charter – implies that 'territorial integrity' can be limited to allow for lawful occupations while simultaneously prohibiting unlawful military occupations.

As a further example, States can voluntarily change borders or boundaries through a peaceful settlement. 'Territorial integrity' therefore prohibits the *forcible* change of borders, not peaceful and consensual alterations. The change of borders through a peaceful settlement or treaty would be a valid limitation of the application of the principle of territorial integrity of that State.

It is therefore submitted that the provisions of the UN Charter, as a form of 'permanent' consent to the powers of the Council, constitute an inherent limitation of the principle of territorial integrity when applied in the context of the use of force by the Council.

[145] See also Bowett (n 144) 152.

[146] See eg: *Friendly Relations Declaration* (n 11) Annex, Principle 1; Conference on Security and Co-operation in Europe, Helsinki Final Act, (1975) 14 ILM 1292, 1294, ch 1(a), s IV.

[147] See eg Y Dinstein, *International Law of Belligerent Occupation* (Cambridge, Cambridge University Press, 2009) 37–38; See also generally A Roberts, 'What Is Military Occupation?' (1984) 55 *British Yearbook of International Law* 249.

3.1.1. Addressing Notable Case Law and 'Territorial Sovereignty'

It is worth at this point addressing the compatibility of such 'inherent qualifications' with a number of cases at the ICJ that have been interpreted as countering any restrictive or dynamic interpretation of 'territorial integrity'. The most notable is the *Corfu Channel* case,[148] which is often read as rejecting any narrow interpretation of territorial integrity. But this could not be further from the truth.

This case involved a dispute between the United Kingdom and Albania, where the UK undertook a minesweeping operation in Albanian territorial waters, without the consent of Albania. In their arguments to the court, while Albania argued that the UK's actions violated Article 2(4), the UK argued on the contrary: '[O]ur action … threatened neither the territorial integrity nor the political independence of Albania. Albania suffered thereby neither territorial loss nor any part of its political independence.'[149]

The UK also made a *separate* argument that a right of self-help still existed in international law, albeit in a limited form, and that in this case there was an urgent necessity to safeguard evidence for the purposes of justice, and therefore that international law should allow for such a limited form of intervention.[150] The ICJ rejected this argument outright, citing the possibility of serious abuses and the perversion of international justice.[151] The court also determined that the UK's actions within Albanian waters were a violation of Albania's 'territorial *sovereignty*'.[152]

Some commentators wrongly interpret the court's rejection of this 'right of intervention', and the Court's findings in favour of Albania, also as a rejection of the UK's *separate* argument relating to the narrow interpretation of Article 2(4). For example, Chesterman suggests that '[t]hough the argument was not specifically addressed in the judgment, the Court's finding that the operation violated Albanian sovereignty impliedly rejects it'.[153] However, Article 2(4) is not once referred to in the judgment of the court, and neither is territorial integrity as a concept.

In fact, when the court did make a limited referral to the use of force, it said:

> It does not consider that the action of the British Navy was a demonstration of force for the purpose of exercising political pressure on Albania. The responsible naval commander, who kept his ships at a distance from the coast, cannot be reproached

[148] *Corfu Channel* case (Merits) (*United Kingdom v Albania*), Judgment of 4 April 1949, [1949] ICJ Reports 4.

[149] *Corfu Channel* case (Pleadings, Oral Arguments, Documents) (*United Kingdom v Albania*), Oral Proceedings (First Part) vol III, Statement by Sir Eric Beckett (United Kingdom) at Public Sitting of 12 November 1948, 296.

[150] ibid; see also *Corfu Channel* Judgment (n 148) 34.

[151] *Corfu Channel* Judgment (n 148) 35.

[152] *Corfu Channel* Judgment (n 148) 35.

[153] Chesterman (n 130) 50.

> for having employed an important covering force in a region where twice within a few months his ships had been the object of serious outrages.[154]

Corten submits that the Court seems to be suggesting here that the UK military operation was not serious enough to come under the prohibition of force – and Corten himself considers the case as a precedent illustrating the need for force to cross a certain threshold of gravity before it can be characterised as a 'use of force' against a state under Article 2(4).[155]

In truth, this case does not *in itself* clarify the scope of Article 2(4), but it has often been used by commentators to conflate the Court's finding of a violation of 'territorial *sovereignty*' with a rejection of a more nuanced understanding of 'territorial integrity'.[156] This also has the unhelpful effect of conflating territorial integrity with territorial *sovereignty*. Asrat goes further and argues that the judgment as a whole was a judgment on the construction of Article 2(4), despite the fact that the Court did not mention the provision at all.[157] The fact remains that the Court did not address Article 2(4), or the UK's argument relating to territorial integrity.

The ICJ returned to the issue in the more recent case of *Construction of a Road in Costa Rica*.[158] Costa Rica claimed that Nicaragua had breached 'fundamental principles of territorial integrity and the prohibition of use of force under the Charter of the United Nations and the Charter of the Organization of American States' due to Nicaragua's alleged incursion into and occupation of Costa Rican territory.[159] Conversely, Nicaragua claimed that Costa Rica had violated Nicaragua's territorial integrity,[160] in particular, by the construction of the road which allegedly caused damage to the San Juan River, which is purportedly within Nicaragua's jurisdiction.[161]

When considering Costa Rica's arguments, the Court noted that Costa Rica alleged a breach of *sovereignty* and *territorial integrity*, and moved forward by first addressing whether there had been a breach of *territorial sovereignty*.[162] Ultimately, the Court decided:

> It is not contested that Nicaragua carried out various activities in the disputed territory since 2010, including excavating three caños and establishing a military presence in parts of that territory. These activities were in breach of Costa Rica's territorial sovereignty.[163]

[154] ibid.

[155] Corten (n 3) 69–70.

[156] See eg Moir (n 19) 7–8; Rosalyn Higgins, *Problems and Process: International Law and How We Use It* (Oxford, Oxford University Press, 1994) 240.

[157] Asrat (n 3) 123–24.

[158] *Certain Activities Carried Out by Nicaragua in the Border Area* (*Costa Rica v Nicaragua*) and *Construction of a Road in Costa Rica along the San Juan River* (*Nicaragua v Costa Rica*) (Judgment) 16 December 2015, [2015] ICJ Rep 665.

[159] ibid, [46].

[160] ibid, [50].

[161] ibid, [174].

[162] ibid, from [65].

[163] ibid, [93].

From this, it is clear that a 'military presence' within a state can breach territorial *sovereignty*. The Court moved on to consider the request by Costa Rica to find that Nicaragua breached 'the prohibition of the threat or use of force under Article 2(4) of the Charter of the United Nations and Article 22 of the Charter of the Organization of American States'.[164] However, even in light of this request, the Court said:

> The relevant conduct of Nicaragua has already been addressed in the context of the Court's examination of the violation of Costa Rica's territorial sovereignty. The fact that Nicaragua considered that its activities were taking place on its own territory does not exclude the possibility of characterizing them as an unlawful use of force. This raises the issue of their compatibility with both the United Nations Charter and the Charter of the Organization of American States. However, in the circumstances, given that the unlawful character of these activities has already been established, the Court need not dwell any further on this submission.[165]

Considering the Court's reasoning that Costa Rica's injury 'will in all events have been sufficiently addressed'[166] by a simple declaration of a violation of territorial sovereignty, it is very disappointing that the Court did not seize a valuable opportunity to clarify the interpretation of the Charter and expand upon whether there was a violation of *territorial integrity*, and thus Article 2(4) of the Charter, especially in light of the fact that Costa Rica explicitly requested such a pronouncement. This was also criticised in Judge Robinson's Separate Opinion, who considered that 'It is … the Court's responsibility, as the "principal judicial organ of the United Nations", to take on the sometimes difficult and sensitive task of identifying the contours of international law's prohibition of the use of force.'[167]

Nevertheless, the Court went further and refused to also make a finding on whether Nicaragua's presence on its territory was the object of military occupation contrary to Article 21 of the Charter of the Organization of American States for the very same reason.[168]

While it is now clear that the Court considers territorial integrity and territorial sovereignty as two separate legal principles, it unfortunately considered its role as simply declaring whether Nicaragua's conduct was unlawful or not. This position was again criticised, where one judge considered that the Court should have placed greater emphasis on the serious nature of Nicaragua's apparent violation of territorial integrity.[169]

However, when the Court considered Nicaragua's claim of a violation of territorial integrity by Costa Rica, there was a little hint by the Court as to

[164] ibid, [96].
[165] ibid, [97].
[166] ibid.
[167] ibid, Separate Opinion of Judge Robinson, 7–8.
[168] ibid, [98]–[99].
[169] ibid, Separate Opinion of Judge Ad Hoc Dugard, 2.

what a violation of territorial integrity might look like. Rejecting Nicaragua's theory that Costa Rica could have violated Nicaragua's territorial integrity by the creation of deltas by sediment, the Court said: 'There is no evidence that Costa Rica *exercised any authority* on Nicaragua's territory or *carried out any activity therein*.'[170]

Based upon this very short snippet of the judgment, it suggests that the 'exercise of authority' on another state's territory is at least a test for a violation of territorial integrity. This seems, to the current author, to be hinting at military occupation as a threshold for violating territorial integrity – after all, exercising authority within a State suggests the military force has some degree of control over the area in which they are based.

3.1.2. Confirmation in the Historical Use of 'Territorial Integrity'

The following examples provide further evidence of a more restrictive interpretation of 'territorial integrity' as supported above. Following the First World War, according to Korman, there was a 'moral turning point' where attitudes towards the right of states to acquire territory by conquest or military victory undoubtedly began to shift.[171] From this shift in attitude, US President Woodrow Wilson advocated for mutual guarantees between States of political independence and territorial integrity for 'great and small states alike' in his 'Fourteen Points' speech.[172]

Eventually, the guarantee of 'territorial integrity' was put into several treaties, including in Article 10 of the Covenant of the League of Nations.[173] As D'Amato highlights,[174] similar phrasing was also inserted into several bilateral and multilateral treaties over the years, many of them 'Treaties of Guaranty', including some examples decades before the League of Nations such as in the Treaty of Paris of 30 March 1856 relating to the Ottoman Empire.[175]

D'Amato argues that the states were simply guaranteeing each other that they would not attempt to capture, seize or annex land belonging to another state – which, critically, involves the changing or diminishing in some way of state borders.[176] More importantly, D'Amato highlights that some treaties

[170] ibid, Judgment, [221]–[223], emphasis added.

[171] S Korman, *The Right of Conquest: The Acquisition of Territory by Force in International Law and Practice* (Oxford, Clarendon Press, 1996) 132–78, 161 (as cited in MW Zacher, 'The Territorial Integrity Norm: International Boundaries and the Use of Force' (2001) 55 *International Organization* 215, 219).

[172] Speech given by President Woodrow Wilson, 'President Woodrow Wilson's Fourteen Points' (8 January 1918) available at The Avalon Project, Yale Law School, http://avalon.law.yale.edu/20th_century/wilson14.asp (accessed 31 July 2019).

[173] Covenant of the League of Nations (adopted 29 April 1919, entered into force 10 January 1920) [1919] UKTS 4 (Cmd 153).

[174] D'Amato (n 125) 58–64.

[175] ibid, 58.

[176] ibid.

specifically include *both* an obligation to respect territorial integrity *and* territorial inviolability, such as in the non-aggression treaty between Lithuania and the then-USSR of 28 September 1926.[177] This particular treaty required: 'The Lithuanian Republic and the Union of Socialist Soviet Republics undertake to respect in all circumstances each other's sovereignty and territorial integrity and inviolability.'[178] The most interesting feature here is that the treaty refers to the notion of territorial 'inviolability', alongside territorial integrity, thus treating the two as related, but nevertheless *distinct*, characteristics of a State. D'Amato's research highlights several other non-aggression pacts adopted through the 1930s that very much reflect the same pattern[179] – and while it is impossible to highlight them all here, it is worth noting that a large number of the treaties referred to both territorial integrity and inviolability in their key provisions.

This pattern continued even after the adoption of the UN Charter. For example, the Inter-American Treaty of Reciprocal Assistance[180] requires the parties to 'formally condemn war and undertake in their international relations not to resort to the threat or the use of force in any manner inconsistent with the provisions of the Charter of the United Nations or of this Treaty'.[181] However, when prescribing how parties should respond to to *aggression* which is not an armed attack, Article 6 refers to potential situations where

> the inviolability or the integrity of the territory or the sovereignty or political independence of any American State should be affected by an aggression which is not an armed attack or by an extra-continental or intra-continental conflict, or by any other fact or situation might endanger the peace of America.[182]

The reference to inviolability of territory here clearly relates to an act of aggression, as with the other non-aggression pacts, but includes specifically 'aggression which is not an armed attack' – in other words, aggressive acts nor necessarily involving the use of force. Furthermore, this is a good example of how the principle of territorial inviolability it is not *explicitly* referred to following the adoption of the UN Charter as part of the new principle prohibiting force in international relations. Clearly territorial inviolability is an obligation still owed to all States, and is also part of the definition of an aggressive act, but it is not clear that it forms part of the prohibition of force in Article 2(4).

[177] Treaty of Non-Aggression between the Republic of Lithuania and the Union of Soviet Socialist Republics Signed at Moscow, September 28, 1926 (adopted 28 September 1926) 60 LNTS 145 (no 1410), English translation at 152 onwards.

[178] ibid, Art 2.

[179] D'Amato (n 125) 64–68.

[180] Inter-American Treaty of Reciprocal Assistance and Final Act of the Inter-American Conference for the Maintenance of Continental Peace and Security (adopted 2 February 1947, entered into force 3 December 1948) 21 UNTS 77 (No 324).

[181] ibid, Art 1.

[182] ibid, Art 6.

Finally, it is worth highlighting the Helsinki Final Act of 1975.[183] As a Cold War agreement on security and cooperation in Europe,[184] it treats the very principles of territorial integrity and the inviolability of frontiers as two separate, but obviously related, principles of international law.

The inviolability of frontiers, as detailed by section III,[185] is much wider in prohibiting the 'assault' of frontiers (which seems to denote the incursion of forces over borders without consent), *as well as* the seizure of territory (which refers to the capture, and exercise of authority, over that territory).

However, section IV[186] – entitled 'Territorial Integrity of States' – repeats wording similar to Article 2(4) of the Charter, and adds some emphasis on the 'unity' of States. Section IV then expands upon territorial integrity, emphasising that states refrain from 'making each other's territory the object of military occupation or other direct or indirect measures of force 'in contravention of international law'. The emphasis is clearly on *unlawful* force against territorial integrity and political independence of States, giving examples such as military occupation, acquisition and direct or indirect force *against that territory*.

The key qualification here is that the forcible measures are directed *against* the territory of the State, and not simply *on* the territory of the State. Accordingly, such force simply within a territory could be against the *political independence* of that State, even when not specifically directed against the territory, but not necessarily against the territorial integrity of that State. The difference is subtle, and may not have any real practical implications when determining a violation of Article 2(4), but it certainly offers a plausible explanation of the very precise legal mechanics of Article 2(4).

The separate treatment of these two principles is consistent with this idea that territorial integrity is a much more precise term than territorial inviolability. Its inclusion within Article 2(4) should not be conflated with the 'inviolability' of frontiers on the basis of that term alone. Returning to Lauterpacht's assertion that territorial integrity is synonymous with territorial inviolability, Lauterpacht adds that this is 'especially where coupled with political independence'.[187] This author does not disagree that *the coupling* of these two terms can be considered as reflecting the inviolability of frontiers, or indeed being synonymous with sovereignty in general. However, it is submitted that territorial integrity, as a *standalone* principle of international law, is much more precise, and relates only to the changes of borders or boundaries, or the *illegal* occupation of territory.

[183] Conference on Security and Co-operation in Europe, Helsinki Final Act (1975) 14 ILM 1292, 1294.

[184] Although the Helsinki Final Act is not strictly speaking a treaty and applied to the situation in Europe before the fall of the Soviet Union, it does help to highlight a consensus between some States at the time regarding some of these legal principles.

[185] Helsinki Final Act, ch 1(a), s III.

[186] ibid, s IV.

[187] Lauterpacht (n 137).

3.2. Inherent Qualifications of Political Independence

According to a relatively consistent consensus among commentators, 'political independence' refers to 'the autonomy in the affairs of the state with respect to its institutions, freedom of political decisions, policy making, and in matters pertaining to its domestic and foreign affairs'.[188] The Draft Declaration on the Rights and Duties of States[189] similarly declares: 'Every State has the right to independence and hence to exercise freely, without dictation by any other state, all its legal powers, including the choice of its own form of government.'[190]

Corten describes independence as 'a notion that implies at the very least that each State exercises full executive power in its territory without external interference'.[191] Corten suggests that even if a use of force was not aimed at overthrowing or changing the government of the target State, then it would still be incompatible with the concept of independence in what is most fundamental about it.[192]

Consent also plays a role in 'limiting' the political independence of a State. Bowett also refers to the inherent limitations of political independence, arguing that the right of political independence is not absolute, but subject to the rights of other States.[193]

Referring this back to the UN Charter, Bowett suggests that:

> Perhaps the most important limitation on the rights of political independence today is the right of intervention assumed by the Security Council in the general interest of the international community as a whole.
>
> ...
>
> This means, therefore, that the right of political independence is conditional upon it not constituting a 'threat to the peace, breach of the peace, or act of aggression' within the terms of Article 39.[194]

This is a very convincing argument, especially in light of the preceding findings of this chapter. Like territorial integrity, political independence also seems to be inherently limited by the consent of States, and any existing international law applying to a State. Bowett also notes that a State's political independence is also

[188] See eg SKN Blay, 'Territorial Integrity and Political Independence' in R Wolfrum (ed), *Max Planck Encyclopaedia of Public International Law* (online edn, March 2010).

[189] UNGA Res 375 (IV), *Draft Declaration on the Rights and Duties of States* (6 December 1949) UN Doc A/RES/375(IV). Although this was never formally adopted, it is illustrative of the attitude of States in the early practice of the UN.

[190] ibid, Annex, Art 1.

[191] Corten (n 3) 499.

[192] ibid.

[193] Bowett (n 144) 51.

[194] ibid, 51–52.

limited by the right of self-defence in international law.[195] Even if not a member of the UN Charter, a State must expect that any armed attack it conducts against a State will be subject to the right of the victim State to respond in self-defence. Therefore, its decision to conduct an external policy of force against a State is not protected by its political independence, because this right has been limited by the very existence of the right of self-defence.

According to the arguments made above, 'absolute' territorial integrity or political independence is only possible with 'absolute' sovereignty. However, as soon as a State is subject to international law, sovereignty is immediately qualified. For example, any new State would be already subject to respecting the sovereignty of other States, which inherently limits the political independence of the new State to conduct a foreign policy of annexation and territorial expansion. These are no longer accepted practices in international law and are no longer protected by the principle of political independence so long as those laws exist.

3.3. Consistency with the Purposes of the United Nations

3.3.1. The 'Catch-All' Provision

The final part of Article 2(4) restricts the use of force in any other manner inconsistent with the purposes of the United Nations. Dinstein[196] argues that this last sentence is a residual 'catch-all' provision that would prohibit all other uses of force, including those already against the territorial integrity or political independence of a State.[197] In other words, the effect of the final provision is the same as would have been intended under the original Dumbarton Oaks Proposal, as discussed above.

In support of this, Dinstein cites Lachs,[198] who originally conceded in 1980 that the final sentence is 'at first sight a residual "catch-all" provision'.[199] However, Lachs continued to suggest that 'it may render the operation of the Article more specific, since it serves to prohibit the substitution of a forcible solution for any process decided upon by the United Nations, in pursuance of its purposes, for the settlement of a particular issue'.[200]

[195] ibid, 51–55. A similar idea is briefly explored by Kaghan who suggests that Art 2(4) 'includes and incorporates the right to use such force in self-defence'. C Kaghan, '*Jus Cogens* and the Inherent Right to Self-Defence' (1996–97) 3 *ILSA Journal of International and Comparative Law* 767, 788.

[196] Y Dinstein, *War, Aggression and Self-Defence*, 5th edn (Cambridge, Cambridge University Press, 2012).

[197] Dinstein (n 196) 90, [241]–[243].

[198] M Lachs, 'The Development of General Trends of International Law in Our Time' (1980) 169 *Recueil des cours de l'Académie de droit international* 9.

[199] ibid, 162.

[200] ibid.

Corten is more explicit in suggesting that the final sentence is an *objective* prohibition of any force used in a manner inconsistent with the stated Purposes of the UN.[201] Similarly, Chesterman agrees that this provision is inclusive of all uses of force whether or not they violate the territorial integrity or political independence of a State.[202]

The current author also adopts a similar 'catch-call' interpretation of this part of Article 2(4), but with the same interpretation as that offered by the drafters of the Charter. That is, all force is caught by the provision, except lawful uses of force that are *consistent* with the purposes of the United Nations. While some may argue that this is too lenient and could leave room for unilateral uses of force, this author's response would be that unilateral force is excluded by the very purpose of the United Nations itself, as will now be explained.

3.3.2. The Purposes of the United Nations

The purposes of the UN are set out in Article 1 of the Charter. One key purpose, according to Article 1(1), is the maintenance of international peace and security through effective collective measures.

Tesón argues that unilateral action – humanitarian intervention in particular – can survive this 'purposes' test, casing his argument on the fact that a primary purpose of the UN is the promotion of human rights.[203] To support this, Tesón cites Article 1(3) of the UN Charter, which emphasises that a purpose of the United Nations is:

> To achieve international cooperation in solving international problems of an economic, social, cultural, or humanitarian character, and in promoting and encouraging respect for human rights and for fundamental freedoms for all without distinction as to race, sex, language, or religion.

Tesón argues that the promotion of human rights is just as important as the maintenance of international peace and security, and so the use of force or humanitarian intervention to remedy serious human rights violations is in accordance with the purposes of the UN.[204] But Tesón's argument is fundamentally flawed. Chesterman argues that Tesón's interpretation stretches the words of the Charter too far, and highlights that the purpose cited by Tesón in Article 1(3) is to achieve *international cooperation* in its aims, while *promoting and encouraging* respect for human rights.[205] Indeed, using the word 'protect' rather than 'promote' could have granted a stronger mandate in enabling States to defend human rights. Simons also raises this point and highlights the fact that

[201] Corten (n 3) 499–500.
[202] Chesterman (n 130) 52–54.
[203] Tesón (n 126) 152–57.
[204] ibid, 152–57.
[205] Chesterman (n 130) 52–53.

the proposal to use the word 'protect' was ultimately rejected out of fear that it would raise hopes of going beyond what the UN could achieve effectively.[206] Emphasising these facts, Chesterman argues that there is no room in this provision to allow for a unilateral right to humanitarian intervention.[207]

On the other hand, Simon alludes to the possibility that the Charter creates a fundamental obligation on States to respect and protect human rights, purportedly making a unilateral humanitarian intervention consistent with the purposes of the Charter that Article 2(4) requires.[208]

But the current author does not find this persuasive for the following reasons. First, unilateral uses of force – ie force without the authorisation of the UN – inherently threaten international peace and security, are ineffective for this purpose and are not sufficiently 'collective' for the purposes of Article 1(1). Secondly, the rarely cited Article 1(4) provides a strong basis for arguing that unilateral action is inconsistent with the purposes of the Charter. This purpose provides that the United Nations is to be 'a center for harmonising the actions of nations' for the attainment of the other purposes of the UN. This author submits that unilateral action would also be inconsistent with the purpose of harmonising the collective maintenance of international peace and security, because the Security Council, as stated in Article 24, acts on behalf of Member States in its responsibility for the maintenance of international peace and security. Action through the United Nations is the only way to harmonise the actions of the nations in response to a crisis – and any unilateral action would clearly be inconsistent with that aim. Therefore, unilateral uses of force are inconsistent with the purposes of the UN – especially such action that does not engage the body with primary responsibility for the maintenance of international peace and security.

This is confirmed by the discussions during the drafting of the Charter, as outlined above, where the Report of the Committee drafting Article 2(4) expressly stated that 'the unilateral use of force or similar coercive measures is not authorized or admitted'.[209] Most revealing, perhaps, is how the report continues to explain that 'The use of force, therefore, *remains legitimate only to back up the decisions of the Organization* at the start of a controversy or during its solution in the way that the Organization itself ordains.'[210] It is notable that the drafters refer to the use of force to back up decisions of the *Organisation*, rather than the *Security Council* specifically, perhaps leaving room for another competent organ of the United Nations beyond the Security Council to authorise the use of force.

[206] Simon (n 88) 133.
[207] ibid.
[208] ibid, 136–37.
[209] *Report of Rapporteur of Committee 1, Commission I* (9 June 1945) Doc 885, I/1/34, 6 *UNCIO* 387, 400.
[210] ibid, emphasis added.

4. FORCE BEYOND THE SECURITY COUNCIL?

4.1. Questions Concerning Action by the General Assembly

Based upon the analysis above, this interpretation of Article 2(4) may have implications on explaining the legality of the use of force by the UN General Assembly. In 1950, due to deadlock in the Security Council, the General Assembly adopted the Uniting for Peace procedure.[211] In short, this purportedly allowed the General Assembly to recommend enforcement action beyond the Security Council.

One recommendation to use force was passed outside of this procedure by the General Assembly in relation to the Korean War.[212] But the Uniting for Peace Resolution itself has only been used rarely and almost exclusively for peacekeeping missions, which are based on the consent of States anyway.[213]

This author's proposed interpretation of Article 2(4), based upon the position of the drafters of the Charter, may explain the ability of the General Assembly to recommend force. However, this would only be the case if: (i) the General Assembly has the requisite competences under the Charter to do so, ie so that the force would not infringe political independence or territorial integrity,[214] and (ii) it remains in conformity with the purposes of the United Nations. These questions remain to be more rigorously examined in Chapter VI. In terms of conformity with the purposes of the United Nations, based on the analysis above, there seems to be no reason to suggest that a Resolution by the General Assembly recommending the use of force, so long as it is competent to do so, would not 'harmonise the actions of nations' in accordance with Article 1(4) any less than an 'authorisation' by the Security Council itself to do the very same thing. Both methods, it seems, are consistent with the purposes of the Charter in Article 1, and so in accordance with the terms of Article 2(4), hence demonstrating that the General Assembly may well also have the power to recommend force in accordance with its competences and procedures.

[211] UNGA Res 377(V), *Uniting for Peace* (3 November 1950) UN Doc A/RES/377(V).

[212] See UNGA Res 376(V), *The Problem of the Independence of Korea* (7 October 1950) UN Doc A/RES/376(V); and UNGA Res 498(V), *Intervention of the Central People's Government of the People's Republic of China in Korea* (1 February 1951) UN Doc A/RES/498(V), preamble [1], and operative [4].

[213] See eg Report of the Secretary-General, *Summary Study of the Experience Derived from the Establishment and Operation of the Force* (9 October 1958) UN Doc A/3943, [13]–[19], [154]–[193]; see also Department of Peacekeeping Operations and Department of Field Support, *United Nations Peacekeeping Operations: Principles and Guidelines* (New York, 2008) 31.

[214] See eg N White and N Tsagourias, *Collective Security: Theory, Law, and Practice* (Cambridge, Cambridge University Press, 2013) 100–14; N White, 'The Relationship between the UN Security Council and General Assembly in Matters of International Peace and Security' in M Weller (ed), *The Oxford Handbook of the Use of Force In International Law* (Oxford, Oxford University Press, 2015).

4.2. Questions Concerning Regional Enforcement

Finally, this interpretation of Article 2(4) may also be used to investigate certain forms of treaty-based 'consent' to use force in regional organisations. For example, in Article 4(h) of the Constitutive Act of the African Union,[215] the African Union has agreed to take enforcement action against States in response to possible acts of genocide and other atrocity crimes. Questions have been raised as to whether this could be a form of treaty-based consent.[216] If so, this could form a treaty-based limitation of territorial integrity and political independence, and thus pass the first hurdle of conformity with Article 2(4).

However, such action may still require the authorisation of the Security Council, as this requirement still exists separately under Chapter VIII of the Charter within Article 53(1). Olivier Corten suggests that this may be possible, since regional organisations are to be construed as within the 'control' (for want of a better word) of the Security Council itself.[217]

Therefore, this chapter's interpretation of Article 2(4) still upholds the long-standing belief that unilateral uses of force, without the authorisation of the United Nations, are a violation of the prohibition. The difference with regional organisations is that, although members of such arrangements may have limited their political independence and territorial integrity through treaty-based consent, the regional organisation's actions must still be consistent with the purposes of the United Nations (which do not allow for such unilateral action), and the *additional* requirement contained in Article 53(1) that no enforcement action may be taken without Security Council authorisation.

5. CONCLUSIONS

This chapter has demonstrated, through an in-depth analysis of the prohibition of force in international law, that there are potential gaps in this rule whereby action could be taken to implement the tertiary responsibility to protect. However, this interpretation, based upon the preparatory works of the Charter, does not allow for unilateral uses of force such as humanitarian intervention.

Therefore, the use of force remains legal only when: (i) it does not violate the territorial integrity or political independence of a State, which could be

[215] Constitutive Act of the African Union (adopted 11 July 2000, entered into force on 26 May 2001) 2158 UNTS 3.

[216] For a thorough overview of this, and debates surrounding Art 4(h) in general, see D Kuwali and F Viljoen (eds), *Africa and the Responsibility to Protect: Article 4(h) of the African Union Constitutive Act* (Abingdon, Routledge, 2014).

[217] Corten (n 3) 210–11, 341–48.

inherently limited or qualified by the prior consent of that State or a rule of customary international law; and (ii) it is consistent with the purposes of the United Nations, which implies that any *unilateral* action beyond the UN would be illegal.

Having established the legal *space* for the tertiary responsibility to protect, it is left to determine whether this responsibility can be *implemented* by the relevant actors, which will be discussed in Chapter VI.

V

The Tertiary Responsibility and Non-Forcible Measures

THIS CHAPTER WILL apply the theory of a tertiary responsibility to protect to the legality of non-forcible, but still coercive, measures beyond the Security Council. Primarily, the chapter will be concerned with the use of 'sanctions' – defined broadly as encompassing economic sanctions such as asset freezes and trade restrictions, as well as other coercive methods.

To do so, this chapter will address the meaning and scope of the principle of non-intervention in customary international law. It finds that the principle of non-intervention does not prohibit the use of certain coercive methods, regardless of anyone's preferred interpretation of 'intervention', so long as the intervention is not 'essentially within the domestic jurisdiction' of a State. It argues that any norm of international law allowing for coercive measures or sanctions is, by definition, not within such 'domestic jurisdiction' of a State, nor is it an intervention in the 'internal or external affairs' of that State because a State's competences in those affairs are inherently 'limited' by the limitation of sovereignty that naturally occurs following the acceptance of, or being subject to, a rule of international law. Therefore, the book takes the position that measures provided for in international law itself may be legally permissible. The chapter specifically highlights the doctrine of countermeasures as allowing proportionate measures in response to prior breaches of international obligations by other States.

Addressing countermeasures, the limitations of the doctrine as a method of implementing a tertiary responsibility to protect are considered, particularly focusing on the question of whether actors not directly injured by a prior breach of an international obligation may take measures in response to breaches of obligations *erga omnes*, as relevant to the responsibility to protect. By addressing this alternative legal avenue beyond the Security Council, the book finds further legal space for the tertiary responsibility to protect to fill, providing more evidence of the concept's viability and utility.

1. THE PRINCIPLE OF NON-INTERVENTION

The UN Charter recognises the principle of non-intervention in a limited form in Article 2(7), where it states:

> Nothing contained in the present Charter shall authorize the United Nations to intervene in matters which are essentially within the domestic jurisdiction of any state or shall require the Members to submit such matters to settlement under the present Charter; but this principle shall not prejudice the application of enforcement measures under Chapter VII.

This principle applies to the United Nations, preventing it from acting within the 'domestic jurisdiction' of a State. A similar, all-encompassing, principle of non-intervention is also recognised in customary international law and applies to all States – as evidenced in several General Assembly Resolutions. For example, the *Declaration on the Inadmissibility of Intervention*, '[r]eaffirming the principle of non-intervention,'[1] insists that: '[D]irect intervention, subversion and all forms of indirect intervention are contrary to these principles and, consequently, constitute a violation of the Charter of the United Nations.'[2] And also declares:

> No State has the right to intervene, directly or indirectly, *for any reason whatever*, in the internal or external affairs of any other State. Consequently, armed intervention and all other forms of interference or attempted threats against the personality of the State or against its political, economic and cultural elements, are condemned.[3]

The *Declaration on Friendly Relations* introduces the general principle as: 'The principle concerning the duty not to intervene in matters *within the domestic jurisdiction* of any State, in accordance with the Charter.'[4]

Importantly, the *Declaration on Friendly Relations* also reiterates that: 'No State *or group of States* has the right to intervene, directly or indirectly, *for any reason whatever*, in the internal or external affairs of any other State.'[5] This declaration clarified that such interventions were a violation of international law,[6] rather than simply being 'condemned' as they were in the earlier declaration. The ICJ has accepted that this declaration was representative of customary international law.[7]

[1] UNGA Res 2131(XX), *Declaration on the Inadmissibility of Intervention in the Domestic Affairs of States and the Protection of Their Independence and Sovereignty* (21 December 1965) UN Doc A/RES/2131(XX), preamble.

[2] ibid, preamble.

[3] ibid, [1] (emphasis added).

[4] UNGA Res 2625(XXV), *Declaration on Principles of International Law concerning Friendly Relations and Co-operation among States in accordance with the Charter of the United Nations* (24 October 1970) UN Doc A/RES/2625 (XXV), Annex, principle 3 (emphasis added).

[5] ibid, principle 3.

[6] ibid.

[7] *Case Concerning Military and Paramilitary Activities in and against Nicaragua (Nicaragua v USA)* (Merits) [1986] ICJ Rep 14 (*Nicaragua* case) 106–07, [202]; *Case Concerning Armed Activities on the Territory of the Congo (Democratic Republic of the Congo v Uganda)*, Judgment of 19 December 2005 (2005) ICJ Reports 168, [162].

During the drafting debates of the *Declaration on Friendly Relations*, there were opposing views as to whether the principle of non-intervention left room for coercive measures beyond the Security Council. A proposal by the United Kingdom included the ultimately prevailing phrase prohibiting 'intervention in matters within the domestic jurisdiction of any other State'.[8] Commentary to this proposal explained that '"intervention" connotes in general forcible or dictatorial interference'.[9] Importantly, however, the UK's commentary stressed that:

> In considering the scope of 'intervention', it should be recognized that in an interdependent world, it is inevitable and desirable that States will he concerned with and will seek to influence the actions and policies of other States, and that the objective of international law is not to prevent such activity but rather to ensure that it is compatible with the sovereign equality of States and self-determination of their peoples.[10]

This difference between 'intervention' and legitimate 'influence' was addressed in the pursuing debates. There were suggestions that intervention could be practised by the processes of diplomacy, and where the coercive nature of an act of interference rendered that act an 'intervention'.[11] On the other hand, one representative suggested that there was a difference between 'permissible' and 'impermissible' intervention.[12] This was supported by others, who suggested that they must be careful not to categorise as intervention action which would form part of normal diplomatic activities, and supported the idea that at least some forms of 'pressure' could be permissible.[13]

In the 1966 session, an attempt was made by some States to include the recognition of a freedom of States to seek to influence the policies and actions of other States 'in accordance with international law and settled international practice'.[14] This was argued as not allowing for intervention, but to allow necessary *influence* in accordance with the law, for example to try to encourage States to follow policies consistent with the maintenance of international peace and security or the fulfilment of human rights.[15] However, this was seen by others as possibly legitimising intervention, and was therefore unacceptable, so the focus should therefore be on defining not when influence was lawful, but when influence was most certainly *unlawful*.[16]

[8] See UNGA, 'Report of the Special Committee on Principles of International Law concerning Friendly Relations and Co-operation among States' (16 November 1964) UN Doc A/5746, 110–11.
[9] ibid, 111.
[10] ibid.
[11] ibid, 125.
[12] ibid.
[13] ibid, 126.
[14] UNGA, 'Report of the 1966 Special Committee on Principles of International Law concerning Friendly Relations and Co-operation among States' (27 June 1966) UN Doc A/6230, [329]–[333].
[15] ibid, [331].
[16] ibid, [333].

When considering the meaning of 'domestic jurisdiction', it seemed generally accepted that this included both internal and external decisions of a State,[17] and the only exception was where 'such jurisdiction was restricted by obligations undertaken by one State towards other States'.[18] This also implied that because of rights and obligations emerging in customary international law or treaty, 'the domestic jurisdiction of States in the legal sense had been continually reduced as the real interest of States in the territory of others had been recognized and given legal protection'.[19] While there was disagreement about how the inclusion of a reference to prohibiting intervention in the 'external affairs' of a State might have unduly restricted legitimate interference on the international plain,[20] this did not seem to be fully settled after two subsequent sessions of the Special Committee did not touch upon the principle due to a lack of time,[21] and there were no detailed recorded discussions of the principle in the final negotiations of the *Declaration on Friendly Relations*.[22]

These fundamental questions continue to be debated in the academic literature. Early work by Thomas and Thomas detailed the stark contrasts in academic opinion.[23] They highlight the divide between arguments that suggest even the slightest interference in a State's affairs, such as a mere correspondence or criticism regarding a State's actions, could amount to unlawful intervention, compared to arguments in favour of a strict application of the principle to only forcible and dictatorial interference.[24]

Thomas and Thomas reject the notion that a State could only be subject to pressure or coercion through the use of force, believing the approach to be too narrow.[25] According to their view, actions taken by a State to 'impose its will' upon another, with attempts to ensure compliance with this will, are an intervention.[26] They refer to a State's 'supreme authority to control all persons

[17] Hence why the language prohibiting intervention in the 'internal or external affairs' of a State was maintained in both Declarations.

[18] Report of the Special Committee (1964) (n 8) 123–24.

[19] ibid, 124.

[20] See eg Report of the Special Committee (1966) (n 14) [306]–[307]; see also UNGA, 'Report of the Special Committee on Principles of International Law concerning Friendly Relations and Co-operation among States' (26 September 1967) UN Doc A/6799, [343]–[348].

[21] See UNGA 'Report of the Special Committee on Principles of International Law Concerning Friendly Relations and Co-operation among States' (1968) UN Doc A/7326, [204]; UNGA, 'Report of the Special Committee on Principles of International Law Concerning Friendly Relations and Co-operation among States' (1969) UN Doc A/7619, [15]; UNGA, 'Report of the Special Committee on Principles of International Law Concerning Friendly Relations and Co-operation among States' (1970) UN Doc A/8018, [19]–[22].

[22] Report of the Special Committee (1970) (n 21) [58]–[59].

[23] AW Thomas and AJ Thomas, Jr, *Non-Intervention: The Law and its Import in the Americas* (Dallas, TX, Southern Methodist University Press, 1956) 68.

[24] ibid; for an overview of the contrasting legal positions between scholars prior to the *Friendly Relations Declaration*, see ibid, 75–78.

[25] ibid, 68.

[26] ibid, 68–69, 72.

and things within its boundaries *subject only to rules of general international law and obligations assumed by international treaty*'.[27] They thus seem to accept the underlying exception that a State's freedom from intervention can be subject only to rules of international law. However, their position seems to be a little more nuanced than this. Thomas and Thomas argue that 'intervention' should not just include 'illegal' intervention, but also that which might be considered 'legal' intervention. They suggest that although classifying differently acts of the same character might allow for 'all intervention' to be condemned categorically and unequivocally under this interpretation, this perhaps 'complicates a problem that is already confused', and so they argue it may be better to classify all acts of the same nature as 'intervention' and *then* recognise that certain interventions are legal by international law.[28]

If this was the accepted interpretation of the principle, the phrase referring to intervention in the 'domestic jurisdiction' of a State would not limit the principle at all. As we have seen above, the *Declaration on Friendly Relations* clearly considers 'domestic jurisdiction' to include the internal *and* external affairs of a State, and Thomas and Thomas rightly note that 'no valid distinction can be made between intervention in internal and external affairs'.[29] Notably, the 'affairs' of a State, whether internal or external, could still be limited by those international agreements or treaties Thomas and Thomas refer to, or even customary international law itself.

In more recent research, Aloupi[30] maintains that it is unclear what is included in the principle of non-intervention, and that its limits and precise extent are open to debate.[31] Taking a clear stance on the interpretation of non-intervention, Aloupi supports the position that the prohibition is limited to those issues that are within the 'domestic jurisdiction' of States, or where the exercise of its discretionary powers are not limited in any way by customary or conventional international law.[32]

This view is certainly consistent with the viewpoints of many States that were outlined during the drafting of the *Declaration on Friendly Relations*, but we must at least identify what forms the basic makeup of a State's 'domestic jurisdiction' or what might be protected as part of its 'internal or external

[27] ibid, 68 (emphasis added).

[28] ibid, 70–71; although, see 72, where they suggest that advice, or official communication requesting a State not to take certain action would not necessarily constitute an 'intervention'.

[29] ibid, 70.

[30] N Aloupi, 'The Right to Non-Intervention and Non-Interference' (2015) 4(3) *Cambridge Journal of International and Comparative Law* 566.

[31] ibid, 570–71. While Aloupi refers to non-intervention as both a 'right' and a 'prohibition', this study draws no distinction and treats non-intervention as a principle of international law.

[32] ibid, 573–75; while Aloupi distinguishes between non-interference and non-intervention, this study does not adopt such a position, and instead treats 'non-interference' as falling within the principle of non-intervention as was adopted in the *Friendly Relations Declaration*.

affairs'. Indeed, the ICJ in the *Nicaragua* case made some attempt to expand upon this when it suggested that:

> A prohibited intervention must accordingly be one bearing on matters in which each State is permitted, by the principle of State sovereignty, to decide freely. One of these is the choice of a political, economic, social and cultural system, and the formulation of foreign policy.[33]

Interestingly, the ICJ went on to say that: 'Intervention is wrongful when it uses methods of coercion *in regard to such choices*, which must remain free ones.'[34]

It may seem that this leaves room for coercion involving choices no longer within the 'domestic jurisdiction' of a State, but such a conclusion would perhaps miss the point. For example, in situations engaging the responsibility to protect, the fact that a State does not have the sovereign power to commit mass atrocities amounting to breaches of international obligations, including war crimes, genocide and crimes against humanity, does not automatically imply that coercion may be used against that State just because those crimes themselves are not exclusively within the 'domestic jurisdiction' of a State. The perpetrating State may have surrendered jurisdiction over the legality of those crimes, but this is not the same as consenting to be subject to coercive methods by other States – at least not by reference to those crimes alone. This is because the methods of coercion we shall go on to discuss do not directly regulate the actual atrocities at hand, but instead relate to the ability of a State to govern and enjoy separate activities, such as international travel, trade, its financial assets and securing its economy. The atrocities are clearly unlawful under international law, and that is a legal aspect no longer exclusively within the 'domestic jurisdiction' of the State – however, the legality of being subject to coercive measures does not automatically follow from *these* international obligations.[35] Before we consider whether international law does permit such action, we must first address how the coercive methods in question may first seemingly fall foul of the general principle of non-intervention.

1.1. Coercion and 'Sanctions'

Because this chapter is concerned with 'coercive' measures short of force, it is first necessary to determine what types of action are included in this, and whether and how they could fall foul of the principle of non-intervention. These are methods short of force which undoubtedly have coercive effects, but their

[33] *Nicaragua* case (n 7) [205].
[34] ibid (emphasis added).
[35] Whether other rules of international law permit such coercive measures, and thus render those measures outside the scope of the domestic jurisdiction of a State, and therefore the principle of non-intervention, is discussed further below.

compatibility with non-intervention, or other rules of international law, seem at odds. Therefore, we must address the extent to which so-called 'economic coercion' is either prohibited or permitted in international law.

Some coercive methods might be justified on the basis that they form part of the sovereign discretion of a State taking those measures, such as domestic legislation or executive acts within the territory of that State. Actions falling into this category have been labelled acts of 'retorsion'. The International Law Commission has described such acts as '"unfriendly" conduct which is not inconsistent with any international obligation of the State engaging in it', which could be in response to an internationally wrongful act by another State.[36] Dawidowicz also highlights this distinction,[37] but notes the inherent problem that in the absence of adequate documentation, it may be difficult to assess whether or not a unilateral coercive measure taken by a State actually affects the rights of the target State so as to correctly categorise it as an act of retorsion or otherwise.[38] The ILC suggested that acts of retorsion 'may include the prohibition of or limitations upon normal diplomatic relations or other contacts, embargoes of various kinds or withdrawal of voluntary aid programmes'.[39]

Acts of retorsion, by definition, would fall outside the scope of this research. That is not to say such acts could not be 'coercive' in nature, such as the use of 'coercive' diplomacy. But this is where we must be careful with the language we use to describe such measures because, as we have seen above, 'influence' might be legitimate, but 'coercion' may not be permitted without legal justification.

1.1.1. Economic Coercion in Customary International Law

The use of 'sanctions' has been a source of controversy in international law, especially the use of 'unilateral sanctions'.[40] The *Declaration on Friendly Relations* did refer to the use of measures for coercion when it declared:

> No State may use or encourage the use of economic, political or any other type of measures to coerce another State in order to obtain from it the subordination of the exercise of its sovereign rights and to secure from it advantages of any kind.[41]

[36] See ILC, 'Draft Articles on Responsibility of States for Internationally Wrongful Acts, with Commentaries', 128, [3], http://legal.un.org/ilc/texts/instruments/english/commentaries/9_6_2001.pdf (accessed 31 July 2019); also included in ILC, 'Report of the International Law Commission on the Work of its Fifty-Third Session' (23 April–1 June and 2 July–10 August 2001) UN Doc A/56/10, reproduced in [2001] (Vol II, Part Two) *Yearbook of the International Law Commission*, 31ff.

[37] M Dawidowicz, 'Public Law Enforcement Without Public Law Safeguards? An Analysis of State Practice on Third-Party Countermeasures and their Relationship to the UN Security Council' (2006) 77 *British Yearbook of International Law* 333, 349.

[38] ibid.

[39] See ILC Articles on Responsibility of States (Commentaries) (n 36) 128, [3].

[40] 'Unilateral sanctions', for the purposes of this study, refers to the use of sanctions by States or an international organisation outside a multilateral framework such as the UN Security Council, or a Regional Treaty, where their use may be explained by the prior consent of the Member States.

[41] *Friendly Relations Declaration* (n 5) Principle 3, [2]; this was also reiterated in the *Declaration on the Inadmissibility of Intervention* (n 1) [2].

This part of the declaration was set out *within* the principle of non-intervention, and certainly seems to indicate that economic coercion would be prohibited within that principle. However, the declaration does seem to limit this to economic coercion that has the aim of subordinating the exercise of a State's sovereign rights, and securing advantages from that State.

Since these early declarations, economic coercion remained an issue of concern for States, especially against developing nations. For example, a similar general principle was adopted in Article 32 of the Charter of Economic Rights and Duties of States in 1974.[42] Subsequently, States regularly reiterated their rejection of unilateral coercive measures, and unilateral economic measures in particular, through the regular adoption of UN General Assembly Resolutions from as early as 1983.[43] These Resolutions regularly denounced the use of economic or political coercion against developing States.

From 1983, developed States such as the US, the UK, Australia, France, Italy, Norway and Japan consistently voted against these Resolutions.[44] By 1997, the US was alone in voting against the Resolutions when other developed nations switched to simply abstaining instead.[45] There were a small number of instances where other States would join the US in voting against the Resolutions, but these were not accompanied by any explanation of their votes in the General Assembly meetings.[46] By 2007, Israel joined the US in being the only two States that

[42] See Charter of Economic Rights and Duties of States, adopted in UNGA Res 3281 (XXIX) *Charter of Economic Rights and Duties of States* (12 December 1974) UN Doc A/RES/3281(XXIX) Annex.

[43] See UNGA Resolutions titled 'Economic Measures as a Means of Political and Economic Coercion against Developing Countries' (1983–96) or 'Unilateral Economic Measures as a Means of Political and Economic Coercion against Developing Countries' (1998–2017): UNGA Res 38/197 (20 December 1983) UN Doc A/RES/38/197; UNGA Res 39/210 (18 December 1984) UN Doc A/RES/39/210; UNGA Res 40/185 (17 December 1985) UN Doc A/RES/40/185; UNGA Res 41/165 (5 December 1986) UN Doc A/RES/41/165; UNGA Res 44/215 (22 December 1989) UN Doc A/RES/44/215; UNGA Res 46/210 (20 December 1991) UN Doc A/RES/46/210; UNGA Res 48/168 (22 February 1994) UN Doc A/RES/48/168; UNGA Res 50/96 (2 February 1996) UN Doc A/RES/50/96; UNGA Res 52/181 (4 February 1998) UN Doc A/RES/52/181; UNGA Res 54/200 (20 January 2000) UN Doc A/RES/54/200; UNGA Res 56/179 (24 January 2002) UN Doc A/RES/56/179; UNGA Res 58/198 (30 January 2004) UN Doc A/RES/58/198; UNGA Res 60/185 (31 January 2006) UN Doc A/RES/60/185; UNGA Res 62/183 (31 January 2008) UN Doc A/RES/62/183; UNGA Res 64/189 (9 February 2010) UN Doc A/RES/64/189; UNGA Res 66/186 (6 February 2012) UN Doc A/RES/66/186; UNGA Res 68/200 (15 January 2014) UN Doc A/RES/68/200; UNGA Res 70/185 (4 February 2016) UN Doc A/RES/70/185; UNGA Res 72/201 (17 January 2018) UN Doc A/RES/72/201.

[44] See, for example, voting records in UNGA Verbatim Record, 104th Plenary Meeting (20 December 1983) UN Doc A/38/PV.104 (OR) 1682; UNGA Verbatim Record, 119th Plenary Meeting (17 December 1985) UN Doc A/40/PV.119, 32; UNGA Verbatim Record, 98th Plenary Meeting (5 December 1986) UN Doc A/41/PV.98, 11.

[45] See UNGA Verbatim Record, 77th Plenary Meeting (18 December 1997) UN Doc A/52/PV.77, 7–8.

[46] For example, Germany and the Marshall Islands joined the US in 1999 in voting against, UNGA Verbatim Record, 87th Plenary Meeting (22 December 1999) UN Doc A/54/PV.87, 7; Uganda joined the US and Israel in 2009 in voting against, UNGA Verbatim Record, 66th Plenary Meeting (21 December 2009) UN Doc A/64/PV.66, 12.

consistently voted against the Resolutions, right up to the most recent instances in 2015 and 2017.[47]

Explanations of these votes were rare. At the first vote, the representative of the German Democratic Republic, on behalf of Eastern European States, argued that nothing could justify measures of economic coercion, that they were opposed to the UN Charter, the *Declaration on Friendly Relations*, and run counter to the norms and practices of international law.[48]

In 1999, Russia used the vote as an opportunity to condemn sanctions taken by the US and the EU against Yugoslavia.[49] Russia argued:

> The use of such economic measures, which are not sanctioned by the Security Council, and the imposition of compliance with them on third States – which is incompatible with the United Nations Charter and generally recognized principles of international law – contradict the basic principles of the system of multilateral trade and undermine the processes of settlement. They also seriously destabilize the situation in the Balkan region.[50]

Russia also stressed its position on the unacceptability of the unilateral use of economic measures 'aimed at a specific country that harm the economic interests of others'.[51] There was no counter to this from the States taking those measures at the time. Only in 2005[52] and 2007[53] did the US defend its voting position, rejecting the Resolutions, and arguing that 'every sovereign State has the right to decide with whom it will or will not trade'.[54] The US suggested that the resolution was 'aimed at undermining the international community's ability to respond effectively to acts that by their very nature and enormity are offensive to international norms'.[55] If there were no consequences for such actions, the US argued, offending States would have no incentive or reason to abandon them.[56] It was put that unilateral and multilateral economic sanctions 'can be an effective means to achieve legitimate foreign policy objectives' and that they 'constitute an influential diplomatic tool'.[57] In 2007, the US went even further to argue:

> Every State has the sovereign power to restrict or cut off trade or other commerce with particular nations when the State believes it is in its national economic or

[47] See UNGA Verbatim Record, 78th Plenary Meeting (19 December 2007) UN Doc A/62/PV.78, 10, for the first instance of Israel voting against; and see UNGA Verbatim Record, 81st Plenary Meeting (22 December 2015) UN Doc A/70/PV.81, 5–6; and UNGA Verbatim Record, 74th Plenary Meeting (20 December 2017) UN Doc A/72/PV.74, 10–11, for the most recent vote.

[48] UNGA Verbatim Record A/38/PV.104 (n 44) 1683, [26].

[49] UNGA Verbatim Record A/54/PV.87 (n 46) 8.

[50] ibid.

[51] ibid.

[52] UNGA Verbatim Record, 68th Plenary Meeting (22 December 2005) UN Doc A/60/PV.68, 7–8.

[53] UNGA Verbatim Record A/62/PV.78 (n 47) 11–12.

[54] UNGA Verbatim Record A/60/PV.68 (n 53) 7.

[55] ibid.

[56] ibid, 8.

[57] ibid.

> security interest to do so or when it serves values about which the nation feels strongly. The suggestion that there is any international legal prohibition against such a right is at best fatuous. That is why so many countries have abstained from supporting the resolution today.[58]

Although the US rejected the existence of a 'legal prohibition' to take 'legitimate' unilateral sanctions, the resolutions themselves only seemed to establish a general position that economic coercion was illegal when inconsistent with the UN Charter or a violation of another rule of international law. They are silent on the possibility of international law providing for a legal justification for such action, but crucially, they leave this door open.

The series of Resolutions were often accompanied by Reports of the Secretary-General on the matter, detailing individual States' concerns at the imposition of such measures by more developed States, most of which suggested that such measures were incompatible with international law or the UN Charter.[59] On a few occasions, however, the reports did address the legal position explicitly, some by reference to expert groups. In 1987, the report acknowledged that international law did not explicitly cover the issue of unilateral coercive economic measures at that time, and that there was no generally agreed interpretation when it came to discussions about the prohibition of force in Article 2(4) of the Charter possibly providing a basis for a prohibition of economic coercion.[60] In 1989, the Secretary-General attached a report by a panel of experts convened by the United Nations Conference on Trade and Development (UNCTAD),[61] which was clear in suggesting that international law lacked a clear consensus as to when such unilateral measures were improper.[62] By 1995, the legal issues were framed by focusing on the principles of non-intervention and non-discrimination, and the report concluded that the strict observation of these basic principles establishes a generally applicable rule prohibiting the application of coercive economic measures 'as instruments of intervention, including any attempts at an exterritorial application of coercive economic measures'.[63]

[58] UNGA Verbatim Record A/62/PV.78 (n 47) 11.

[59] See eg Report of the Secretary General, 'Adoption and Effects of Economic Measures Taken by Developed Countries as a Means of Political and Economic Coercion against Developing Countries' (1984) UN Doc A/39/415. See also Reports of the Secretary General, 'Economic Measures as a Means of Political and Economic Coercion against Developing Countries' (1986) UN Doc A/41/739; (1987) UN Doc A/42/660; (1989) UN Doc A/44/510; (1995) UN Doc A/50/439; (1997) UN Doc A/52/459. See also Reports of the Secretary General, 'Unilateral Economic Measures as a Means of Political and Economic Coercion against Developing Countries': (1999) UN Doc A/54/486; (2001) UN Doc A/56/473; (2003) UN Doc A/58/301; (2005) UN Doc A/60/226; (2007) UN Doc A/62/210; (2009) UN Doc A/64/179; (2011) UN Doc A/66/138; (2013) UN Doc A/68/218; (2015) UN Doc A/70/152; (2017) UN Doc A/72/307.

[60] Report of the Secretary General (1987) A/42/660 (n 59) 7, [23]–[24].

[61] Report of the Secretary General (1989) A/44/510 (n 59) Annex.

[62] ibid, 7, [4]. This conclusion was repeated in Note by the Secretary-General, 'Economic Measures as a Means of Political and Economic Coercion against Developing Countries' (25 October 1993) UN Doc A/48/535, [2].

[63] Report of the Secretary General (1995) A/50/439 (n 59) 13–14, [45].

The report did recognise, however, that there were evolving norms of international law that may allow for the legitimate use of such unilateral measures.[64]

Subsequently, the 1997 report considered it now 'generally accepted' that international law prohibits, as a general rule, 'the use by one State of economic coercion against another State', and also highlighted a number of allowable exceptions and circumstances that they labelled 'legitimacy indicators'.[65] This time, the report highlighted a lack of consensus and controversy surrounding the application of domestic measures which have extraterritorial effects.[66] In other words, there seemed to be growing concern about measures of 'retorsion', which are apparently within the internal sovereignty of a State, having potentially unlawful effects beyond that State's jurisdiction.[67]

Finally, 1999 was the final instance where the Secretary-General's Report made use of a panel of experts to explicitly address the legal position.[68] The experts largely reaffirmed the previous report, and this time seemed readier to accept the doctrine of countermeasures as an exception to the general rule, but did highlight some concern at certain measures which were being imposed against developing States, such as US legislation imposing measures against Cuba, Iran and Libya.[69]

Unfortunately, States' responses to these legal opinions, as detailed in these and subsequent Secretary-General Reports, did not explicitly address the legal exceptions outlined in any detail, if at all. Only recently did one State address the doctrine of countermeasures in this context, when Brazil disputed 'the interpretation that unilateral sanctions act as "countermeasures" to induce a State to end the infringement of certain norms of international law'.[70] In its contribution to the 2017 Report, the European Union countered the usual arguments against unilateral economic coercion by suggesting that 'the content of this question is misleading and that in future questionnaires, it could be formulated in a manner that is in line with international law'. The EU went on to suggest that:

> [I]n appropriate circumstances, targeted economic measures imposed in accordance with international law are a legitimate part of the Common Foreign and Security Policy of the European Union.
>
> Targeted economic measures may be used to seek to prevent activities in third countries, including proliferation of serious violations of human rights, which pose a threat to the security of the European Union and its member States.[71]

Separately from in the General Assembly, this repetitive rhetoric surrounding 'unilateral economic coercion' can also be seen where some large blocs of

[64] ibid, [46]–[47]; see also a discussion of the early work of the ILC on countermeasures at [29].
[65] Report of the Secretary General (1997) A/52/459 (n 59) 20, [72] and 21–22, [76]–[78].
[66] ibid, [72], [79]–[81].
[67] ibid, [79]–[81].
[68] Report of the Secretary General (1999) A/54/486 (n 59) 9–10, [48]–[50].
[69] ibid, see also s 2.
[70] Report of the Secretary General (2013) A/68/218 (n 59) 6 (Brazil).
[71] Report of the Secretary-General (2017) UN Doc A/72/307, 9.

States have declared 'unilateral sanctions', generally, to be illegal. For example, the Non-Aligned Movement has rejected, on multiple occasions, the use of 'unilateral coercive measures' or sanctions.

More recently, the Movement has been consistently referring to 'unilateral economic sanctions' as a measure which could 'undermine international law and international legal instruments'.[72] In this regard, the Movement undertook to 'refrain from recognising, adopting or implementing such measures' which 'seek to exert pressure on Non-Aligned Countries – threatening their sovereignty and independence, and their freedom of trade and investment – and prevent them from exercising their right to decide, by their own free will, their own political, economic and social systems'.[73] Importantly, this condemnation seems limited to 'where such measures or laws constitute flagrant violations of the UN Charter, international law, the multilateral trading system as well as the norms and principles governing friendly relations among States'. This was also the case in the Movement's separate declaration in 2016, where 'unilateral sanctions' were directly condemned, but particularly referred to as unilateral coercive measures 'in violation of the Charter of the United Nations and international law, particularly the principles of non-intervention, self-determination and independence of States subject of such practices'.[74]

The Movement also declared that such unilateral measures by a specific State or group for political and economic purposes 'violates the Charter of the United Nations and undermines international law and the rules of the World Trade Organization and also severely threatens freedom of trade and investment, and constitutes an interference in the internal affairs of other countries'.[75] This issue was also referred to within the context of human rights, when the Movement declared that the use of such unilateral coercive measures could 'hinder the well-being of populations of the affected countries and … create obstacles to the full realization of their human rights'.[76]

Earlier summits of the Non-Aligned Movement similarly declared their opposition to unilateral sanctions, but again these condemnations referred to such measures 'where such measures or laws constitute flagrant violations of the UN Charter, international law, the multilateral trading system as well as

[72] Non-Aligned movement, 'Final Outcome Document: Ministerial Meeting of the Coordinating Bureau of the Non-Aligned Movement' (20–21 July 2019, Caracas, Bolivarian Republic of Venezuela) Doc NAM 2019/CoB/Doc.1, https://mnoal.org/cobmm/Caracas%20Final%20Document%20(2019).pdf (accessed 31 July 2019) [30] and [30.4]; see also Non-Aligned Movement, 'Final Outcome Document: 17th Summit of Heads of State and Government of the Non-Aligned Movement' (17–18 September 2016, Island of Margarita, Venezuela) Doc NAM 2016/CoB/Doc.1. Corr.1, https://mnoal.com/docs/documents/NAM%20Margarita%20Declaration.pdf (accessed 31 July 2019) [21], [21.4].

[73] XVII NAM Final Outcome (n 72) [21.4].

[74] Non-Aligned Movement, 'Declaration of the XVII Summit of Heads of State and Government of the Non-Aligned Movement' (17–18 September 2016) Doc NAM2016/CoB/Doc.11, 4, [6].

[75] XVII NAM Final Outcome (n 72) [600].

[76] ibid, [750.2].

the norms and principles governing friendly relations among States',[77] or much simply referring to just those sanctions 'in contradiction with international law and the purposes and principles of the United Nations Charter'.[78]

Similarly, a recent joint declaration by Russia and China,[79] in the wake of the crises in Syria and Ukraine,[80] stated:

> The Russian Federation and the People's Republic of China share the view that good faith implementation of generally recognized principles and rules of international law excludes the practice of double standards or imposition by some States of their will on other States, and consider that imposition of unilateral coercive measures not based on international law, also known as 'unilateral sanctions', is an example of such practice. The adoption of unilateral coercive measures by States in addition to measures adopted by the United Nations Security Council can defeat the objects and purposes of measures imposed by the Security Council, and undermine their integrity and effectiveness.[81]

There are a few interesting points about this statement. Firstly, it does not categorically declare *every* imposition of unilateral sanctions illegal – it carefully refers to unilateral coercive measures 'not based on international law', but unhelpfully labels these as 'unilateral sanctions'. The latter part of the statement indeed does warn against the practical effects that sanctions taken beyond the UN Security Council might have on *existing* UN sanctions, but it does not clarify whether Russia and China view this practice as illegal.

Dupont[82] also highlights the widespread opposition to such unilateral measures, but also notes the concerns over the 'improper use' of measures of retorsion.[83] For example, Dupont refers to a position paper by China and the Group of 77 at the 13th United Nations Conference on Trade and Development.[84]

[77] Non-Aligned Movement, 'Declaration of the XVI Summit of Heads of State or Government of the Non-Aligned Movement' (30–31 August 2012, Tehran) Doc NAM 2012/Doc.7, 6, [8] (hereinafter 'the Tehran Declaration'); see also Non-Aligned Movement, 'Final Outcome Document: 16th Summit of Heads of State or Government of the Non-Aligned Movement' (26–31 August 2012, Tehran, Iran) Doc NAM 2012/Doc.1/Rev.2, [24.4], [468]; and Non-Aligned Movement, 'Final Outcome Document: XV Summit of Heads of State and Government of the Non-Aligned Movement' (16 July 2009) Doc NAM2009/FD/Doc.1, [18.4].

[78] See eg Non-Aligned Movement, 'Sharm El Sheikh Summit Declaration: 15th Summit Conference of Heads of State and Government of the Non-Aligned Movement' (15–16 July 2009, Sharm El Sheikh, Egypt) Doc NAM2009/SD/Doc.4, 3.

[79] Ministry of Foreign Affairs of the Russian Federation, 'The Declaration of the Russian Federation and the People's Republic of China on the Promotion of International Law' (25 June 2016) Press Release No 1202-25-06-2016, www.mid.ru/en/foreign_policy/news/-/asset_publisher/cKNonkJE02Bw/content/id/2331698/ (accessed 31 July 2019) (hereinafter 'the Russia–China Declaration').

[80] See below for sanctions in this context.

[81] Russia–China Declaration (n 79) [21].

[82] P-E Dupont, 'Countermeasures and Collective Security: The Case of the EU Sanctions Against Iran' (2012) 17(3) *Journal of Conflict & Security Law* 301.

[83] ibid, 316.

[84] ibid; see United Nations Conference on Trade and Development, 'Group of 77 and China Position Paper: Position Paper of the Group of 77 and China on the Draft Outcome Document for the Thirteenth Session of the United Nations Conference on Trade and Development (UNCTAD-XIII) Doha, Qatar', UNCTAD-XIII (Doha, 12–16 April 2012) (27 October 2011) UN Doc TD/455.

This joint paper called for a study into unilateral economic, financial or trade measures, contrary to international law and WTO rules. China and the Group of 77 considered such measures to 'hinder market access, investments, freedom of transit, and the welfare of the population of the affected countries',[85] and called upon the Conference to

> strongly urge States to refrain from enacting and implementing unilateral economic, financial or trade measures that are not in accordance with international law or the Charter of the United Nations and that hamper the full achievement of economic and social development as well as trade, particularly in developing countries.[86]

While Dupont highlights these calls as improper measures of 'retorsion', it is clear from the statements themselves that they are referring to measures which are illegal – and not necessarily those which are inherently lawful.

The Group of 77 and China's proposals were incorporated into the 'Doha Mandate',[87] where the Conference did urge States to refrain from 'promulgating and applying any unilateral economic, financial or trade measures not in accordance with international law and the Charter of the United Nations',[88] but also called for 'addressing' non-tariff measures including unilateral measures 'where they may act as unnecessary trade barriers'.[89] While this does not disallow measures usually considered retorsion, as addressed by Dupont, it does certainly highlight a hesitance over the imposition of certain legal measures that may have negative practical effects on trade.

However, a clear divide seems to have emerged at the UNCTAD conference in 2016. The 'zero document' of that conference, which was the starting point for negotiating the final outcome, did incorporate these previous sentiments urging States to refrain from unilateral coercive measures contrary to international law.[90] This was later revised to strengthen the negotiating text, adding references to the most recent UN General Assembly Resolution[91] and also condemning the effect of such unilateral measures as having 'a destabilizing effect on the global economy' and highlighting that they 'artificially create dividing lines in the sphere of international economic relations and are a means of unfair competition on the world market'.[92] However, these references to the General Assembly Resolution and the stronger language were deleted from the final text, which

[85] 'Group of 77 and China Position Paper' (n 84) [45].

[86] ibid.

[87] United Nations Conference on Trade and Development, 'The Doha Mandate', UNCTAD-XIII (Doha, 21–26 April 2012) (31 May 2012) UN Doc TD/500/Add.1.

[88] ibid, para [25].

[89] ibid, [25].

[90] United Nations Conference on Trade and Development, 'Pre-Conference Negotiating Text', UNCTAD-XIV (Geneva, 12 February 2016) UN Doc TD/XIV/PC/1, [31].

[91] UNGA Res 70/185 (n 43).

[92] United Nations Conference on Trade and Development, 'Pre-Conference Negotiating Text, Revised', UNCTAD-XIV (Geneva, 13 June 2016) (16 June 2016) UN Doc TD(XIV)/PC/1/Rev.1, [50].

merely settled for a version nearly identical to that adopted in the previous Doha Mandate.[93]

The Group of 77 and China again issued a declaration in this context,[94] but this time their language was much stronger than their previous Position Paper:

> We stress that unilateral coercive measures and legislation are contrary to international law, international humanitarian law, the United Nations Charter, the norms and principles governing peaceful relations among States and the rules and principles of the World Trade Organization. These measures impede the full achievement and further enhancement of the economic and social development of all countries, particularly developing countries, by imposing unconscionable hardships on the people of the affected countries.[95]

Here, the declaration is unequivocal in establishing that unilateral coercive measures, in their view, are contrary to international law *from the outset*. This time, there is no restriction of their condemnation to *only* measures that are illegal – instead, the position seems to be that *all* unilateral coercive measures are illegal *generally*.

The declaration also firmly rejected 'the imposition of laws and regulations with extraterritorial impact and all other forms of coercive economic, financial and trade measures, including unilateral sanctions against developing countries'.[96] While this clearly expresses opposition to what Dupont categorised as measures of retorsion, it does not express an opinion on whether such measures are, or should be, contrary to international law. Yet, the earlier references to 'legislation' being contrary to international law, are possibly a nod towards this.

Taking all of this evidence collectively, these statements, coupled with the resolutions of the General Assembly, are not incorrect. However, they are certainly misleading. Unilateral sanctions, *without justification*, seem to be illegal in general terms – but this depends on the 'sanction' imposed.[97] Indeed, all of these statements might even be taken as supporting a general principle that 'sanctions' are prima facie unlawful because they interfere with the principle of non-intervention, constitute economic coercion, or otherwise, in the absence of a legal justification. Yet, they do not necessarily shed light on whether they consider there to be any legal justifications for their use – they simply do not

[93] United Nations Conference on Trade and Development, 'Nairobi Maafikiano – From Decision to Action: Moving Towards an Inclusive and Equitable Global Economic Environment for Trade and Development', UNCTAD-XIV (Nairobi, 17–22 July 2016) (5 September 2016) UN Doc TD/519/Add.2, [34].

[94] United Nations Conference on Trade and Development, 'Ministerial Declaration of the Group of 77 and China to UNCTAD XIV', UNCTAD-XIV (Nairobi, 17–22 July) (12 July 2016) UN Doc TD/507.

[95] Group of 77 and China Ministerial Declaration (n 94) [16].

[96] ibid, [39].

[97] For a similar analysis, see DH Joyner, 'International Legal Limits on the Ability of States to Lawfully Impose International Economic/Financial Sanctions' in N Ronzitti (ed), *Coercive Diplomacy, Sanctions and International Law* (Leiden, Brill Nijhoff, 2016) 194–99.

touch upon this issue. What is clear, however, is the fact that 'unilateral sanctions' are indeed likely to fall foul of the principle of non-intervention, or the corollary of this principle prohibiting economic coercion.[98]

Carter has argued that 'economic sanctions themselves are rarely, if ever, unlawful',[99] and rejects that a rule of customary international law has emerged prohibiting economic coercion, noting the efforts of developing and non-aligned States in the General Assembly and elsewhere, but considering that they have been unsuccessful in establishing a general rule prohibiting economic *sanctions*.[100] To support this, Carter cites the ICJ's decision in the *Nicaragua* case, where the court addressed certain economic measures by the US against Nicaragua, concluding quite simply that: '[T]he Court has merely to say that it is unable to regard such action on the economic plane as a breach of the customary-law principle of non-intervention.'[101] Carter also refers to the 1993 Note by the UN Secretary-General,[102] part of the series of Reports and expert conclusions discussed above, which concluded that: '[T]here is no clear consensus in international law as to when coercive measures are improper, despite relevant treaties, declarations, and resolutions adopted in international organizations which try to develop norms limiting the use of these measures.'[103]

Carter's conclusions are slightly misleading here. The ICJ did consider the US's action as compatible with the principle of non-intervention, but this can be explained on the basis that those measures were merely methods of retorsion and did not constitute prohibited economic coercion. Nicaragua had argued that the US's cessation of economic aid and 90 per cent reduction in the sugar quota for US imports from Nicaragua, and a trade embargo, were 'indirect' interventions in the internal affairs of Nicaragua.[104] The ICJ admitted it did not have jurisdiction over questions of the compatibility of the trade measures with multilateral treaties, due to the US's multilateral treaty reservation in that case.[105] However, the measures Nicaragua complained about in the first place were measures within the US's jurisdiction – measures which counsel for Nicaragua had admitted were not unlawful in themselves.[106]

Therefore, the ICJ's rejection of Nicaragua's argument cannot be interpreted as a rejection of the existence of a prohibition of economic coercion, or that economic coercion does not fall within the principle of non-intervention – such an assertion would go directly against the widely accepted *Declaration on*

[98] Although see A Tzanakopoulos, 'The Right To Be Free from Economic Coercion' (2015) 4(3) *Cambridge Journal of International and Comparative Law* 616.

[99] BE Carter, 'Economic Sanctions' in *Max Planck Encyclopedia of Public International Law* (online edn, April 2011) [32].

[100] ibid, [29]–[32].

[101] *Nicaragua* case (n 7) [244].

[102] Note by the Secretary General (1993) A/48/535 (n 62).

[103] Carter (n 99) [30]; see also Note by the Secretary General (1993) A/48/535 (n 62) [2].

[104] *Nicaragua* case (n 7) [244].

[105] ibid, [245].

[106] ibid, [244].

Friendly Relations itself. The only inference we may confidently draw from that case is that the measures adopted by the US were either not 'interventions', or if they were then they were not interventions in the 'domestic jurisdiction' of Nicaragua.

In terms of Carter's reference to the 1993 Note of the Secretary-General, unfortunately this point omits the subsequent reports in this series which eventually noted that it was 'generally accepted' that a rule prohibiting economic coercion existed in international law.[107] While it is true that there is no general rule prohibiting 'economic *sanctions*' specifically, there can be no doubt that there is a prohibition of 'economic coercion' by virtue of the principle of non-intervention. The legality of economic sanctions, as widely addressed in the series of expert reports for the Secretary-General on this issue, is based upon the *exceptions* to that general rule. The question is, therefore: what 'economic sanctions' constitute unlawful 'economic coercion', and *then* when do such coercive measures find justification in international law?

Of course, the law is more nuanced than this general rule, and indeed not all 'sanctions' would fall within this general prohibition of intervention. And so, before we consider what circumstances render the taking of sanctions lawful in international law, the next section will outline the specific types of coercive action at issue. These include: asset freezes; travel bans; trade embargos or restrictions; and the suspension of international agreements.

1.2. Methods of Coercion

1.2.1. Asset Freezes

Asset freezes involve the blocking of any use or disposition of assets, including financial assets such as bank accounts. These are typically targeted at officials of State who have assets within the jurisdiction of a State taking 'coercive' measures, but can sometimes target assets specifically owned by the target State itself. At first glance, it may seem that asset freezes, taking place within the jurisdiction a State taking such measures, are inherently lawful by virtue of the sovereign discretion of that State, so long as the freezes are consistent with the internal laws of that State.

However, it has been argued that asset freezes, because they can target assets belonging to another State, generally fall foul of the principle of non-intervention. For example, Criddle[108] argues that the freezing of foreign assets by a State constitutes a form of intervention.[109] He suggests that these

[107] See eg Report of the Secretary General (1997) A/52/459 (n 59) 20, [72] and 21–22, [76]–[78].
[108] EJ Criddle, 'Humanitarian Financial Intervention' (2013) 24(2) *European Journal of International Law* 583.
[109] ibid, 584.

measures purposefully interfere in the domestic affairs of a target State, undermining their political independence and 'transgressing legal protections for the fair and equitable treatment of foreign investment'.[110] Accordingly, the fact that a State may operate exclusively within its own territorial jurisdiction when it freezes foreign assets 'does not absolve it of international responsibility because the purpose and effect of its actions are transparently interventionist: to subordinate a foreign state and its assets to the host state's superintendent power'.[111]

Criddle tried to draw a distinction between acts of retorsion and acts of 'wrongful intervention', utilising his 'wrongful means theory' to suggest that only acts that are prima facie wrongful under international law constitute wrongful intervention.[112] His theory proposes that asset freezes constitute a form of wrongful expropriation, falling foul of the principle of non-intervention, because they fall foul of the 'international minimum standard' of 'fair and equitable treatment' in international investment law.[113] For this, Criddle is referring to a possible customary international law obligation that he says includes respect for due process (eg access to justice, non-arbitrariness) and good faith (eg consistency, transparency, non-arbitrariness, respecting reasonable expectations).[114]

While it is unclear whether such legal standards derive from the principle of non-intervention itself, it cannot be denied that similar standards have been recognised in international agreements, meaning that these obligations may well exist separately to the principle of non-intervention too. For example, Bothe argues[115] that restrictions on money transfers fall within the regulatory regime of the International Monetary Fund (IMF),[116] and when relating to financial services may fall within the General Agreement on Trade in Services (GATS).[117]

In particular, Article VIII(2)(a) of the IMF agreement prohibits Members from imposing 'restrictions on the making of payments and transfers for current international transactions' without IMF approval. In 1952, the IMF clarified that: 'Article VIII, Section 2(a), in conformity with its language, applies to all restrictions on current payments and transfers, irrespective of their motivation and the circumstances in which they are imposed.'[118] Article VIII(3) also stipulates that Members shall not engage in 'any discriminatory currency arrangements'

[110] ibid. Criddle calls this 'humanitarian financial intervention' when the measures are used 'to promote cosmopolitan humanitarian values abroad'.

[111] ibid, 591–92.

[112] ibid, 592.

[113] ibid.

[114] ibid.

[115] M Bothe, 'Compatibility and Legitimacy of Sanctions Regimes' in Ronzitti (n 97) 37.

[116] Articles of Agreement of the International Monetary Fund 1944 (adopted 22 July 1944, entered into force 27 December 1945) 2 UNTS 39, as amended.

[117] General Agreement on Trade in Services (GATS) (adopted 15 April 1994, entered into force 1 January 1995) 1869 UNTS 183.

[118] IMF Decision No 144-(52/51) (14 August 1952) available in IMF, *Selected Decisions and Selected Document of the International Monetary Fund* (Thirty-Eighth Issue, Washington, DC, 29 February 2016) 573–74.

except as authorised by the IMF or in particular cases stipulated by the Agreements. Bothe notes that no practice seems to have arisen where the IMF has allowed such action.[119]

In terms of the GATS framework, Article II provides for the 'Most-Favoured-Nation Treatment' whereby Members shall accord to services and service suppliers of any other Member treatment no less favourable than that it accords any other country. On the face of it, it does indeed seem that financial measures such as asset freezes could fall foul of this general principle.

These provisions do seem to provide a sound basis for suggesting that financial restrictions such as asset freezes, if they do not in the circumstances violate the general principle of non-intervention, then they may still violate these popular agreements. Of course, not all States may be members of the IMF or the WTO, but at the same time it is not possible to provide an exhaustive account of all bilateral agreements providing for similar trade or investment rights. Depending on the circumstances of a dispute, these types of financial measures are likely to fall foul of such obligations owed by one State to another. In any case, there is still a convincing possibility that they may constitute economic coercion and thus fall foul of the principle of non-intervention.

1.2.2. Travel Bans

Travel bans are decisions on allowing or disallowing persons to enter the territory of the State imposing restrictive measures. Often, this can affect the ability of target-State officials to conduct business within the territory of that State, or even to attend international political events that are held within that territory, making diplomacy and international affairs more difficult for the target State. Generally, these may be acts of retorsion – as Bothe points out,[120] there is a human right to leave a country,[121] but there is no corresponding right to enter a country other than in the case of the non-refoulment of refugees, or perhaps even the right of return for refugees.[122]

Nevertheless, on occasion, such bans may fall foul of an international agreement or treaty which, for example, calls for States to allow each other's officials into the other's territory for the purposes of a cooperation agreement. Recently, for example, when the US took restrictive measures against Russia following

[119] Bothe (n 115) 37.

[120] Bothe (n 115) 39.

[121] International Covenant on Civil and Political Rights 1966 (adopted 15 December 1966, entered into force 23 March 1976), 999 UNTS 171, available in UNGA Res 2200 (XXI) *International Covenant on Economic, Social and Cultural Rights, International Covenant on Civil and Political Rights and Optional Protocol to the International Covenant on Civil and Political Rights* (16 December 1966) UN Doc A/RES/2200(XXI) Annex, Art 12(2).

[122] Bothe (n 115) 39; see also The Convention Against Torture and Other Cruel, Inhuman or Degrading Treatment or Punishment (adopted 10 December 1984, entered into force 26 June 1987) 1465 UNTS 85, Art 3.

the events in Ukraine, Russia argued[123] that the cancellation of events and bilateral meetings related to nuclear energy was a violation of Article IV(3) and Article X(1) of the Agreement between the Government of the United States of America and the Government of the Russian Federation on Cooperation in Nuclear- and Energy-Related Scientific Research and Development.[124] It is unclear whether individuals who would have attended such meetings were subject to the travel bans imposed by the US.

Nevertheless, it is clear that some bilateral agreements such as this could well provide a basis for suggesting that travel bans may in certain circumstances fall foul of international obligations,[125] but each restriction can only be judged on a case-by-case basis depending on the bilateral or multilateral agreements agreed upon by the States involved.

1.2.3. Trade Restrictions or Embargos

Trade restrictions or embargos on imports or exports are often used as 'sanctions' to coerce another State into changing a particular course of action. Bothe argues that there is no general rule of customary international law forbidding trade restrictions, and nor is there any general right to 'commercial intercourse'.[126] Similarly, the ICJ in *Nicaragua* opined that a trade embargo does not necessarily fall foul of the principle of non-intervention,[127] and that a State 'is not bound to continue trade relations longer than it sees fit to do so, in the absence of a treaty commitment or other specific legal obligation'.[128]

However, States have increasingly agreed to principles relating to trade. The General Agreement on Trade and Tariffs (GATT),[129] and the GATS,[130] alongside the creation of the World Trade Organization (WTO), establish a number of general principles of world trade that, on the face of it, may seem to be violated by the imposition of certain trade restrictions or embargos. Bothe suggests

[123] Government Decision, 'Suspending the Russian–US Agreement on Cooperation in Nuclear- and Energy-Related Scientific Research and Development' (5 October 2016) http://government.ru/en/docs/24766/ (accessed 31 July 2019).

[124] Agreement between the Government of the United States of America and the Government of the Russian Federation on Cooperation in Nuclear- and Energy-Related Scientific Research and Development (adopted 16 September 2013, entered into force 24 January 2014) TIAS 14-124.

[125] Bothe (n 115) 39.

[126] ibid, 35; for a similar point, see Carter (n 99) [29]–[32], who is of the view that a rule prohibiting economic coercion generally has not emerged despite the regular attempts by the blocs of nations, as outlined above.

[127] *Nicaragua* case (n 7) [244]–[245].

[128] ibid, [276]; see also Tzanakopoulos (n 98) 626.

[129] General Agreement on Tariffs and Trade 1947 (GATT 1947) (adopted 30 October 1947, entered into force 1 January 1948), 55 UNTS 187, amended by the Marrakech Agreement Establishing the World Trade Organization (adopted 15 April 1994, entered into force 1 January 1995), 1867 UNTS 154, and the General Agreement on Tariffs and Trade 1994 (GATT 1994) (adopted 15 April 1994, entered into force 1 January 1995) 1867 UNTS 187; provisions of the GATT 1947, as incorporated by GATT 1994, hereinafter simply referred to as 'GATT'.

[130] GATS (n 117).

that more than 90 per cent of international merchandise trade is covered by the GATT regime.[131]

Article I of GATT provides for the Most-Favoured-Nation rule, reflecting that discussed above in the GATS regime, instead essentially providing that contracting parties should afford all other contracting parties the same favourable treatment or terms on imports and exports. Any 'sanction' which restricts or bans such trade would be a very clear prima facie breach of this provision, since a State being sanctioned is very clearly being treated less favourably than other contracting parties. Trade restrictions and bans could also fall foul of Article XI(1), which provides that:

> No prohibitions or restrictions other than duties, taxes or other charges, whether made effective through quotas, import or export licences or other measures, shall be instituted or maintained by any contracting party on the importation of any product of the territory of any other contracting party or on the exportation or sale for export of any product destined for the territory of any other contracting party.

While it was suggested by the ICJ in *Nicaragua* that measures such as a trade embargo did not, at that point, violate the principle of non-intervention, it was unable to pronounce on the application of GATT to those measures due to a lack of jurisdiction. The Court did, however, decide that the trade embargo imposed by the US was contrary to the object and purpose of the US–Nicaragua Treaty of Friendship, Commerce and Navigation 1956,[132] and in particular violated Article XIX on that agreement on the equal treatment of commercial vessels in both States.[133] This of course indicates that even if a State is not a member of the WTO or GATT, certain trade measures could still be inconsistent with bilateral agreements adopted between the target State and the State imposing restrictive measures.

Without seeking to settle the issue as to whether trade embargos constitute economic coercion or unlawful intervention on the face of it, it is also clear that States taking such measures against another State when they are both members of the WTO and GATT would be a prima facie breach of these obligations.

1.2.4. Intentional Suspension of Treaty Obligations

In certain circumstances, States may suspend the application of an international agreement between itself and a target State to impose certain coercive measures – or sometimes as a coercive measure itself. This type of action may by justified via Article 60 of the VCLT,[134] which allows agreements to be suspended

[131] Bothe (n 115) 35.

[132] Treaty of Friendship, Commerce and Navigation between the United States of America and the Republic of Nicaragua (adopted 21 January 1956, entered into force 24 May 1958) 367 UNTS 3.

[133] *Nicaragua* case (n 7) [279]–[280], [282].

[134] Vienna Convention on the Law of Treaties, (adopted 23rd May 1969, entered into force 27th January 1980) 1155 UNTS 331, Art 60.

or terminated but only where there is a 'material breach' of that treaty.[135] Such a material breach requires either: (i) a repudiation of the treaty not sanctioned by the present Convention; or (ii) the violation of a provision essential to the accomplishment of the object or purpose of the treaty.[136]

However, the suspension of an international agreement may take place *without* there actually being a material breach of that agreement by the target State in the first place. For example, an agreement might be suspended by an imposing State in retaliation for the breach of a separate obligation by the target State.[137] This type of action would fall outside of the scope of Article 60 VCLT, and may only be justified by legal justifications elsewhere in general international law, in particular the doctrine of countermeasures in certain circumstances, as will be discussed below.[138]

Indeed, when it comes to measures taken in response to the threat or commission of mass atrocities under the responsibility to protect, States may not necessarily suspend the treaties that provide for some of those obligations, such as regional human rights instruments, or even the Genocide Convention.[139] Such a suspension would likely have little to no effect on coercing the State responsible – firstly, the target State would have already breached that instrument itself; and, secondly, such treaty obligations do not provide many, if any, direct political or economic advantages to that State which would compel a State in breach of such obligations to cease their course of action in favour of protecting those benefits. For example, the ICJ recognised the absence of such individual advantages and disadvantages in the Genocide Convention in its Advisory Opinion[140] on reservations to that treaty:

> In such a convention the contracting States do not have any interests of their own; they merely have, one and all, a common interest, namely the accomplishment of those high purposes which are the *raison d'être* of the convention. Consequently, in a convention of this type *one cannot speak of individual advantages and disadvantages to States*, or of the maintenance of a perfect contractual balance between rights and duties. The high ideals which inspired the Convention provide, by virtue of the common will of the parties, the foundation and measure of all its provisions.[141]

[135] ibid, Art 60(1) and (3).

[136] ibid.

[137] This was seemingly the case when the EU suspended its cooperation agreement with Syria, as discussed below, section 2.2.3.

[138] For the difference between suspension and the 'breach' of an obligation via countermeasures, see ILC Articles on Responsibility of States (Commentaries) (n 36) 128, [4].

[139] Convention on the Prevention and Punishment of the Crime of Genocide 1948 (adopted 9 December 1948, entered into force 12 January 1951) 78 UNTS 277 (hereinafter referred to as 'the Genocide Convention'); even then, such suspensions, according to Art 60(5) VCLT, 'do not apply to provisions relating to the protection of the human person contained in treaties of a humanitarian character'.

[140] *Reservations to the Convention on the Prevention and Punishment of the Crime of Genocide* (Advisory Opinion of 28 May 1951) [1951] ICJ Rep 15.

[141] ibid, 23 (emphasis added).

Coercive measures have focused on *economic* or *trade* matters, and treaties protecting populations from atrocities do not themselves provide these economic rights or duties that have been used as tools to pressure other States. Therefore, if a State does decide to suspend or 'violate' a treaty obligation to coerce another, it would not necessarily suspend the treaties relevant to the breach in the first place, and so such a suspension would not fall within Article 60 VCLT.

1.3. Legal Justifications

Legal justifications available for the taking of coercive measures depend upon the measures imposed, and the international agreements between the disputing States. In terms of the collective security framework, such measures may be taken by Member States of the UN when this action is authorised or imposed by the Security Council under Article 41 of the UN Charter.[142] In other cases, measures may be permissible by an agreement between the States themselves, perhaps as part of an agreement between Member States of a regional organisation.[143] However, such regional instruments would not apply when the regional organisation seeks to take coercive measures against a non-member, for example. Therefore, it is worth highlighting in brief the possible legal justifications for truly 'unilateral' coercive measures before embarking on an analysis of the law of countermeasures.

1.3.1. WTO/GATT Security Exceptions

In terms of restrictive trade measures, for WTO and GATT Members the security exceptions in Article XXI of GATT permit a Member 'to take any action which it considers necessary for the protection of its essential security interests'[144] which either: (i) relates to fissionable materials or the materials from which they are derived;[145] (ii) relates to arms, ammunitions and related trade for supplying a military establishment;[146] or (iii) is 'taken in time of war or other emergency in international relations'.[147] More generally, GATT also excludes 'any action in pursuance of its obligations under the United Nations Charter for the maintenance of international peace and security'.[148] Article XIV*bis* of GATS provides for largely the same security exceptions in relation to services,

[142] See also N Ronzitti, 'Sanctions as Instruments of Coercive Diplomacy: An International Law Perspective' in Ronzitti (n 97) 15–16; see also, Thomas and Thomas (n 23) 205–07.
[143] See Chapter VI, section 2.3.1. See also Ronzitti (n 142) 16–17; Thomas and Thomas (n 23) 210–12 on the Organization of American States.
[144] GATT, Art XXI(b).
[145] ibid, Art XXI(b)(i).
[146] ibid, Art XXI(b)(ii).
[147] ibid, Art XXI(b)(iii).
[148] ibid, Art XXI(c).

except for a requirement that the Council for Trade in Services must be informed of such measures when taken and terminated.[149]

Most relevant to our debate relating to the prevention and cessation of mass atrocities, measures taken 'in time of war or other emergency in international relations' seems to be the most appropriate fit. However, this must still be action which the State 'considers necessary' for the protection of *its own* 'essential security interests'. The first concern here is that action taken to protect populations of *other States* may not always be necessary to protect the national security interests of the State taking such measures. Secondly, it is important to understand what the provision means by 'necessary' action, and what standard must be applied to this.

Neuwirth and Svetlicinii[150] highlight the fact that these provisions refer to actions Members 'consider necessary', and rightly question whether this provides for a *self-judging* test.[151] They raise the ICJ's decisions in *Nicaragua* and *Oil Platforms*,[152] where bilateral agreements provided for similar exceptions that allowed parties to take measures 'necessary' to protect the essential security interests of the State concerned.[153] In *Nicaragua*, the ICJ noted that there was a difference in the wordings of Article XXI of GATT and Article XXI(1)(d) of the bilateral agreement between the US and Nicaragua, where GATT referred to action which a party 'considers necessary' for its national security, whereas the 1956 US–Nicaragua Treaty referred simply to 'necessary' measures and not those 'considered' by a party as such.[154] It was on this basis that the Court considered itself to have jurisdiction over determining the nature of the measures it was considering.[155] The Court then also considered what affect this construction would have on the substantive interpretation of that provision; it made clear that because it used the word 'necessary' instead of the phrase 'considers necessary', the assessment was not 'purely a question for the subjective judgment of the party'.[156] In *Oil Platforms*, the Court made the same assessment relating to

[149] GATS, Art XIV*bis* (2); but see in relation to GATT Art XXI: GATT Council, *Decision Concerning Art XXI of the General Agreement* (2 December 1982) L/5426, which suggested that 'contracting parties should be informed to the fullest extent possible of trade measures taken under Article XXI'.

[150] R Neuwirth and A Svetlicinii, 'The Economic Sanctions over the Ukraine Conflict and the WTO: "Catch-XXI" and the Revival of the Debate on Security Exceptions' (2015) 49(5) *Journal of World Trade* 891.

[151] ibid, 903–08 generally.

[152] *Case Concerning Oil Platforms* (*Islamic Republic of Iran v United States of America*) (Judgment) [2003] ICJ Rep 161.

[153] In *Nicaragua*, it has been detailed above that this related to the Treaty of Friendship, Commerce and Navigation (n 132) Art XXI(1)(d); in *Oil Platforms*, this related to the Treaty of Amity, Economic Relations and Consular Rights 1955 (adopted 15 August 1955, entered into force 16 June 1957) 284 UNTS 93, Art XX(1)(d); see Neuwirth and Svetlicinii (n 150) 906.

[154] *Nicaragua* case (n 7) [222].

[155] ibid, [222]–[223].

[156] ibid, [282].

Article XX of the Iran–US bilateral agreement, and cited this as the reason why the necessity of the measures therein could be assessed by the Court.[157]

Although the ICJ did not pronounce on the interpretation of the corresponding GATT or GATS provisions, its judgments might be utilised by those arguing that those provisions are self-judging because of the remarks by the ICJ on the phrase 'considers necessary'. However, Neuwirth and Svetlicinii highlight the very real possibility that, if this exception was self-judging, the risks of abuse of these provisions is very real.[158] Even so, they point out that the self-judging nature of these provisions had never been expressly confirmed by a WTO Panel or even previously under the 1947 GATT dispute settlement system, until very recently.[159] When the US's measures against Nicaragua were reviewed within the previous GATT framework, although the US excluded an examination of its reliance on Article XXI from the terms of reference of the Panel, the Panel did raise concerns about the possible self-judging interpretation of the provision, questioning how such an interpretation could ensure that it is not invoked excessively or for purposes other than those set out in the provision itself.[160]

But the law became a little clearer in 2019, when a WTO Panel ruled on a dispute between Russia and Ukraine.[161] In this dispute, Ukraine complained to the WTO about Russian restrictions on rail and road transit routes across the Ukraine–Russia border for specific goods destined for other States and territories including Kazakhstan, the Kyrgyz Republic, Mongolia, Tajikistan, Turkmenistan, Uzbekistan, and Belarus.[162] Russia invoked Article XXI(b)(iii) of the GATT 1994, arguing that the measures were those that Russia considers necessary for the protection of its essential security interests, which Russia took '[i]n response to the emergency in international relations that occurred in 2014 that presented threats to the Russian Federation's essential security interests'.[163] Russia argument was that 'the explicit wording of Article XXI confers sole discretion on the Member invoking this Article to determine the necessity, form, design, and structure of the measures taken pursuant to Article XXI'.[164] Accordingly, Russia argued, the Panel lacked jurisdiction to address the matter.[165]

[157] *Oil Platforms* (n 152) [43].

[158] Neuwirth and Svetlicinii (n 150) 904–06.

[159] ibid, 906. For the recent decision at the WTO, see below n 161 and accompanying text.

[160] *United States – Trade Measures Affecting Nicaragua* (13 October 1986) L/6053, [5.17], www.wto.org/gatt_docs/English/SULPDF/91240197.pdf (accessed 31 July 2019).

[161] *Russia – Measures Concerning Traffic in Transit* (5 April 2019) WT/DS512/R (Panel Report), www.wto.org/english/tratop_e/dispu_e/512r_e.pdf (accessed 31 July 2019).

[162] ibid, [7.1.a]–[7.1.d].

[163] ibid, para [7.4]. This 'emergency' is a reference to Russia's intervention in Ukraine and annexation of Crimea, and the tensions between the two States following these incidents; see also ibid, [7.27], [7.112], [7.115]–[7.126].

[164] ibid, [7.28].

[165] Ibid, [7.4], [7.28] and [7.57].

The Panel made several important conclusions. On whether Article XXI(b) is self-judging, the Panel took a relatively nuanced approach. The Panel conceded that Article XXI(b) 'qualifies action that a Member may not be prevented from taking as that "which [the Member] considers necessary for the protection of its essential security interests"'.[166] To the Panel, the phrase 'which it considers' indicates the existence of some form of discretion afforded to WTO Members deciding to take the measures in question.[167] This discretion, however, is not unlimited to make the provision totally self-judging.[168]

On the question as to whether a measure was 'necessary for the protection of its essential security interests', it was down to WTO Members to define what its own 'essential security interests' are.[169] But the Panel was careful to highlight that this still does not grant an unlimited discretion to Members to take security measures as it sees fit. In particular, the Panel said that any judgment by a State of its 'essential security interests' is still subject to the overarching obligation of good faith.[170] In other words, a State cannot in bad faith term anything and everything an essential security interest, and therefore a Member is *not* 'free to elevate any concern to that of an "essential security interest"'.[171] Furthermore, a member must 'articulate the essential security interests said to arise from the emergency in international relations sufficiently enough to demonstrate their veracity'.[172] In this regard, a 'sufficient level of articulation' implies that the Member's assertions cannot be 'obscure or indeterminate'.[173] Linked to this, the Panel also said that the obligation of good faith also applies to the connection between the Member's purported security interests and the measures adopted by a Member to protect them. In other words, Article XXI(b) requires that 'the measures at issue meet a minimum requirement of plausibility in relation to the proffered essential security interests, ie that they are not implausible as measures protective of these interests'.[174]

On the question as to what measures are 'necessary' to protect a Member's essential security interests, the Panel said that it is for the Member to decide this question too,[175] because there is no conditioning or qualification of this discretion in the wording of Article XXI(b),[176] and such a reading is purportedly confirmed by the negotiating history of the provision.[177]

[166] ibid, [7.62], brackets in original.
[167] ibid, [7.63]–[7.65].
[168] ibid, [7.102].
[169] ibid, [7.130]–[7.131].
[170] ibid, [7.132]–[7.133].
[171] ibid, [7.132].
[172] ibid, [7.134]–[7.135].
[173] ibid, [7.136].
[174] ibid, [7.138].
[175] ibid, [7.146].
[176] ibid, [7.146]–[7.147]
[177] ibid, s 7.5.3.1.2, and [7.92].

Importantly, there are further limitations to this discretion under Article XXI. Firstly, those measures may only be taken in the three scenarios outlined in Article XXI(b)(i)–(iii) – to repeat they are where a situation: (i) relates to fissionable materials or the materials from which they are derived;[178] (ii) relates to arms, ammunitions and related trade for supplying a military establishment;[179] or (iii) is taken in time of war or other emergency in international relations.[180] To the Panel, these circumstances may be objectively determined and it is therefore for the WTO Panel to conclude on whether they apply.[181] In other words, '[F]or action to fall within the scope of Article XXI(b), it must objectively be found to meet the requirements in one of the enumerated subparagraphs of that provision.'[182]

In light of the above, while some measures taken in response to mass atrocities, under a tertiary responsibility to protect, may fit with the exceptions under Article XXI(b), this may not always be the case. Not all sanctions or coercive measures will fall within the conditions of Article XXI(b)(i)–(iii), particularly the Article XXI(b)(iii) scenario where the measures are 'taken in time of war or other emergency in international relations' to protect that State's own security interests. Firstly, measures taken in order to coerce a target State to halt or avoid atrocity crimes may not be intended to protect the adopting State's own security interest, but to coerce the target State into taking an alternative course of action. The commission of atrocity crimes themselves may well threaten international peace and security, and so it could be argued that their prevention is an 'essential security interest' of the State taking the measures, but it is unclear as to whether this would apply so easily. Furthermore, as outlined above, the WTO Panel was clear that there had to be some connection between the measures taken and the protection of the security interest of the State, but collective measures to uphold or implement the responsibility to protect may not always be aimed at protecting a State's own interests directly, but instead be based on securing accountability, the cessation of hostilities, or any other collective strategic interests. It would still be useful, then, to explore further lines of enquiry relating to other possible legal justifications beyond the WTO regime. Of course, in any case, not all coercive measures are exclusively related to trade, and so alternative legal avenues would need to be found for non-trade-related measures.

1.3.2. IMF Security Exceptions

In relation to asset freezes, we have seen that the IMF may approve members taking restrictions on current transactions and payments. In the 1952

[178] GATT, Art XXI(b)(i).
[179] ibid, Art XXI(b)(ii).
[180] ibid, Art XXI(b)(iii).
[181] *Russia – Measures Concerning Traffic in Transit* (n 161) [7.68]–[7.77], [7.82].
[182] ibid, [7.101].

IMF decision,[183] it was considered that, in terms of restrictions imposed for the preservations of national or international security, the IMF 'does not, however, provide a suitable forum for discussion of the political and military considerations leading to actions of this kind'.[184] It therefore took the policy decision that a member intending to impose restrictions *not authorised* by Article VII(3)(b) or Article XIV(2) of the IMF Agreement should notify the Fund before imposing such restrictions whenever possible.[185] The decision also makes clear that such restrictions must be *solely* related to the preservation of national or international security, but such a decision is 'in the judgment of the member' concerned.[186] The decision then stipulated that:

> Unless the Fund informs the member within 30 days after receiving notice from the member that it is not satisfied that such restrictions are proposed solely to preserve such security, the member may assume that the Fund has no objection to the imposition of the restrictions.[187]

Although such an avenue is possible through the IMF, the asset freezes, as outlined above, may still be subject to the principle of non-intervention for non-members. Of course, even for members of the IMF, there does not seem to have been any instance where the Fund has allowed such measures.[188]

1.3.3. Limits of these Exceptions

The exceptions in these particular WTO and IMF regimes only apply as a defence to prima facie breaches of the rights and duties of those regimes therein – they do not provide a standalone legal justification for the breach of another international obligation, for example either in general international law, such as the principle of non-intervention, or a bilateral treaty provision between the relevant parties.[189] In other words, although coercive measures may violate the GATT, GATS or IMF agreements, if they also violate the principle of non-intervention, then further justification may be required beyond the exceptions in those specialist regimes that would only render them compatible with the obligations in those regimes. Of course, as addressed above, the principle of non-intervention would not be necessarily violated if the exceptions to

[183] IMF Decision No 144-(52/51) (n 118).
[184] ibid.
[185] ibid, operative [1].
[186] ibid.
[187] ibid.
[188] Bothe (n 115) 37.
[189] This, of course, does not apply where a treaty explicitly provides for the taking of such measures in response to threats to peace and security or otherwise, as may be found in regional security arrangements (see Chapter VI, section 2.3.1) or even in the UN Charter itself (see Chapter VI, section 1.3.1).

these regimes apply, because such matters are no longer within the 'domestic jurisdiction' of that State by virtue of their membership of such bodies, and their consent to the relevant security exceptions. This 'limitation' of 'domestic jurisdiction', however, is restricted to coercive measures being in accordance with the exceptions discussed above. If they are not, and the exceptions do not apply or have been exceeded, the principle of non-intervention still applies, and any legal justification for these measures must be based upon the residual rules of customary international law – in particular, the doctrine of countermeasures.

It is, however, clear that these exceptions, either to the *lex specialis* treaty regimes, or to the principle of non-intervention in general, have their limits. Coercive measures in response to mass atrocities cannot *always* be justified under these regimes – for example, these exceptions do not provide for the legality of such measures in cases when the Security Council is paralysed, and has failed in its responsibilities to protect and maintain international peace and security; where the measures under GATT or GATS are not necessary to protect the security interests of a State, but are nevertheless considered necessary for some other reason; or where the measures by a regional organisation are taken against a *non-member*, and therefore cannot be justified on the basis of their founding instrument alone.

Nevertheless, there are still avenues that States and regional organisations may take to justify legally the taking of such coercive measures. This avenue is provided by the doctrine of countermeasures.

2. COUNTERMEASURES

2.1. Basic Legal and Procedural Requirements

In basic terms, the doctrine of countermeasures acts as a legal 'defence' that renders lawful a breach of an international obligation that would be otherwise unlawful. To further understand the limitations of any kind of coercive measure, this section will outline the scope of the law of countermeasures, and how far this doctrine may be utilised to adopt coercive measures beyond the Security Council.

The lawfulness of the taking of countermeasures in certain circumstances has been recognised for many years. Early practice of international legal proceedings, such as the arbitration decision in the *Air Services* case,[190] recognised at the very least the ability of States to take certain measures against another State in response to a prior breach of an international obligation by that State.[191]

[190] *Case Concerning the Air Service Agreement of 27 March 1946 between the United States of America and France* (Decision of 9 December 1978) (1978) 18 RIAA 417–93.

[191] ibid, 443, [80]–[84].

Since then, practice and doctrine has developed to specify procedural and substantive limitations on the ability of States to take such measures. The ILC worked on this issue for many years,[192] and several draft reports and Draft Articles on State Responsibility sought to consolidate the historical practice on the law of countermeasures.[193]

Some of the ILC's earlier work was cited by the ICJ. For example, in the decision in *Gabčíkovo-Nagymaros*,[194] the court recognised a number of conditions for taking countermeasures, including: (i) a countermeasure 'must be taken in response to a previous international wrongful act of another State and must be directed against that State';[195] (ii) the injured State must call upon the State committing the wrongful act to 'discontinue its wrongful conduct or to make reparation for it';[196] (iii) the countermeasure must be proportionate, or, as the court put it, 'the effects of a countermeasure must be commensurate with the injury suffered';[197] and (iv) the purpose of the countermeasure must be to induce the wrongdoing State to comply with its obligations under international law, and so the countermeasure much therefore be reversible.[198]

These conditions have been further expanded upon by the ILC in its revised Articles on the Responsibility of States for Internationally Wrongful Acts.[199]

Article 22 of these Articles recognises the use of countermeasures as a circumstance precluding the wrongfulness of an act of a State which is not in conformity with an international obligation towards another State, so long as those countermeasures are in accordance with the legal safeguards laid down in Chapter II of Part Three of those Articles.

Chapter II of Part Three of the Articles details further requirements countermeasures must meet. This includes the requirement that '[a]n injured State may only take countermeasures against a State which is responsible for an internationally wrongful act in order to induce that State to comply with its obligations',[200] as well as a limitation of countermeasures to 'the non-performance for the time being of international obligations of the State taking the measures towards the responsible State'.[201] Article 49(3) confirms the requirement that

[192] The ILC's mandate was given in 1953 by UNGA Res 799 (VIII), *Request for Codification of the Principles of International Law Governing State Responsibility* (7 December 1953) UN Doc A/RES/799(VIII).

[193] For a full collection of the relevant works of the ILC on this topic from 1953 to 2001, see ILC, 'Analytical Guide to the Work of the International Law Commission: State Responsibility' (12 January 2016) http://legal.un.org/ilc/guide/9_6.shtml (accessed 31 July 2019).

[194] *Gabčíkovo-Nagymaros Project (Hungary / Slovakia)*, Judgment of 25 September 1997, [1997] ICJ Rep 7.

[195] ibid, 55, [83].

[196] ibid, 56, [84].

[197] ibid, 56, [85].

[198] ibid, 56–57, [87].

[199] See, generally, UNGA Res 56/83, *Responsibility of States for Internationally Wrongful Acts* (28 January 2002) UN Doc A/RES/56/83, Annex.

[200] ibid, Art 49(1).

[201] ibid, Art 49(2).

countermeasures should be reversible, as far as possible, so as to permit the resumption of performance of the obligations in question. Similarly, Article 52 requires countermeasures to be terminated once the responsible State has complied with its relevant international obligations.

Article 50 sets out substantive limitations of countermeasures, ensuring that countermeasures cannot involve the use of force, or affect obligations such as the protection of fundamental rights, and norms of *jus cogens*. Article 51 confirms the requirement that countermeasures must adhere to the principle of proportionality.

Notwithstanding some of the more procedural obligations relating to countermeasures, such as the condition that an injured State shall call upon the responsible State to comply with its international obligations, seek to negotiate, and notify the responsible State of its decision to take countermeasures all prior to adopting such measures,[202] there are some more fundamental conditions on the legality of countermeasures that require particular scrutiny, especially in relation to the issue of utilising such measures as a means of implementing a tertiary responsibility to protect.

The ILC's works on the ability of States to take countermeasures, and also the ability of international organisations to do the same, only address the possibility of an *injured* State or organisation utilising this doctrine. Therefore, the ILC Articles leave unanswered the question as to whether non-directly injured States or international organisations are able to utilise countermeasures in a situation where they are entitled to invoke the responsibility of the wrongdoer, but are not directly *injured* by their breach.[203] This issue is particularly relevant when we consider whether a party is able to take countermeasures in response to a breach of an obligation *erga omnes* – ie an obligation owed to the international community at large.

The second key issue that will be explored is the general requirement that only a *prior breach* of an international obligation may give rise to an ability to take countermeasures. Based upon an analysis of more recent State practice, the following discussion will also identify the types of obligations that may give rise to a right to take collective countermeasures when breached. This analysis will culminate in an assessment of whether breaches of obligations *erga omnes* may give rise to legal and legitimate recourse to countermeasures beyond the Security Council.

2.2. Injured State or Organisation and Obligations *Erga Omnes*

A key requirement of countermeasures, as accepted by the work of the ILC, is that they may only be undertaken by a State, or organisation, injured by the

[202] See ibid, Arts 49–53 generally.
[203] See section 2.2.

breach of an international obligation. Article 49(1) of the ILC Articles on the Responsibility of States refers to this.[204] The ILC's more recent works on the Responsibility of International Organisations for Internationally Wrongful Acts also refers to the ability of International Organisations to take countermeasures.[205] Article 51 of the International Organisations Articles again makes direct reference to 'an injured State or an injured international organisation' taking lawful countermeasures.[206]

However, both works of the ILC make clear that they do not attempt to answer the question as to whether non-directly injured parties may utilise countermeasures.[207] This is evident for two reasons. Firstly, both works contain 'saving clauses' that reference the ability of such non-directly injured parties to take *lawful* measures to invoke the responsibility of a wrongdoing party where they are entitled to do so. For example, Article 57 of the International Organisations Articles clarifies:

> This Chapter does not prejudice the right of any State or international organization, entitled under article 49, paragraphs 1 to 3, to invoke the responsibility of another international organization, to take lawful measures against that organization to ensure cessation of the breach and reparation in the interest of the injured State or organization or of the beneficiaries of the obligation breached.[208]

Secondly, the commentaries accompanying both works explain that the Commission did not have enough evidence of State practice at the time to make an assessment either way on this question. In the commentaries accompanying the State Responsibility Articles,[209] the Commission conducts a detailed review of the available State practice at the time, and concludes that:

> [T]he current state of international law on countermeasures taken in the general or collective interest is uncertain. State practice is sparse and involves a limited number of States. At present, there appears to be no clearly recognized entitlement of States referred to in article 48 to take countermeasures in the collective interest.[210]

Therefore, the Commission decided that it was not appropriate at that time to include a provision on whether non-directly injured parties may utilise

[204] ILC Articles on State Responsibility (n 199) Art 49(1).
[205] See, generally, UNGA Res 66/100, *Responsibility of International Organisations* (9 December 2011) UN Doc A/RES/66/100, Annex.
[206] ibid, Art 51(1).
[207] While the ILC did not make a decision on the question of non-injured party countermeasures (also called 'third-party countermeasures' or 'solidarity measures'), a number of authors have addressed this topic in depth, including eg: M Dawidowicz, *Third-Party Countermeasures in International Law* (Cambridge, Cambridge University Press, 2017); E Katselli Proukaki, *The Problem of Enforcement in International Law: Countermeasures, the Non-Injured State and the Idea of International Community* (Abingdon, Routledge, 2010).
[208] Art 54 of the ILC Articles on State Responsibility also contains a similar provision relating to the taking of lawful measures *by* States, *against* responsible States.
[209] ILC (n 36).
[210] ibid, 139, Art 54 Commentary, [6].

countermeasures, but instead adopted the saving clause which 'reserves the position and leaves the resolution of the matter to the further development of international law'.[211]

In the commentaries accompanying the International Organisations Articles,[212] it is similarly stated that the ILC was not intending to decide either way on the question as to whether non-injured States or international organisations, who are entitled to invoke the responsibility of another international organisation, would have the right to resort to countermeasures.[213] The Commission again based this decision on the fact that practice in this area, at the time of writing, was limited and sparse, and examples of such countermeasures actually being taken against an *international organisation* were not found.[214] It was still emphasised, however, that this lack of practice did not necessarily imply that the law prohibited such countermeasures either.[215]

Although the International Organisations Articles address only the issue as to whether States or international organisations may take countermeasures against another *international organisation* in detail, the Commission pointed out in its commentary that the provisions of the International Organisations Articles refer to international law for the conditions concerning countermeasures taken against *States* by an international organisation.[216] The ILC suggests that one may apply by analogy the conditions for countermeasures set out in the Articles on State Responsibility.[217]

With these issues in mind, the following subsections will address: (i) the ILC's position on only injured States utilising countermeasures, and what 'injury' falls within the scope of this coverage; (ii) the relevant State practice prior to the adoption of the 2011 ILC Articles on the Responsibility of International Organisations relevant to non-injured party countermeasures; and (iii) relevant State practice post-2011 relevant to non-injured party countermeasures.

2.2.1. *The International Law Commission's Position on 'Injured States'*

The ILC in 2001 made a distinction between 'injured States', and those entitled to 'invoke' responsibility for the purpose of determining who was entitled to

[211] ibid. See discussion below for the various positions of States prior to the adoption of this saving clause by the ILC.

[212] ILC, 'Draft Articles on the Responsibility of International Organisations, with Commentaries', http://legal.un.org/ilc/texts/instruments/english/commentaries/9_11_2011.pdf (accessed 31 July 2019); also included in ILC, 'Report of the International Law Commission on the Work of its Sixty-Third Session' (26 April–3 June and 4 July–12 August 2011) UN Doc A/66/10, 69ff.

[213] ibid, 89, Art 57 Commentary, [2].

[214] ibid.

[215] ibid.

[216] ibid, 47, Art 22 Commentary, [2].

[217] ibid. Further discussion on the ability of international organisations to take countermeasures, especially concerning Member States of that organisation, is set out below.

utilise countermeasures.[218] Article 42 of the State Responsibility Articles deals with the right of an injured State to invoke responsibility, where the obligation breached is owed to that State individually, or to a group of States including that State. Where there is an obligation owed to a group of States, or the international community as a whole, Article 42 requires the breach: (i) to specifically affect that State;[219] or (ii) to be of such a character as radically to change the position of all States owed that obligation with regard to the further performance of that obligation.[220]

According to the Commission, a breach of an obligation owed directly to a State individually 'injures' that State concerned, seemingly by virtue of that breach alone.[221] This is the case whether the obligation is owed on a bilateral basis based upon a bilateral treaty, a multilateral treaty owing obligations to a specific State, or originating from a principle of general international law that establishes bilateral obligations owed directly by one State to another.[222] The key factor is that the obligation is somehow owed on an individual basis to the State.

When addressing 'collective obligations' – obligations owed not to one State individually but to a group of States or the international community as a whole – the Commission determined that a State must be 'specifically affected' to be injured by a violation of such an obligation.[223] When considering the meaning of being 'specifically affected' the Commission stated:

> This will have to be assessed on a case-by-case basis, having regard to the object and purpose of the primary obligation breached and the facts of each case. For a State to be considered injured, it must be affected by the breach in a way which distinguishes it from the generality of other States to which the obligation is owed.[224]

When addressing Article 42(b)(ii), where a breach injures the State parties when it 'is of such a character as radically to change the position of all the other States to which the obligation is owed', the Commission suggests that this deals with a special category of obligation, a breach of which *must* be considered as affecting per se every State owed the obligation.[225] Examples given by the Commission include a disarmament treaty or a nuclear-free zone treaty.[226] This type of obligation is summarised as a 'treaty where each party's performance is effectively conditioned upon and requires the performance of each of the others'.[227]

[218] ILC (n 36) 137, Art 54 Commentary, [1].
[219] ILC Articles on State Responsibility (n 199) Art 42 (b)(i).
[220] ibid, Art 42 (b)(ii).
[221] ibid, Art 42(a); See also ILC (n 36) 118, Art 42 Commentary, [6]–[10].
[222] The ILC uses the general international law governing diplomatic or consular relations as an example: see ILC (n 36) 118, Art 42 Commentary, [10].
[223] ibid, 119, Art 42 Commentary, [12].
[224] ibid.
[225] ibid, [13].
[226] ibid.
[227] ibid.

With such obligations, the Commission considered that all State parties must be individually entitled to react to a breach, whether or not a State party is particularly affected or has suffered any quantifiable damage.[228]

Obligations protecting the collective interests of the international community *as a whole* have been recognised by the ICJ in *Barcelona Traction*, where all States are said to have a legal interest in their protection.[229] However, the ILC made it clear that Article 42(b)(ii) must be narrow in scope,[230] excluding the possibility of every obligation that may be considered *erga omnes* from falling within the scope of this injury test, and seemingly only considering a State 'injured' in such circumstances when they satisfy the aforementioned 'radically affected' test.

On first reading, it might seem unclear *why* such a distinction is necessary – after all, if an obligation is owed to a State, whether through a multilateral treaty or via an obligation *erga omnes*, why would one not consider that State 'injured' or 'affected' due to a breach of that obligation? The very specific injury threshold has two important consequences. Foremost, it restricts the ability of a third State to take countermeasures – a State who is not owed an obligation at all, nor has any recognised legal interest in the obligation. This, however, has the effect of also disallowing the taking of countermeasures by States who *do* have a legal interest in compliance, but who may not suffer damage following a breach. The reason for such a distinction seems based on several considerations.

Firstly, when the General Assembly's Sixth Committee considered the ILC's work shortly before its final draft of the Articles on State Responsibility, some States raised concerns that the general scheme of countermeasures, and especially countermeasures by non-injured States, posed a notable risk of abuse.[231] Arguments were put that a broad scope of discretion by non-injured States could provide a further pretext for power politics.[232]

Some States have highlighted this inherent risk of abuse as being one of the main concerns with the system of countermeasures generally, but most specifically concerning the prospect of countermeasures by non-injured States, and even States that did support countermeasures recommended their strict regulation.[233]

[228] ibid, 119, Art 42 Commentary, [14].

[229] *Case Concerning Barcelona Traction, Light and Power Company, Limited (Belgium v Spain)* (Judgement) [1970] ICJ Rep 3, (hereinafter *Barcelona Traction*) 32, [33].

[230] ILC (n 36) 119, Art 42 Commentary, [15].

[231] See generally ILC, 'Topical Summary of the Discussion Held in the Sixth Committee of the General Assembly During its Fifty-Fifth Session' (2001) UN Doc A/CN.4/513, [150] and [174]–[175]. See also ILC, 'Fourth Report on State Responsibility by Mr James Crawford, Special Rapporteur' (2001) UN Doc A/CN.4/517, [55] and [72].

[232] Sixth Committee Topical Summary (n 231) [175].

[233] See eg: UNGA Sixth Committee (55th Session), 'Summary Record of the 15th Meeting' (13 November 2000) UN Doc A/C.6/55/SR.15, [63] (Botswana); UNGA Sixth Committee (55th Session), 'Summary Record of the 14th Meeting' (10 November 2000) UN Doc A/C.6/55/SR.14, [54] (Germany) and [67] (Japan); UNGA Sixth Committee (55th Session), 'Summary Record of the

Some believed the risks of abuse or subjectivity were inherent in the nature of countermeasures, or at least in the vague approach taken by the previous drafts of the ILC. India, for example, as well as raising concerns about the potential for abuse, argued that the distinction between injured States and those 'not directly affected' was too subtle a distinction.[234] Similarly, Cyprus cited the need for countermeasures to be narrowly defined because of this possibility of abuse.[235] Cuba seemed the most outspoken on this point, suggesting that the lack of precision in the provisions proposed in the draft articles might have led to the justification of collective sanctions or collective interventions, and thus serve as a pretext for the adoption of unilateral armed reprisals and other types of intervention.[236]

While understanding the general need for countermeasures by directly injured States, some States feared that 'collective countermeasures' by non-directly injured States would only be used by more powerful States with their own agendas. For example, China suggested that only powerful States and blocs were in a position to take countermeasures, usually against weaker nations.[237] Tanzania went further to argue that countermeasures were a threat to small and weak States, and raised concerns that countermeasures could be made punitively in order to satisfy the political and economic interests of the State claiming to be injured or affected.[238]

Another concern with the idea of countermeasures by non-injured parties was that such measures, in and of themselves, would be disproportionate in some cases and therefore contrary to one of the key safeguards of countermeasures. Germany raised concerns that disproportionate unilateral acts, not justified by the interest they sought to protect, could be disguised as countermeasures.[239] Cuba was explicitly concerned that countermeasures by non-injured States involved more risks than benefits, and ran counter to the principle of proportionality.[240] Similarly, China stated that '"collective countermeasures" were inconsistent with the principle of proportionality … for they would become tougher when non-injured States joined in, with the undesirable consequence that countermeasures might greatly outweigh the extent of the injury'.[241]

There were calls from States that any countermeasures in the collective interest should be governed by the existing provisions of the UN Charter,[242] regulated

16th Meeting' (13 November 2000) UN Doc A/C.6/55/SR.16, [57] (Hungary); UNGA Sixth Committee (55th Session), 'Summary Record of the 23rd Meeting' (14 November 2000) UN Doc A/C.6/55/SR.23, [4] (Columbia).

[234] UNGA Sixth Committee, 15th Meeting (n 233) [29]–[30] (India).

[235] UNGA Sixth Committee (55th Session), 'Summary Record of the 18th Meeting' (4 December 2000) UN Doc A/C.6/55/SR.18, [32] (Cyprus).

[236] ibid, [59]–[60] (Cuba).

[237] UNGA Sixth Committee, 14th Meeting (n 233) [40] (China).

[238] ibid, [46] (United Republic of Tanzania).

[239] ibid, para [54] (Germany).

[240] UNGA Sixth Committee, 18th Meeting (n 235) [61] (Cuba).

[241] UNGA Sixth Committee, 14th Meeting (n 233) [41] (China).

[242] See eg UNGA Sixth Committee, 18th Meeting (n 235) [61] (Cuba).

by the UN Security Council, or a regional organisation where appropriate. On this point, Libya argued,

> collective countermeasures could be legitimate only in the context of intervention by the competent international or regional institutions. In that respect, no delegation of power – in other words the handing over of the right to take countermeasures to a group of countries which would exercise that right outside any constitutional framework based on international legitimacy – would be acceptable. Recourse to collective countermeasures must not turn into collective reprisals, in other words action with political aims.[243]

These concerns led the Special Rapporteur, James Crawford, to conclude that the thrust of the governments' response to the insertion of a provision allowing 'collective countermeasures' by non-injured States, even in response to breaches of obligations *erga omnes*, was that such a provision had 'no basis in international law and would be destabilizing'.[244] Tams,[245] on the other hand, does not come to the same conclusion – he believes the views of States during the Sixth Committee debates were much more nuanced than Crawford observed.[246]

While accepting that States did raise these concerns over abuse and subjectivity, and some States were certainly against the idea of countermeasures by non-injured States, Tams suggests that a greater majority of States accepted the basic idea that all States could respond to serious *erga omnes* breaches by way of countermeasures.[247] The concerns some raised, he suggests, were to highlight the need for further restrictions or modifications of the proposals.[248]

Indeed, Tams was right to highlight this fact – there were a considerable number of States who saw the utility in such countermeasures. Even the representative for Costa Rica, who expressly declared that he would have preferred a complete ban on the use of countermeasures because of fears of a power imbalance, welcomed the proposals of the ILC, stating that 'since the international community did not yet have a central authority to enforce the fulfilment of States' obligations, the usefulness of countermeasures must be acknowledged'.[249]

However, even for those States that did not support countermeasures by non-directly injured States, some of their concerns may be alleviated in a number of ways. Firstly, relating to the argument that collective countermeasures would render their utility disproportionate, this concern seems misplaced.

[243] UNGA Sixth Committee (55th Session), 'Summary Record of the 22nd Meeting' (1 December 2000) UN Doc A/C.6/55/SR.22, [52] (Libya).

[244] ILC, 'Fourth Report on State Responsibility by Mr James Crawford, Special Rapporteur' (2001) UN Doc A/CN.4/517, [72].

[245] CJ Tams, *Enforcing Obligations Erga Omnes in International Law* (Cambridge, Cambridge University Press, 2005).

[246] ibid, 246.

[247] ibid, 247.

[248] ibid, 247.

[249] UNGA Sixth Committee (55th Session), 'Summary Record of the 17th Meeting' (14 November 2000) UN Doc A/C.6/55/SR.17, [64] (Costa Rica).

Logically speaking, if additional measures by non-injured States were taken, and measured collectively in addition to any countermeasures taken by the State directly injured by the prior breach, rendering the response disproportionate, then this would imply that those collective measures were *not* countermeasures, because they fell short of the principle of proportionality.

It is also unconvincing that *any* additional non-injured State countermeasure, in every situation, would render the application of countermeasures automatically disproportionate, as seemed to be suggested by China.[250] While it is impossible to hypothesise on every breach of an *erga omnes* obligation, it may well be the case that collective measures are indeed an appropriate response to a serious breach of international law. This is certainly not an inconceivable possibility. The point is that the proportionality of the measures depends on the breach itself and the measures proposed in response.

The specific obligations that may fall within the scope of non-injured party countermeasures will be outlined below, but first we must assess the practice of States on the point as to whether such parties have standing to react to breaches of obligations *erga omnes*.

2.2.2. Pre-2011 State Practice

Practice on non-injured party countermeasures before 2011, when the ILC released its Articles on the Responsibility of International Organisations, has been covered in great depth on numerous occasions and in several detailed studies,[251] and it is not necessary to repeat such assessments in detail here. It is, however, useful to outline the position of some commentators who assess pre-2011 practice differently to the ILC, before examining more recent practice to determine whether there has been any development in international practice since then.

To recall, the ILC described State practice on countermeasures by non-injured parties in response to breaches of obligations *erga omnes* as limited and sparse.[252] Special Rapporteur Crawford similarly described such practice as 'embryonic',[253] 'selective'[254] and dominated by the practice of 'Western States'[255]

[250] UNGA Sixth Committee, 14th Meeting (n 233) [41] (China).

[251] See eg: M Dawidowicz, 'Public Law Enforcement Without Public Law Safeguards? An Analysis of State Practice on Third-Party Countermeasures and their Relationship to the UN Security Council' (2006) 77 *British Yearbook of International Law* 333; J Frowein, 'Reactions by Not Directly Affected States to Breaches of Public International Law' (1994) 248 *Recueil des cours de l'Académie de droit international* 353, 416–22; Tams (n 245) 207–28; see also Dawidowicz (n 207) and Katselli Proukaki (n 207).

[252] See above, at nn 210–14 and accompanying text.

[253] Crawford, 'Fourth Report' (n 244) [71].

[254] ILC, 'Third Report on State Responsibility by Mr James Crawford, Special Rapporteur' (2000) UN Doc A/CN.4/507, [396] and [399].

[255] ibid, [396]; Dawidowicz (n 251) 408.

(rather than a general practice, as required to establish a generally applicable norm of customary international law).[256]

On the point that the State practice was allegedly limited, embryonic and selective, Dawidowicz makes the point that the ILC itself only identified six examples of such practice on third-party/non-injured State countermeasures, whereas Dawidowicz himself provides 27 examples of practice, and five statements, that he says strongly suggests that State practice is neither limited nor embryonic.[257]

Indeed, the ILC did provide six examples of State practice, and two examples of 'other cases' where States 'similarly suspended treaty rights in order to exercise pressure on States violating collective obligations. However, they did not rely on a right to take countermeasures, but asserted a right to suspend the treaty because of a fundamental change of circumstances.'[258] Crawford provided the very same examples.[259] Even so, some of the additional examples that Dawidowicz highlighted are worth mentioning, particularly for their very close relevance the underlying themes of the current study.

Firstly, Dawidowicz refers to the Iranian hostage crisis at the US embassy in Tehran in 1979–1980.[260] This example is particularly relevant because an attempt was made to adopt a UN Security Council Resolution which would have imposed a total trade embargo and political sanctions on Iran.[261] However, this resolution was vetoed by the Soviet Union.[262] In response, European Community States and others unilaterally suspended all commercial contracts with Iran that were entered into after the date of the hostage taking.[263] While Dawidowicz

[256] On this point, see Tams (n 245) 235; on the requirement of a general opinio juris and evidence of settled practice for customary international law, see *North Sea Continental Shelf (Federal Republic of Germany/Netherlands; Federal Republic of Germany/Denmark)* (Judgment) [1969] ICJ Rep 3, [75]–[77].

[257] Dawidowicz (n 251) 408–09; the examples of practice Dawidowicz refers to are at 350–98, and the statements are outlined at 398–40; see also Dawidowicz (n 207) 242–45.

[258] ILC (n 36) 137–39, Art 54 Commentary, [3]. Practice cited by the ILC includes: measures taken by the US against Uganda in response to the alleged commission of genocide in 1978; measures taken by the US and other 'western States' against Poland and the Soviet Union in 1981 after the imposition of martial law and the suppression of demonstrations; the imposition of trade restrictions and embargos by the European Community, Australia, Canada, and New Zealand against Argentina following the invasion of the Falkland Islands in 1982; the suspension of landing rights of South African Airlines by the US following the declaration of a state of emergency in South Africa in 1985; collective measures, including embargoes and asset freezes, taken against Iraq in 1990 following its invasion of Kuwait; and, in response to the humanitarian crisis in Kosovo in 1998, asset freezes and flight bans imposed by France, Germany and the United Kingdom, as a non-performance of bilateral aviation agreements, against the Federal Republic of Yugoslavia.

[259] Crawford, 'Third Report' (n 254) [391(a)–(f)].

[260] Dawidowicz (n 251) 408–09.

[261] UNSC Draft Resolution S/13735 (10 January 1980) UN Doc S/13735.

[262] UNSC Verbatim Record, 2191st Meeting (11 and 13 January 1980) UN Doc S/PV.2191ANDADD.1 (OR); France, Jamaica, Niger, Norway, Philippines, Portugal, Tunisia, the UK, the US and Zambia voted in favour, the German Democratic Republic and the Soviet Union voted against, with Bangladesh and Mexico abstaining.

[263] Dawidowicz (n 251) 402–03.

recognises that these actions are likely to be categorised as measures of retorsion, because Iran was not a member of GATT and there were purportedly no violations of any bilateral agreements, he does highlight that statements made by the European Parliament and Council of Ministers suggested that the possibility of adopting countermeasures in this situation was implied.[264]

Looking to the statements referred to,[265] there was certainly an explicit statement of willingness to implement the measures that were provided for in the draft resolution that did not pass at the Security Council.[266] This, of course, does indicate a willingness to go beyond the Security Council in this situation. As Frowein notes, 'It is not absolutely clear whether the implementation of this decision amounted to a neglect of otherwise applicable rules of public international law',[267] and so it cannot be said for sure that this was an expression on the legality of non-injured State countermeasures. Tams suggests that the Council of Ministers took the view that general international law 'permitted the imposition of coercive measures' in this case.[268] However, such a statement was not made explicitly or in those terms, either by the Council or by the European Parliament.[269] The Foreign Ministers of the Nine, however, did seek to impose the sanctions 'in accordance with international law'.[270] While it is unclear whether this calls for *only* actions that would be 'in accordance with international law' or is evidence that they consider *any* such sanctions to be so, it is certainly clear that the European Community considered it legitimate to impose sanctions against Iran.

Dawidowicz argues that, on the basis of the test for international custom requiring evidence of a widespread acceptance of the practice of States, although practice may be *dominated* by Western States it is not *limited* to these States.[271] Importantly, Dawidowicz asserts that even the Group of 77 – a group very clearly in favour of a general prohibition of coercive measures and unilateral sanctions, as discussed above – had expressed support, albeit implicitly, through a number of positions and declarations they have taken.[272] Dawidowicz refers to the situation in South Africa in the 1960s,[273] noting that the Second Conference of African Independent States recommended that all African States institute a trade embargo against South Africa in response to its policy of apartheid.[274] A similar recommendation was made by the Non-Aligned Movement in 1964,

[264] ibid, 403; on this point see also Frowein (n 251) 417.
[265] Bulletin of the European Communities, 'The Community and the Member States and the events in Iran' [1980] 13(4) EC Bull [1.2.6], [1.2.7]–[1.2.9].
[266] ibid, [1.2.9].
[267] Frowein (n 251) 417.
[268] Tams (n 245) 226–27.
[269] See EC Bull 1980 (4) (n 265) [1.2.6]–[1.2.9].
[270] ibid, [1.2.7], declaration [5].
[271] Dawidowicz (n 251) 410; see also *North Sea Continental Shelf* (n 256).
[272] Dawidowicz (n 251) 410–11.
[273] ibid, 352–54.
[274] ibid, 352.

which called upon all States to boycott all South African goods and to refrain from exporting goods, and also to deny airport and overflying facilities to aircraft and port facilities to ships proceeding to and from South Africa.[275] Most relevantly, the UN General Assembly also adopted a Resolution requesting such a trade embargo,[276] for which most developing nations voted in favour, and most *developed* nations either voted against or abstained.[277]

Dawidowicz notes that, in the absence of any rights under general international law or specific treaty commitments, such measures may be regarded as 'retorsion', yet many States were already parties to GATT, and so he argues 'the call for a trade embargo in the resolutions expressed at least a willingness to contemplate a *prima facie* violation of international law'.[278] He also argues that none of the States that took such measures invoked the security exceptions in Article XXI of GATT, and although no justifications made based upon general international law or countermeasures either, this instance may provide support for State practice that non-injured parties may take such countermeasures.[279] Such action was taken *before* the UN Security Council finally recommended,[280] and then subsequently requested under Chapter VII of the Charter in 1977,[281] that certain sanctions be imposed, and indeed the action itself was unrelated to the actual sanctions requested by the Security Council therein. Therefore, as Dawidowicz argued, it could be suggested that States did not at this time consider the Security Council to be the *exclusive* bearer of 'a right to respond to serious breaches',[282] or perhaps even as having the sole legal competence to do so.

2.2.3. Post-2011 State Practice

Since 2011, and especially following the so-called 'Arab Spring', State practice in this area has arguably increased exponentially. As deadlock crept into the

[275] Non-Aligned Movement, 'Programme for Peace and International Co-operation: Declaration Adopted by the Conference' (10 October 1964, Cairo) Doc NAM-II/HEADS/5; available in UNGA, 'Letters Dated 28 October 1964 from the Permanent Representative of the United Arab Republic to the United Nations Addressed to the Secretary General' (29 October 1964) UN Doc A/5763, Annex, 12–13.

[276] UNGA Res 1761 (XVII), *The Policies of Apartheid of the Government of the Republic of South Africa* (6 November 1962) UN Doc A/RES/1761(XVII), [3]; see also Chapter VI, section 1.3.

[277] See UNGA Verbatim Record, 1165th Plenary Meeting (6 November 1962) UN Doc A/PV.1165, 679.

[278] Dawidowicz (n 251) 353.

[279] ibid, 354.

[280] UNSC Res 181 (1963) (7 August 1963) UN Doc S/RES/181(1963) [3], calling for a voluntary arms embargo; and UNSC Res 182 (1963) (4 December 1963) UN Doc S/RES/182(1963) [5], calling for the cessation of sales and shipments of equipment and materials for the manufacture and maintenance of arms and ammunition.

[281] UNSC Res 418 (1977) (4 November 1977) UN Doc S/RES/418(1977) [3].

[282] ibid, 354.

UN Security Council from 2011 concerning the Syrian crisis, and the subsequent situation in Ukraine in 2014, States seemed to have no choice but to move beyond the UN.

The following analysis will focus on three cases that are particularly relevant to whether there is legal space for the tertiary responsibility to protect to operate. As well as addressing situations where States have acted beyond the level of measures called for by the UN Security Council, this section will also focus on situations where the Security Council has been faced by deadlock in recent years, and where States have taken it upon themselves to impose their own countermeasures collectively in response to these situations. It shall also address States' initial reactions to the situation in Libya, measures adopted following Security Council deadlock over Syria, and will point out a number of instances where regional organisations such as the European Union[283] have taken measures against non-Member States particularly with regard to the situation in Ukraine. Finally, more recent measures adopted in response to the atrocities that have taken place in Myanmar and the failure of the Security Council provide a fitting, albeit unacceptable, context for establishing the legal space for the tertiary responsibility to protect.

2.2.3.1. Libya (2011)

As discussed in Chapter II, the international response to impending atrocities in Libya in 2011 was one of the starting hopes that the responsibility to protect would be put into practice. Notwithstanding some of the overstretches of military action, and a lack of practical planning for the aftermath, some States did take economic and coercive action short of force even before the UN Security Council imposed its own sanctions.

US President Barack Obama issued an Executive Order[284] on 25 February 2011 which found that Colonel Muammar Qadhafi had taken 'extreme measures against the people of Libya' including 'wanton violence against unarmed civilians', and declared a national emergency in response to the 'deterioration in the security of Libya' which posed 'a serious risk to its stability, thereby constituting an unusual and extraordinary threat to the national security and foreign policy of the United States'.[285] The Order imposed asset freezes on Libyan government officials and others close to Qadhafi.[286]

This action was taken *before* the UN Security Council issued Resolution 1970 the following day, which among other things imposed travel bans, arms embargos, asset freezes, and referred the situation to the International

[283] Although, the legality of these measures and their compatibility with the countermeasures regime will be further discussed below, in Chapter VI, section 2.3.2.

[284] Executive Order 13566 of February 25, 2011, 76 Fed Reg 11315 (2 March 2011).

[285] ibid.

[286] ibid, see also Annex.

Criminal Court.[287] Therefore, the US would have needed a legal basis in international law to impose the asset freezes, but the US did not explicitly provide one.

Similarly, on 22 February 2011, the League of Arab States suspended the Libyan delegation from the organisation.[288] As will be assessed below in relation to Syria, there seems to be no basis for such action in the organisation's founding document, and so this action by the Arab League could be considered unlawful, unless there is some justification elsewhere, such as in the law of countermeasures.

2.2.3.2. Responses to the Situation in Syria (2011–Present)

The general outline of the situation in Syria and the deadlock faced by the Security Council has been set out in Chapter II.[289] However, it is necessary to assess in some detail States' reactions to the situation beyond Council deadlock, and how this may indicate a development of State practice relating to non-injured State countermeasures.

The United States first imposed unilateral measures in response to the emerging crisis in Syria in April 2011. US President Barack Obama extended a previous executive order, which initially established a sanctions programme against Syria in 2004,[290] by a new executive order freezing assets of targeted individuals and entities.[291] This executive order justified the measures on the grounds that 'the Government of Syria's human rights abuses, including those related to the repression of the people of Syria … constitute an unusual and extraordinary threat to the national security, foreign policy, and economy of the United States'.[292]

The European Union also adopted its own framework of measures in May 2011, starting with action that included an arms embargo, travel bans and asset freezes.[293] In deciding on these measures, the Council of the EU cited its 'grave concern about the situation unfolding in Syria and the deployment of military and security forces in a number of Syrian cities',[294] and based its decision on the 'violent repression against the civilian population in Syria'.[295]

[287] UNSC Res 1970 (2011) (26 February 2011) UN Doc S/RES/1970 (2011).

[288] See League of Arab States, Council Meeting at the Level of Delegates of 22 February 2011 (Emergency Meeting, 22 February 2011) www.lasportal.org/en/councils/lascouncil/Pages/LasCouncilEnvoyDetails.aspx?RID=88 (accessed 31 July 2019); see also 'Arab League suspends Libya delegation – TV' *Reuters* (22 February 2011) www.reuters.com/article/libya-protests-league-idUSLDE71L2GK20110222 (accessed 31 July 2019).

[289] Chapter II, section 3.2.2.

[290] Executive Order 13338 of 11 May 2004, 69 Fed Reg 26751 (12 May 2004).

[291] Executive Order 13572 of 29 April 2011, 76 Fed Reg 24787 (3 May 2011).

[292] ibid.

[293] Council Decision 2011/273/CFSP of 9 May 2011 concerning restrictive measures against Syria [2011] OJ L121/11; see also Council Regulation (EU) No 442/2011 of 9 May 2011 concerning restrictive measures in view of the situation in Syria [2011] OJ L121/1. The actual legal bases for such action will be considered in Chapter VI, section 2.3.1

[294] Council Decision 2011/273/CFSP (n 293), preamble [2].

[295] ibid, preamble [3].

The Council of the EU added further measures, including an embargo of oil imports and exports from Syria.[296] This was accompanied by a partial suspension of the Cooperation Agreement between the European Economic Community and the Syrian Arab Republic[297] by the Council.[298] The Council justified this decision by stating that 'the Union considers that the current situation in Syria is in clear violation of the principles of the United Nations Charter which constitute the basis of the cooperation between Syria and the Union'.[299] The Council then went on to refer to the international obligations it considered breached, stating:

> Considering the extreme seriousness of the violations perpetrated by Syria in breach of general international law and the principles of the United Nations Charter, the Union has decided to adopt additional restrictive measures against the Syrian regime.[300]

What is crucial about this line of reasoning is that fact that the Council did not expressly consider Syria to have breached the Cooperation Agreement itself, but *separate* principles of international law that 'constitute the basis' of that cooperation. This suggests that the legal basis for suspending the agreement is not Article 60 of the VCLT.[301] As detailed above, the suspension of a treaty requires a 'material breach' of that instrument, and such a material breach requires either: (i) a repudiation of the treaty not sanctioned by the present Convention; or (ii) the violation of a provision essential to the accomplishment of the object or purpose of the treaty.[302]

The problem with the Cooperation Agreement in question is that there seems to have been no material breach or violation of such a provision. The Cooperation Agreement is 'based on' the 'common desire of the Parties to maintain and strengthen friendly relations in accordance with the principles of the United Nations Charter'.[303] As the Council puts it, this may be a political and diplomatic purpose of the agreement, but it is by no means a legal requirement of that agreement itself because the obligations therein do not derive from, and are

[296] Council Decision 2011/522/CFSP of 2 September 2011 amending Decision 2011/273/CFSP concerning restrictive measures against Syria [2011] OJ L228/16, preamble [5], and Art 1(1); see also Council Regulation (EU) No 878/2011 of 2 September 2011 amending Regulation (EU) No 442/2011 concerning restrictive measures in view of the situation in Syria [2011] L228/1.

[297] Cooperation Agreement between the European Economic Community and the Syrian Arab Republic [1978] OJ L269/2. Although Syria was not a member of the WTO or GATT, the measures considered by the EU could have been considered prima facie breaches of corresponding provisions of this agreement.

[298] Council Decision 2011/523/EU of 2 September 2011 partially suspending the application of the Cooperation Agreement between the European Economic Community and the Syrian Arab Republic [2011] OJ L228/19.

[299] ibid, preamble [9].

[300] ibid, preamble [10].

[301] VCLT, Art 60.

[302] ibid.

[303] Council Decision 2011/523/EU (n 298) preamble [2].

not specifically required by, any provision of that treaty. The Preamble certainly refers to this desire to uphold these principles *through* the agreement,[304] but such obligations themselves are found in separate sources of international law.

Article 42 of the agreement does allow for action 'which it considers essential to its security in time of war or serious international tension'. But this has not been invoked by the EU. Nor did the Council specifically justify the legality of the suspension on grounds of Article 60 of the VCLT. In fact, there are a number of indicators which certainly seem to suggest that it is the law of countermeasures that the Council is utilising as a legal basis for this action.

Firstly, this decision, and subsequent decisions expanding the suspension of the agreement,[305] emphasise that the suspensions were taken 'until the Syrian authorities put an end to the systematic violations of human rights and can again be considered as being in compliance with general international law and the principles which form the basis of the Cooperation Agreement'.[306] This particularly highlights the intended temporary nature of the measures, giving the Syrian government the opportunity to comply with its international obligations to have the measures reversed.[307] Secondly, these decisions specifically require Syria to be notified of the decision to suspend the treaty.[308] Additionally, the decisions were intended to be limited in nature, stating that 'the suspension should aim at targeting the Syrian authorities only and not the people of Syria, [and] the suspension should be limited'.[309] In terms of the oil embargo, this was justified by the fact that since 'crude oil and petroleum products are at present the products whose trade most benefits the Syrian regime and which thus supports its repressive policies, the suspension of the Agreement should be limited to crude oil and petroleum products'.[310]

These limitations on the suspension suggest the Council was at least aiming to act in conformity with the procedural and substantive conditions for the taking of countermeasures.[311] The fact that this is a measure taken by an international organisation, not 'directly injured' by Syria's violations of the outlined

[304] Cooperation Agreement (n 297) preamble [1]; see also Council Decision 2011/523/EU (n 298) preamble [9].

[305] See eg Council Decision 2012/123/CFSP of 27 February 2012 amending Decision 2011/523/EU partially suspending the application of the Cooperation Agreement between the European Economic Community and the Syrian Arab Republic [2012] OJ L54/18, extending the suspension to allow for restrictions on gold, precious metals and diamonds.

[306] Council Decision 2011/523/EU (n 298) preamble [11]; Council Decision 2012/123/CFSP (n 305) preamble [2].

[307] As consistent with the requirements set out above, see section 2.1.

[308] Council Decision 2011/523/EU (n 298) Art 2; Council Decision 2012/123/CFSP (n 305) Art 2.

[309] Council Decision 2011/523/EU (n 298) preamble [12]; see also Council Decision 2012/123/CFSP (n 305) preamble [4].

[310] Council Decision 2011/523/EU (n 298) preamble [12]; a very similar wording was used in reference to the restrictions on gold, precious metals and diamonds in Council Decision 2012/123/CFSP (n 305) preamble [4].

[311] As consistent with the requirements set out above, see section 2.1.

obligations, suggests that the EU considers such measures to be available by such parties in these circumstances, specifically in response to these violations of international obligations.

The Conclusions of the European Council in October 2011 determined that the EU would impose further and more comprehensive measures against the Assad regime 'as long as the repression of the civilian population continues'.[312]

However, so-called 'Western States' were not the only bloc to adopt measures in response to the crisis in Syria. The Arab League took unprecedented action in November 2011 when it firstly suspended Syria from the organisation on 12 November,[313] and then subsequently imposed 'sanctions' against it on 27 November.[314]

These measures, although called 'sanctions' in the media[315] and in States' remarks about them,[316] are not 'sanctions' in the sense that they have been adopted as part of a multilateral treaty or institution that has the power to take such measures against its members. The Arab League's founding Pact[317] does not grant the organisation any powers to take 'sanctions' or other coercive measures short of force, and so it cannot be said that Syria may be bound by such actions on the basis of its consent to this instrument.

Syria argued at the UN Security Council that:

> It considers the resolution adopted by the meeting of the Council of the League of Arab States a violation of its national sovereignty, a flagrant interference in its internal affairs and a blatant violation of the purposes for which the League of Arab States was established. It is also a violation of article 8 of the Charter of the League of Arab States.[318]

Article 8 of the Pact requires that every Member State respect the 'form of government obtaining in the other States of the League', and 'recognise the form

[312] European Council, 'Conclusions of 23 October 2011' (CO EUR 17/CONCL 5) EUCO 52/11, Document Number ST 52 2011 REV 1, [17].

[313] League of Arab States, Council Resolution 7438 (Extraordinary Session, 12 November 2011) www.lasportal.org/ar/councils/lascouncil/Pages/LasCouncilMinistrialDetails.aspx?RID=61 (in Arabic) (accessed 31 July 2019).

[314] League of Arab States, Council Resolution 7442 (Extraordinary Session, 27 November 2011) www.lasportal.org/ar/councils/lascouncil/Pages/LasCouncilMinistrialDetails.aspx?RID=58 (in Arabic) (accessed 31 July 2019); see also Syria's complaint containing a list of these restrictive measures in, Report of the Secretary-General, 'Unilateral Economic Measures as a Means of Political and Economic Coercion against Developing Countries' (9 August 2017) UN Doc A/72/307, 20–21.

[315] See eg 'Syria Unrest: Arab League Adopts Sanctions in Cairo' *BBC News* (27 November 2011) www.bbc.co.uk/news/world-middle-east-15901360 (accessed 31 July 2019); N MacFarquar and N Bakri, 'Isolating Syria, Arab League Imposes Broad Sanctions' *New York Times* (27 November 2011) www.nytimes.com/2011/11/28/world/middleeast/arab-league-prepares-to-vote-on-syrian-sanctions.html (accessed 31 July 2019).

[316] See eg UNSC Verbatim Record, 6710th Meeting (31 January 2012) UN Doc S/PV.6710, 3 (Qatar), 24 (Russia), 25 (China). Incidentally, France also referred to the EU measures imposed on Syria as 'sanctions' in this meeting: 15 (France).

[317] Pact of the League of Arab States (adopted 22 March 1945, entered into force 10 May 1945) 70 UNTS 237, English translation from 248.

[318] UNSC Meeting 6710 (n 316) 12 (Syria).

of government obtaining as one of the rights of those States', and furthermore for States to pledge 'not to take any action tending to change that form'. Exclusion of members is to be taken under Article 18 of the Pact, which provides that:

> The Council of the League may consider any State that is not fulfilling the obligations resulting from this Pact as excluded from the League, by a decision taken by a unanimous vote of all the States except the State referred to.

However, Resolution 7438 of the Council only seems to 'suspend' Syria, and even considering this language the Resolution was not adopted unanimously. Dawidowicz also highlights a similar point in relation to the suspension of Libya, arguing that Article 18 only allows for such action when the Member State is 'not fulfilling the obligations' under the Pact, and that since the Pact 'does not refer to any obligation incumbent upon Arab League Member States to comply with international human rights and humanitarian law', the suspensions could not be justified under the Pact.[319]

The League can take binding decisions on States where there is a dispute *between* two or more members,[320] or where there is an act of aggression by one member against another.[321] However, there is no provision in the Pact to determine the powers of the League in a situation reflecting that in Syria at the time. In fact, the Pact itself makes clear that cases where decisions are reached by a majority, 'shall only bind those that accept them'.[322] Therefore, there is no way that the resolutions passed by the Council in the Arab League could bind Syria *legally* – thus any measures taken against it cannot be 'institutional sanctions' rendered lawful by its prior consent.

Nor can these measures be considered as acts of retorsion. The key feature of acts of retorsion is that they are inherently lawful, but unfriendly. The actions taken by the Arab League, especially the freezing of Syrian government assets, are to be considered as unlawful acts under general international law requiring some basis in custom or otherwise to render them lawful.

Therefore, on what other basis could the actions of the Arab League be taken if not customary international law, and in particular the law of countermeasures? With no basis in the Arab League Pact, the law of countermeasures would be the only other option – and that would require us to accept that States may take such measures in situations where they are not directly injured.

[319] M Dawidowicz, 'Third-Party Countermeasures: A Progressive Development of International Law?' *Questions of International Law* (30 June 2016) www.qil-qdi.org/third-party-countermeasures-progressive-development-international-law/ (accessed 31 July 2019); see also, in relation to the Syria suspensions, M Dawidowicz, 'Third-Party Countermeasures: Observations on a Controversial Concept' in C Chinkin et al, *Sovereignty, Statehood and State Responsibility* (Cambridge, Cambridge University Press, 2015) 348, 361; and Dawidowicz (n 207) 220–38.

[320] Arab League Pact, Art 5.

[321] ibid, Art 6.

[322] ibid, Art 7.

2.2.3.3. Responses to the Situation in Ukraine (2014–Present)

When Russia invaded and annexed Crimea from Ukraine, there was international outcry that the incident was an act of aggression, and violated the sovereignty, territorial integrity and political independence of Ukraine, rendering the annexation also a gross violation of the UN Charter.[323] With Russia having a permanent seat and a veto on the Security Council, it might be considered impossible to take any action in response to this through the UN, whether by sanctions or otherwise, owing to the near-certainty that Russia would block such action against it.

The European Union was early to respond when the situation was still developing, before Crimea was formally 'annexed', but it was clear that there was a presence of troops on the peninsula, new 'leaders' in Crimea had called for a referendum on the future status of the territory, and the situation was developing quickly. In a statement, EU Heads of State called for Russia and Ukraine to rectify the situation quickly and for negotiations to produce results 'within a limited timeframe'.[324] The Heads of State then warned that if no results were produced, the EU would decide on measures such as travel bans, asset freezes and the cancellation of an upcoming EU–Russia summit.[325] They also said that the EU 'has a special responsibility for peace, stability and prosperity in Europe'.[326]

When the Crimean 'referendum' went ahead anyway, the EU responded the next day when the Foreign Affairs Council adopted conclusions on the developing situation.[327] The Council rejected the legitimacy and legality of the referendum, deploring the developments as violations of Ukraine's sovereignty and territorial integrity.[328] The Council expressed its regret that a resolution in the UN Security Council was blocked by a Russian veto,[329] emphasising that constructive dialogue was still possible, and warning against any annexation by Russia of Crimea which it would consider as a violation of international law.[330] On the same day, the Council of the EU once again acted within its Common

[323] See eg statements in UNSC Verbatim Record, 7144th Meeting (19 March 2014) UN Doc S/PV.7144.

[324] European Council, 'Statement of the Heads of State or Government on Ukraine' (Brussels, 6 March 2014) [5], www.consilium.europa.eu/en/meetings/european-council/2014/03/06/ (accessed 31 July 2019).

[325] ibid.

[326] ibid, [3]; this was also reiterated later in European Council, 'Conclusions on Ukraine Approved by the European Council' (Brussels, 20 March 2014) [8], www.consilium.europa.eu/uedocs/cms_data/docs/pressdata/en/ec/141707.pdf (accessed 31 July 2019).

[327] Council of the European Union, 'Council Conclusions on Ukraine', Foreign Affairs Council Meeting (Brussels, 17 March 2014) www.consilium.europa.eu/uedocs/cms_data/docs/pressdata/EN/foraff/141601.pdf (accessed 31 July 2019).

[328] ibid, [1].

[329] ibid, [3].

[330] ibid, [4].

Foreign and Security Policy framework and imposed 'restrictive measures' on Russia, placing travel restrictions and asset freezes on both Russian and Crimean officials.[331]

The UN General Assembly issued a Resolution stating that the referendum had no validity,[332] and called upon States not to recognise the result.[333] The Resolution 'welcomed' the efforts of 'other international and regional organizations to assist Ukraine in protecting the rights of all persons in Ukraine', but did not specifically highlight whether this was directed at the EU measures.[334] The EU Foreign Affairs Council welcomed this resolution,[335] and warned that 'any further steps by the Russian Federation to destabilise the situation in Ukraine would lead to additional and far reaching consequences for relations in a broad range of economic areas'.[336] The Council continued to condemn Russia's stance on the matter, and also 'any attempt to circumvent the sanctions regime',[337] further expanding its targets for restrictive measures,[338] and calling for further trade, economic and financial measures.[339] What is also interesting is that the Council also called on UN Member States 'to consider similar measures in line with UNGA Resolution 68/262', even though that resolution did not mention such measures explicitly.[340]

The UN Office of the High Commissioner for Human Rights (OHCHR) began producing reports detailing allegations of growing violence, torture, and violations of human rights and international humanitarian law in Eastern

[331] Council Decision 2014/145/CFSP of 17 March 2014 concerning restrictive measures in respect of actions undermining or threatening the territorial integrity, sovereignty and independence of Ukraine [2014] OJ L78/16; see also Council Regulation (EU) No 269/2014 of 17 March 2014 concerning restrictive measures in respect of actions undermining or threatening the territorial integrity, sovereignty and independence of Ukraine [2014] OJ L78/6; and, Council Implementing Regulation (EU) No 284/2014 of 21 March 2014 implementing Regulation (EU) No 269/2014 concerning restrictive measures in respect of actions undermining or threatening the territorial integrity, sovereignty and independence of Ukraine [2014] OJ L86/27.

[332] UNGA Res 68/262, *Territorial Integrity of Ukraine* (1 April 2014) UN Doc A/RES/68/262, [5].

[333] ibid, [6].

[334] ibid, [4].

[335] Council of the European Union, 'Council Conclusions on Ukraine', Foreign Affairs Council Meeting (Luxembourg, 14 April 2014) [2], www.consilium.europa.eu/uedocs/cms_data/docs/pressdata/EN/foraff/142223.pdf (accessed 31 July 2019).

[336] ibid, [6].

[337] Council of the European Union, 'Council Conclusions on Ukraine', Foreign Affairs Council Meeting (Brussels, 12 May 2014) [5], www.consilium.europa.eu/en/meetings/fac/2014/05/12/ (accessed 31 July 2019).

[338] ibid, [9]; see also Council Decision 2014/265/CFSP of 12 May 2014 amending Decision 2014/145/CFSP concerning restrictive measures in respect of actions undermining or threatening the territorial integrity, sovereignty and independence of Ukraine [2014] OJ L137/9; and, Council Regulation (EU) No 476/2014 of 12 May 2014 amending Regulation (EU) No 269/2014 concerning restrictive measures in respect of actions undermining or threatening the territorial integrity, sovereignty and independence of Ukraine [2014] OJ L137/1.

[339] Conclusions of 12 May 2014 (n 337) [10].

[340] ibid, [10].

Ukraine, calling for independent investigations into the allegations.[341] With this a growing concern for the EU Foreign Affairs Council in the backdrop of the annexation of Crimea,[342] the Council decided to prohibit the import of goods originating from Crimea or the city of Sevastopol into the European Union.[343]

When fighting in the east of Ukraine continued, and the Malaysian Airlines passenger flight MH17 was shot down over the area of conflict on 17 July 2014, the EU increased the scope of its asset freezes and travel bans to targets who supported, materially or financially, actions undermining or threatening the territorial integrity, sovereignty and independence of Ukraine.[344] Eventually, the Council targeted Russian financial institutions and the defence sector, and imposed an arms embargo.[345] This was further expanded to target the Russian oil sector.[346] This Regulation expressly stated that its aim was to 'put pressure on the Russian Government'.[347] Similar measures and further restrictions continued to be imposed upon Russia up to the time of writing.[348]

Dawidowicz[349] is of the opinion that the financial measures imposed by the EU would generally fall foul of Article II of the GATS,[350] providing for

[341] See eg United Nations Office of the United Nations High Commissioner for Human Rights (OHCHR), 'Report on the Human Rights Situation in Ukraine' (15 June 2014) www.ohchr.org/Documents/Countries/UA/HRMMUReport15June2014.pdf (accessed 31 July 2019).

[342] Council of the European Union, 'Council Conclusions on Ukraine', Foreign Affairs Council Meeting (Luxembourg, 23 June 2014) [3] and [4], www.consilium.europa.eu/en/meetings/fac/2014/06/23/ (accessed 31 July 2019).

[343] Council Decision 2014/386/CFSP of 23 June 2014 concerning restrictions on goods originating in Crimea or Sevastopol, in response to the illegal annexation of Crimea and Sevastopol [2014] OJ L183/70; see also Council Regulation (EU) No 692/2014 of 23 June 2014 concerning restrictions on the import into the Union of goods originating in Crimea or Sevastopol, in response to the illegal annexation of Crimea and Sevastopol [2014] OJ L183/9.

[344] Council Decision 2014/475/CFSP of 18 July 2014 amending Decision 2014/145/CFSP concerning restrictive measures in respect of actions undermining or threatening the territorial integrity, sovereignty and independence of Ukraine [2014] OJ L214/28; see also Council Regulation (EU) No 783/2014 of 18 July 2014 amending Regulation (EU) No 269/2014 concerning restrictive measures in respect of actions undermining or threatening the territorial integrity, sovereignty and independence of Ukraine [2014] OJ L214/2.

[345] Council Decision 2014/512/CFSP of 31 July 2014 concerning restrictive measures in view of Russia's actions destabilising the situation in Ukraine [2014] OJ L229/13; see also Council Regulation (EU) No 833/2014 of 31 July 2014 concerning restrictive measures in view of Russia's actions destabilising the situation in Ukraine [2014] OJ L229/1.

[346] Council Decision 2014/659/CFSP of 8 September 2014 amending Decision 2014/512/CFSP concerning restrictive measures in view of Russia's actions destabilising the situation in Ukraine [2014] OJ L271/54; see also Council Regulation (EU) No 960/2014 of 8 September 2014 amending Regulation (EU) No 833/2014 concerning restrictive measures in view of Russia's actions destabilising the situation in Ukraine [2014] L271/3.

[347] Regulation (EU) No 833/2014 (n 346) preamble [6].

[348] For a full timeline of measures, up to date at the time of writing, see European Council/Council of the European Union, 'Timeline – EU Restrictive Measures in Response to the Crisis in Ukraine' (*European Union*, updated regularly) www.consilium.europa.eu/en/policies/sanctions/ukraine-crisis/history-ukraine-crisis/ (accessed 31 July 2019).

[349] Dawidowicz (n 319); for a detailed review of this practice, see also Dawidowicz (n 207) 231–38.

[350] General Agreement on Trade in Services (GATS) (adopted 15 April 1994, entered into force 1 January 1995), 1869 UNTS 183.

'Most-Favoured-Nation Treatment' whereby Members shall accord to services and service suppliers of any other Member treatment no less favourable than that it accords any other country. He also notes that none of the security exceptions in Article XIV*bis* of the same agreement have been invoked by the EU, and therefore argues that the only explanation of these measures would be to accept the legality of non-injured State countermeasures.[351] Similarly, he also argued in terms of the GATT[352] that:

> The limited export embargo applicable to energy-related goods also amounts to a quantitative trade restriction which is *prima facie* unlawful under Article XI GATT. Again, EU Member States did not invoke the national security exception in Article XXI GATT as possible justification for their otherwise unlawful conduct.[353]

Of course, just because the EU does not *invoke* the security exceptions in GATS, or the similar security exceptions in GATT Article XXI, does not necessarily mean that they do not apply. As discussed above, the exceptions provided for in Article XIV*bis* GATS and Article XXI GATT are quite vague and it is not clear whether they are to be interpreted as self-judging, or at least subject to some form of objective review criteria.[354] If the provisions were to be interpreted objectively, the question is whether the actions taken by the EU are 'necessary for the protection of its essential security interests', even if it could be readily accepted that the Ukraine crisis is an 'emergency in international relations'. Part of that assessment, as highlighted by the WTO Panel, is whether the measures imposed are sufficiently connected to the protection of those interests, and whether they are invoked in good faith.[355] This interpretation, incorporating the obligation of good faith, could render the security exceptions to GATT and GATS less prone to abuse, since the party relying on them must *actually* believe the exceptions apply. Based on this interpretation, Dawidowicz may well have a point in highlighting the lack of an invocation of these exceptions by the EU, because it may be used to indicate whether or not the EU genuinely believes that these exceptions apply.

[351] Dawidowicz (n 319).

[352] General Agreement on Tariffs and Trade 1947 (GATT 1947) (adopted 30 October 1947, entered into force 1 January 1948), 55 UNTS 187, amended by the Marrakech Agreement Establishing the World Trade Organization (adopted 15 April 1994, entered into force 1 January 1995), 1867 UNTS 154, and the General Agreement on Tariffs and Trade 1994 (GATT 1994) (adopted 15 April 1994, entered into force 1 January 1995) 1867 UNTS 187; provisions of the GATT 1947, as incorporated by GATT 1994, hereinafter simply referred to as 'GATT'.

[353] Dawidowicz (n 319).

[354] See section 1.3.

[355] See *Russia – Measures Concerning Traffic in Transit* (n 161) [7.130]–[7.133]. But see also Neuwirth and Svetlicinii (n 150) 905–06, where they highlight an argument, at n 93, by Schloemann and Ohlhoff that 'Although "consideration" must be exercised in good faith, showing that a government acted in bad faith is next to impossible in practice'; see also HL Schloemann and S Ohlhoff, '"Constitutionalization" and Dispute Settlement in the WTO: National Security as an Issue of Competence' (1999) 93 *American Journal of International Law* 424, 445.

As discussed above,[356] if one of the exceptions to GATT or GATS applies, this renders the measures in question compatible with the GATT or GATS regimes in international law, so long as they are also consistent with other general principles of international law such as non-intervention, human rights and the prohibition of force.

Neuwirth and Svetlicinii discussed this issue particularly in relation to the measures taken in response to the Ukraine crisis.[357] They highlight the 'rational choice theory' which supports the position that 'states do not abuse the security exception, because by doing so, they would encourage other states to follow suit'.[358] By extension, it could be argued that parties may not *invoke* the security exception explicitly, where they are really relying on it on duplicitous or contentious grounds, out of the same fear that other States may do the same. The reality is, if States or international organisations really do want to secure the observance of human rights norms or the law concerning mass atrocities by utilising coercive measures, it would certainly be more legitimate and legally sound for them to justify their action as it is, rather than stretching the meaning of 'essential security interests' beyond its logical and ordinary meaning.

Other measures taken in response to the Ukraine crisis include similar economic measures by States including the US,[359] Australia,[360] Canada[361] and Japan.[362] The US Executive Orders referred to the deployment of Russian forces into Ukraine as 'an unusual and extraordinary threat to the national security and foreign policy of the United States'[363] and the first Order declared a 'national emergency' in response.[364] Canada's measures viewed Russia's actions as 'a grave breach of international peace and security that has resulted or is likely to result in a serious international crisis'.[365]

356 See section 1.3.
357 Neuwirth and Svetlicinii (n 150).
358 ibid, 909.
359 See eg: Executive Order 13660 of 6 March 2014, 79 Fed Reg 13493 (10 March 2014); Executive Order 13661 of 16 March 2014, 79 Fed Reg 15535 (19 March 2014); Executive Order 13662 of 20 March 2014, 79 Fed Reg 16169 (24 March 2014); and, Executive Order 13685 of 19 December 2014, 79 Fed Reg 77357 (24 December 2014).
360 See eg Autonomous Sanctions (Russia, Crimea and Sevastopol) Specification 2015 (31 March 2015) www.legislation.gov.au/Details/F2015L00390 (accessed 31 July 2019).
361 Special Economic Measures (Russia) Regulations SOR/2014–58 (17 March 2014) http://laws.justice.gc.ca/eng/regulations/SOR-2014-58/FullText.html (accessed 31 July 2019).
362 Ministry of Foreign Affairs of Japan, 'Statement by the Minister for Foreign Affairs of Japan on the Sanctions against Russia over the situation in Ukraine' *MOFA Japan* (29 April 2014) www.mofa.go.jp/press/release/press4e_000281.html (accessed 31 July 2019); Ministry of Foreign Affairs of Japan, 'Statement by the Minister for Foreign Affairs of Japan on the Additional Measures over the situation in Ukraine' *MOFA Japan* (28 July 2014) www.mofa.go.jp/press/release/press2e_000003.html (accessed 31 July 2019); and Ministry of Foreign Affairs of Japan, 'Statement by the Minister for Foreign Affairs of Japan on the Additional Measures Imposed on Russia in Connection with the Ukraine Situation' *MOFA Japan* (25 September 2014) www.mofa.go.jp/press/release/press4e_000445.html (accessed 31 July 2019).
363 Executive Orders 13660, 13661 and 13662 (n 359).
364 ibid, Executive Order 13660.
365 Regulations SOR/2014-58 (n 361).

Despite questioning the legality of sanctions outside of the UN Charter and the Security Council,[366] Russia adopted several 'counter-sanctions'[367] in response to these measures. For example, President Putin issued an executive order limiting the import of agricultural products, raw materials and foodstuffs from States that imposed 'economic sanctions against Russian legal entities' and also individuals who joined such action.[368] The latest versions of the Russian measures imposed restrictions upon the US, the EU, Canada, Australia, Norway, Ukraine, Albania, Montenegro, Iceland and Liechtenstein up until 31 December 2017.[369]

Similarly, Russia suspended[370] its 2013 Agreement with the US on Cooperation in Nuclear and Energy Related Scientific Research and Development.[371] According to the official statement on this decision, Russia considered that the ongoing extensions of sanctions by the US against Russia 'requires the adoption of countermeasures in relation to the US'.[372] It further underscored:

> Under this approach, the international legal framework of cooperation with the United States will be preserved. Russia will preserve the possibility of resuming cooperation under the Agreement when that is justified by the general context of relations with the United States.[373]

Based upon this particular statement, it does seem that Russia is justifying its action as a countermeasure within the international law meaning of that phrase. However, as Hofer has rightly pointed out, Russia could only rely on the doctrine of countermeasures if the sanctions they are responding to are illegal

[366] For a detailed overview of Russia's apparently contradictory position on countermeasures specifically with regard to this crisis, see Dawidowicz (n 207) 237–38.

[367] The phrase 'counter-sanctions' is used here only to indicate the nature of Russia imposing measures in response to other international measures against it, without deciding on whether or not these measures by Russia are legal 'countermeasures'.

[368] See eg Executive Order (Decree) No 560, 'On the Application of Certain Special Economic Measures to Ensure the Security of the Russian Federation' (6 August 2014) http://en.kremlin.ru/acts/news/46404 (accessed 31 July 2019); see also Government Resolution No 778, 'On Measures to Implement the Presidential Executive Order on Adopting Special Economic Measures to Provide for Security of the Russian Federation' (7 August 2014) http://government.ru/en/docs/14195/ (accessed 31 July 2019).

[369] See Executive Order (Decree) No 305, 'On the Prolongation of the Application of Certain Special Economic Measures to Ensure the Security of the Russian Federation' (29 June 2016); see also Government Resolution No 778 (n 368), as amended, http://government.ru/en/docs/23584/ (accessed 31 July 2019).

[370] See, Government Decision, 'Suspending the Russian–US Agreement on Cooperation in Nuclear- and Energy-Related Scientific Research and Development' (5 October 2016) http://government.ru/en/docs/24766/ (accessed 31 July 2019).

[371] Agreement between the Government of the United States of America and the Government of the Russian Federation on Cooperation in Nuclear- and Energy-Related Scientific Research and Development (signed at Vienna on 16 September 2013).

[372] Government Decision of 5 October 2016 (n 370).

[373] ibid.

in the first place.[374] This is precisely the question at hand, and on the basis of the preceding analysis it does seem that there is growing evidence of State practice in support of non-injured party countermeasures, indicating the legal space in which a tertiary responsibility to protect beyond the failures of the Security Council could operate.

2.2.3.4. Responses Following Atrocity Crimes in Myanmar (2016–Present)

Chapter II outlined in detail the latest developments in Myanmar and Rakhine State and the evidence of atrocity crimes, including possible genocide, that have taken place in recent years.[375] The inaction of the UN Security Council in response to these atrocities indicates a possible failure of the Council's responsibility to protect and even arguably its responsibility to maintain international peace and security. Therefore, the international response beyond the Security Council is particularly relevant in the context of this investigation to find any legal space for coercive measures to implement the responsibility to protect beyond the Security Council.

The European Union has been the most prolific entity to have utilised coercive measures against Myanmar actors in response to the recent atrocities. In 2013, although Myanmar still had spouts of violence, the EU responded to what it called a 'remarkable process of reform' and a transition towards democracy in Myanmar by easing all pre-existing sanctions while maintaining an arms embargo on the country.[376] Against this backdrop, the Council of the EU urged that 'the government should continue to pursue and implement durable solutions to the underlying causes of the tensions that include addressing the status of the Rohingya'.[377]

Following the harrowing crackdown on the Rohingya population in August 2017, as detailed above,[378] the Council of the EU adopted conclusions on 16 October 2017.[379] Here, the EU expressed that the 'humanitarian and human

[374] A Hofer, 'Russia's Unilateral Suspension of the 2013 Agreement on Nuclear Cooperation with the United States' *EJIL: Talk!* (27 October 2016) www.ejiltalk.org/russias-unilateral-suspension-of-the-2013-agreement-on-nuclear-cooperation-with-the-united-states/ (accessed 31 July 2019).

[375] See above, Chapter II, section 3.2.3.

[376] Council of the European Union, 'Council Conclusions on Myanmar/Burma', 3236th Foreign Affairs Council Meeting (Luxembourg, 22 April 2013) www.consilium.europa.eu/uedocs/cms_data/docs/pressdata/EN/foraff/136918.pdf (accessed 31 July 2019); see also Council Decision 2013/184/CFSP of 22 April 2013 concerning restrictive measures against Myanmar/Burma and repealing Decision 2010/232/CFSP [2013] OJ L111/75; and Council Regulation (EU) No 401/2013 of 2 May 2013 concerning restrictive measures in respect of Myanmar/Burma and repealing Regulation (EC) No 194/2008 [2013] OJ L121/1.

[377] Conclusions of 22 April 2013 (n 376) [4].

[378] See above, Chapter II, Section 3.2.3.

[379] Council of the European Union, 'Outcome of the Council Meeting', 3566th Council Meeting, Foreign Affairs (Luxembourg, 16 October 2017) Doc 13032/17, www.consilium.europa.eu/media/22071/st13032en17-vf.pdf (accessed 31 July 2019).

rights situation in Rakhine State is extremely serious'.[380] In light of what the Council labelled 'the disproportionate use of force carried out by the security forces', the EU suspended invitations to Myanmar military forces and reviewed its defence cooperation with those forces.[381] The Council also confirmed that the arms embargo was to remain in place so that such arms and equipment could not be used for 'internal repression' and warned that it would adopt additional measures should the situation not improve.[382]

In further conclusions adopted in February 2018,[383] the Council invited the EU's High Representative to make proposals for the extension of the existing arms embargo,[384] and proposals for targeted restrictive measures against 'senior military officers of the Myanmar armed forces (Tatmadaw) responsible for serious and systematic human rights violations without delay'.[385] By April 2018, the EU had strengthened the arms embargo, and set out a framework for imposing measures such as travel bans and asset freezes on members of the Myanmar Armed Forces who may be found responsible for serious human rights violations, obstructing the conduct of independent investigations into such violations, or obstructing access to humanitarian assistance.[386] In June 2018, the EU targeted seven members of the armed forces for these measures,[387] with the reasons for listing primarily being that each of the targets was 'responsible for the atrocities and serious human rights violations committed against Rohingya population in Rakhine State'.[388]

Following the report of the UN Human Rights Council's Independent International Fact-Finding Mission on Myanmar,[389] the EU extended the restrictive measures to a further seven members of the Myanmar Armed Forces.[390] By February 2019, several States had aligned themselves with the restrictive

[380] ibid, 6, [1].
[381] ibid, 7, [6].
[382] ibid.
[383] Council of the European Union, 'Council Conclusions on Myanmar/Burma', 3598th Meeting, Foreign Affairs, (26 February 2018) http://data.consilium.europa.eu/doc/document/ST-6418-2018-INIT/en/pdf (accessed 31 July 2019).
[384] ibid, [11].
[385] ibid, [12].
[386] Council Decision (CFSP) 2018/655 of 26 April 2018 amending Decision 2013/184/CFSP concerning restrictive measures against Myanmar/Burma [2018] OJ L108/29; see also Council Regulation (EU) 2018/647 of 26 April 2018 amending Regulation (EU) No 401/2013 concerning restrictive measures in respect of Myanmar/Burma [2018] OJ L108/1.
[387] Council Implementing Regulation (EU) 2018/898 of 25 June 2018 implementing Regulation (EU) No 401/2013 concerning restrictive measures in respect of Myanmar/Burma [2018] OJ L160/1.
[388] ibid, Annex.
[389] See above, Chapter II, section 3.2.3; see also Council of the European Union, 'Council Conclusions on Myanmar/Burma', 3662nd Meeting, Foreign Affairs (10 December 2018) [1], www.consilium.europa.eu/media/37409/st15033-en18.pdf (accessed 31 July 2019).
[390] Council Decision (CFSP) 2018/2054 of 21 December 2018 amending Decision 2013/184/CFSP concerning restrictive measures against Myanmar/Burma [2018] OJ L327/5; see also Council Implementing Regulation (EU) 2018/2053 of 21 December 2018 implementing Regulation (EU) No 401/2013 concerning restrictive measures in respect of Myanmar/Burma [2018] OJ L327/1, Annex.

measures against Myanmar, including: Turkey, Macedonia, Montenegro, Albania, Bosnia and Herzegovina, Iceland, Liechtenstein, Norway, Moldova and Armenia.[391] In April 2019, the council extended the restrictive measures until 30 April 2020.[392]

Other States also took restrictive measures against Myanmar or Myanmar military targets. In the United States, the House of Representatives passed a Resolution condemning 'ethnic cleansing of the Rohingya and calling for an end to the attacks in and an immediate restoration of humanitarian access to the state of Rakhine in Burma'.[393] The Resolution went further to call on 'the President to impose sanctions on those responsible for human rights abuses, including members of Burma's military and security services'.[394] The US imposed travel bans on the highest ranks of the Myanmar military in July 2019, including the Commander-in-Chief Min Aung Hlaing.[395] Canada, on the other hand, imposed targeted asset freezes against senior members of the Myanmar military.[396] Australia also imposed travel bans and targeted financial sanctions on members of the Myanmar military following the UN Fact-Finding Mission's report.[397]

The UN Fact-Finding Mission on Myanmar took the step of urging the international community to sever financial ties with the Myanmar military

[391] See Council of the European Union, 'Declaration by the High Representative on behalf of the EU on the alignment of certain countries with Council Decision concerning restrictive measures against Myanmar/Burma', Press Release 73/19 (7 February 2019) www.consilium.europa.eu/en/press/press-releases/2019/02/07/declaration-by-the-high-representative-on-behalf-of-the-eu-on-the-alignment-of-certain-countries-with-council-decision-concerning-restrictive-measures-against-myanmar-burma/pdf (accessed 31 July 2019).

[392] Council Decision (CFSP) 2019/678 of 29 April 2019 amending Decision 2013/184/CFSP concerning restrictive measures against Myanmar/Burma [2019] OJ L114/18; see also Council Implementing Regulation (EU) 2019/672 of 29 April 2019 implementing Regulation (EU) No 401/2013 concerning restrictive measures in respect of Myanmar/Burma [2019] OJ L114/1.

[393] United States Congress, 'Condemning Ethnic Cleansing of the Rohingya and Calling for an End to the Attacks in and an Immediate Restoration of Humanitarian Access to the State of Rakhine in Burma', House of Representatives H.Con.Res.90 (7 November 2017) www.congress.gov/115/bills/hconres90/BILLS-115hconres90ih.pdf (accessed 31 July 2019).

[394] ibid, operative [8].

[395] US State Department, 'Public Designation, Due to Gross Violations of Human Rights, of Burmese Military Officials', Press Statement (16 July 2019) www.state.gov/public-designation-due-to-gross-violations-of-human-rights-of-burmese-military-officials/ (accessed 31 July 2019).

[396] See eg Regulations Amending the Special Economic Measures (Burma) Regulations: SOR/2018-135 (25 June 2018) www.gazette.gc.ca/rp-pr/p2/2018/2018-07-11/html/sor-dors135-eng.html (accessed 31 July 2019); see also Global Affairs Canada, 'Canada Imposes Further Sanctions in Response to Ongoing Crisis in Myanmar', News Release, *Global Affairs Canada* (25 June 2018) www.canada.ca/en/global-affairs/news/2018/06/canada-imposes-further-sanctions-in-response-to-ongoing-crisis-in-myanmar.html (accessed 31 July 2019).

[397] See T Westbrook and S Lewis, 'Australia Slaps Sanctions on Myanmar Army Top Brass' *Reuters* (23 October 2018) www.reuters.com/article/us-australia-myanmar/australia-slaps-sanctions-on-myanmar-army-top-brass-idUSKCN1MX0O8 (accessed 31 July 2019); for the most up-to-date sanctions, see Australian Government, Department of Foreign Affairs and Trade, 'Sanctions Regimes: Myanmar', https://dfat.gov.au/international-relations/security/sanctions/sanctions-regimes/Pages/myanmar.aspx (accessed 1 July 2019).

and to financially isolate the military commanders, in order to bring them before a court to answer 'charges of war crimes, crimes against humanity and genocide'.[398] Although it is not clear whether the members of the Mission were encouraging States to take countermeasures, or simply cut off existing financial funding as a measure of retorsion, their encouragement of 'financial isolation' was very clear. Similar calls for tougher targeted sanctions have also been made by human rights groups such as Human Rights Watch.[399]

It is clear that many of these coercive measures are aimed at encouraging accountability for the atrocities that took place in Rakhine State, especially the spike in violence from August 2017. Indeed, even the Prosecutor at the ICC has attempted to find creative ways of establishing that the ICC has jurisdiction over the atrocities, and has sought to open an investigation into the situation.[400] Myanmar is not a Member of the ICC, but Bangladesh – where refugees have fled to – is a Member State. Therefore, the ICC's Pre-Trial Chamber decided that the Court may exercise jurisdiction over the alleged deportation of the Rohingya people from Myanmar to Bangladesh.[401]

Undoubtedly, the accountability aspect of the responsibility to protect is essential to maintain a continuum of protection and forms an integral part of *rebuilding* a society after atrocity crimes. However, with reports that atrocity crimes may still be taking place,[402] the coercive measures taken by the EU and other States may need to be strengthened or reviewed accordingly.

Myanmar's neighbouring States and larger powers such as Russia and China have not adopted any coercive response to the atrocities within Myanmar. The Association of Southeast Asian Nations (ASEAN), at each of the Summits since the crisis spiralled in August 2017, tended to respond to the crisis in Myanmar with carefully worded statements, which often omitted some of the more pressing issues. For example, at the 31st ASEAN Summit in November 2017, the Chairman's Statement of the Summit supported Myanmar's 'efforts to bring about peace' and welcomed the government's commitment to 'take immediate

[398] UN Human Rights Council, 'UN Independent International Fact-Finding Mission on Myanmar Urges Financial Isolation of Myanmar Military', Press Release (Geneva, 14 May 2019) www.ohchr.org/EN/HRBodies/HRC/Pages/NewsDetail.aspx?NewsID=24608&LangID=E (accessed 31 July 2019).

[399] See eg Human Rights Watch, 'Burma: US Should Promote Justice for Rohingya' *Human Rights Watch* (25 September 2018) www.hrw.org/news/2018/09/25/burma-us-should-promote-justice-rohingya, (accessed 31 July 2019); M Ganguly and B Adams, 'For Rohingya Refugees, There's No Return in Sight' *Human Rights Watch* (5 June 2019) www.hrw.org/news/2019/06/05/rohingya-refugees-theres-no-return-sight, (accessed 31 July 2019).

[400] International Criminal Court, Office of the Prosecutor, 'Notice Pursuant to Regulation 45 of the Regulations of the Court', OTP2019/014274 (12 June 2019).

[401] Decision on the 'Prosecution's Request for a Ruling on Jurisdiction under Article 19(3) of the Statute', Pre-Trial Chamber 1, ICC-RoC46(3)-01/18 (6 September 2018).

[402] Amnesty International, *'No One Can Protect Us': War Crimes and Abuses in Myanmar's Rakhine State*, (London, Amnesty International, 2019) www.amnesty.org/download/Documents/ASA1604172019ENGLISH.PDF (accessed 31 July 2019).

steps to end the violence in Rakhine'.[403] In April 2018, ASEAN concentrated largely on the efforts to return displaced persons to Rakhine State, omitting any mention of accountability or the allegations against Myanmar itself, and once again supported the Myanmar government's 'efforts' to 'promote harmony and reconciliation among the various communities'.[404] These warm words were largely repeated in November 2018 at the 33rd Summit, where it expected 'the Independent Commission of Enquiry established by the Government of Myanmar to seek accountability by carrying out an independent and impartial investigation of the alleged human rights violations and related issues', seemingly ignoring the UN Fact-Finding Mission and its findings.[405] In June 2019, the Summit finally committed to 'a more visible and enhanced role of ASEAN to support Myanmar in providing humanitarian assistance, facilitating the repatriation process with regard to the situation in Rakhine State', but offered no further indication of any real action or response to the ongoing atrocities in this respect.[406]

And so, the measures taken by the European Union and other States do seem to indicate some support for taking coercive action beyond the inaction of the Security Council, and therefore an indication of practice consistent with non-injured party countermeasures. However, ASEAN's response as the main regional organisation in this area has been disappointing, indicating perhaps that the problem of inaction and a lack of political will to criticise an ally or a neighbour extends beyond the membership of the Security Council.

2.2.4. Preliminary Conclusions on the Viability of Non-Injured Party Countermeasures

Based on the analysis above, it is submitted that the requirement that a State or international organisation must be 'injured' before it is able to take countermeasures against a breach of an obligation *it is owed*, and has a legal interest in preserving, seems somewhat misplaced. It has been clear from early State practice that the party taking countermeasures must be a victim of a breach – but the advent of the requirement of 'injury' is unclear. Hesitance against allowing

[403] ASEAN, 'Chairman's Statement of the 31st ASEAN Summit: Partnering for Change, Engaging the World' (Manila, Philippines, 13 November 2017) [87], https://asean.org/storage/2017/11/final-chairmans-statement-of-31st-asean-summit.pdf (accessed 31 July 2019).

[404] ASEAN, 'Chairman's Statement of the 32nd ASEAN Summit' (Singapore, 28 April 2018) [17], https://asean.org/wp-content/uploads/2018/04/Chairmans-Statement-of-the-32nd-ASEAN-Summit.pdf (accessed 31 July 2019).

[405] ASEAN, 'Chairman's Statement of the 33rd ASEAN Summit' (Singapore, 13 November 2018) [37], https://asean.org/storage/2018/11/33rd_ASEAN_Summit_Chairman_s_Statement_Final.pdf (accessed 31 July 2019).

[406] ASEAN, 'Chairman's Statement of the 34th ASEAN Summit: Advancing Partnership for Sustainability' (Bangkok, 23 June 2019) [42]–[43], https://asean.org/storage/2019/06/Final_Chairs-Statement-of-the-34th-ASEAN-Summit_as-of-23-June-2019-12....pdf (accessed 31 July 2019).

all States with a *legal interest* in preserving an obligation to enforce that obligation through countermeasures have consistently cited the potential for abuse as a concern. However, in the view of this author, it seems that the requirement of 'injury' as the ILC defines it goes too far in limiting the application of countermeasures.

If a State is owed an obligation by virtue of that obligation being owed to the international community as a whole – and that obligation is breached, but there is no 'victim State' that has been directly injured – the use of countermeasures would still be subject to the requirement of proportionality. As addressed in relation to Libya and China's fears above,[407] there is a need to avoid countermeasures and the risk of abuse where there is only a 'minor' or 'technical' breach of an obligation. However, it seems this concern goes too far. The requirement of proportionality would surely be enough of a legal stopper to prevent the use of countermeasures where it would be wholly disproportionate or inappropriate. To respond to a technical breach of an obligation with a far-reaching substantive breach of another, in itself, would be disproportionate and therefore illegal. In other words, if *any* countermeasure would be disproportionate in response to a breach, then that must be a legal indication that countermeasures are legally unavailable in the first place.

In light of more recent practice, it seems much clearer that States are of the position that countermeasures may be taken in response to breaches of obligations *erga omnes* by States not directly affected. Whether these States consider themselves as 'specifically affected' or 'injured' is unclear, but the countermeasures were utilised nonetheless.

Elagab[408] highlighted this very point in 1988 when he argued that, although he believed there was no support in State practice *at that time* for countermeasures in response to 'international crimes',[409] there may be a legal argument for reactions to obligations *erga omnes*:

> None the less, the *erga omnes* principle may be applied to widen the category of 'an aggrieved party' so as to include all States where the violated obligation has an *erga omnes* character. Accordingly, all States, including those which have not been injured directly, will be deemed to have a right to impose counter-measures against the perpetrator of the breach. That said, it needs, however, to be recognised that measures taken in such circumstances might exceed the limits of proportionality. It follows, therefore, that difficulties would arise when the legality of such measures is being considered.[410]

[407] See section 2.2.1.

[408] OY Elagab, *The Legality of Non-Forcible Counter-Measures in International Law* (Oxford, Clarendon Press, 1988).

[409] This was a rejected category of responsibility in earlier drafts of the ILC Articles: see eg ILC, 'Frist Report on State Responsibility by Mr James Crawford, Special Rapporteur' (1998) UN Doc A/CN.4/490, [46]–[51] and [70]–[95].

[410] Elagab (n 408) 59.

This, of course, is not to say that there would be no risks of abuse if non-injured parties could take countermeasures freely and at their own choosing. Crawford stressed the balance that needs to be met, highlighting the difficulty in situations where breaches of human rights obligations are owed to the international community as a whole but affect only the nationals of the responsible State:

> The difficulty here is that, almost by definition, the injured parties will lack representative organs which can validly express their wishes on the international plane, and there is a substantial risk of exacerbating such cases if third States are freely allowed to take countermeasures based on their own appreciation of the situation. On the other hand it is difficult to envisage that, faced with obvious, gross and persistent violations of community obligations, third States should have no entitlement to act.[411]

Crawford is clearly stressing the difficult choice between allowing non-injured State countermeasures and the risks of abuse.[412] Alland outlines the same concerns that countermeasures 'may be merely a way of imposing a partial, biased and subjective view of international *ordre public*' and that 'they may allow the domination of a few states over others to be legitimized, since countermeasures retain their self-assessed nature'.[413] Some have argued that allowing non-injured State countermeasures would be 'an invitation to chaos' which would legitimise 'mob-justice', 'vigilantism' and 'power politics'.[414] However, if there is a clear need to allow such action in genuine circumstances, there is no reason why these measures cannot be allowed with the requisite safeguards in place.[415] Proportionality, as argued, is just one of those safeguards alongside the other procedural and substantive limitations outlined by the ILC in Articles 49–53 of its State Responsibility Articles.[416]

Indeed, perhaps some States are right when they highlighted during the General Assembly's Sixth Committee debates on this issue that collective countermeasures of this kind should at least be authorised by a competent international or regional organisation.[417] There was of course a clear preference by some States such as Mexico[418] that collective measures should be taken by the

[411] Crawford, 'Third Report' (n 254) [403].

[412] On this point, see also D Alland, 'Countermeasures of General Interest' (2002) 13(5) *European Journal of International Law* 1221.

[413] ibid, 1236.

[414] See the arguments and authors cited by Dawidowicz (n 251) 344; see also Tams (n 245) 199 and 240.

[415] See on the need for safeguards for countermeasures generally, eg ILC, 'Report of the International Law Commission on the Work of its Fifty-Third Session' (23 April–1 June and 2 July–10 August 2001) UN Doc A/56/10, 324–27, particularly [6]; see also Alland (n 412) 1225.

[416] See ILC Articles on State Responsibility (n 199) Arts 49–53 generally. For an in-depth review of the safeguards against abuse, see Dawidowicz (n 207) ch 6.

[417] See above (n 243) and discussion therein.

[418] UNGA Sixth Committee (55th Session), 'Summary Record of the 20th Meeting' (14 November 2000) UN Doc A/C.6/55/SR.20, [35]–[36] (Mexico).

UN Security Council. There were also cautious warnings by others that unilateral action should not be taken while the Security Council is seized of a matter, for the risk of undermining or marginalising the Security Council itself.[419] Iran expressed a wider view, suggesting that 'where there had been a serious breach of an essential obligation owed to the international community as a whole, countermeasures must be coordinated by the United Nations'.[420] It is not clear whether Iran meant through the Security Council, or whether this coordination could have been done by another competent body of the UN.

Such institutional safeguards certainly increase the legitimacy of collective countermeasures. But in our case, where the Security Council has failed to respond, inaction could have dire consequences. As we shall discuss in Chapter VI, a requirement that action should be green-lit by the General Assembly may well satisfy the thirst for safeguards, but this of course depends upon the competences of the Assembly under the UN Charter.[421] Like the failure of the Security Council, the UN General Assembly may not always have the political will to act, or the UN *in general* may not be in a position to respond quickly enough to *prevent* atrocity crimes from taking place, whereas a regional organisation might be. The responsibility to protect still does not end, and so we must also consider whether action *beyond* the UN could come with sufficient safeguards to allow such emergency responses by regional organisations.[422]

Leaving aside these questions for now, we must address whether there are grounds to accept that this category of non-injured party countermeasures has been accepted as a legal justification for coercive measures. The main problem, of course, is that State practice may indicate an implied belief that this is so, but their statements are not explicit or exact enough to categorically demonstrate evidence of opinio juris, and their actions might also be based upon purely political or moral grounds rather than legal ones.[423] Dawidowicz seeks to explain this criticism by using what he describes as the ICJ's own method for assessing the existence of opinio juris, as purportedly adopted by the ILC: that 'in the absence of evidence of non-normative intent (opinio non juris), the ICJ has often presumed that consistent practice is accompanied by normative intent (opinio juris)'.[424] Dawidowicz earlier explained that: '[T]he method implicit in their assessment could be described as a process of elimination: in the absence

[419] See UNGA Sixth Committee (55th Session), 'Summary Record of 17th Meeting' (14 November 2000) UN Doc A/C.6/55/SR.17, [85] (Greece); and UNGA Sixth Committee (55th Session), 'Summary Record of 24th Meeting' (16 November 2000) UN Doc A/C.6/55/SR.24, [63]–[64] (Cameroon).

[420] UNGA Sixth Committee (55th Session), 'Summary Record of the 15th Meeting' (13 November 2000) UN Doc A/C.6/55/SR.15, [17] (Iran).

[421] See Chapter VI, section 1.3.

[422] See Chapter VI, section 2.

[423] See, for example, points made by Crawford, where he highlights that States have sometimes had implied preference for alternative justifications such as grounds for the suspension or termination of treaties: Crawford, 'Third Report' (n 254) [396(a)]; see also Tams (n 245) 238–39.

[424] Dawidowicz (n 207) 255.

of indications of outright illegality or alternative legal justifications, a particular act has been presumed lawful as a third-party countermeasure.'[425] He goes on:

> On this basis, by demonstrating that alternative and converging justifications are unavailable in each case, the better view is arguably that there is a presumption of legality attached to the generally uniform conduct assessed in this study. The view that *prima facie* unlawful unilateral coercive measures taken in defence of the most serious breaches of international law should be regarded as merely 'politically motivated measures' is thus not borne out by international practice.[426]

Dawidowicz has expanded and updated this argument more recently, when he argued that:

> [I]f any State practice motivated by political considerations were dismissed …, there would not be much potential for law to make a contribution to international affairs. A politically motivated practice is still susceptible to legal analysis and evaluation, and can constitute valuable evidence of a rule of custom. … The key question is whether practice is motivated by extra-legal considerations. A negative answer must be provided to this question. Even if States have not explicitly invoked the concept of third-party countermeasures, the practice examined … nevertheless demonstrated that they have relied on it in substance.[427]

Dawidowicz makes a very strong argument here. Indeed, Tams makes a very similar point, suggesting that: '[I]n the absence of specific indications to the contrary, the conduct of States will be based on an accompanying legal conviction; *opinio juris* thus can usually be inferred from State practice'.[428] Tams also argues politically motivated conduct does not necessarily lack opinio juris, because a State's assessment of a situation is often still legally relevant.[429] It leads one to conclude that customary international law may well have developed to indicate that non-injured parties may have standing to take countermeasures, but only in response to certain breaches of international obligations, and only on the basis that there are certain safeguards to prevent abuse.

While a purely Western or developed-State centric practice was a key criticism of the ILC's research, it has already been highlighted above that developing and non-Western States have also utilised coercive measures that could be explained as examples of non-injured party countermeasures.[430] In any case, there does seem a logical explanation for why smaller States do not always utilise coercive measures. Simply, sanctions such as asset freezes and trade restrictions depend on the economies and relationships between the target State and the States using coercive measures. It is more likely that some measures by larger States will be

[425] Dawidowicz (n 251) 412–15, particularly 415.
[426] ibid, 415 (footnote omitted).
[427] Dawidowicz (n 207) 252.
[428] Tams (n 245) 238.
[429] ibid, 239.
[430] See also Dawidowicz (n 207) 242–45.

more effective than if taken by smaller States, because more developed nations such as the US or trade blocs like the EU may have a much deeper trading or financial relationships with the target State than smaller States with little or no trade links. This could especially be the case if the target State was a much larger economy itself. Indeed, larger economies may be more willing and able to take the economic hit that comes with pausing such relationships in pursuit of upholding their collective responsibilities than a smaller economy could endure. Of course, all of this depends on the States in question, and their individual relationships, because there may be some links between smaller neighbouring States that could induce a more effective economic and political coercive pressure than the simple freezing of assets abroad by a larger economic power. This might include, for example, important transport links or use of key infrastructure of the smaller State. The fact that more developed States seem more likely to take coercive measures should not be the sole measure of support for non-injured party countermeasures. What this pattern may indicate, however, is the need for all States to be more creative with the coercive methods they utilise in order to make them more effective in inducing a target State to uphold its responsibility to protect.

Even if this is not the case, and customary international law has not yet developed to extend countermeasures to *non-injured* parties, the current author submits that all States could be considered 'injured' in cases of widespread or systematic atrocities such as those that come within the responsibility to protect. Therefore, the question becomes not whether the law of countermeasures allows non-injured parties to take such action, but whether breaches of *certain* obligations *erga omnes* actually do cause injury to a State concerned, or even the international community as a whole. This depends, of course, on the obligation breached – a question to which we shall now turn.

2.3. Identifying a 'Prior Breach' of an International Obligation *Erga Omnes*

As outlined above, one of the most fundamental requirements for countermeasures to be available is that there is a prior breach of an international obligation by the party that is to be subject to such measures. The varieties of obligations one might expect to be breached when the responsibility to protect is engaged, especially in a situation where the Security Council has failed in its responsibilities,[431] could include violations of human rights obligations, or even the commission of the atrocity crimes themselves. Such obligations may be considered obligations *erga omnes* – owed to the international community as a whole. But since the responsibility to maintain international peace and security

[431] As discussed in Chapter III.

was also identified as a legal responsibility in Chapter III, it is also important to address the application of this obligation in this context too.

As mentioned above, obligations *erga omnes* were recognised by the ICJ in *Barcelona Traction*.[432] The court said in this regard:

> In particular, an essential distinction should be drawn between the obligations of a State towards the international community as a whole, and those arising vis-à-vis another State in the field of diplomatic protection. By their very nature the former are the concern of all States. In view of the importance of the rights involved, all States can be held to have a legal interest in their protection; they are obligations *erga omnes*.[433]

The ICJ gave as examples of obligations *erga omnes*, 'the outlawing of acts of aggression, and of genocide … the principles and rules concerning the basic rights of the human person, including protection from slavery and racial discrimination',[434] and also noted that such obligations may be conferred by general international law as well as 'international instruments of universal or quasi-universal character'.[435]

Regarding the use of countermeasures in response to breaches of such obligations, there seems to be support in commentary for an additional safeguard, namely that these measures may only be used in response to *widespread* or *serious* violations of obligations *erga omnes*. Rather than allowing countermeasures for a simple or technical breach of an *erga omnes* obligation alone, this additional step requiring a threshold of seriousness is supported by a number of writers. For example, Crawford highlighted a pattern in State practice whereby, he supposes, the violation of an obligation had been seen to have reached a certain threshold.[436] Tams in particular highlights States' responses to the ILC's earlier work, and determines that a general right to take countermeasures would be restricted to serious breaches of obligations *erga omnes*.[437] This threshold seems to be widely accepted by other commentators on this issue too.[438]

[432] *Case Concerning Barcelona Traction, Light and Power Company, Limited* (*Belgium v Spain*) (Judgment) [1970] ICJ Rep 3 (hereinafter *Barcelona Traction*) 32, [33].

[433] ibid, 32, [33].

[434] ibid, 32, [34]; see also: *East Timor* (*Portugal v Australia*) (Judgment) [1995] ICJ Rep 90, 102, [29], confirming self-determination as erga omnes; *Application of the Convention on the Prevention and Punishment of the Crime of Genocide* (*Bosnia and Herzegovina v Yugoslavia*) (Preliminary Objections) [1996] ICJ Rep 595, 615–16, [31], confirming the crime of genocide as erga omnes.

[435] ibid.

[436] Crawford, 'Third Report' (n 254) [399] and [404]–[406].

[437] Tams (n 245) 248–49.

[438] See eg: M Payandeh, 'With Great Power Comes Great Responsibility? The Concept of the Responsibility to Protect Within the Process of International Lawmaking' (2010) 35(2) *Yale Journal of International Law* 470, 513; Dawidowicz (n 251) 342, 347; Criddle (n 108) 597. For a discussion of the distinction more generally, see LA Sicilianos, 'The Classification of Obligations and the Multilateral Dimension of the Relations of International Responsibility' (2002) 13(5) *European Journal of International Law* 1127.

Tams supports this additional threshold of 'seriousness', and argues that it provides another safeguard against abuse.[439] He similarly argues that States thus seem prepared to accept the risk of abuse inherent with non-injured party countermeasures in exchange for the increased possibility of responding against particularly serious wrongful conduct.[440]

But this 'seriousness' threshold is evidently ambiguous and raises more questions than answers.[441] While it is not the purpose of this study to investigate the exact threshold of when violations become 'serious', the ILC commentaries may provide some guidance. In particular, Part Two, Chapter III of the Articles on State Responsibility sets out some consequences for *serious breaches* of obligations under peremptory norms of international law (*jus cogens*). Although it is not entirely clear whether *jus cogens* and obligations *erga omnes* (owed to the international community as a whole) are the same, the ILC acknowledges that there is certainly a substantial overlap between them.[442] Therefore, this author submits that the threshold between serious and technical breaches of *jus cogens* would, by analogy, shed some light on what constitutes serious breaches of obligations *erga omnes*, notwithstanding any substantive difference between the two types of norm.

With this in mind, it is useful to highlight that Article 40(2) of the Articles on State Responsibility suggests '[a] breach of such an obligation is serious if it involves a gross or systematic failure by the responsible State to fulfil the obligation'. When explaining this further, the ILC commentaries state:

> The word 'serious' signifies that a certain order of magnitude of violation is necessary in order not to trivialize the breach and it is not intended to suggest that any violation of these obligations is not serious or is somehow excusable. But relatively less serious cases of breach of peremptory norms can be envisaged, and it is necessary to limit the scope of this chapter to the more serious or systematic breaches. Some such limitation is supported by State practice. For example, when reacting against breaches of international law, States have often stressed their systematic, gross or egregious nature.[443]

The ILC further elaborated that a 'systematic' violation of obligations would be carried out in an organised and deliberate way, whereas a 'gross' violation would denote a flagrant breach, 'amounting to a direct and outright assault on the values protected by the rule', and these terms are not necessarily mutually exclusive.[444] With some obligations, such as genocide, the ILC noted that the

[439] Tams (n 245) 250.
[440] Tams (n 245) 251.
[441] See ibid, 248; and also the concerns outlined by States during the ILC's drafting of the ARS with regard to similar language used in Part Two, Chapter III of ARS: Crawford, 'Fourth Report' (n 244) [48].
[442] ILC (n 36) 111, Part Two, Chapter III General Commentary, [7].
[443] ibid, 113, Art 40 Commentary, [7].
[444] ibid, 113, Art 40 Commentary, [8].

obligations themselves by their very nature require an intentional violation on a large scale, seemingly satisfying this 'seriousness' threshold automatically.[445]

On this basis, particular types of obligation can now be assessed. Before this, however, it is worth noting that this 'seriousness' threshold does seem to be another clandestine manifestation of the principle of proportionality in the guise of another test for standing to take countermeasures. The fact that State practice seems to indicate that States cannot take countermeasures in response to 'minor or isolated breaches of obligations *erga omnes*'[446] has resonance with the concerns outlined above that were expressed by other States, regarding the need to limit countermeasures to injured States to prevent the use of these measures against 'technical' breaches of obligations. The question as to whether such breaches must be 'widespread' or 'systematic' again does not seem a suitable application of assessing whether States have legal standing to take countermeasures, but instead this question seems more relevant to whether those countermeasures are *proportionate*. This, in turn, would still assess whether the countermeasures were legally suitable to be taken in the first place.

With this in mind, there may be a number of obligations that would be breached prior to or during the occurrence of atrocity crimes, bringing the use of countermeasures within the toolbox of the responsibility to protect.

2.3.1. Human Rights

In *Barcelona Traction*, it is clear that the ICJ considers 'the basic rights of the human person' to constitute an obligation *erga omnes*.[447] Ragazzi,[448] for example, highlights this language to suggest that it is only 'basic' human rights that are owed *erga omnes*.[449] In other words, Ragazzi reads the court's dictum as indicating that *erga omnes* obligations do not 'apply indiscriminately to all principles and rules protecting human rights'.[450] On the other hand, a 1989 Resolution of the Institut de droit international considered the general obligation to ensure the protection of human rights as *erga omnes*.[451] While Ragazzi rejects this wider view,[452] Dinstein[453] supports it by arguing that such a distinction is 'without foundation in the theory and practice of human rights' especially since

[445] ibid, 113, Art 40 Commentary, [8].

[446] Tams (n 245) 248, see also 230.

[447] *Barcelona Traction* (n 432) 32, [34];

[448] M Ragazzi, *The Concept of International Obligations Erga Omnes* (Oxford, Oxford University Press, 2000).

[449] ibid, 140–41.

[450] ibid.

[451] Institut de droit international, 'The Protection of Human Rights and the Principle of Non-Intervention in Internal Affairs of States' (Session of Santiago de Compostela, 13 September 1989) Art 1, www.idi-iil.org/app/uploads/2017/06/1989_comp_03_en.pdf (accessed 31 July 2019).

[452] Ragazzi (n 448) 141.

[453] Y Dinstein, 'The *Erga Omnes* Applicability of Human Rights' (1992) 30(1) *Archiv des Völkerrechts* 16.

'all human rights are interchangeably depicted as "fundamental freedoms"'.[454] Moreover, Dinstein argues that the Institut's Resolution supports the view that all the rights deriving from the Universal Declaration of Human Rights[455] are *erga omnes*, and argues further that rights recognised subsequent to the adoption of the Universal Declaration may not be regarded as such.[456]

Perhaps Ragazzi's reliance on the word 'basic' in the ICJ's judgment reads too much into the Court's intentions. However, it is not the current author's intention to settle this divide here and determine what specific human rights obligations are *erga omnes*. For our purposes, it is enough to suggest that no matter which position prevails, the violations of human rights that would be associated with the responsibility to protect, leading to, or in preparation of, mass atrocity crimes, would *always* be violations of even the most 'basic' rights. The problem, as addressed above, is identifying the threshold at which the 'seriousness' criterion exists, where 'grave' violations of human rights take place, so that countermeasures may be available. Therefore, the distinction between types of human rights and what particular obligation is *erga omnes* would perhaps not have much consequence in these circumstances if this 'seriousness' threshold still persists in any case.

And so, notwithstanding these debates and subtle distinctions, it is more pertinent for us to concentrate on those situations where human rights violations may become a concern for the responsibility to protect – and that is when violations of human rights could evolve into the commission of genocide, war crimes, crimes against humanity and ethnic cleansing. But we must also not forget that we are specifically concerned with these violations as part of the *tertiary* responsibility to protect, and thus only when the UN Security Council has failed or is failing in its responsibilities. The indicators that the UN Security Council might have failed in its responsibility to protect, or its responsibility to maintain international peace and security, would suggest that 'less serious', non-widespread violations of human rights would be more readily dealt with earlier before they reach the threshold of a 'threat to international peace and security' and therefore engage the Council's obligations under the Charter.[457] With this in mind, the tertiary responsibility to protect is less likely to be activated or engaged at the point of technical human rights violations, because it is less likely that the Security Council can be said to have failed or is failing in its responsibilities. The question left open is *when* the Security Council could be said to have failed in its responsibilities when human rights violations are occurring, but the answer depends entirely on the circumstances of a given case and cannot be fully hypothesised here.

[454] ibid, 17.
[455] Universal Declaration of Human Rights (adopted 10 December 1948), in UNGA Res 217(A), UN Doc A/Res/217(III).
[456] Dinstein (n 453) 17–18.
[457] See Chapter III generally.

It may seem a contradiction in terms that the responsibility to protect is primarily concerned with the *prevention* of atrocity crimes, yet it would seem that the *tertiary* responsibility to protect, and the use of countermeasures as a tool in that regard, comes at a point where grave violations of human rights have already occurred. Unfortunately, that is the only legal basis on which countermeasures beyond the Security Council may be utilised, indicating further that the tertiary responsibility to protect may be seen more as part of the 'responsibility to react' or 'Pillar III' of the framework.

This is not to say that the role of prevention is excluded completely. Where there are serious violations of human rights that have not yet become violations of the atrocity crimes, countermeasures may then be utilised as a tool to prevent those crimes from taking place. Criddle details how financial measures may be imposed on States to 'incapacitate' them, for example by utilising asset freezes to limit the capacity of human rights violators.[458] Criddle argues that:

> Even when international asset freezes do not render foreign actors financially incapable of violating human rights, they may shift the political dynamic within a target state, empowering rights-respecting factions to introduce reforms that would narrow the legal authority and practical capacity of state and non-state actors to violate human rights.[459]

However, Criddle also notes that the law of countermeasures may prohibit States from permanently freezing foreign assets.[460] This is because countermeasures are only meant to be *temporary* measures;[461] thus Criddle writes: 'States may freeze foreign assets only temporarily to compel a target State to abandon unlawful practices and furnish appropriate remedies.'[462] Criddle therefore rules out incapacitation as a purpose of countermeasures. However, although countermeasures may only be imposed for the duration and until the State concerned resumes its legal obligations and ceases the relevant breach, this does not stop the use of countermeasures to freeze assets for a *temporary* incapacitation, so long as those measures are proportionate. Therefore, if incapacitation *and* coercion are possible in a given situation, serious violations of human rights may provide grounds for the use of countermeasures as a preventative tool for the responsibility to protect, incapacitating a State by freezing assets central to its ability to commit atrocity crimes.

Legally speaking, these measures could in theory be available to States or other parties,[463] before the Security Council can be said to have *failed* in its responsibility to protect or maintain international peace and security. The Security Council may be taking other measures, diplomatic or otherwise, of

[458] Criddle (n 108) 587.
[459] ibid.
[460] ibid, 597.
[461] As set out above in section 2.1.
[462] Criddle (n 108) 597. Criddle labels this as 'coercion' rather than prevention or incapacitation.
[463] See Chapter VI, sections 2.3 and 2.4.1.

its own, yet the situation has crossed the threshold where serious violations of obligations *erga omnes* have given rise to the option for States to take their own proportionate countermeasures in response. The question in this situation is whether it is *legitimate* for States to do this, or whether their taking of countermeasures while the Security Council is still the main bearer of responsibility would assist, improve, or threaten the situation further.[464] Importantly, in these cases, countermeasures would not form part of the tools of the *tertiary* responsibility to protect until the Security Council has failed or is paralysed. While they may be legal, they are not recommended at this point, because the tertiary toolbox has not yet been opened.

2.3.2. Atrocity Crimes

Several atrocity crimes have been recognised as *erga omnes* obligations. For example, the ICJ recognised as *erga omnes* the general obligation to prevent and punish genocide,[465] as recognised in Article I of the Genocide Convention.[466] In fact, the ICJ recognised that *all* rights and obligations enshrined by this Convention were *erga omnes*, and these obligations to prevent and punish were not territorially limited by the Convention.[467]

Elements of international humanitarian law are also considered obligations *erga omnes*. For example, the ICJ recognised in the *Construction of a Wall* case[468] that Israel had violated certain obligations *erga omnes*, which is said to include 'certain of its obligations under international humanitarian law'.[469] In recognising this, the Court recalled its Advisory Opinion on the *Legality of the Threat or Use of Nuclear Weapons*[470] where it recognised international humanitarian law as 'elementary considerations of humanity'[471] that are 'to be observed by all States whether or not they have ratified the conventions that contain them, because they constitute intransgressible principles of international customary law'.[472] It was on this basis that the Court viewed these principles as

[464] On this point, see Ministry of Foreign Affairs of the Russian Federation, 'The Declaration of the Russian Federation and the People's Republic of China on the Promotion of International Law' (25 June 2016) Press Release No 1202-25-06-2016, www.mid.ru/en/foreign_policy/news/-/asset_publisher/cKNonkJE02Bw/content/id/2331698/ (accessed 31 July 2019).

[465] *Application of the Convention on the Prevention and Punishment of the Crime of Genocide (Bosnia and Herzegovina v Yugoslavia)* (Preliminary Objections) [1996] ICJ Rep 595, 615–16, [31].

[466] See Genocide Convention (n 139).

[467] *Application of the Convention on Genocide* (n 465) [31]. This has also been widely accepted by commentators: see eg Ragazzi (n 448) 92–104.

[468] *Legal Consequences of the Construction of a Wall in the Occupied Palestinian Territory* (Advisory Opinion of 9 July 2004) [2004] ICJ Rep 136.

[469] ibid, [155].

[470] *Legality of the Threat or Use of Nuclear Weapons* (Advisory Opinion of 8 July 1996) [1996] ICJ Reports 226 (hereinafter *Legality of Nuclear Weapons*).

[471] This phrase was also used by the ICJ in *Corfu Channel Case* (Merits) (*United Kingdom v Albania*), Judgment of 4 April 1949, [1949] ICJ Reports 4, 22.

[472] *Legality of Nuclear Weapons* (n 470) 257, [79].

erga omnes.[473] Indeed, it seems on face value that the ICJ considered all of international humanitarian law as *erga omnes*. Whether these customary law principles reflect all four Geneva Conventions,[474] the Additional Protocols,[475] is secondary to the issue as to whether 'war crimes' in particular constitute obligations *erga omnes*.

Although some have viewed *any* breach of international humanitarian law as a war crime, the more widely accepted approach is to treat only *serious* or *grave* breaches of international humanitarian law as such.[476] The Geneva Conventions themselves adopt the 'grave breaches' approach for war crimes.[477] 'War Crimes' are listed in the Rome Statute of the ICC[478] as: grave breaches of the Geneva Conventions;[479] other serious violations of the laws and customs applicable in international armed conflict;[480] serious violations of Article 3 common to the four Geneva Conventions, in the context of a non-international armed conflict;[481] and 'other serious violations of the laws and customs applicable in armed conflicts not of an international character'.[482] Each of these categories was accompanied by a select list of breaches therein, usually including acts such as wilful or indiscriminate killing, torture and the taking of hostages.

Logically, if those customary rules relating to IHL are obligations *erga omnes*, then these 'serious breaches' amounting to war crimes are also breaches of obligations *erga omnes*. Tams notes that war crimes and crimes against humanity are

[473] *Construction of a Wall* (n 468) [157].

[474] Geneva Conventions I–IV: Geneva Convention for the Amelioration of the Condition of the Wounded and Sick in Armed Forces in the Field (adopted August 12 1949, entered into force 21 October 1950) 75 UNTS 31; Geneva Convention for the Amelioration of the Condition of Wounded, Sick and Shipwrecked Members of Armed Forces at Sea (adopted 12 August 1949, entered into force 21 October 1950) 75 UNTS 85; Geneva Convention Relative to the Treatment of Prisoners of War (adopted 12 August 1949, entered into force 21 October 1950) 75 UNTS 135; Geneva Convention Relative to the Protection of Civilian Persons in Time of War (adopted 12 August 1949, entered into force 21 October 1950) 75 UNTS 287.

[475] Additional Protocols I–III: Protocol Additional to the Geneva Conventions of 12 August 1949, and Relating to the Protection of Victims of International Armed Conflicts (Protocol I) (adopted 8 June 1977, entered into force 7 December 1977) 1125 UNTS 3; Protocol Additional to the Geneva Conventions of 12 August 1949, and Relating to the Protection of Victims of Non-International Armed Conflicts (Protocol II) (adopted 8 June 1977, entered into force 7 December 1978) 1125 UNTS 609; Protocol Additional to the Geneva Conventions of 12 August 1949, and Relating to the Adoption of an Additional Distinctive Emblem (Protocol III) (adopted 8 December 2005, entered into force 14 January 2007) 2404 UNTS 261.

[476] For an overview of this issue, see R Cryer, 'War Crimes' in ND White and C Henderson, *Research Handbook on International Conflict and Security Law*: Jus ad Bellum, Jus in Bello, *and* Jus post Bellum (Cheltenham, Edward Elgar, 2013).

[477] For example, see Geneva Convention I (n 474) Arts 49 and 50; and more recently see Additional Protocol I (n 475) Art 85, with Art 85(5) referring explicitly to such grave breaches as 'war crimes'.

[478] Rome Statute of the International Criminal Court (adopted 17 July 1998, entered into force 1 July 2002) 2187 UNTS 90, since amended.

[479] ibid, Art 8(2)(a).

[480] ibid, Art 8(2)(b).

[481] ibid, Art 8(2)(c).

[482] ibid, Art 8(2)(e).

widely considered *erga omnes*, but authority for this is 'not abundant', and the ICJ's judgments on such issues may be too sweeping to have general support.[483] Yet he does highlight evidence in the jurisprudence of the International Criminal Tribunal for the Former Yugoslavia (ICTY) and discussions during the drafting of the VCLT that these atrocity crimes are considered *jus cogens*, which may provide a basis for arguing they are also *erga omnes*.[484]

Similarly, the Commission of Experts for Yugoslavia considered crimes against humanity applicable to the conflicts during the Yugoslav crisis in the 1990s, seemingly on the basis that they apply in customary international law.[485] Notably, the Commission defined crimes against humanity as 'gross violations of fundamental rules of humanitarian and human rights law' linked to a party to the conflict.[486]

This author would argue, very simply, on the basis that such crimes are 'elementary considerations of humanity', and so widely accepted by States, that the case for their *erga omnes* status is very strong indeed, if not inherent in their very nature.

Notably, crimes against humanity also seem to have a threshold of 'seriousness' built into the definition of the crime itself. No such criterion was evident in Article 5 of the Statute of the ICTY.[487] However, Article 3 of the Statute of the International Criminal Tribunal for Rwanda[488] required crimes against humanity to be 'committed as part of a widespread or systematic attack against any civilian population'. Similarly, Article 7(1) of the Rome Statute requires a 'widespread or systematic attack', and Article 7(2)(a) further defines an attack against a civilian population to be 'pursuant to or in furtherance of a State or organizational policy to commit such attack'.

The apparent absence of the criterion in the ICTY Statute was addressed by the Trial Chamber,[489] where the requirement of an attack against the 'civilian population' implied crimes of a collective nature,[490] and was to be interpreted to imply that such an attack should be widespread or systematic in nature.[491] The prosecution even argued that a 'widespread or systematic attack' was part of the elements of crimes against humanity.[492]

[483] Tams (n 245) 144–45.
[484] ibid, 145, and the extensive sources listed therein.
[485] Commission of Experts for Yugoslavia, *Interim Report of the Commission of Experts Established Pursuant to Security Council Resolution 780 (1992)* (10 February 1993) UN Doc S/25274, [49].
[486] ibid, [49].
[487] See, for the original Statute, Report of the Secretary General, *Report of the Secretary-General Pursuant to Paragraph 2 of Security Council Resolution 808 (1993)* (3 May 1993) UN Doc S/25704, Annex; statute adopted in UNSC Res 827 (1993) (25 May 1993) UN Doc S/RES/827(1993) [2].
[488] UNSC Res 955 (1994) (8 November 1994) UN Doc S/RES/955(1994), and Annex: Statute of the International Tribunal for Rwanda.
[489] *Prosecutor v Dusko Tadić* (Merits) ICTY-94-1-T (7 May 1997).
[490] ibid, [644].
[491] ibid, [646]–[647].
[492] ibid, [626].

From the above, it is clear that the atrocity crimes associated with the responsibility to protect already have a 'seriousness' threshold within their definition. Therefore, this author submits that the commission of atrocity crimes automatically reach the threshold of a 'serious' violation of an *erga omnes* obligation for the purpose of non-injured party countermeasures. A 'serious' breach of an obligation that is already, by definition, 'serious' and 'widespread', in this author's view, does not have to go any further to allow the use of non-injured State countermeasures. And so, the prior-breach criterion for non-injured party countermeasures is established on the commission of atrocity crimes.

2.3.2.1. The Question of the Perpetrator

A critical issue to note is the legal connection between the *target* of the proposed countermeasures and the *violator* of the obligations at hand. For example, if a State is committing the atrocity crimes, the issue is relatively clear cut – countermeasures may be taken to coerce the State into ceasing such activity, or temporarily restraining the ability of the State to do so by freezing assets or taking other financial measures. However, if a *non-State actor* commits the crimes, the use of financial measures depends upon the circumstances at hand. Unilateral coercive measures against a non-State actor responsible for atrocity crimes are beyond the scope of this study. However, there are still legal issues that must be addressed in such circumstances should other States seek to adopt coercive measures against the State in which the crimes are taking place – especially if that State is unwilling or unable to halt the atrocities.[493]

Measures against the State in which the crimes are taking place depend on a number of factors. If the State is failing, or has failed in its responsibility to protect, and the Security Council is paralysed, it depends whether the failure of the host State is down to their *unwillingness* or their *inability* to prevent or suppress the atrocity crimes. In terms of genocide in particular, a breach of the obligation to *prevent* a genocide (committed by a non-State actor) could provide grounds to take countermeasures against the failing State. However, such countermeasures would not be useful if that State is *unable* to prevent further genocide – there would be no point in coercing a State to do something it is unable to achieve realistically. However, if the State is simply *unwilling* to do so, and would otherwise be able to suppress the atrocities, or has some influence over the responsible non-State actors, countermeasures could provide a useful tool for coercing that State into adhering to its obligations and hopefully preventing further crimes from taking place.

Of course, if atrocity crimes are already being committed or are underway, this undermines the primary aim of the responsibility to protect to *prevent* such atrocities. Countermeasures would not be available solely on the basis that the

[493] See, generally, ND White, 'Sanctions Against Non-State Actors' in Ronzitti (n 97).

atrocity crimes are *about* to take place – there has been no *prior* breach yet – unless there can be said to have been a breach of the Genocide Convention and the *erga omnes* obligation to prevent and punish genocide. It remains unclear whether there are other specific obligations on States to prevent *all* atrocity crimes, of the same character as that within the Genocide Convention.[494] Without an *erga omnes* obligation to prevent the other relevant atrocity crimes, genocide remains the only recognised atrocity whereby countermeasures could be used prior to its occurrence, without any other international obligations being breached beforehand that could provide an alternative basis for such measures. However, the possible existence of an *erga omnes* obligation to maintain international peace and security could fill this gap, as will now be explained.

2.3.3. The Maintenance of International Peace and Security as an Erga Omnes *Obligation?*

The current author argued in Chapter III that the nature of the responsibility for the maintenance of international peace and security was a legal responsibility capable of being assumed by an actor with residual responsibility, which includes the international community.[495] It was also determined that the atrocity crimes within the remit of the responsibility to protect can in most circumstances reach such a threshold whereby this more general responsibility for the maintenance of international peace and security is engaged.[496]

If we accept that the responsibility to maintain international peace and security, although normally vested primarily with the Security Council, is also vested on an ancillary basis to the international community in general, we must also logically accept the legal corollary to that position – that all States must not *endanger* international peace and security. While a general obligation *not to endanger* international peace and security has not been explicitly verbalised by States – at least to the author's knowledge – there are ample references to these general and inherent responsibilities of States to maintain peace. There is also a specific obligation, in Article 2(3) of the Charter, for States not to endanger international peace and security – but this is articulated with specific regard to the *peaceful settlement of disputes*:[497]

> All Members shall settle their international disputes by peaceful means in such a manner that international peace and security, and justice, are not endangered.

[494] Although UN Secretary-General Ban Ki Moon in his first report on the responsibility to protect suggested that: 'Under conventional and customary international law, States have obligations to prevent and punish genocide, war crimes and crimes against humanity.' See Report of the Secretary-General, *Implementing the Responsibility to Protect* (12th January 2009) UN Doc A/63/677, [3].

[495] See generally Chapter III.

[496] See Chapter III, section 1.2.

[497] On this point, see S O'Connor and CM Bailliet, 'The Good Faith Obligation to Maintain International Peace and Security and the Pacific Settlement of Disputes' in CM Bailliet and KM Larsen (eds), *Promoting Peace Through International Law* (Oxford, Oxford University Press, 2015).

Consider all the specific obligations surrounding collective security: for example, the prohibition of force, the prohibition of intervention, the peaceful settlement of disputes, the crime of aggression, and the responsibility to maintain international peace and security itself. Given the character of these obligations, this author submits that it would not be much of a stretch to suggest that States are indeed under a general obligation not to endanger international peace and security. If there were such an obligation, this would undoubtedly be *erga omnes* in character, because all States have an interest in international peace and security being maintained. A similar notion was expressed by the UN Secretary-General's High-Level Panel on Threats, Challenges and Change, which stated that: '[A]ll States have an interest in forging a new comprehensive collective security system that will commit all of them to act cooperatively in the face of a broad array of threats.'[498]

In the context of countermeasures and the requirement of a *prior breach of an obligation*, the crucial point is that a breach of this obligation arguably *does* injure a State, and arguably *does* 'specifically affect' all parties to which the obligation is owed. Threats to international peace and security, or breaches of international peace and security, have very practical and very real-world effects. International emergencies can have far-reaching effects on States' economies – even States who are not necessarily involved in or geographically close to that emergency. International trade can be disrupted, or emergencies can affect the supply and demand of important goods or commodities. Refugee crises may erupt, creating huge financial and practical problems for those States who offer to help and must take measures themselves to accommodate thousands, if not millions, of people into their territory. Fundamentally, the national security of neighbouring countries may be endangered by an overspill of violence, and they may have to take preventative steps to secure borders, provide relief, ease tensions or protect their own populations.

The point to note is that when violations of other obligations transcend into the endangerment of international peace and security, States may be considered 'specifically affected' as defined by the ILC so as to be considered an 'injured State' for the purposes of countermeasures.[499] Furthermore, Article 42(b)(ii) of the ILC State Responsibility Articles highlights that a State may be injured by a breach of an obligation owed to the international community as a whole where the breach of that obligation 'is of such a character as radically to change the position of all the other States to which the obligation is owed with respect to the further performance of the obligation'. According to the ILC's own commentaries, this could include the breach of a disarmament treaty, or a nuclear-free zone treaty, where 'each party's performance is effectively conditioned upon and

[498] High-Level Panel on Threats, Challenges and Change, *A More Secure World: Our Shared Responsibility* (New York, UN Publications, 2004) [28].

[499] ILC (n 36) 119, Art 42 Commentary, [12]; see also ILC Articles on State Responsibility (n 199) Art 42 (b)(i).

requires the performance of each of the others'.[500] The Commentaries further suggest that a State is only considered injured under this provision 'if the breach is of such a character as radically to affect the enjoyment of the rights or the performance of the obligations of all the other States to which the obligation is owed'.[501]

Under an obligation *not to endanger* international peace and security, all States would essentially be owed an obligation to exist free from threats to international peace and security caused by another State. The ILC's example of a breach of a disarmament treaty seems to be an example of a breach of an obligation that has little practical effect to 'injure' or 'cause damage' to a State, but still perhaps creates a significant endangerment to a State's national security. Therefore, why should the endangerment of *international peace and security* not be considered to have the same injurious effects? The practical effects that an endangerment of international peace and security could entail, as outlined above, is certainly 'of such a character as radically to affect the enjoyment of the rights' provided by an obligation to maintain international peace and security.

No doubt, there would be many concerns that the breach of an obligation not to endanger international peace and security might be used surreptitiously to justify unwarranted or illegitimate countermeasures. This very much reflects the same concerns raised by States for the use of non-injured party countermeasures we explored above. Usually, the obligation to maintain international peace and security is vested in the security institutions such as the UN, the Security Council or regional mechanisms. But when these institutions fail, can we really deny that such an obligation continues to exist? While it may not be for individual states acting alone to maintain international peace and security, the overarching obligation *not* to endanger international peace and security surely remains a steadfast obligation owed to the other Member States of the international community in any instance. If such an obligation does exist, a breach of it would provide a very clear basis for the taking of *proportionate* countermeasures. If it does not, then the obligations explored above regarding atrocity crimes and human rights still provide such a basis to utilise countermeasures in the circumstances outlined therein.

3. CONCLUSION ON COERCIVE MEASURES

This chapter has sought to demonstrate that there are legal avenues available to utilise coercive, non-forcible measures, such as asset freezes and trade restrictions, beyond the UN Security Council in response to mass atrocities. The doctrine of countermeasures could provide a legal basis for the taking of such

[500] ILC (n 36) 119, Art 42 Commentary, [13]–[14].
[501] ibid, [15].

measures, subject to the stringent legal safeguards set out therein. The more controversial issue as to whether these measures can be taken in response to violations of obligations *erga omnes*, by actors who have not been 'directly injured', is addressed by this study in the following ways: (i) much more widespread practice has emerged of the taking of coercive measures that are, prima facie, unlawful (and therefore would require justification via the law of countermeasures), supporting the claim that non-injured party countermeasures are available as proportionate responses to violations of *erga omnes* obligations; and (ii) violations of these obligations, especially with regard to the responsibility to protect, are likely to 'injure' interested States, providing them with a legal basis for the taking of countermeasures in any case.

While this chapter has sought to address some issues relating to the problem of countermeasures being abused by States, it is for the following discussion to specifically answer these issues in full. At this stage, however, it is argued that this problem of potential abuse further highlights the need for a division of primary, secondary and tertiary responsibilities, especially given the fact that countermeasures may be available to some actors to utilise even *before* the Security Council has failed in its responsibilities. In this regard, although actions may be legally available, the compartmentalisation of different responsibilities provides further safeguards to their abuse by providing a clear framework as to *when* these measures would be available. This does not mean that they would be appropriate – only that, upon assuming their tertiary responsibility, that compartment of the toolbox would be opened for these actors to consider whether they are competent to do so.

Having established this alternative legal avenue, there is certainly legal space for the tertiary responsibility to protect to continue to exist and be implemented beyond the failures of the Security Council. What is left to address is the question as to whether this responsibility is *capable* of being implemented by those actors involved based upon their legal competences and other legal limitations. Addressing this question will not only establish the viability of the tertiary responsibility to protect framework, but will also be used to address the hesitations relating to the use of countermeasures and their susceptibility to abuse without institutional safeguards.

VI

Implementing the Tertiary Responsibility to Protect

HAVING ESTABLISHED IN previous chapters that there is scope for the responsibility to protect to continue beyond the failures of the Security Council in the form of a 'tertiary' responsibility to protect, especially where the threat or act of atrocity crimes also engages the responsibility for the maintenance of international peace and security, this chapter will now investigate whether and how this responsibility beyond the Council may be implemented. Focusing on the questions left open in the previous analysis of the legality of forcible and non-forcible coercive measures, this chapter will consider the legality of these measures being utilised both within the UN framework (specifically by the General Assembly), and outside of this framework (by regional organisations or States individually). While this book has so far identified possible legal avenues relating to the prohibition of force and the principle of non-intervention (and the doctrine of countermeasures therein), for the tertiary responsibility to exist, these avenues must actually be capable of being implemented by actors who have the competence to do so. Not only will this chapter address the questions surrounding the legal competences of the relevant actors, but it will also consider whether the framework of a 'tertiary responsibility to protect' provides a suitable and viable avenue for implementing the responsibility to protect beyond the Security Council.

As previously argued, by establishing the legal space for the responsibility to protect to continue through the use of legal measures, and identifying the particular actors and procedures that may be utilised in this regard, it is much easier to determine that the international community's general responsibility to protect continues even in the face of Security Council failure.

1. THE TERTIARY RESPONSIBILITY WITHIN THE UN

This chapter will first address the possibility of the tertiary responsibility continuing beyond the Security Council, but still remaining within the UN Collective Security framework. In this regard, one would repeat the recognition of the ICJ in the *Certain Expenses*[1] case that the responsibility of the Security Council for the maintenance of international peace and security under Article 24 of the Charter was a 'primary' but not 'exclusive' responsibility.[2] This may be compared to the Court's opinion in the *Construction of a Wall* case,[3] where it suggested that Article 24 referred to a primary, but not exclusive, *competence* in the maintenance of international peace and security.[4] Therefore, the court has acknowledged that both the *responsibility* to maintain peace and security, and the legal *competence* to do so, does not lie solely with the Security Council.

Nevertheless, there is a delicate balance to be met when considering when these 'residual' responsibilities and competencies can and should be engaged. Indeed, the ICJ highlighted the phrase in Article 24 that the Security Council was conferred *primary* responsibility 'in order to ensure prompt and effective action', and stressed that '[i]t is only the Security Council which can require enforcement by coercive action against an aggressor'.[5]

In contrast to this, the General Assembly's *Uniting for Peace* Resolution[6] recognises a very clear role for the Assembly in the maintenance of international peace and security, alongside the ability to recommend enforcement action. Firstly, in the preamble to the Resolution, the Assembly is:

> *Conscious* that failure of the Security Council to discharge its responsibilities on behalf of all the Member States, particularly those responsibilities referred to in the preceding paragraphs [the maintenance of international peace and security], does not relieve Member States of their obligations or the United Nations of its responsibility under the Charter to maintain international peace and security.[7]

The Resolution then went on to recognise that 'such a failure does not deprive the General Assembly of its rights or relieve it of its responsibility under the Charter in regard to the maintenance of international peace and security'.[8] Therefore, as previously established, it is clear that the General Assembly, and indeed the Member States,[9] have a residual responsibility for the maintenance of international peace and security. This much is relatively uncontroversial.

Relating this to the responsibility to protect, when a situation involving the atrocity crimes associated with the responsibility to protect crosses the threshold to become a matter for the responsibility for the maintenance of international peace and security,[10] the General Assembly's residual responsibility would still be

[1] *Certain Expenses of the United Nations (Article 17, paragraph 2 of the Charter)* (Advisory Opinion of 20 July 1962) [1962] ICJ Rep 151 (hereinafter *Certain Expenses*).

[2] *Certain Expenses* (n 1) 163.

[3] *Legal Consequences of the Construction of a Wall in the Occupied Palestinian Territory* (Advisory Opinion of 9 July 2004) [2004] ICJ Rep 136 (hereinafter *Construction of a Wall*).

[4] ibid, [26].

[5] *Certain Expenses* (n 1) 163.

[6] UNGA Res 377(V), *Uniting for Peace* (3 November 1950) UN Doc A/RES/377(V).

[7] ibid, Resolution A, preamble [7].

[8] ibid, Resolution A, preamble [8].

[9] On this point, see Chapter III, section 1.2, and further below, section 2.

[10] As previously established in Chapter III, section 1.2.

engaged here. Therefore, there is also a role for the General Assembly in addressing the *responsibility to protect* beyond the inaction of the Security Council.

What is controversial, however, is the extent of the role the General Assembly should play in implementing its residual responsibilities. The *Uniting for Peace* Resolution went further in this regard, declaring:

> [I]f the Security Council, because of a lack of unanimity of the permanent members, fails to exercise its primary responsibility for the maintenance of international peace and security in any case where there appears to be a threat to the peace, breach of the peace, or act of aggression, the General Assembly shall consider the matter immediately with a view to making appropriate recommendations to Members for collective measures, including in the case of a breach of the peace or act of aggression the use of armed force when necessary, to maintain or restore international peace and security. If not in session at the time, the General Assembly may meet in emergency special session within twenty-four hours of the request thereof. Such emergency special session shall be called if requested by the Security Council on the vote of any seven members, or by a majority of the Members of the United Nations.[11]

This Resolution evidently envisaged a role for the Assembly to take action to maintain or restore international peace and security. However, the compatibility of the *Uniting for Peace* Resolution with the Charter itself is far from clear. To determine the extent of this responsibility, and therefore the *tertiary* responsibility to protect, we must address the legal powers and competences of the General Assembly for the maintenance of international peace and security.

In this regard, this section argues that the tertiary responsibility to protect *does* continue within the UN, establishing that the General Assembly has both residual responsibility and legal competence to adopt it. In terms of being capable of taking measures to implement this responsibility, it is argued that the General Assembly is both able to recommend forcible measures, and non-forcible measures in certain circumstances. Recommendations to use force by the Assembly render such military measures compatible with the prohibition of force by: (i) inherently qualifying the principles of territorial integrity and political independence by virtue of a State's consent to this power, and the purpose of the Charter in Article 1(1) to take effective collective measures; and (ii) rendering this action consistent with the Purposes of the Charter by being such an effective collective measure and harmonising the actions of nations for this objective. In this regard, it will be argued below that Security Council authorisations to use force find their origin in the Council's general ability to 'make recommendations' under Article 39, which explains the non-binding nature of such measures, and also the ability of the General Assembly to make such recommendations.

Recommendations to take other coercive measures are within the scope of the Assembly's general power to make recommendations for the maintenance of international peace and security, demonstrated by State practice, and where

[11] *Uniting for Peace* (n 6) Resolution A, operative [1].

such measures violate international agreements, they would be permissible as a circumstance precluding wrongfulness when taken in accordance with the doctrine of countermeasures in customary international law.

1.1. Legal Competences of the General Assembly

There are several ways that the UN Charter grants the General Assembly a role in the maintenance of international peace and security, but there are also ways in which this is curtailed in favour of the Security Council's primary role too. In particular, Article 10 grants the General Assembly the general power to 'discuss any questions or any matters within the scope of the present Charter' and, subject to Article 12,[12] to 'make recommendations to the Members of the United Nations or to the Security Council or to both on any such questions or matters'.

Article 11 further provides for particular powers in relation to the maintenance of international peace and security.[13] This includes the ability of the General Assembly to discuss general principles of cooperation in this regard;[14] the power to discuss 'any questions' relating to the maintenance of international peace and security, and make recommendations therein;[15] and to call the attention of the Security Council to situations which are likely to endanger international peace and security.[16] Even at the outset we can see that the Assembly's powers are significantly different to those afforded to the Security Council – the Assembly's powers to recommend are inherently non-binding, unlike the compulsory measures that may be utilised by the Security Council in Chapter VII and binding on Member States via Article 25.

However, regarding the General Assembly's specific power to make recommendations relating to peace and security, Article 11(2) requires that: 'Any such question on which action is necessary shall be referred to the Security Council by the General Assembly either before or after discussion.' Furthermore, Article 12 stipulates that the Assembly shall not make any recommendation with regard to a dispute or situation while the Security Council is exercising its functions assigned to it in the Charter with regard to that dispute or situation.[17]

Therefore, before addressing the specific measures that may be taken by the General Assembly to implement its tertiary responsibility to protect, these legal obstacles must first be addressed.

[12] See section 1.1.2.

[13] See also Arts 13 and 14 relating to specific powers to recommend measures relating to the other duties of the Assembly.

[14] Art 11(1).

[15] Art 11(2).

[16] Art 11(3).

[17] Art 12(1).

1.1.1. Requirement to Refer when 'Action' is Required

Article 11(2) could have a paralysing effect on the ability of the General Assembly to assume any real role in the maintenance of peace and security, especially where a situation requires 'action'. The requirement that a situation be referred to the Security Council in such cases raises some critical questions. Firstly, what does the provision mean by 'action', and would this preclude the General Assembly from 'acting' or recommending measures? Secondly, does this provision still apply even in a situation where the Security Council has already considered a matter or situation but has failed in its responsibility to maintain international peace and security, and its responsibility to protect?

Regarding the interpretation of 'action', the ICJ's opinion in *Certain Expenses* offers some guidance. The Court clarified that 'the kind of action referred to in Article 11, paragraph 2, is coercive or enforcement action'.[18] It further stated that:

> The word 'action' must mean such action as is solely within the province of the Security Council. It cannot refer to recommendations which the Security Council might make, as for instance under Article 38, because the General Assembly under Article 11 has a comparable power.[19]

Accordingly, the Court suggested, Article 11(2) does not apply where the necessary action is not 'enforcement action'.[20]

The Court takes a very specific definition of 'action' here that applies precisely in the context of Article 11(2). It also seems evident that any 'action' that is available to the General Assembly by virtue of the Charter is not included within this provision – it refers to 'action' via powers that *only* the Security Council has. Tsagourias and White[21] highlight that the Court makes reference to the kind of 'action' that is within the exclusive ambit of the Security Council, particularly pointing out that the Court said, 'only the Security Council … can *require* enforcement by coercive action'[22] and that 'it is the Security Council which, exclusively, may *order* coercive action'.[23] It is on this basis that they argue that it is only *compulsory* or *binding* action that is exclusively within the ambit of the Security Council, and because the General Assembly makes non-binding recommendatory measures, then there is no restriction on the General Assembly

[18] *Certain Expenses* (n 1) 164.
[19] ibid, 165.
[20] ibid.
[21] N Tsagourias and ND White, *Collective Security: Theory, Law and Practice* (Cambridge, Cambridge University Press, 2013).
[22] *Certain Expenses* (n 1) 163 (emphasis added).
[23] ibid, 163 (emphasis added); Tsagourias and White (n 21) 104.

taking non-binding 'action' for the purposes of Article 11(2).[24] This argument has also been adopted by others such as Carswell[25] and Kenny.[26]

Hailbronner and Klein[27] take this analysis further, to investigate the meaning of 'enforcement action' in this context, arguing:

> There is a decisive difference between the recommendation of enforcement action, and the actual taking of such measures. This is illustrated by the formal definition of the term 'enforcement', according to which the existence of an 'enforcement action' is not determined by the character of the action itself but by the binding nature of the measure taken. Therefore, a non-binding recommendation is not to be considered as 'action', so that the GA [General Assembly] is not prevented by Art 11(2) cl 2 from recommending coercive measures. This norm only recalls the fact that the GA shall not take any enforcement measures binding on all member States.[28]

The logic flowing from this argument is that the General Assembly can, in theory, recommend or 'request' the Security Council to take such binding enforcement action within Chapter VII of the Charter, although the Council would not be bound to do so.[29]

Unfortunately, while these arguments are persuasive, they do overlook one important statement by the ICJ in *Certain Expenses* that may undermine this whole line of argument. Later in the judgment, when the Court is considering the nature of UNEF[30] as a peaceful measure and therefore not 'enforcement action', it sheds further light on another type of 'action' which it considers as belonging exclusively to the Security Council when it concludes:

> It could not therefore have been patent on the face of the resolution that the establishment of UNEF was in effect "enforcement action" under Chapter VII which, in accordance with the Charter, could be *authorized* only by the Security Council.[31]

Based upon the assertions above, it seems a contradiction in terms that the Court should consider the *authorisation* of 'enforcement action' to be an exclusive power of the Security Council. Authorisations, by definition, do not legally oblige Member States to take action – they are permissible, not compulsory.[32]

[24] Tsagourias and White (n 21) 104–05.

[25] AJ Carswell, 'Unblocking the UN Security Council: The *Uniting for Peace* Resolution' (2013) 18(3) *Journal of Conflict and Security Law* 453, 474.

[26] C Kenny, 'Responsibility to Recommend: The Role of the UN General Assembly in the Maintenance of International Peace and Security' (2016) 3(1) *Journal on the Use of Force and International Law* 3, 25.

[27] K Hailbronner and E Klein, 'Article 10' in B Simma (ed), *The Charter of the United Nations: A Commentary* (Oxford, Oxford University Press, 2002).

[28] ibid, 264–65.

[29] K Hailbronner and E Klein, 'Article 11' in Simma (n 27) 283.

[30] United Nations Emergency Force.

[31] *Certain Expenses* (n 1) 171 (emphasis added).

[32] On this point, see discussion of the basis of 'authorisations' in the Charter, section 1.2.2.

Furthermore, this particular provision of the judgment indicates that 'authorisations' of 'enforcement action', according to the Court, can only be done by the Security Council. If non-binding, permissive enforcement measures are apparently exclusive to the Security Council, this may indicate that the General Assembly may *not* recommend such measures in any case. However, it is also worth pointing out that the Court specifically cites 'enforcement action' under Chapter VII in relation to this assertion, perhaps explaining the apparent contradiction, since it is of course only the Security Council that can authorise *Chapter VII* measures. The General Assembly would, if it had the power, utilise powers under Chapter IV, not Chapter VII, and so this assertion by the ICJ technically would not prohibit authorisations of powers found elsewhere in the Charter.

Notwithstanding these substantive issues, considering the test provided by the ICJ for the meaning of 'action' within Article 11(2), it is clear that the Court determined this as action *solely* within the competence of the Security Council. What should be remembered, and indeed this is acknowledged by Hailbronner and Klein,[33] is that Article 11(2) is not a *substantive* restriction on the types of recommendations that the General Assembly can make, but a procedural obligation to refer a situation to the Security Council when 'action' is necessary. It does not expressly prevent the Assembly from 'acting' itself. Indeed, Article 11(4) explicitly stipulates that: 'The powers of the General Assembly set forth in this Article shall not limit the general scope of Article 10.'

When considering a situation where the Security Council has already been made aware of a situation, and cannot act because of deadlock or a failure to uphold its responsibilities, Hailbronner and Klein rightly argue that the obligation on the Assembly to refer no longer applies.[34] Similarly, the current author submits that, in any case, such an obligation would be fulfilled once the Security Council has at least attempted to address the situation, because of the very fact that the obligation in Article 11(2) is no more than a procedural obligation to give effect to the primacy of the Security Council in the maintenance of international peace and security. Once the Security Council fails in that responsibility, there would be no need for the General Assembly to refer a situation that the Council has already failed to address.

Where Article 11(2) may present a hurdle to the Assembly would be *before* the Council has had a chance to address the issue, because such a referral would activate the restrictions in Article 12,[35] as we will discuss. However, this is very much the point of the provision. It is only when a referral to the Council would be futile that the requirement to refer becomes unnecessary.

[33] Hailbronner and Klein (n 27) 266; Hailbronner and Klein (n 29) 283.
[34] Hailbronner and Klein (n 27) 266.
[35] K Hailbronner and E Klein, 'Article 12' in Simma (n 27) 289.

1.1.2. *Exclusivity of Security Council Action under Article 12*

Article 12(1) of the Charter provides:

> While the Security Council is exercising in respect of any dispute or situation the functions assigned to it in the present Charter, the General Assembly shall not make any recommendation with regard to that dispute or situation unless the Security Council so requests.

This clearly provides for the primacy of the Security Council in the maintenance of peace and security, ensuring the Assembly does not interfere while the Council is acting. Tsagourias and White suggest that it was settled practice in the early life of the UN that the Security Council was deemed to be 'exercising its functions' within the meaning of Article 12(1) when a particular situation was placed onto the Council's agenda.[36] This, they suggest, links Article 12(1) with Article 12(2), which requires the Secretary-General to notify the Assembly of matters that are being dealt with by the Security Council and when the Council has ceased to deal with them. Tsagourias and White therefore argue that: 'The theory behind the list of matters which the UN Secretary-General submits to the GA is that it tells the GA the issues it is not allowed to discuss because they are receiving attention in the SC.'[37]

However, the ICJ in the *Construction of a Wall* Opinion noted that the interpretation of Article 12 has evolved subsequently.[38] In this regard, the Court referred to an opinion of the UN Legal Counsel in response to a question on the matter at the General Assembly's Third Committee in 1968, where the Legal Counsel clarified the Assembly's interpretation of Article 12:

> The matters relating to South Africa, Southern Rhodesia and the Territories under Portuguese rule were on the agenda of the Security Council and, in principle, the General Assembly could not make any recommendations. However, the Assembly had interpreted the words 'is exercising' as meaning 'is exercising at this moment'; consequently, it had made recommendations on other matters which the Security Council was also considering.[39]

The ICJ further noted that the General Assembly and the Security Council increasingly dealt in parallel with the same matter concerning the maintenance of international peace and security,[40] and noted that while the Council dealt with peace and security matters, the Assembly tended to take a much broader view and considered the wider humanitarian, social and economic aspects of

[36] Tsagourias and White (n 21) 102–03; see also, *Construction of a Wall* (n 147) [27]; and Hailbronner and Klein (n 35) 290.

[37] Tsagourias and White (n 21) 102.

[38] *Construction of a Wall* (n 147) [27].

[39] UNGA Third Committee (23rd Session), 'Official Records, 1637th Meeting' (12 December 1968) UN Doc A/C.3/SR.1637, [9].

[40] *Construction of a Wall* (n 147) [27]; the Court gave as examples the UN's responses to matters relating to Cyprus, South Africa, Angola, Southern Rhodesia, Bosnia and Herzegovina, and Somalia.

each situation.[41] The Court therefore considered such practice consistent with Article 12.[42]

Kenny interprets the Court's judgment as confirming that 'the prohibition of simultaneous action by the General Assembly and the Security Council has been superseded by practice'.[43] But this may be an oversimplification of the Court's opinion. There are two observations that can be made that suggest the Court's judgment is more nuanced than this. The interpretation of 'exercising functions' within Article 12 has become much more literal over the years – the Council simply being 'seized' of a matter and holding a situation on its agenda is not enough to preclude consideration by the Assembly. This, of course, indicates that there may still be instances where the Assembly may not make recommendations where they would undermine or go against specific measures adopted by the Security Council. The current interpretation of Article 12 may allow for simultaneous action or recommendations of a different character, but it may still preclude the *same* action taken simultaneously.

In situations most relevant to this book and the failures of the Security Council in this context, the restriction of Article 12 does not seem to be an insurmountable hurdle. If the Security Council has failed in its responsibilities, as established in Chapter III, and is subject to deadlock and inaction, then the Council certainly would not be 'exercising its functions' within the meaning of Article 12. This is especially true if we adopt the Assembly's own literal interpretation, as advocated by the Legal Counsel, that the Council is not exercising functions 'at that moment'. In other words, Security Council deadlock, and failure in its responsibilities, deems any subsequent action by the General Assembly as consistent with Article 12, so long as the Council remains paralysed or inactive.

It is in this respect that Carswell argues that the *Uniting for Peace* Resolution is specifically aimed at situations where Article 12(1) does not apply.[44] On this point, he rightly rejects arguments that *any* veto by a permanent member stops the Council 'exercising' is functions within the meaning of Article 12(1).[45] Of course, Carswell is right in recognising that the use of the veto alone could not legitimately establish that the Council has ceased to function – for better or worse, the veto power is still a part of the collective security system,[46] and the use of it should not be regarded as leaving room for the General Assembly to step in, or as a sole indicator of the Council's failure.[47] Article 12 could not be

[41] ibid; for a further examination of State practice in this regard, see Hailbronner and Klein (n 35) 290.

[42] *Construction of a Wall* (n 147) [28].

[43] Kenny (n 26) 6.

[44] Carswell (n 25) 469.

[45] ibid.

[46] In this context see Hailbronner and Klein (n 35) 291.

[47] Carswell (n 25) 469.

reconciled with Article 27(3), which provides for the veto power, if that were the case. As discussed in Chapter III, much more is required than one single use of the veto to establish Council failure.

But Carswell might go too far in interpreting the *Uniting for Peace* Resolution as imposing a requirement that the veto must be at least used, *and* cause the Council to fail in its responsibilities, before the General Assembly can step in. It is true that the *Uniting for Peace* Resolution permits the Assembly to act 'if the Security Council, because of lack of unanimity of the permanent members, fails to exercise its primary responsibility'.[48] However, this should not be seen as imposing a restriction on the General Assembly. The changes that this Resolution made to the General Assembly's Rules of Procedure did *not* include any substantive need for Council failure.[49] In establishing an Emergency Special Session, all that is required is a procedural vote of the Security Council, or a request from a majority of Members of the UN[50] – the substantive restrictions would have to come from the Charter itself.

Moreover, the *Uniting for Peace* Resolution was a non-binding recommendatory act of the Assembly.[51] Other than the changes made to the Rules of Procedure, and perhaps any evidence of subsequent agreement or practice it provides for the interpretation of the Charter,[52] there is no legal reason why the General Assembly could not adopt a subsequent 'Uniting for Peace' resolution with alternative requirements, so long as it remains within its powers granted by the Charter.

Indeed, following on from this, the veto and paralysis is only *one* way in which the Council may fail in its responsibilities. Simple inaction and indifference in the face of atrocity crimes – as discussed in Chapter III – could indicate a very real failure to protect, and a failure to maintain international peace and security. Therefore, while it is very likely that failures of the Council will involve the use of the veto, Carswell's assertion that a veto is a *requirement* before the General Assembly can act is not convincing.

Hailbronner and Klein refer to this idea when they suggest that, although the *Uniting for Peace* Resolution does not cover non-veto failures, there seems no reason why, according to the philosophy behind the Resolution, the alleged 'better judgment' of the Assembly should not prevail even over an inactive

[48] *Uniting for Peace* (n 149) operative [1].

[49] See *Uniting for Peace* (n 149) Annex, for the amendments to the Rules of Procedure.

[50] ibid.

[51] For further detailed insight into the Uniting for Peace Resolution itself, see Y Nahlawi, 'Overcoming Russian and Chinese Vetoes on Syria through Uniting for Peace' (2019) 24(1) *Journal of Conflict and Security Law* 111; see also, in the context of recent events, R Barber, 'Uniting for Peace not Aggression: Responding to Chemical Weapons in Syria Without Breaking the Law' (2019) 24(1) *Journal of Conflict and Security Law* 71.

[52] Within the meaning of Art 31(3)(a) and Art 31(3)(b) of the VCLT (adopted 23 May 1969, entered into force 27 January 1980) 1155 *UNTS* 331.

majority of the Security Council.[53] The current author would take a slightly different view to Hailbronner and Klein, however, and argue that it is not the 'better judgment' of the Assembly which makes a compelling case for this, but the very fact that the Assembly has a residual responsibility to maintain international peace and security, and that it is in fact the Assembly's *duty* at least to consider a dispute or situation in the face of the Council's failure. In other words, if the Charter *allows* the General Assembly to make recommendations in the face of Council failure, then the residual responsibility of the Assembly indicates that it *should* make any recommendations appropriate when it assumes this residual responsibility. Like the arguments made in Chapter III, this is not to dictate or determine *how* the General Assembly should act, but instead indicates on the basis of its residual responsibilities that it should not ignore the situation.

On the basis of the preceding analysis, it is submitted that a failure of the Security Council in its responsibility for the maintenance of international peace and security, to be established by the procedures and tests outlined in Chapter III, renders any subsequent action by the General Assembly compatible with the restrictions of Article 12.

1.2. Forcible Measures

The legality of the recommendation of forcible measures by the General Assembly depends on two factors. Firstly, it must be within the legal powers of the Assembly to make such recommendations. Secondly, the actual implementation of that recommendation must be compatible with the prohibition of force enshrined in Article 2(4) of the Charter. While some arguments suggest that 'recommendations' have no legal effect, this author uses the analogy of Security Council 'authorisations', arguing that they themselves are based on the Council's power to 'recommend' under Article 39, and therefore that the General Assembly also has an analogous legal power to do the same.

1.2.1. Assessing General Assembly Competences to Recommend Force

As outlined above, the legal bases in the Charter that might allow the General Assembly to recommend the use of forcible measures would be either: (i) the general power in Article 10 to make recommendations to members or the UN itself concerning any question or matter within the scope of the Charter; or (ii) the specific power under Article 11(2) to make recommendations regarding any questions relating to the maintenance of international peace and security. Based on a very wide reading of these provisions, and especially in light of Article 10's general nature, there seems to be no reason why such recommendations

[53] Hailbronner and Klein (n 35) 291.

should not include a recommendation to take 'effective collective measures' to maintain or restore international peace and security, as recognised as a fundamental Purpose of the UN in Article 1(1).

In this regard, the ICJ recognised in *Certain Expenses* that 'when the Organization takes action which warrants the assertion that it was appropriate for the fulfilment of one of the stated purposes of the United Nations, the presumption is that such action is not *ultra vires* the Organization'.[54] Similarly, in its *Namibia* Advisory Opinion, the Court suggested that:

> A resolution of a properly constituted organ of the United Nations which is passed in accordance with that organ's rules of procedure, and is declared by its President to have been so passed, must be presumed to have been validly adopted.[55]

Unless there is reason to rebut this presumption,[56] any Resolution utilising or referencing the purported ability of the General Assembly to recommend forcible action may be referenced as evidence of an interpretation of the Assembly's powers in favour of the existence of such a power.

1.2.1.1. Practice Recognising a Power to Recommend Force

The clearest example of the General Assembly considering its ability to recommend force is the *Uniting for Peace* Resolution itself. As outlined above, the Resolution recognised that in the face of Security Council failure:

> [T]he General Assembly shall consider the matter immediately with a view to making appropriate recommendations to Members for collective measures, including in the case of a breach of the peace or act of aggression the use of armed force when necessary, to maintain or restore international peace and security.[57]

Henderson[58] suggests that the adoption of the *Uniting for Peace* Resolution, and the level of support for this, could be an example of an act of subsequent practice in the interpretation of the Charter.[59] In other words, it may be used as a basis of interpreting the powers of the General Assembly in accordance with Article 31(3)(b) of the VCLT. This is not to say that there were no dissenting voices in the adoption of this Resolution. For example, the Soviet Union was perhaps the strongest voice denouncing the legality of the Resolution.[60]

[54] *Certain Expenses* (n 1) 168.

[55] *Legal Consequences for States of the Continued Presence of South Africa in Namibia (South West Africa) Notwithstanding Security Council Resolution 276 (1970)* (Advisory Opinion), 21 June 1971, [1971] ICJ Rep 16, [20].

[56] *Construction of a Wall* (n 147) [35].

[57] *Uniting for Peace* (n 149) Resolution A, operative [1].

[58] C Henderson, 'Authority without Accountability? The UN Security Council's Authorization Method and Institutional Mechanisms of Accountability' (2014) 19(3) *Journal of Conflict and Security Law* 489.

[59] Henderson (n 58) 506.

[60] See UNGA Verbatim Record, 301st Plenary Meeting (2 November 1950) UN Doc A/PV.301.

Further evidence of the ability of the Assembly to recommend force may be found in Resolution 376(V),[61] adopted *prior* to *Uniting for Peace*, in response to the developing situation on the Korean peninsula in 1950. This Resolution recommended that States take 'all appropriate steps' to achieve stability throughout Korea.[62] Later, the General Assembly also passed Resolution 498(V),[63] which reaffirmed the UN military action in Korea, and called upon all States to continue to assist the United Nations in taking this action.[64]

These recommendations came after the Security Council initially took steps to recommend the use of military measures in response to an armed attack by North Korean forces against South Korea.[65] The Security Council's Resolutions 82 and 83 (1950) were passed while the Soviet Union was absent from the Security Council and therefore unable to cast its veto. However, once the Soviet Union returned, the Security Council was paralysed again, compelling States to act through the General Assembly, and ultimately to adopt the *Uniting for Peace* Resolution.

Frowein and Krisch suggest that the Security Council simply recommended that States act in collective self-defence in response to the armed attack by North Korean forces.[66] Others reject this position, pointing out that Resolution 83 (1950) does not only call upon States to repel the armed attack, but also recommends that States take action to *restore* peace and security to the area[67] – a security task much wider than self-defence.[68] With this in mind, it could be argued that the subsequent General Assembly Resolutions are not simply 'reaffirming' this right to take self-defence, but also the necessity to take action to restore international peace and security.

De Wet notes a fundamental issue with the possibility of the Korean action being labelled as a UN enforcement measure, because both Koreas were not at the time Members of the UN, and so the legal basis for taking enforcement action could only be found in general international law beyond the UN system – they had not consented to the powers of the UN at that time.[69]

It is not for this study to investigate the legal basis for the UN action in Korea. However, it should be noted with caution that the international legal system governing the use of force at that time is relatively unclear. In particular, it is not clear whether the *customary* prohibition of force as it is found today

[61] UNGA Res 376(V), *The Problem of Independence of Korea* (7 October 1950) UN Doc A/RES/376(V).

[62] ibid, [1].

[63] UNGA Res 498(V), *Intervention of the Central People's Government of the People's Republic of China in Korea* (1 February 1951) UN Doc A/RES/498(V).

[64] ibid, [3] and [4].

[65] See UNSC Res 82 (1950) (25 June 1950) UN Doc S/RES/82(1950); see also UNSC Res 83 (1950) (27 June 1950) UN Doc S/RES/83(1950).

[66] J Frowein and N Krisch, 'Article 39' in Simma (n 27) 727–28.

[67] UNSC Res 83 (1950) [6].

[68] See eg Tsagourias and White (n 21) 71–72, 110.

[69] E De Wet, *The Chapter VII Powers of the United Nations Security Council* (Oxford, Hart Publishing, 2004) 278–80.

had yet been established in custom at that time, notwithstanding that a majority of States had accepted the rule in Article 2(4) of the UN Charter. Therefore, it is not clear whether there remained a legal basis for the UN to act based upon a separate right of customary international law that had not yet been extinguished by the development of Article 2(4). Furthermore, the Security Council itself apparently did not consider North Korea to be a State at the time, and so any protections afforded by such a status did not apply.[70] Even the Soviet Union viewed the situation as a 'civil war' between two competing governments.[71]

What the Korean action demonstrates is a belief on the part of the General Assembly that it had the power to recommend the use of forcible measures. Notwithstanding the debate regarding the legal basis for such force, it is still clear that there exists a power of the Assembly to recommend the use of force. Whether these recommendations are compatible with the prohibition of force will be addressed below.

Further evidence of the Assembly's powers in this regard reappeared during the development of the responsibility to protect itself. For example, the ICISS[72] acknowledged the possibility of utilising the General Assembly for military action in the face of Security Council failure.[73] Subsequently, the Secretary-General's very first report on the responsibility to protect highlighted the *Uniting for Peace* procedure as a possible avenue for the General Assembly to authorise 'collective measures' to implement the responsibility to protect.[74]

Most notably, Brazil's 'Responsibility While Protecting' initiative[75] expressly provided in its framework that:

> The use of force, including in the exercise of the responsibility to protect, must always be authorized by the Security Council, in accordance with Chapter VII of the Charter, or, in exceptional circumstances, by the General Assembly, in line with its resolution 377 (V).[76]

These examples, taken collectively with the *Uniting for Peace* Resolution itself, it is submitted, reveal a practice that demonstrates that the General Assembly does indeed have a power to recommend forcible measures.

[70] H Kelsen, 'Recent Trends in the Law of the United Nations', a supplement to *The Law of the United Nations* (first published New York, FA Praeger, 1950; reprint, Lawbook Exchange 2000, 2011) 933; see also UNSC Res 82 (1950) (25 June 1950) UN Doc S/RES/82(1950) preamble [1].

[71] UNSC Verbatim Record, 483rd Plenary Meeting (4 August 1950) UN Doc S/PV.483, 2 (USSR).

[72] International Commission on Intervention and State Sovereignty,

[73] ICISS, *The Responsibility to Protect*, (Ottawa, International Development Research Centre, 2001) [6.29]–[6.30].

[74] Report of the Secretary-General, *Implementing the Responsibility to Protect* (12 January 2009) UN Doc A/63/677, [56], although this was notably missing from subsequent reports, and was seemingly contradicted in Report of the Secretary-General, *Mobilizing Collective Action: The Next Decade of the Responsibility to Protect*, (22 July 2016) UN Doc A/70/999–S/2016/620, [46].

[75] See UNGA, 'Letter Dated 9 November 2011 from the Permanent Representative of Brazil to the United Nations Addressed to the Secretary-General' (11 November 2011) UN Doc A/66/551–S/2011/701, Annex.

[76] ibid, Annex, [11(c)].

1.2.2. The Legal Effect of Recommendations to Use Force

Having established that there is sufficient evidence of practice in favour of a power of the General Assembly to recommend the use of force, we must now address the legal effects of this power in order to then understand how it would be compatible with the prohibition of force.

In this regard, we must address the issue as to whether such recommendations could only be acted upon where there is an independent 'legal title' to use force – such as collective self-defence – or whether such recommendations in themselves have a 'legalising effect' whereby they render the use of force compatible with the prohibition in Article 2(4).

Dinstein[77] argues that 'when the General Assembly adopts a recommendation for action by States in the realm of international peace and security, such a resolution – while not bereft of political significance – does not alter the legal rights and duties of those States'.[78] Similarly, Corten[79] argues that 'there is nothing to show that the General Assembly can authorise States to conduct military action in the territory of another State without that action being otherwise based on an autonomous legal title'.[80]

The logic behind these positions seems to be that non-binding recommendations, by definition, cannot affect State sovereignty in themselves, and cannot provide a standalone basis for the use of force. According to this argument, recommendations by the Assembly do not have the effect of 'legalising' an otherwise unlawful use of force and making it compatible with Article 2(4). This immediately causes this author to question: how then does a similar non-binding 'authorisation' to use force by the Security Council differ from this? If a non-binding recommendation does not alter the legal rights or duties of States, it would seem contradictory to suggest that a non-binding authorisation would have the opposite effect, because the lack of legal effect would come from the non-binding nature of the act or declaration therein.

While it is not the primary purpose of this study to explain the legal basis for Security Council authorisations to use force, it is nevertheless necessary to delve into this debate briefly to shed light on the General Assembly's analogous ability to recommend force. To understand the legal effect of recommendations, we must also understand the place of 'authorisations' within the Charter and how these non-binding, permissive acts seemingly 'make lawful' an otherwise unlawful use of force, and whether or not they are different to 'recommendations' to do the same. Based upon the analysis to follow, this author believes

[77] Y Dinstein, *War, Aggression and Self-Defence*, 6th edn (Cambridge, Cambridge University Press, 2017).

[78] ibid, 367, [964].

[79] O Corten, *The Law Against War: The Prohibition on the Use of Force in Contemporary International Law* (Oxford, Hart Publishing, 2012).

[80] ibid, 330–31.

that the Security Council's power to authorise force originates from its ability to 'make recommendations' to maintain or restore international peace and security under Article 39 of the Charter. Therefore, by extension, and based upon the subsequent practice of States, a 'recommendation' by the General Assembly to do the same would logically and necessarily have the same legal effect in permitting the use of force.

1.2.2.1. The Debate Regarding Security Council 'Authorisations' of Force

Conflated Definitions of Authorisations and Delegations

Proponents of the position that General Assembly recommendations have no legal effect must also explain the analogous ability of the Security Council to 'authorise' the use of force. To do so, Corten argues, for example, that the reason Security Council 'authorisations' are legal is because they are in fact 'delegations' of its Chapter VII powers.[81]

Much of the theory on this issue derives from Sarooshi, whose work on the delegation of Security Council powers is widely cited in support of this argument.[82] Sarooshi suggests that the power of the Security Council to delegate its powers originates from general international law,[83] and uses this theory to explain the legality of recent Council resolutions allowing to Member States to use force.[84]

This is despite the fact that the Security Council has consistently used the term 'authorise' when granting States the ability to undertake military measures.[85] Sarooshi suggests: 'The Council may be using the term "authorization", but what it is doing in substance is delegating its Chapter VII powers to Member States.'[86] Chesterman[87] similarly described the Security Council's use of the term 'authorise' in its resolutions as 'misleading'.[88]

This author, however, does not believe that the Security Council's choice of language should be dismissed out of hand. For example, Sarooshi cites the European Court of Justice case of *Meroni v High Authority*[89] in support of the Security Council's apparent general competence to delegate its powers.[90]

[81] ibid, 331, see also 314–15.

[82] See generally D Sarooshi, *The United Nations and the Development of Collective Security: The Delegation by the UN Security Council of its Chapter VII Powers* (Oxford, Oxford University Press, 1999).

[83] ibid, 16–19.

[84] ibid, 13; see also Chapter 5 generally.

[85] For an overview of the relevant practice in this regard, see Sarooshi (n 82), ch 5, 167ff.

[86] ibid, 13.

[87] S Chesterman, *Just War or Just Peace: Humanitarian Intervention and International Law* (Oxford, Oxford University Press, 2001).

[88] ibid, 165.

[89] Case 9/56 *Meroni v High Authority* [1958] ECR 133.

[90] Sarooshi (n 82) 8–9, 17.

But even in this case, the general principle that powers can be delegated required such a delegation to be expressly provided, and leaving no room for inference:

> A delegation of powers cannot be presumed and even when empowered to delegate its powers the delegating authority must take an express decision transferring them.[91]

The Security Council's 'authorisations' similarly should not be used to imply a delegation. There is no clear reason why we should dismiss the language chosen by the Security Council itself in its resolutions – if the Security Council wished to delegate its powers, there is no reason to suggest it would not have done so more explicitly; similarly, if the Security Council simply wants to authorise and permit a course of action, short of the actual transfer of powers, there is no reason to *disbelieve* this. This is one reason why the delegation theory is not convincing.

This is especially important because 'authorisations' and 'delegations' are very distinct legal acts, and so for the sake of legal certainty, we must be sure which the Security Council would be utilising. In ordinary terms, an 'authorisation' means 'the action of authorising a person or thing; formal permission or approval' or 'the action of making legally valid'.[92] By contrast, to 'delegate' means 'to entrust, commit of deliver (authority, a function, etc) to another as an agent or deputy'.[93] In legal doctrine, even Sarooshi concedes that there is a legal distinction between these two.[94] In this regard. Sarooshi submits:

> An authorization is more limited than a delegation of powers: both in terms of the specification of the objectives to be achieved and the qualitative nature of the powers transferred to achieve the designated objective. … An authorization, thus, may represent the conferring on an entity of a very limited right to exercize [*sic*] a power, or part thereof; or the conferring on an entity of the right to exercize a power it already possesses, but the exercize of which is conditional on an authorization that triggers the competence of the entity to use the power.[95]

Sarooshi goes on to argue that the single distinguishing characteristic of a delegation of power is that it is a transfer of a power of broad discretion.[96] Based on this alone, this distinction is evident when one considers the actual powers which the Security Council is purported to delegate. Those in favour of the delegation theory argue that the Security Council would be delegating its Article 42 powers to Member States.[97] However, Article 42 is a broad discretionary power. It refers

[91] *Meroni* (n 89) judgment [9], and 151.
[92] *Oxford English Dictionary* definition, www.oed.com/view/Entry/13351 (accessed 31 July 2019).
[93] *Oxford English Dictionary* definition, www.oed.com/view/Entry/49313 (accessed 31 July 2019).
[94] Sarooshi (n 82) 11–12.
[95] ibid, 12–13.
[96] ibid, 13.
[97] See eg E De Wet, *The Chapter VII Powers of the United Nations Security Council* (Oxford, Hart Publishing, 2004) 260–64; Sarooshi (n 82) 146–49; Corten (n 79) 315–16; see Chesterman

to the Council's general ability to 'take action' using measures that amount to the use of force.[98] Importantly, it is a broad power to take such action 'as may be necessary to maintain or restore international peace and security'.

In reality, when the Security Council authorises Member States to use force, it does so in relation to a very specific situation, and often with other limitations. It may give States discretion as to how the measures are implemented, such as the tactics and operational command that are utilised – however, this discretion is simply not broad enough to reflect a delegation of powers in Article 42. Therefore, the Council does not transfer its Article 42 powers – the Council is permitting States to use force in a specific situation for a specific objective. It does not grant States the general ability to use force for the general maintenance of international peace and security. By Sarooshi's own logic, this must be a simple authorisation, rather than a delegation.

Erroneous Definition of 'Authorisation' in Legal Discourse

Regarding the definition of 'authorisation', De Wet takes a slightly different approach, suggesting that the term authorisation 'should be reserved for situations where the organ creates subsidiary organs and "authorises" them to perform functions which it may not perform itself, but which it may nonetheless authorise under the Charter'.[99] Conversely, De Wet argues that the term delegation should be reserved for situations where an organ empowers another entity to exercise one of its own functions.[100]

This idea that an authorisation is restricted to functions which the authorising body may not perform itself was adopted by the ECtHR in *Behrami v France*,[101] when the court considered whether it had jurisdiction over the acts of members of KFOR (the 'Kosovo Force') during the international operations in Kosovo. When addressing the nature of the Security Council resolutions authorising KFOR,[102] the Court considered:

> While this Resolution used the term 'authorise', that term and the term 'delegation' are used interchangeably. Use of the term 'delegation' in the present decision refers to the empowering by the UNSC of another entity to exercise its function as opposed to 'authorising' an entity to carry out functions which it could not itself perform.[103]

(n 87) 165–66, and 167–69 who notes that the precise legal basis for delegation remains in dispute, but offers a number of options; see also J Frowein and N Krisch, 'Action with respect to Threats to the Peace, Breaches of the Peace and Acts of Aggression' in Simma (n 27) 712–13, who suggest the legal basis for delegation of these powers is Art 42 itself.

[98] Art 42 refers to 'action by air, sea, or land forces', and stipulates that this may include 'demonstrations, blockade, and other operations by air, sea, or land forces of Members of the United Nations'.

[99] De Wet (n 97) 259.

[100] ibid.

[101] *Behrami v France; Saramati v France, Germany and Norway* (2007) 45 EHRR SE10.

[102] See eg UNSC Res 1244 (1999) (10 June 1999) UN Doc S/RES/1244(1999).

[103] *Behrami v France* (n 101) [43].

The Court does not explain why it adopted this definition, but the Court does rely heavily on De Wet and Sarooshi's works, among others, later in the judgment when it discussed and determined the basis of the Security Council's supposed 'delegation' of power to KFOR.[104]

The source of confusion seems to be the ICJ's Advisory Opinion in *Application for Review*,[105] a case De Wet herself refers to in support of the definition of 'authorisation'.[106] In this case, the ICJ referred to the distinction between a delegation and an authorisation when it considered the nature of a General Assembly subsidiary body's[107] power to request an Advisory Opinion of the Court. In particular, the Court considered the Committee's power to be based upon an 'authorisation' rather than a 'delegation' of the General Assembly's own power to request an Advisory Opinion.[108] In this regard, the distinction comes down to the interpretation of Article 96 of the Charter, whereby Article 96(1) empowers the General Assembly to request an Advisory Opinion on 'any legal question', and Article 96(2) allows the General Assembly to 'authorise' other organs of the UN to request such opinions on 'legal questions arising within the scope of their activities'. The Court explicitly considered that the Committee's power was *not* a delegation of the Assembly's own broader power, precisely because the Committee's powers were more limited, and so did not actually reflect the Assembly's own broad competence under Article 96(1).[109] Indeed, the Court also noted that the limited nature of the Committee's competences also did not restrict the Assembly's power to authorise such organs to request Advisory Opinions in Article 96(2).[110]

The erroneous definition of 'authorisation' may originate from Sarooshi's mistaken reading of the case that:

> The Court found that since the General Assembly could not perform the same function as the Committee – the review of decisions of the Administrative Tribunal – the source of the Committee's power to request an advisory opinion was not as a result of a delegation of the Assembly's own power under Article 96(1).[111]

Unfortunately, Sarooshi seems to be conflating a power to review decisions of the Administrative Tribunal with the very distinct legal power of requesting Advisory Opinions – the two are not the same, and the reference the Court made

[104] ibid, [130] and [132].

[105] *Application for Review of Judgement No 158 of the United Nations Administrative Tribunal* (Advisory Opinion), 12 July 1973, [1973] ICJ Rep 166.

[106] De Wet (n 97) 259, see also her fn 15.

[107] The UN Committee on Applications for Review of Administrative Tribunal Judgments (hereinafter 'the Committee').

[108] *Application for Review* (n 105) [19]–[23].

[109] ibid, [20]; see also Sarooshi (n 82) 12–13.

[110] *Application for Review* (n 105) [20].

[111] Sarooshi (n 82) 12; this is surprising, because Sarooshi himself immediately goes on to recognise the broader power available to the General Assembly compared to that conferred on the Committee.

to delegation in this regard related only to the question of the latter power. Indeed, the ICJ has already recognised that there is a distinction between the delegation of the Assembly's own functions and the exercise of a power which creates a body with powers the General Assembly itself does not hold.[112] The fact that the General Assembly did not have the power to review Tribunal decisions does not in any way affect its power to request Advisory Opinions on *any* legal question under Article 96(1).

Unfortunately, Sarooshi's statement, and De Wet's subsequent submission following his analysis,[113] seems to have provided the basis for misunderstanding the legal nature of authorisations in a number of judicial decisions, including as discussed in the *Behrami* case,[114] and later also endorsed further in *Al-Jedda* by the UK's House of Lords.[115]

Problems with the Doctrine of Delegated Powers when applied to the Security Council

One of the key restrictions of the general principle of delegation, as advocated by Sarooshi,[116] is that the delegator must remain in 'ultimate' or 'overall' 'authority and control' of the exercise of the delegated powers.[117] However, there are a few problems with this restriction.

Firstly, as noted by Sarooshi himself, the very existence of the permanent five's veto power could mean that any termination of a delegation of powers could be blocked, in effect meaning that the Security Council is no longer in 'ultimate control' of its delegation.[118] However, Sarooshi seeks to explain this by arguing that Security Council delegations could terminate automatically, especially once the objectives determined by the Council have been achieved.[119] Similarly, the ECtHR in *Behrami* indicated that the veto power alone was not sufficient to conclude that the Security Council did not retain ultimate authority and control.[120]

[112] *Effect of Awards of Compensation Made by the United Nations Administrative Tribunal* (Advisory Opinion), 13 July 1954, [1954] ICJ Rep 47, 61; see also *Application for Review* (n 105) [17], which explains the judgment of the Court in this regard.

[113] De Wet (n 97) 259.

[114] *Behrami v France* (n 101) [43].

[115] See, for example, the dissenting judgment of Lord Roger of Earlsferry in the UK House of Lords case *R (Al-Jedda) v Secretary of State for Defence* [2008] 1 AC 332, [79] onwards, where Lord Roger seems to mistake the General Assembly's creation of a subsidiary body with powers that it does not itself possess, with the authorisation of a limited power (ie the Committee's limited scope to request Advisory Opinions) – a much broader version of which the Assembly already possesses (ie the Assembly's power to request Advisory Opinions on *any* legal question). Other judges who endorsed the *Behrami* test for 'authorisation', based upon Sarooshi's work, include Lord Bingham at [21] and [23], and Lord Brown at [143].

[116] Sarooshi (n 82) 35–41.

[117] *Behrami v France* (n 101) [133].

[118] Sarooshi (n 82) 40–41.

[119] Sarooshi (n 82) 41, 156–59.

[120] *Behrami v France* (n 101) [134].

De Wet also seeks to explain this problem by arguing that a mandate to use force will cease when it becomes clear that it no longer enjoys the support of the majority of Security Council members.[121] In this regard, De Wet seems to suggest that the 'intention' of the Security Council might be inferred from a draft resolution that receives the support of a majority of members, but is vetoed by a permanent member.[122] In other words, a draft resolution terminating the mandate, which would have passed but for the veto of a permanent member, may indicate the true 'will' of the Council itself. Unfortunately, this author believes De Wet goes too far to suggest this may result in a presumption that a mandate to use force is terminated – this would completely ignore the voting procedures of the Council which, for better or worse, are still legally binding.

However, her argument is convincing on the point that it may indicate the will of the Council itself. Constructing this 'will' of the Security Council does help to understand the point that the Council itself is not the bearer of ultimate authority or control when it confers a mandate to use force with no point of termination or expiration. Indeed, this is also true when we consider a situation where the Council may be unable to change or edit a mandate in response to a developing situation, and that would be the will of the Council but for the fact that such an alteration to the mandate may be vetoed. This problem of vetoing terminations or alterations is especially significant in the situation where the authorisation to use force is granted to, or includes, one of the permanent members – it would seem a complete legal fiction to suggest that the Security Council has overall authority and control when the delegate has the final say as to whether it surrenders power back to the delegator. As Frowein and Krisch highlight,[123] in practice the Council enacts Chapter VII Resolutions usually for an unlimited period and terminating them requires a positive decision by the Council which is still subject to what they call the 'reverse veto'.

Tsagourias and White similarly reject the argument that periodic reports provide a sufficient form of oversight by the Security Council, viewing this mechanism as too weak to amount to proper supervision.[124] Moreover, they are clear in establishing that Security Council authorisations simply do not adhere to many of the requirements of the delegation doctrine, especially where the mandates are not sufficiently defined to adhere with the general criterion outlined in *Meroni*.[125]

Moreover, more recent case-law has accepted that some Security Council mandates simply do not provide for the ultimate authority or control of the Council. While the ECtHR in *Behrami* considered the Security Council still to be in ultimate authority and control of KFOR, when *Al-Jedda* reached the ECtHR

[121] De Wet (n 97) 270.
[122] ibid.
[123] Frowein and Krisch (n 97) 714.
[124] Tsagourias and White (n 21) 291.
[125] ibid; see *Meroni* (n 89) at 151–154.

it decided differently on the facts.[126] The Court considered the Multi-National Force (MNF) in Iraq, authorised to 'to take all necessary measures to contribute to the maintenance of security and stability in Iraq',[127] was not under the 'effective control nor ultimate authority and control' of the UN Security Council.[128] Therefore, by extension, these mandates cannot be considered delegations, and so they must be simple authorisations. It is also worth noting the ILC's support for this decision in its commentaries on its Draft Articles on the Responsibility of International Organisations,[129] and its subtle criticism of the earlier case-law therein.[130]

Not only does this demonstrate that 'authorisations' (in their ordinary meaning) are possible by the Security Council, but it also indicates that such authorisations are consistent with the prohibition of force and State sovereignty.

1.2.2.2. Article 39 as the Alternative Legal Basis for Security Council Authorisations

Having established that Security Council authorisations to use force are not delegations of its Chapter VII powers, this section will offer an explanation for the legal basis of this power. Article 53(1) in Chapter VIII of the Charter explicitly references the ability of the Council to 'authorise' enforcement action by regional agencies or arrangements. But there is no express provision in the Charter granting the Security Council this power, or the power to authorise Member States generally. Therefore, there must be some provision in Chapter VII of the Charter that leaves room for the Council to 'authorise' action.[131] This author argues that Article 39 provides for such a power. But first, we shall address arguments in favour of alternatives.

[126] *Al-Jedda v United Kingdom* (2011) 53 EHRR 23.

[127] UNSC Res 1511 (2003) (16 October 2003) UN Doc S/RES/1511(2003) para [13]; see also UNSC Res 1546 (2004) (8 June 2004) UN Doc S/RES/1546(2004) [9].

[128] *Al-Jedda v United Kingdom* (n 126) [84]; see also *R (Al-Jedda) v Secretary of State for Defence* (n 115) [22]–[24] per Lord Bingham.

[129] ILC, 'Draft Articles on the Responsibility of International Organisation, with Commentaries', http://legal.un.org/ilc/texts/instruments/english/commentaries/9_11_2011.pdf (accessed 31 July 2019); also included in ILC, 'Report of the International Law Commission on the Work of its Sixty-Third Session' (26 April–3 June and 4 July–12 August 2011) UN Doc A/66/10, from 69 (hereinafter 'DARIO Commentaries').

[130] ILC DARIO Commentaries (n 129), Commentary to Art 7, [10]–[13]; see also its assertion regarding the lack of attribution to the UN of the conduct of forces authorised by the Security Council, at General Commentary to Chapter II, [5].

[131] Chapter VII is specifically assigned to 'actions relating to threats to the peace, breaches of the peace, and acts of aggression', and so in accordance with Art 24(2), listing the Chapters where the Council's powers are found, Chapter VII would be the only logical place to find this power.

Chesterman highlights one argument that the Council possesses a general *implied* power in the Charter to authorise force.[132] This is based upon an assertion by the ICJ in the *Reparation for Injuries*[133] Advisory Opinion, where it said:

> Under international law, the Organization must be deemed to have those powers which, though not expressly provided in the Charter, are conferred upon it by necessary implication as being essential to the performance of its duties.[134]

Unfortunately, as Chesterman rightly notes, this view results in a complete lack of legal certainty about any limitations or scope of the Security Council's powers to authorise force.[135] Furthermore, the context of the ICJ's statement was very specific as to the possibility of the UN bringing claims for reparations on the behalf of its agents in the circumstances of that case – this is very different to implying a power to authorise the use of force against a Member State. As such, it would be preferable to investigate a basis for this power within the provisions of the Charter as opposed to a general inference.

As highlighted above, some authors believe Article 42 provides a sound legal basis for the authorisation model. For example, Corten argues that the word 'action' in Article 42 is wide enough to cover the Council's recent practice of authorising States to use force.[136]

Of course, Article 42, as originally intended, was meant to allow the Security Council *itself* to use force, taking action by controlling the forces of UN Member States, as determined by agreements that were to be concluded on the basis of Article 43, and as determined by the Military Staff Committee under Articles 46 and 47. As is well known, the Article 43 agreements were never concluded.

In *Certain Expenses*, the ICJ noted that the failure to reach such agreements did not leave the Security Council impotent in the face of an emergency.[137] It is on this basis that some argue that Article 42 may be interpreted to allow the Security Council to 'authorise' force, rather than take action itself.[138] Nevertheless, there are still those who consider Article 42 as strictly confined to military action taken by the Security Council itself in fulfilment of the dormant security apparatus in Article 47 of the Charter.[139]

[132] Chesterman (n 87) 168; see also, for a similar point, H Freudenchuß, 'Between Unilateralism and Collective Security: Authorizations of the Use of Force by the UN Security Council' (1994) 5 *European Journal of International Law* 492, 526.

[133] *Reparation for Injuries Suffered in the Service of the United Nations* (Advisory Opinion), 11 April 1949, [1949] ICJ Rep 174.

[134] ibid, 182.

[135] Chesterman (n 87) 168.

[136] Corten (n 79) 315–16.

[137] *Certain Expenses* (n 1) 167.

[138] See eg J Frowein and N Krisch, 'Article 42' in Simma (n 27) 756–57; De Wet (n 97) 260.

[139] See eg B Conforti and C Focarelli, *The Law and Practice of the United Nations*, 4th edn (Leiden, Koninklijke Brill, 2010) 280.

White,[140] however, while noting the plausibility of Article 42 as a legal basis for such action, also notes the equal plausibility of this action deriving from 'recommendations' under Article 39 of the Charter.[141] Article 39, as discussed in Chapter III, obliges the Security Council to determine the existence of threats to, or breaches of, the peace or acts of aggression, and then either to make recommendations or take decisions under Articles 41 and 42 for the maintenance or restoration of international peace and security.

The making of 'recommendations' – a non-binding act – may well provide a basis for the Security Council's power to authorise Member States to take military action.[142] Dinstein, for example, argues that while recommendations can only urge Member States to take action, 'if Member States choose to heed a Council's recommendation authorizing them to take measures predicated on a binding determination concerning the existence of a threat to the peace etc, these measures must be considered lawful notwithstanding their permissive character'.[143] He then goes on to argue that permissive action of this kind can only be anchored in Article 39, and not Article 48.[144] Indeed, referencing the arguments that Article 42 is the basis for Council authorisation, Dinstein also rejects this, noting that both authorisations and recommendations are of a non-mandatory nature and thus neither action comes within the rubric of Article 42.[145] To him, there is no genuine distinction between an authorisation and a recommendation, and an authorisation is no less permissive than a recommendation.[146]

After the Security Council first 'recommended' the use of military measures in response to the situation in Korea in 1950,[147] Kelsen[148] doubted whether this corresponded to the intentions of the drafters of the Charter.[149] However, he did admit that the wording of Article 39 does not exclude the possibility of the Security Council recommending enforcement measures, and it was only if this interpretation was accepted that the Security Council's Resolution doing so in Korea could be considered constitutional.[150]

[140] N White, 'From Korea to Kuwait: The Legal Basis of United Nations' Military Action' (1998) 20(3) *International History Review* 597.

[141] ibid, 605, 608, 613; see also ND White and Ö Ülgen, 'The Security Council and the Decentralised Military Option: Constitutionality and Function' (1997) 44(3) *Netherlands International Law Review* 378, 385 and 387.

[142] But see, in the International Criminal Tribunal for the former Yugoslavia (ICTY) *Prosecutor v Tadić* (Jurisdiction) Case IT-94-1AR72 (2 October 1995) [29] and [31], where the Tribunal suggests that recommendations in Art 39 simply reflect a continuation of those available to the Council concerning the peaceful settlement of disputes in Chapter VI of the Charter.

[143] Dinstein (n 77) 331, [869].

[144] ibid, 341, [894].

[145] ibid, 359, [946].

[146] ibid, 359, [946].

[147] UNSC Res 83 (1950) (27 June 1950) UN Doc S/RES/83(1950).

[148] Kelsen (n 70).

[149] ibid, 932.

[150] ibid, 933.

During Security Council meetings which addressed this action, the UK representative considered the proper legal basis to be Article 39, arguing:

> Had the Charter come fully into force and had the agreement provided for in Article 43 of the Charter been concluded, we should, of course, have proceeded differently, and the action to be taken by the Security Council to repel the armed attack would no doubt have been founded on Article 42. As it is, however, the Council can naturally act only under Article 39, which enables the Security Council to recommend what measures should be taken to restore international peace and security.[151]

Not only does this suggest actions under Article 42 were considered as actions only to be taken directly by the Security Council, but it supports the argument that Article 39 may be the proper legal basis for authorisations to use force.[152] As noted by White, the French and US delegations also accepted this position.[153]

One argument against this interpretation might be to suggest that recommendations are of lesser legal importance than authorisations, or that recommendations do not have the same 'legalising' effect as authorisations. However, based on the ordinary meaning of these terms, logic tells us otherwise. We have determined that an 'authorisation' grants official permission,[154] whereas to recommend means to 'present (a thing, course of action) to a person etc, as being desirable or advisable'.[155] Therefore, a 'recommendation' involves urging a party to do something, and this, it is submitted, necessarily implies that the body doing the recommending *permits* such an act to be done. A recommendation, therefore, goes beyond a simple permission to undertake an act – it actively encourages it. It is by this argument that one considers a recommendation to necessarily *imply* a relevant authorisation where it is considered legal for the body in question to authorise such action in the first place.

In this context, if an official body such as the Security Council recommended that States use force in a situation, it must necessarily follow that it permits such action, and therefore authorises it. This issue can be highlighted by reference to Security Council Resolution 2249 (2015), where the Council 'called upon' States to use all necessary measures to prevent and suppress terrorist acts committed by terrorist group 'Islamic State in Syria' or 'Da'esh'.[156] While there have been

[151] UNSC Verbatim Record, 476th Meeting (7 July 1950) UN Doc S/PV.476, 3; reference to the Charter not being 'fully in force' seems to be a colloquial reference to the missing agreements under Art 43, not necessarily the legally binding force of the Charter itself.

[152] See also UNSC Verbatim Record, 486th Meeting (11 August 1950) UN Doc S/PV.486, 6.

[153] White (n 140) 613.

[154] See above, n 92.

[155] *Oxford English Dictionary* definition, www.oed.com/view/Entry/159715 (accessed 31 July 2019).

[156] UNSC Res 2249 (2015) (20 November 2015) UN Doc S/RES/2249(2015) [5]; for similar language in the context of the crisis in Southern Rhodesia, see UNSC Res 221 (1966) (9 April 1966) UN Doc S/RES/221(1966) [5], where the Council 'called upon' the UK to prevent, by the use of force if necessary, the arrival of ships at Beira reasonably believed to be carrying oil destined for Southern Rhodesia.

debates regarding the ambiguous language of this Resolution,[157] some States certainly interpreted the Resolution as providing a legal basis in and of itself for military action notwithstanding possible alternative claims of collective self-defence against the terrorist groups.[158] With this in mind, the current author argues that it would be reckless for a body such as the Security Council, with the power to authorise the use of far-reaching measures, to recommend the use of forcible measures when it did not also intend to authorise such measures. Of course, there may be political reasons behind the ambiguous language of a Resolution,[159] as is to be expected when it is necessary for the Members of the Council (especially the five permanent members) to compromise. But, legally speaking, if the Council does not intend to authorise force, it should not encourage States to use such force in a way that suggests it is permissible to do so.

On this basis, it is submitted that the legal basis for Security Council authorisations to use force is inherent in its ability to *recommend* force in Article 39. Having established this, we may now address the analogous ability of the General Assembly to do the same.

1.2.2.3. General Assembly Recommendations

Dinstein seems to accept the legality of Security Council recommendations to use force, but not the legality of General Assembly recommendations to do the same, suggesting that only a Security Council decision can validate an otherwise unlawful use of force.[160] This returns to the debate that the non-binding nature of recommendations do not provide a standalone legal title to use force, a point that Tsagourias and White find unconvincing.[161]

However, this assumes that the legality of the use of force in pursuance of a recommendation by a competent body is not inherent in the power to recommend force in the first place. Instead, it is logically preferred to consider the lawfulness of a use of force as based upon the consent of a State to the power of the relevant body to make such recommendations. In other words, the power to make recommendations in Article 39 may now be considered, by virtue of subsequent practice and agreement to the ability of the Council to authorise force, as *including* the power to recommend the use of force. If a target State has

[157] See eg D Akande and M Milanovic, 'The Constructive Ambiguity of the Security Council's ISIS Resolution' *EJIL: Talk!* (21 November 2015) www.ejiltalk.org/the-constructive-ambiguity-of-the-security-councils-isis-resolution/ (accessed 31 July 2019); see also A Lang, 'Legal Basis for UK Military Action in Syria' (House of Commons Briefing Paper No 7404, UK House of Commons Library, 1 December 2015).

[158] For an overview of the State arguments, and actions subsequent to this Resolution, see T Ruys et al, 'Digest of State Practice: 1 July–31 December' (2016) 3(1) *Journal on the Use of Force and International Law* 126, 150–54.

[159] ibid.

[160] Dinstein (n 77) 367, [965].

[161] Tsagourias and White (n 21) 292–93; for a different explanation, see Nahlawi (n 51) 117–19.

accepted such a power by virtue of their Membership of the United Nations, although not of a mandatory nature, it must also logically follow that the State accepts the consequences of the use of that power – the consequence being the use of force against them.

This submission follows from the interpretation of Article 2(4) of the Charter, as investigated in Chapter IV, that the use of force is legal when it is consistent with Article 2(4), rather than falling within a defined selection of 'exceptions' to a general rule. It is the compatibility with Article 2(4) of the General Assembly's purported power to recommend force, and the use of it therein, that we shall now address.

1.2.3. Compatibility with Article 2(4)

On the basis of an analysis of Article 2(4) of the Charter, it was argued in Chapter IV that the prohibition was not an all-encompassing general prohibition of all uses of force, but a carefully constructed prohibition which allowed for very narrow uses of force where they are compatible with the prohibition itself. Therefore, the so-called 'exceptions' to the prohibition of self-defence and the powers of the Security Council were explained not as exceptions per se but circumstances that did not violate the prohibition of force.

To be compatible with Article 2(4), Assembly recommendations, and the actions taken in pursuit of them, must: (i) not violate the territorial integrity or political independence of the target State; and (ii) be consistent with the Purposes of the United Nations.

1.2.3.1. Territorial Integrity and Political Independence

As outlined above, territorial integrity and political independence – foundational principles of State sovereignty itself – may be inherently qualified by the consent of a State, or by a rule of customary international law limiting the scope of those principles.[162] Applying this to recommendations of the General Assembly to use force, this power must be established as part of the Charter regime, or the use of force in pursuit of such recommendations must be provided for on the basis of a State's consent to such action provided elsewhere in the Charter.

In Chapter IV, the powers of the Security Council were explained as a form of permanent consent by Members to the ability of the Security Council to take or authorise such measures. This is quite uncontroversial, as this is clearly foreseen as one of the main reasons the United Nations was founded. The ability of the General Assembly to recommend such action, however, is not explicit, and so must be explained.

[162] See Chapter IV, section 3.1 and section 3.2.

There are two possible bases for the consent of Members to the use of force in pursuance of a recommendation of the General Assembly. This could be: (i) an interpretation of the General Assembly's powers under either Article 10 or Article 11 of the Charter, based upon subsequent agreement or practice implying that the recommendations therein include recommendations to use force; or (ii) a general principle of the Charter granting effective collective measures, such as the use of force, when taken in accordance with the procedures and competences of the organs of the organisation.

As for the first possibility, it is clear from the practice outlined above that the General Assembly's powers have subsequently been considered to include the ability to recommend force, especially considering the *Uniting for Peace* Resolution.[163] Of course, this power has only been utilised in practice once, and the international community has been hesitant to utilise the General Assembly outside of peacekeeping since the 1950s. The competence of the Assembly only being secondary for the maintenance of peace and security, it is evident that any precedents would be rare, and this should not necessarily reflect the international community's support (or lack of) for the legality of such actions.

The second possibility has been advocated, in a sense, by Tsagourias and White, when they suggest that the 'exception' to the prohibition of force allowing the Security Council to take action is not an exception just for the Council, but also for the 'organs representing the membership of the UN in matters of peace and security' in general.[164] In this regard, White argues that the question of which organ authorises action is an internal issue.[165] Thus, in accordance with this argument, the legality of the organ taking such measures is an internal matter to be determined by the internal procedures and divisions of competence within the organisation.

While this author does not quite agree that this construction is an 'exception' to Article 2(4), it is certainly possible that the Charter itself provides a basis for the UN in general to have the power to use force, rather than exclusively the Security Council. Such an argument may be drawn out by reference to the preamble of the Charter, where it considers that the use of force should not be used 'save in the common interest', or indeed by Article 1(1) itself, which provides that the primary purpose of the United Nations is:

> To maintain international peace and security, and to that end: *to take effective collective measures* for the prevention and removal of threats to the peace, and for the suppression of acts of aggression or other breaches of the peace.[166]

It could well be argued, on this basis, that States have consented to the role of the United Nations in taking forcible measures, especially since one of its main purposes has been explicitly regarded as taking 'effective collective measures'.

[163] See above, section 1.2.1.1.

[164] Tsagourias and White (n 21) 111; see also N White, 'The Legality of Bombing in the Name of Humanity', (2000) 5(1) *Journal of Conflict and Security Law* 27, 28, 39–41.

[165] White (n 164) 39.

[166] Emphasis added.

So long as the secondary rules providing for the competences and the procedures of the organs of the Organisation are upheld, this is sufficient to render such action to be compatible with the inherently limited principles of territorial integrity and political independence.

This argument, coupled with the support outlined for the competence of the General Assembly to recommend force, would render such action compatible with the first requirement of Article 2(4).

1.2.3.2. Consistency with the Purposes of the United Nations

As for the second requirement of Article 2(4), prohibiting force inconsistent with the purposes of the United Nations, it will be recalled from Chapter IV that this clause of the provision effectively prohibits all unilateral uses of force.[167] It was argued therein that Article 1(4), detailing the purpose of the UN to be a centre for harmonising the actions of nations, for the attainment of the purpose of maintenance of international peace and security in Article 1(1), implies that any forcible measures must be sufficiently 'harmonised' and 'collective' to be consistent with these purposes and thus Article 2(4).

Considering the very fact that action authorised by the Security Council is compatible with these purposes, it is also submitted here that a recommendation by the General Assembly can also be considered as such. Moreover, since the General Assembly represents every Member of the UN, the adoption of a Resolution recommending such action could certainly be considered as 'harmonising' the actions of nations, and rendering the basis of the use of force as sufficiently 'collective' for these purposes.

1.2.4. Compatibility with Article 2(7)

One further issue that should be addressed briefly is the compatibility of this line of action with Article 2(7) of the Charter. While this provision generally prevents the UN from intervening in the domestic jurisdiction of States, as established above, the consent of States to the powers of the Assembly to make these recommendations renders such conduct automatically outside the domestic jurisdiction of Members. Furthermore, the reference in this provision to Chapter VII of the Charter is of little relevance in this regard, since enforcement measures are still clearly envisioned in other parts of the Charter.[168] Therefore, the principle contained in Article 2(7) is, at first glance, contradictory, but nevertheless follows the same pattern as the general principle of non-intervention, still requiring specific powers to justify an 'intervention' into any internal matter.[169]

[167] See Chapter IV, section 3.3.

[168] See eg Chapter VIII and of course the powers of the General Assembly itself in this regard.

[169] See also G Nolte, 'Article 2(7)' in Simma (n 27) 156–57, 160–68, 171; and generally, R Higgins, *The Development of International Law through the Political Organs of the United Nations* (London, Oxford University Press, 1963) 64–130.

1.2.5. *Conclusions on Forcible Measures by the General Assembly*

Considering the above, one would conclude that the General Assembly does have the legal power, in certain circumstances, to recommend the use of force, and the implementation of such a recommendation by Member States would be compatible with the prohibition of force in Article 2(4). As such, this power could indeed provide an alternative measure to implement the responsibility to protect. In this sense, it is worth noting that this power is only compatible with the Charter's protections regarding the primacy of the Security Council in Articles 11(2) and 12 where there is a failure of the Security Council to uphold its responsibility for the maintenance of international peace and security.

Since the use of force, as an 'effective collective measure', is only consistent with the purposes of the Charter in pursuance of the maintenance of international peace and security, it logically follows that the General Assembly's power to recommend such measures is limited to measures specifically for the purposes of preventing or removing threats to the peace and the suppression of acts of aggression.[170] By extension, such recommendations cannot be made to, for example, prevent human rights abuses where those abuses do not also threaten international peace and security. In this sense, the Assembly might be considered under the same restraints as the Security Council is under Article 39. While it does not explicitly need to determine the existence of such threats, breaches or acts of aggression, the powers utilised therein are restricted to these purposes. Therefore, the use of force by the General Assembly may only be a tool of implementing the responsibility to protect, where the prevention or suppression of atrocity crimes also engages the responsibility for the maintenance of international peace and security.

Furthermore, while this identifies a legal alternative to implement the responsibility to protect, this does not necessarily imply that this method would be the most suitable, or the most practical. While General Assembly action to maintain or restore peace provides an alternative basis to prevent inaction, this route would still require a two-thirds majority of the Members States of the UN to support such action.[171]

1.3. Non-Forcible Coercive Measures

This section addresses the ability of the General Assembly to adopt other coercive measures, such as sanctions, asset freezes or trade embargoes, as a method of implementing the tertiary responsibility to protect. Firstly, it will

[170] This is the phrasing used in Art 1(1) of the Charter.

[171] See Art 18(2) of the Charter, where Assembly recommendations relating to the maintenance of peace and security require a two-thirds majority.

explore whether the powers of the Assembly allow such recommendations to be made. Secondly, the compatibility of such a power with the principle of non-intervention will also be explained. In this regard, it is argued that the powers of the Assembly do indeed provide for non-forcible measures, but only in circumstances permitted by international law – in particular, by virtue of the doctrine of countermeasures.

1.3.1. Assessing General Assembly Competences to Recommend Coercive Measures

Having established that the General Assembly may make recommendations for the use of force for the maintenance of international peace and security, it would seem to follow that the General Assembly could also recommend that economic measures are taken. However, before such a conclusion can be drawn, the subsequent agreement and practice of States must indicate whether the Assembly's general powers to make recommendations have been interpreted to include the taking of such measures in the first place.

There are a few instances where the General Assembly has urged States to take economic measures. For example, during the Korean crisis, the General Assembly established an 'Additional Measures Committee' to report on possible measures that could be taken in response to China's intervention in Korea.[172] This Committee produced a report which recommended a Resolution imposing a trade embargo on China.[173] The General Assembly adopted the Committee's suggestion in Resolution 500 (V), recommending that every State apply an arms and strategic trade embargo on China and the North Korean authorities.[174]

Around this time, the General Assembly also adopted several reports of the Coercive Measures Committee.[175] This Committee produced a number of reports in the 1950s, some of which built upon the work of the *Uniting for Peace* Resolution, to suggest routes of action and strategic measures that could be

[172] UNGA Res 498 (V), *Intervention of the Central People's Government of the People's Republic of China in Korea*, (1 February 1951) UN Doc A/RES/498(V) [6].

[173] UNGA, 'Report of the Additional Measures Committee: Intervention of the Central People's Government of the People's Republic of China in Korea' (14 May 1951) UN Doc A/1799.

[174] UNGA Res 500 (V) *Additional measures to be employed to meet the aggression in Korea* (18 May 1951) UN Doc A/RES/500(V) [1].

[175] The Committee was established in *Uniting for Peace* (n 149), operative [11]; its reports were adopted by the General Assembly in: UNGA Res 503 (VI), *Methods which Might be Used to Maintain and Strengthen International Peace and Security in Accordance with the Purposes and Principles of the Charter* (12 January 1952) UN Doc A/RES/503(VI); UNGA Res 703 (VII), *Methods which Might Be Used to Maintain and Strengthen International Peace and Security in Accordance with the Purposes and Principles of the Charter: Report of the Collective Measures Committee* (8 April 1953) UN Doc A/RES/703(VII); UNGA Res 809(IX), *Methods which Might Be Used to Maintain and Strengthen International Peace and Security in Accordance with the Purposes and Principles of the Charter: Report of the Collective Measures Committee* (4 November 1954) UN Doc A/RES/809(IX).

used for the maintenance of international peace and security.[176] Importantly, throughout these reports, the Committee considered *both* the Security Council and the General Assembly to have the ability to take such measures, which included trade embargoes, and the suspension of financial relations.[177]

Similarly, in response to the government of South Africa's policy of apartheid, the Assembly adopted several Resolutions calling for States to take economic measures. For example, Resolution 1761 (XVII)[178] requested States to take measures, including: (i) breaking off diplomatic relations with South Africa; (ii) closing ports to South African-flagged ships; (iii) enacting legislation prohibiting their own ships from entering South African ports; (iv) boycotting South African goods and refraining from exporting goods, arms and ammunition to South Africa; and (v) refusing landing passage and facilities to South African airlines.[179]

Although the Security Council also called upon States to adhere to a voluntary arms embargo,[180] the General Assembly also reiterated further calls for such action, including calling upon States to 'take effective economic and other measures', following developments in Namibia and South Africa's occupation of the territory therein.[181] Later, towards the early 1980s, the General Assembly announced its disappointment that the Security Council had failed to take further economic and other sanctions, under Chapter VII of the Charter, against South Africa as the policy of apartheid continued and further caused the situation to deteriorate.[182] The Assembly therefore adopted its own recommendations, calling for numerous types of action, including economic and other measures, as well as calling for the Security Council to adopt mandatory sanctions.[183]

[176] See UNGA, 'Report of the Collective Measures Committee' (1951) UN Doc A/1891; UNGA, 'Report of the Collective Measures Committee' (1952) UN Doc A/2215; UNGA, 'Report of the Collective Measures Committee: Methods which Might Be Used to Maintain and Strengthen International Peace and Security in Accordance with the Purposes and Principles of the Charter' (30 August 1954) UN Doc A/27130-S/3283.

[177] See eg Collective Measures Committee's First Report (1951) (n 176) [41]–[166] generally.

[178] UNGA Res 1761 (XVII), *The Policies of Apartheid of the Government of South Africa* (6 November 1962) UN Doc A/RES/1761(XVII).

[179] ibid, [4].

[180] See eg UNSC Res 181 (1963) (7 August 1963) UN Doc S/RES/181(1963); UNSC Res 182 (1963) (4 December 1963) UN Doc S/RES/182(1963); and UNSC Res 191 (1964) (18 June 1964) UN Doc S/RES/191(1964); although this was later replaced by a mandatory arms embargo under Chapter VII of the Charter in UNSC Res 418 (1977) (4 November 1977) UN Doc S/RES/418(1977) [2].

[181] UNGA Res 2871 (XXVI), *Question of Namibia* (20 December 1971) UN Doc A/RES/2871 (XXVI) [6(d)].

[182] UNGA Res 34/93, *Policies of Apartheid of the Government of South Africa* (12 December 1979) UN Doc A/RES/34/93, at Section C, preamble para [3] and [4].

[183] UNGA Res 34/93 (n 182) s A, para [12], [14]; Section D generally detailing an arms embargo; Section F, detailing an oil embargo; and Section Q, welcoming State's unilateral measures ceasing investments and loans in South Africa.

The General Assembly reiterated these detailed calls for specific measures and action in further Resolutions.[184]

The General Assembly's recommendations regarding South Africa were cited by the Panel of Experts in the Secretary-General's 1997 report on economic measures in support of the position that such recommendations were a 'legitimacy indicator' for the imposition of coercive economic measures.[185] The Panel considered such recommendations as legitimate where the measures were taken in response to 'clear violations of international law'.[186]

Dawidowicz explains[187] that some of these measures might usually be considered measures of retorsion, but largely they conflict with other obligations, such as those under GATT.[188] Therefore, these recommendations by the General Assembly could demonstrate an opinion on the part of States that the Assembly can recommend measures that would conflict with other obligations in international law. Crucially, Dawidowicz highlights that these recommendations were taken in response to breaches of international obligations – in particular, *erga omnes* obligations.[189] While this practice demonstrates that there is certainly a power for the General Assembly to recommend coercive, non-forcible measures,[190] it does not demonstrate clearly whether the recommendations themselves have a 'legalising' effect on the action in question, as might be the case regarding recommendations to use force.

1.3.2. Legal Basis for Recommendations to Adopt Coercive Measures

It is clear from the practice of the General Assembly that it considers itself able to recommend or request that States adopt coercive economic measures for the maintenance of international peace and security. However, the practice does not demonstrate whether these recommendations provide a legal basis for the taking

[184] See, for example, UNGA Res 35/206, *Policies of apartheid of the Government of South Africa* (16 December 1980) UN Doc A/RES/35/206, particularly s C, [1]–[6]; also UNGA Res 36/172, *Policies of Apartheid of the Government of South Africa* (17 December 1981) UN Doc A/RES/36/172.

[185] Report of the Secretary General, *Economic Measures as a Means of Political and Economic Coercion against Developing Countries* (14 October 1997) UN Doc A/52/459, [76(d)].

[186] ibid.

[187] M Dawidowicz, 'Public Law Enforcement Without Public Law Safeguards? An Analysis of State Practice on Third-Party Countermeasures and their Relationship to the UN Security Council' (2006) 77 *British Yearbook of International Law* 333, 352–53.

[188] General Agreement on Tariffs and Trade 1947 (GATT 1947) (adopted 30 October 1947, entered into force 1 January 1948), 55 UNTS 187, amended by the Marrakech Agreement Establishing the World Trade Organization (adopted 15 April 1994, entered into force 1 January 1995), 1867 UNTS 154, and the General Agreement on Tariffs and Trade 1994 (GATT 1994) (adopted 15 April 1994, entered into force 1 January 1995) 1867 UNTS 187; provisions of the GATT 1947, as incorporated by GATT 1994, hereinafter simply referred to as 'GATT'.

[189] Dawidowicz (n 187) 354.

[190] See further Hailbronner and Klein (n 27) 264–67.

of such measures, or whether the measures must be based upon another foundation in customary international law.

1.3.2.1. A General Legal Basis under the UN Charter

It might be argued that this power has the same effect as the power to recommend force, as discussed above, and so such measures would be rendered legal on a similar basis. The question here is not just whether the legal basis renders the measures compatible with the principle of non-intervention, but also whether they can trump other existing international obligations owed to the target State. As explored in Chapter V, this question could cover obligations relating to trade agreements, financial assets, or other specific bilateral or multilateral agreements between the target State and those taking the measures in question.[191]

Of course, such a basis under the Charter would require an interpretation of the General Assembly's general power to recommend measures for the maintenance of peace as including the power to permit the temporary violation of other international obligations. A power to recommend (or 'authorise') coercive measures could explain some general compatibility with the principle of non-intervention, and State sovereignty by extension, based on State consent to these Charter powers. But this does not easily explain the conflict between this power and other international obligations.

The crux of this issue may come down to the interpretation of Article 103 of the Charter, which provides:

> In the event of a conflict between the obligations of the Members of the United Nations under the present Charter and their obligations under any other international agreement, their obligations under the present Charter shall prevail.

The problem here is that this provision only seems to grant precedence to the UN Charter *obligations*. Recommendations (or *requests*, as some of the Assembly's Resolutions state)[192] are by their very nature non-binding, and therefore *not* obligations. However, some interpretations of Article 103 seek to explain its compatibility with the Security Council's power to 'authorise' measures, and therefore the possibility that conduct usually incompatible with other international obligations can be made legal on the basis of an 'authorisation'. Frowein and Krisch, for example, argue that these authorisations have not been opposed on the ground of conflicting treaty obligations, and the Charter would not achieve its purpose and objective of allowing the Security Council to take the action it deems appropriate and deprive it from the flexibility it is supposed to have in these matters.[193] Of course, Frowein and Krisch do not adopt the interpretation

[191] See Chapter V, section 1.2.
[192] See, for example, UNGA Res 1761 (XVII) (n 178) [4].
[193] Frowein and Krisch (n 66) 728–29; see also Sarooshi (n 82) 149–51.

of 'recommendations' that this author adopts above,[194] and therefore they also consider that action in pursuance of recommendations require a separate legal basis in international law.[195] Similarly, Lord Bingham in *Al-Jedda* accepted the argument put by Frowein and Krisch regarding Article 103, and also suggested that 'obligations' in the provision should not be interpreted narrowly.[196]

Kolb argues that Article 103 should be read to allow 'authorisations' within their scope, but still maintaining a difference between 'authorisations' and 'recommendations' despite both being of a non-mandatory character.[197] On the other hand, in the ILC's study on the fragmentation of international law, its Study Group considered that non-binding resolutions adopted by UN organs, including the Security Council, do not fall within the scope of Article 103.[198] Dawidowicz similarly argues on this basis that measures requested or recommended by the General Assembly could only be justified on the basis of general international law.[199]

In the context of the Security Council's powers, Frowein and Krisch suggest that the power to authorise force, as a 'stronger power', necessarily implies that there must be a power to authorise 'weaker measures'.[200] But even applying that logic to the General Assembly's powers, it simply does not follow that coercive economic measures are 'weaker' or 'less invasive' than the use of force. In fact, in many cases, a general trade embargo could have more far reaching effects on the security and stability of a situation than, for example, a precise and limited military operation. The legal debate surrounding the use of force is often 'limited' to whether the military operation violates the prohibition of force and State sovereignty more generally. It has been demonstrated above how recommendations by a competent UN body can render such measures compatible with these principles. What is not clear, however, is whether such authorised or recommended uses of force violate *other* international agreements. Of course, it is certainly possible for a military operation to take place in such a way without violating trade agreements, or other specific treaties.

In light of this discussion, it is evident that the debate regarding Article 103 is far from settled, but there does seem to be some consensus that recommendations

[194] ie that a recommendation necessarily implies an authorisation, where the body in question has the power to authorise.

[195] Frowein and Krisch (n 66) 728.

[196] *R (Al-Jedda) v Secretary of State for Defence* (n 115) [34] per Lord Bingham. The ECTHR in this case seemed to take a more nuanced interpretation: see *Al-Jedda v United Kingdom* (n 126) [109].

[197] R Kolb, 'Does Article 103 of the Charter of the United Nations Apply only to Decisions or Also to Authorizations Adopted by the Security Council?' (2004) 64 *ZaöRV* 21, www.zaoerv.de/64_2004/64_2004_1_a_21_36.pdf (accessed 31 July 2019).

[198] Report of the Study Group of the International Law Commission, 'Fragmentation of International Law: Difficulties Arising from the Diversification and Expansion of International Law' (13 April 2006) UN Doc A/CN.4/L.682, [331]; This position is also supported by Bernhardt: R Bernhardt, 'Article 103' in Simma (n 27).

[199] Dawidowicz (n 187) 377.

[200] Frowein and Krisch (n 66) 729.

themselves are outside the scope of the provision. In any case, notwithstanding the (rather unconvincing) possibility of applying a wide interpretation of Article 103 to General Assembly recommendations, this author does not believe that there is enough evidence of State practice to determine sufficiently that these recommendations can provide a standalone legal basis for coercive economic measures. Firstly, as Dawidowicz interprets, the practice of the General Assembly seems to indicate its encouragement of the use of countermeasures based on customary international law rather than indicating a belief that it may 'legalise' such actions itself.[201] Secondly, it is important to distinguish between the practice in support of the General Assembly to have the power to recommend or authorise force – thus granting permission to act in a way that would otherwise be contrary to a fundamental principle of the Charter, namely Article 2(4) – and practice suggesting it has the power to allow States to ignore their treaty obligations. While there may be evidence of the first, there does not seem to be a clear indication of the latter.

Even if this question was left open, there is also an issue that must be addressed concerning the use of coercive measures in the context of the responsibility to protect. In particular, the General Assembly's power to recommend coercive measures is likely to be restricted to measures adopted in the pursuance of the maintenance of international peace and security.[202] As highlighted in Chapter V, there may be instances where the use of non-forcible measures could aid the *prevention* of the relevant atrocity crimes, but the situation has not yet reached a threshold to be considered a threat to or breach of international peace and security.[203] This could be where gross violations of human rights are occurring, or there are other breaches of obligations *erga omnes* that have not yet transformed into a threat to international peace and security. Similarly, at this point, the Security Council might not be considered to have *failed* in its responsibility to maintain international peace and security but is certainly *failing* in its similar responsibility to protect. In such circumstances, the only feasible way in which the Assembly's recommendations may be compatible with the principle of non-intervention is where they are based upon the law of countermeasures. This is because, while it might be clear that the General Assembly can take measures for the maintenance of peace, there is no evidence of a comparable power for the general promotion of human rights or other related purposes of the UN.

1.3.2.2. Countermeasures as a Legal Basis

The law and requirements of countermeasures have been outlined in some detail in Chapter V. Recalling the ILC's works on the Responsibility of International

[201] Dawidowicz (n 187) 411–12, 417.
[202] See section 1.2.
[203] See Chapter V, section 2.3.

Organisations for Internationally Wrongful Acts,[204] it is worth remembering that these Articles only address in detail the issue as to whether States or international organisations may take countermeasures against another *international organisation*. In the commentaries accompanying the international organisation Articles,[205] it is also notable that the Commission pointed out in its commentary that the Articles refer to international law for the conditions concerning countermeasures taken against *States* by international organisation,[206] and in this regard the ILC suggested that one may apply by analogy the conditions for countermeasures set out in the Articles on State Responsibility.[207]

The Articles do, however, place some restrictions on the taking of countermeasures by international organisations in any case. For international organisations, the ILC has been much more restrictive in its proposed Articles regarding countermeasures. The ILC recognises, in Article 22 of the IO Articles, that an international organisation may take countermeasures in certain circumstances. However, the Articles provide at the outset four important restrictions, namely: (i) that the substantive and procedural conditions required by international law are adhered to;[208] (ii) that the countermeasures are not inconsistent with the rules of the organisation;[209] (iii) that no appropriate means are available for otherwise inducing compliance with the obligations breached;[210] and (iv) that countermeasures may not be taken by an international organisation in response to a breach of the rules of that organisation, unless so provided for by those rules.[211]

With regard to the General Assembly on these issues, point (ii) essentially means that the General Assembly may not use a breach of the UN Charter as a countermeasure, and therefore the competences and procedural requirements that the General Assembly is bound by still hold firm when utilising countermeasures. More notably, however, point (iv) suggests that the General Assembly may not take countermeasures against breaches of the UN Charter, unless the Charter itself so provides for such measures.

In the context of the responsibility to protect, it was argued above that there certainly is support for the ability of *States* to take proportionate

[204] See, generally, UNGA Res 66/100, *Responsibility of International Organisations* (9 December 2011) UN Doc A/RES/66/100, Annex.

[205] ILC, 'Draft Articles on the Responsibility of International Organisation, with Commentaries', http://legal.un.org/ilc/texts/instruments/english/commentaries/9_11_2011.pdf (accessed 31 July 2019); also included in ILC, 'Report of the International Law Commission on the Work of its Sixty-Third Session' (26 April–3 June and 4 July–12 August 2011) UN Doc A/66/10, 69ff.

[206] ibid, 47, Art 22 Commentary, [2].

[207] ibid.

[208] ILC Articles on Responsibility of International Organisations (n 204), Art 22(1) and Art 22(2)(a).

[209] ibid, Art 22(2)(b).

[210] ibid, Art 22(2)(c).

[211] ibid, Art 22(3).

countermeasures in response to breaches of obligations *erga omnes*, such as systematic violations of human rights, or even the commission of the atrocity crimes themselves. As for such measures by an international organisation, the ILC did note just one possible example of countermeasures being utilised by an international organisation against a State.[212] However, if the General Assembly was simply to recommend in its Resolutions that States take countermeasures *themselves*, then the measures would not be taken by the UN as an organisation, but by the States themselves. Whether a recommendation for States to use countermeasures has any implications for the responsibility of the UN itself is largely irrelevant considering the practice outlined above that suggests it is within the General Assembly's power to do so. This also indicates that such recommendations are also within the restrictions of Article 22 of the international organisation Articles, even if they could be considered countermeasures in themselves.

Therefore, when making recommendations to take coercive economic measures, the General Assembly is well within its power to recommend the taking of non-injured State countermeasures. This does necessitate, however, that the procedural and substantive restrictions on these measures are adhered to by States – and it would certainly be reckless, if not illegal, for the General Assembly to make recommendations which do not also reflect these safeguards. These safeguards stipulate,[213] as outlined above, that the measures recommended must above all be proportionate;[214] their purpose must be to induce the wrongdoing State to comply with its obligations under international law, and in that sense be reversible;[215] they must not involve the use of force, or affect obligations such as the protection of fundamental rights, and norms of *jus cogens*;[216] and, finally, the target of the countermeasures must be given an opportunity to comply with its obligations, and be notified of the decision to take such measures.[217]

One of the biggest fears surrounding the use of non-injured party countermeasures is the risk of abuse that comes with such a comprehensive right. However, by utilising these measures through the recommendations of the General Assembly, not only would this provide an alternative basis for implementing the responsibility to protect beyond the Security Council, but it also

[212] ILC Articles on Responsibility of International Organisations (Commentaries) (n 205) 89, Art 57 Commentary, [2], n 338.

[213] For States, see UNGA Res 56/83, *Responsibility of States for Internationally Wrongful Acts* (28 January 2002) UN Doc A/RES/56/83, Annex, Arts 43 and 49–53 generally; for international organisations, see ILC Articles on Responsibility of International Organisations (n 204) Arts 51–56.

[214] ILC Articles on State Responsibility (n 213) Art 51; ILC Articles on Responsibility of International Organisations (n 204) Art 54.

[215] ILC Articles on State Responsibility (n 213) Art 49; ILC Articles on Responsibility of International Organisations (n 204) Art 51.

[216] ILC Articles on State Responsibility (n 213) Art 50; ILC Articles on Responsibility of International Organisations (n 204) Art 53.

[217] ILC Articles on State Responsibility (n 213) Art 52; ILC Articles on Responsibility of International Organisations (n 204) Art 55.

provides an additional institutional safeguard that was so widely called for by those States initially hesitant to recognise the viability of these measures.[218] Furthermore, the role of the General Assembly in this regard, representing almost the entire international community of States, provides a further legitimising factor for the taking of these measures, and the harmonising of the actions of the international community in pursuance of the responsibility to protect.[219]

1.4. Conclusions on General Assembly Measures

Within the United Nations, in the face of deadlock in the Security Council, and a failure for this organ to live up to its primary responsibility for the maintenance of international peace and security, the organisation itself may still have the opportunity to live up to its primary purpose. The General Assembly can assume its residual responsibility for the maintenance of international peace and security, and while it is not a replacement for the mechanism of the Security Council, it is still able to harmonise the actions of States in pursuance of coercive and forcible measures to maintain or restore international peace and security.

Admittedly there are still questions relating to the compatibility of recommendations generally with Article 103 of the Charter, and whether this indicates any substantive limitation on the legality to use force in pursuance of a recommendation by virtue of pre-existing treaty obligations. Unfortunately, a detailed analysis of this is issue is beyond the scope and capacity of this book. Nevertheless, restricting General Assembly recommendations to use coercive economic measures to the doctrine of countermeasures does provide a sound legal basis to continue. In this author's view, given the scope and impact of these measures, the collective use of countermeasures by States to back up recommendations of the General Assembly could provide an effective and legitimate mechanism to implement a tertiary responsibility to protect. The safeguards therein, it is submitted, seem very well balanced for these purposes.

These methods demonstrate legal avenues to implement the responsibility to protect beyond the inaction or paralysis of the Security Council, especially in situations where mass atrocities also engage the responsibility to maintain international peace and security. In light of this, and the arguments in previous chapters, it is submitted that there is room within the United Nations for a tertiary responsibility to protect. Not only is this a continuation of the responsibility to protect as a political and moral doctrine, but where the maintenance

[218] See Chapter V, section 2.2; see also Dawidowicz (n 187) 415–16, 418.

[219] See again, Panel of Experts in the 1997 Report of the Secretary General on Economic Measures (n 185) [76(d)].

of international peace and security is concerned it is also a continuation of the international community's legal duty not to ignore situations which endanger international peace and security. Again, this does not *require* the use of the measures outlined herein, but simply that the international community must utilise the most appropriate means to prevent breaches of the peace, and the commission of atrocity crimes.

2. THE TERTIARY RESPONSIBILITY BEYOND THE UNITED NATIONS

Implementing a tertiary responsibility to protect beyond the Security Council may also involve measures adopted beyond the United Nations itself. This section will outline the legality (and illegality) of forcible and coercive measures being utilised by regional arrangements and States individually, on a unilateral basis, to prevent or suppress the commission of mass atrocity crimes. It is important to address the legality of action beyond the United Nations even though action may be legal through the General Assembly, simply because the rarity of action through the Assembly and the difficulty in achieving political consensus in this organ could well hamper any international response to a crisis involving mass atrocities if the possibilities of action stopped there. Indeed, where it is evident that the Security Council is manifestly failing in its responsibility to protect, quick and legal action at a regional level could provide and effective preventive response *prior* to more international measures being adopted by the General Assembly. Therefore, this section will identify measures that may be utilised at the regional level so that an effective local response might be identified in the face of inaction and failure at the international level.

It is argued herein that forcible measures by regional organisations are still restricted to being authorised by a competent body of the United Nations, but that there is the possibility of authorisation being granted *after* emergency action has been taken. This does, however, risk the action not being authorised ex post facto and remaining illegal. In terms of non-forcible measures, the doctrine of countermeasures provides a further legal basis for collective coercive action by regional bodies to implement their tertiary responsibility to protect.

2.1. Regional Organisations and the Responsibility to Protect

The place of regional organisations and their role in collective security has been debated in detail by a number of commentators.[220] Indeed, there has also

[220] See eg NI Diab, 'Enforcement Action by Regional Organisations Revisited: The Prospective Joint Arab Forces' (2017) 4(1) *Journal on the Use of Force and International Law* 86.

been much debate in recent years regarding the role of regional organisations in implementing the responsibility to protect, especially with regard to peaceful tools of prevention and assistance.[221]

It is not the place of this study to repeat these debates, or to provide a detailed analysis of their roles of prevention and capacity building. It is important, however, briefly to assess the role and powers of regional organisations in implementing a tertiary responsibility to protect beyond the United Nations, specifically investigating the use of force and other coercive measures for this purpose. In this regard, the argument for the existence of the tertiary responsibility is strengthened by demonstrating that there are legal avenues for regional organisations to implement the responsibility to protect in the face of deadlock in the UN Security Council.

Chapter VIII of the UN Charter clearly recognises a role for regional organisations and arrangements in the maintenance of international peace and security, subject to the proviso in Article 53(1) that any enforcement action be authorised by the Security Council.[222] By extension, in those situations where the responsibility for peace and security overlaps with the responsibility to protect, there is also a role for regional organisations in the prevention and suppression of mass atrocities.

In the *Agenda for Peace* report, the Secretary-General recognised that regional organisations and arrangements could play a crucial role in efforts such as peacekeeping, preventive diplomacy, peacebuilding and peacemaking.[223] The report also noted that the end of the Cold War had ushered in a new era of opportunity for regional organisations to be utilised for the maintenance of international peace and security.[224] This did, however, come with a significant limitation:

> But in this new era of opportunity, regional arrangements and agencies can render great service if their activities are undertaken in a manner consistent with the Purposes and Principles of the Charter, and if their relationship with the United Nations, particularly the Security Council, is governed by Chapter VIII.[225]

[221] See, generally, discussions of the role of regional organisations in: Report of the Secretary-General, *The Role of Regional and Sub-Regional Arrangements in Implementing the Responsibility to Protect* (18 June 2011) UN Doc A/65/877–S/2011/393; Report of the Secretary-General, *Responsibility to Protect: Timely and Decisive Response* (25 July 2012) UN Doc A/66/874–S/2012/578, [35]–[37]; Report of the Secretary-General, *A Vital and Enduring Commitment: Implementing the Responsibility to Protect* (13 July 2015) A/69/981–S/2015/500, [57], [68]; Report of the Secretary-General, *Mobilizing Collective Action: The Next Decade of the Responsibility to Protect* (22 July 2016) UN Doc A/70/999–S/2016/620, [46], [59].

[222] This limitation will be addressed in detail in section 2.3.3.

[223] See, generally, Report of the Secretary-General, *An Agenda for Peace: Preventive Diplomacy, Peacemaking, and Peace-keeping* (17 June 1992) UN Doc A/47/277–S/74111.

[224] ibid, [60]–[62].

[225] ibid, [63].

In his supplement to this report,[226] the Secretary-General stressed the need for coordination between regional organisations and the United Nations in matters of peace and security,[227] and clearly preferred the primacy of the United Nations above any unilateral action when it came to the use of enforcement measures.[228]

In 2004, the High-Level Panel on Threats, Challenges, and Change[229] considered regional organisations 'a vital part of the multilateral system'.[230] One of the Panel's key recommendations in this regard was that '[a]uthorization from the Security Council should in all cases be sought for regional peace operations',[231] keeping in conformity with Chapter VIII of the Charter. However, the recommendation goes on, 'recognizing that in some urgent situations that authorization may be sought after such operations have commenced'.[232] Indeed, in the context of the responsibility to protect, this possibility of ex post facto authorisation for regional enforcement action was endorsed by the original ICISS Report,[233] and even cautiously cited by the Secretary-General in his very first report on the responsibility to protect.[234] While there may be cautious political support for this practice, the legality of such action will be addressed below.[235]

Although regional organisations have a general 'role' to play in the maintenance of peace and protection of populations from mass atrocities, the actual *responsibilities* of these organisations are yet to be determined. Abass[236] makes a proposal regarding the powers of regional organisations specifically in the situation where the Security Council and the General Assembly fail to discharge their responsibilities for the maintenance of international peace and security.[237] He argues that in these circumstances, regional organisations should be able to act in defence of collective interests.[238] Abass bases this argument upon a theory of social contracts[239] whereby, in domestic settings, the people are assumed to have

[226] Report of the Secretary-General, *Supplement to An Agenda for Peace: Position Paper of the Secretary-General on the Occasion of the Fiftieth Anniversary of the United Nations* (25 January 1995) UN Doc A/50/60–S/1995/1.

[227] See ibid, [81]–[96].

[228] See ibid, [80], [88].

[229] High-Level Panel on Threats, Challenges and Change, *A More Secure World: Our Shared Responsibility* (New York, UN Publications, 2004).

[230] ibid, [272].

[231] ibid, [86], [272].

[232] ibid.

[233] ICISS (n 73) [6.5] and [6.35].

[234] Report of the Secretary-General, *Implementing the Responsibility to Protect* (12 January 2009) UN Doc A/63/677, [58].

[235] See section 2.3.3.

[236] A Abass, *Regional Organisations and the Development of Collective Security: Beyond Chapter VIII of the UN Charter* (Oxford, Hart Publishing, 2004).

[237] ibid, 135.

[238] ibid, 135.

[239] While social contract theory is beyond the scope of this study, Abass's argument draws upon the works of philosophers such as: T Hobbes, *Leviathan* [1651] (London, Collins, 1962); J Loke, *Two Treatises of Civil Government* [1690] (London, Everyman, 1924); M Tebbit, *Philosophy of Law: An Introduction* (London, Routledge, 2000); J Rawls, *A Theory of Justice* (Oxford, Oxford University Press, 1972); and D Hume, *A Treatise of Human Nature* [1738] (London, Fontana, 1972).

entered into a social contract with the sovereign, with the sovereign acting by virtue of the consent of the subjects which places certain constraints on the exercise of power.[240] Where the sovereign fails in its responsibilities to the people, the argument goes, the legal powers revert back to the people.[241] Abass argues that the conferral of authority to the Security Council by States for the maintenance of international peace and security, by analogy to this social contract theory, suggests that States themselves can assume authority for the maintenance of peace and security where the Security Council has failed, and thus act through regional organisations for the defence of collective interests.[242] The current author does not necessarily accept or adopt the social contract theory, and the argument that the legal powers of the Security Council can be assumed by States or regional organisations itself is also not convincing. There seems no evidence of an accepted doctrine whereby such a transfer of *power* would take place upon the failure of the Security Council.

On the other hand, when addressing *responsibility* only, the underlying philosophy of Abass's argument does provide a convincing basis for the premise that the legal *responsibilities* of the Security Council are assumed by States where the Security Council fails to uphold them. In this respect, the current author argues that the responsibilities of the Security Council may revert to States when there is a failure to maintain peace and security, or indeed a failure to protect in the context of the responsibility to protect. This follows, and is compatible with, the recognised 'residual' responsibility of the General Assembly, as discussed above. To continue this 'residual' responsibility to States as members of the international community in general seems the next logical step in this 'doctrine' of responsibilities.

While we may accept the roles and responsibilities of regional organisations, the fundamental protections of Article 2(4) and non-intervention cannot be ignored. To truly determine whether the responsibility to protect continues beyond UN inaction to regional organisations, these actors must also have the legal ability to act upon it. We shall apply the findings of Chapter IV relating to the prohibition of force and Chapter V on the use of non-forcible measures to the question of implementing the tertiary responsibility to protect.

2.2. Forcible Measures

It was previously explained in Chapter IV that Article 2(4) of the UN Charter clearly prohibits unilateral uses of force, such as humanitarian intervention, because they are inconsistent with the purposes of the Charter and find no basis

[240] Abass (n 236) 131–33.
[241] ibid, 131–133, 135.
[242] ibid, 132–34, 135.

in contemporary international law. Therefore, there does not seem to be much leeway for actions by regional organisations that may be set up for maintaining regional peace and security. Nevertheless, there are a few plausible arguments in favour of regional enforcement mechanisms being consistent with these fundamental rules, and it is in light of these arguments that this section addresses whether such organisations have any legal basis to utilise forcible measures in this context. This author argues that there is no legal basis for regional mechanisms to take unilateral military measures without UN approval, but notes the contentious possibility of this approval being granted after emergency action has begun.

2.2.1. Regional Enforcement Mechanisms

The legality of regional enforcement mechanisms, and their compatibility with the UN Charter, becomes particularly contentious when an organisation is set up with explicit security powers that seem to allow intervention in a Member State. The most prominent example of this is in the African Union. The Constitutive Act of the African Union[243] provides an unprecedented right to intervene in a Member State under Article 4(h), where it provides, as a principle of the Union, 'the right of the Union to intervene in a Member State pursuant to a decision of the Assembly in respect of grave circumstances, namely: war crimes, genocide and crimes against humanity'.

Additionally, a 2003 amendment to this provision, which has not yet entered into force, included intervention in circumstances of 'a serious threat to legitimate order to restore peace and stability'.[244] Since Article 4(h) allows intervention in response to war crimes, genocide and crimes against humanity, there is clearly a close relationship between this provision and the responsibility to protect.

Similarly, the Economic Community of West African States (ECOWAS) Treaty[245] enables the organisation to institutionalise mechanisms for the maintenance of peace and security in the region.[246] In 1999, ECOWAS adopted a Protocol establishing a mechanism for conflict prevention and security[247] which

[243] Constitutive Act of the African Union, (adopted 11 July 2000, entered into force on 26 May 2001) 2158 UNTS 3 (hereinafter 'AU Constitutive Act').

[244] Protocol on Amendments to the Constitutive Act of the African Union 2003 (adopted by the 1st Extraordinary Session of the Assembly of the Union in Addis Ababa, Ethiopia on 3 February 2003; and by the 2nd Ordinary Session of the Assembly of the Union in Maputo, Mozambique on 11 July 2003) https://au.int/sites/default/files/treaties/35423-treaty-0025_-_protocol_on_the_amendments_to_the_constitutive_act_of_the_african_union_e.pdf (accessed 31 July 2019). For the current status of the Protocol, see *OAU/AU Treaties, Conventions, Protocols & Charters*, www.au.int/en/treaties (accessed 31 July 2019).

[245] Revised Treaty of the Economic Community of West African States (ECOWAS) (adopted 24 July 1993, entered into force 23 August 1995) 2373 UNTS 233.

[246] ibid, Arte 58.

[247] ECOWAS, Protocol Relating to the Mechanism for Conflict Prevention, Management, Resolution, Peacekeeping and Security (Lomé, 10 December 1999) Doc A/P.1/12/99, reprinted in (2005) 5(2) *Journal of Conflict and Security Law* 231.

contained powers of intervention in humanitarian crises. The Protocol established the Mediation and Security Council,[248] which was granted the power under Article 10(2)(c) to 'authorise all forms of intervention and decide particularly on the deployment of political and military missions'. The Protocol also established that the ECOWAS Monitoring Group (ECOMOG) would also assist the Mediation and Security Council,[249] and was charged with the mission of 'humanitarian intervention in support of humanitarian disaster'.[250] Considering these mechanisms, Abass suggests that there is a 'gradual but steady movement of regional organisations towards a more autonomous regime of collective security' and that this 'can no longer be denied in legal analysis'.[251]

At first glance, both mechanisms seem at odds with the requirement of Security Council authorisation under Article 53(1) of the UN Charter, and even the prohibition of force under Article 2(4). By allowing action beyond the United Nations, it could be said that these provisions are incompatible with these obligations under the Charter, and therefore the Charter obligations must prevail in accordance with Article 103. But this would assume that these provisions are to be interpreted as allowing such unilateral intervention. But there are interpretations of these mechanisms that render them compatible with the Charter, and therefore still valid, as will be addressed below.

Another argument in favour of these mechanisms' validity is to suggest that they represent a form of treaty-based consent to the interventions that they purport to allow. In this regard, Abass argues:

> The validity of transforming host state consent into a treaty obligation derives, not only from the existence of affirmative state practice to that effect, but largely from the fact that states made a conscious choice to change the status of the principle from a soft law obligation into treaty law.[252]

The difficulty with this assertion is that the prohibition of force in Article 2(4) is considered *jus cogens* and therefore, as discussed in Chapter IV, any treaty-based derogation from this would be void in accordance with Article 53 of the VCLT. This raises two issues to be addressed: firstly, whether such treaty-based consent could be compatible with Article 2(4), so as not to constitute a prohibited derogation; and, secondly, what effect such treaty-based consent has on the scope of the prohibition of force. A further issue with these mechanisms is the question of their compatibility with the *separate* requirement of Security Council authorisation under Article 53(1) of the Charter.

[248] ibid, Art 8.
[249] ibid, Art 17.
[250] ibid, Art 22(c).
[251] Abass (n 236) 176; for further analysis of the ECOWAS mechanism in particular, see A Abass, 'The New Collective Security Mechanism of ECOWAS: Innovations and Problems' (2000) 5(2) *Journal of Conflict and Security Law* 211.
[252] Abass (n 236) 164.

2.2.2. *Compatibility with Article 2(4)*

In the specific context of the use of force by regional organisations, Abass interprets Article 2(4) in such a way that only 'aggression' is considered *jus cogens*, therefore leaving room for non-aggressive elements of Article 2(4) to be contracted out by State consent.[253] This, accordingly, would explain the ability of regional arrangements to use force and be compatible with Article 2(4).[254]

However, the position of the current author, as outlined in Chapter IV, is that Article 2(4) as a whole is considered *jus cogens*. But this does not mean that consent (whether treaty-based or otherwise) does not have a place in determining the scope of Article 2(4). For example, consent can determine the extent to which territorial integrity and political independence protect the State. However, consent cannot derogate from or contract out of the provision prohibiting force 'in any manner inconsistent with the purposes of the United Nations'. Therefore, consent – based upon treaty or otherwise – cannot grant a use of force that would be inconsistent with Purposes of the United Nations.

The question to be addressed here is therefore whether the use of force by a regional security arrangement, pursued in accordance with a treaty-based consent, is *consistent* with the Purposes of the United Nations.

2.2.2.1. Territorial Integrity and Political Independence

As above, for any use of force by regional organisations to be consistent with Article 2(4), it first must not violate the principles of territorial integrity and political independence. The relevant question here, to determine whether there are any inherent qualifications of these principles in these circumstances, is whether the relevant regional treaty provides a legal basis for such a use of force. In other words, does the relevant treaty provide a treaty-based consent that inherently limits the existing territorial integrity and political independence of the State concerned? Of course, as will be recalled from Chapter IV, this does not mean that the relevant treaty may provide for the *forcible* change of territorial boundaries or even imposing a new political regime – these specific aspects of territorial integrity and political independence seem to have a non-derogable character similar to *jus cogens* when it comes to the use of forcible measures. They are the ultimate protections of the prohibition of force that even the Security Council cannot violate.

Therefore, while the treaty may provide for a State's consent to use force, such force must not impede on the ultimate protections of territorial integrity and political independence. Even then, in accordance with the second part of Article 2(4), the force cannot be used against the State in any manner inconsistent with the Purposes of the United Nations.

[253] ibid, 194–201.
[254] ibid, 201–08.

2.2.2.2. Consistency with the Purposes of the United Nations

The use of force inconsistent with the Purposes of the United Nations includes any unilateral measure that is not authorised by a competent organ of the United Nations.[255] This is because such unilateral action, beyond the UN, is not considered an 'effective collective measure' in accordance with Article 1(1), and also does not harmonise the actions of nations in accordance with Article 1(4). Such a reading was confirmed by the analysis of the drafting of the Charter in Chapter IV. Therefore, for any treaty-based form of intervention in a regional arrangement to be compatible with Article 2(4), it must be capable of being interpreted in a way that provides for the primacy of the United Nations.

Although the African Union Constitutive Act, and the ECOWAS Protocol, do not explicitly provide for the authorisation of the UN in their procedure, it does not seem proportionate to invalidate these treaties simply on the basis that this is missing. Indeed, it is perfectly possible for this procedure still to be adhered to even though it is not specifically provided for. So long as, in practice, the primacy of the UN security mechanism is provided for, such provisions might be considered consistent with the Purposes of the United Nations. The question as to *when* such an authorisation might be provided is a separate matter, as discussed in the following section.

2.2.3. Compatibility with Article 53(1)

Chapter VIII of the UN Charter, while recognising the role of regional organisations in the maintenance of international peace and security, keeps some control over their actions when it comes to enforcement action. For example, Article 52(1), while providing for the existence and role of regional organisations or arrangements in this regard, restricts their activities to being 'consistent with the Purposes and Principles of the United Nations'. Furthermore, Article 53(1) states: 'The Security Council shall, where appropriate, utilize such regional arrangements or agencies for enforcement action under its authority. But no enforcement action shall be taken under regional arrangements or by regional agencies without the authorization of the Security Council.'

It seems clear that the use of force by a regional organisation would be considered 'enforcement action' within the meaning of this provision. Importantly, however, Article 53(1) only prohibits enforcement action being taken without the authorisation of the Security Council – not necessarily prohibiting the existence of the provisions such as Article 4(h) of the AU Constitutive Act. To be compatible with this obligation under the UN Charter, the regional arrangements must at least leave room for, and be compatible with, the authority of the Security Council.

[255] See Chapter IV, section 3.3.

A question that has developed from practice is whether the Security Council's authorisation must come *before* the relevant action is taken or whether it can be granted after the fact.[256] In the context of the responsibility to protect, this would perhaps be arguable in circumstances where an emergency local response is necessary to prevent atrocities, but it would take too long to gain approval from the Security Council. Such an interpretation would mirror what is allowed for self-defence in Article 51, where the State is free to take forcible action *until* the Security Council steps in.

In the African Union's *Ezulwini Consensus*,[257] the Members of the Union declared their willingness as a regional organisation to be bound by the authority of the UN Security Council, but also made clear that the Union was willing to act in circumstances requiring urgent action and achieve the requisite authority from the Security Council *after the fact*.[258]

In the ECOWAS 1999 Protocol, Article 52(3) provides: 'In accordance with Chapters VII and VIII of the United Nations Charter, ECOWAS shall *inform* the United Nations of any military intervention undertaken in pursuit of the objectives of this Mechanism.'[259] This provision only requires that ECOWAS shall 'inform' the United Nations of a military intervention, rather than seeking authorisation for it. This is certainly consistent with Article 54 of the UN Charter, which requires that: 'The Security Council shall at all times be kept fully informed of activities undertaken or in contemplation under regional arrangements or by regional agencies for the maintenance of international peace and security.' Again, just because the mechanism itself does not explicitly provide for Security Council authorisation in accordance with Article 53(1) does not mean that it cannot be adhered to in practice.

However, interviews with officials conducted by Abass certainly reveal some fundamental understandings in this regard. Abass details an interview with the former Director of the Peace and Security department of the African Union,[260] where the Director suggested that the Union would not always seek an authorisation from the Security Council prior to an enforcement action. The Director stated that the African Union was 'not an arm of the United Nations. We accept the UN's global authority, but we will not wait for the UN to authorise an action that we intend to take.'[261] Most revealing of all, the Director went on to state: '[W]e are in a tacit agreement with the United Nations on this and there is an

[256] See above, n 233, and accompanying discussion.

[257] African Union (Executive Council), 'Decision on the Report of the High Level Panel on the Reform of the United Nations' (AU Addis Ababa, Ethopia, 7–8 March 2005) Doc. Ext/EX.CL/Dec.1–3 (VII), adopting African Union (Executive Council), 'The Common African Position on the Proposed Reform of the United Nations: "*The Ezulwini Consensus*"' (AU Addis Ababa, Ethiopia, 7–8 March 2005) Doc Ext/EX.CL/2 (VII).

[258] ibid, 6, s B(i).

[259] Emphasis added.

[260] Ambassador Sam Ibok, interview conducted on 2 February 2004 by Ademola Abass, detailed in Abass (n 236) 166.

[261] ibid.

understanding to that effect.'[262] Abass also suggests that the Director of the ECOWAS Legal Department also gave a similar answer to a similar question in 2000.[263] Of course, it is not clear from these statements alone whether such 'tacit agreements' still exist, or whether these views are shared among States to evidence a subsequent agreement or practice relating to the interpretation of Article 53(1) of the Charter.

The origins of the possibility of ex post facto authorisations seem to come from the actions of ECOWAS itself. Of note, having captured the broad attention of academic commentators, are the ECOWAS interventions in Liberia and Sierra Leonne in the 1990s.

In 1989, Charles Taylor led an uprising and insurgency against President Doe of Liberia, leading the National Patriotic Front of Liberia (NPFL) into Liberia from Côte d'Ivoire.[264] Taking control of up to 90 per cent of Liberian territory by mid-1990, the rebel forces made an advance towards the capital of Monrovia. The UN Security Council did not immediately respond to this situation, despite the Liberian government seeking support from the UN. As a result, in August 1990 ECOWAS called on the warring factions to observe a ceasefire[265] and established its Cease-Fire Monitoring Group (ECOMOG)[266] with powers to conduct military operations 'for the purpose of Monitoring the ceasefire, restoring law and order to create the necessary conditions for free and fair elections'.[267]

ECOMOG, although cited in official documents as a peacekeeping force, managed to secure Monrovia and aided the installation of an interim government under President Sawyer. ECOWAS secured the agreement of all warring factions to a ceasefire on 28 November 1990, where all parties also agreed that the ceasefire was to be monitored by ECOMOG.[268] This was formalised in a ceasefire agreement in February 1991.[269] This ceasefire largely held until August 1992, when fighting erupted again. This prompted ECOMOG once again to defend Monrovia, this time also capturing territory from the NPFL forces.[270]

Although seemingly a 'peacekeeping force', doubts arise given its supposedly loose interpretation of its mandate, its clear preference for one side of the

[262] ibid.

[263] ibid.

[264] For details of this crisis, see C Gray, *International Law and the Use of Force*, 3rd edn (Oxford, Oxford University Press, 2008) 392–94; Chesterman (n 42) 134–37; Abass (n 236) 143–45.

[265] ECOWAS Standing Committee, Decision A/DEC/1/8/90, 'On the Ceasefire and Establishment of an ECOWAS Ceasefire Monitoring Group for Liberia' (7 August 1990) 21 *ECOWAS Official Journal* 6, Art 1; ECOWAS Official Journal available at the University of Ghana: http://ugspace.ug.edu.gh:8080/xmlui/handle/123456789/7052 (accessed 31 July 2019).

[266] ibid, Art 2(1).

[267] ibid, Art 2(2).

[268] ECOWAS, 'Joint Declaration on Cessation of Hostilities and Peaceful Settlement of Conflict' (28 November 1990) 21 *ECOWAS Official Journal* 14, [1] and [2].

[269] ECOWAS, 'Agreement on Cessation of Hostilities and Peaceful Settlement of Conflict – Lomé, Togo' (13 February 1991) 21 *ECOWAS Official Journal* 16; on the acceptance of ECOMOG, see Art 1(2).

[270] See Gray (n 264) 393; Chesterman (n 42) 136.

conflict, and the fact that some of its actions seemed more like peace enforcement than peacekeeping.[271] As Gray points out, not all the warring factions initially consented to the presence of ECOMOG, as is usually expected for peacekeeping missions.[272] Abass suggests that ECOMOG was intended to be an enforcement operation from the outset,[273] and cites the 'all-out military action' taken by ECOMOG to prevent the capture of Monrovia following the death of President Doe as evidence of this.[274]

Notwithstanding this 'quasi-enforcement' role, the legal basis for ECOMOG's actions is also widely disputed. Some authors suggest that President Doe consented to the operation,[275] and therefore the ECOMOG mission was an intervention by invitation which does not require any prior authorisation by the UN Security Council.[276] However, others question the validity of this consent, arguing that Doe did not have effective control over most of Liberia at the time.[277]

De Wet and Nolte suggest that there seems to be no *official* record of President Doe's invitation, but acknowledge that this was widely reported by news media at the time.[278] In fact, the ECOWAS Official Journal now includes the letter containing Doe's invitation,[279] in which he called for ECOWAS to 'take note of [his] personal concerns and the collective wishes of the people of Liberia, and to assist in finding a constitution and reasonable solution to the crisis in our country as early as possible'.[280] Doe also suggested that it was 'time to introduce an ECOWAS Peace-keeping Force into Liberia to forestall increasing terror and tension and to assure a peaceful transitional environment'.[281]

Walter argues that this invitation by President Doe is not very explicit, that it does not clearly demand an intervention and that ECOWAS did not invoke the letter as a justification for its actions.[282] Similarly, Abass argues that such

[271] For an in-depth assessment of these points, see, generally, AC Ofodile, 'The Legality of ECOWAS Intervention in Liberia' (1994) 32(2) *Columbia Journal of Transnational Law* 381.

[272] Gray (n 264) 402–03; see also Ofodile (n 271) 412.

[273] Abass (n 236) 144.

[274] ibid.

[275] See eg De Wet (n 97) 299.

[276] On this point, see also G Nolte, 'Restoring Peace by Regional Action: International Legal Aspects of the Liberian Conflict', (1993) 53 *ZaöRV* 603, 621–22, www.zaoerv.de/53_1993/53_1993_3_a_603_637.pdf (accessed 31 July 2019).

[277] This argument was highlighted, but rejected, by De Wet (n 97) 299; see also C Walter, 'Security Council Control over Regional Action' (1997) 1 *Max Planck Yearbook of United Nations Law* 129, 152–53.

[278] De Wet (n 97) 299; Nolte (n 276) 621.

[279] ECOWAS, 'Text of a Letter Dated 14th July 1990 Addressed by President Samuel K Doe to the Chairman and Members of the Ministerial Meeting of the ECOWAS Standing Mediation Committee' (14 July 1990) 21 *ECOWAS Official Journal* 6.

[280] ibid, [7].

[281] ibid.

[282] Walter (n 277) 152–53; see also B Nkrumah and F Viljoen, 'Drawing Lessons from ECOWAS in the implementation of Art 4(h)' in D Kuwali et al (eds), *Africa and the Responsibility to Protect: Article 4(h) of the African Union Constitutive Act* (Abingdon, Routledge, 2014) 256–57.

an invitation would have been superfluous because ECOWAS had apparently already assumed competence to intervene without this invitation.[283] Frank goes further to suggest that the ECOWAS force was not the force that Doe requested, and so reflected an intervention that would have to be authorised under Article 53(1) of the Charter.[284]

It is perhaps a stretch in logic to suggest that the ECOWAS action could not be based on this invitation because it was not explicitly invoked. Neverthless, there can be no doubt that ECOMOG's monitoring role was accepted by all the warring parties via the November 1990 joint declaration,[285] and the February 1991 ceasefire agreement. The question therefore is whether its intervention *prior* to this was based upon an invitation or not. Evidently, this issue remains a point of contention.

In any case, we must also address the arguments in favour of this practice as a precedent for the ability of the Security Council to authorise such action after the fact. ECOWAS called upon the UN Security Council to support its humanitarian and political action as early as August 1990.[286] Those who do support this intervention as a precedent indicating the viability of ex post facto authorisation argue that the Security Council's subsequent Resolutions commending ECOWAS are sufficient to establish such a subsequent authorisation.[287] Indeed, the Security Council did eventually become involved in the situation, and passed Resolutions which, among other things, commended ECOWAS 'for its efforts to restore peace, security, and stability in Liberia',[288] and welcomed the continued commitment of ECOWAS 'to and the efforts towards a peaceful resolution of the Liberian conflict'.[289] The Council did not explicitly authorise ECOWAS to take enforcement action, merely 'recalling' Chapter VIII of the Charter in the preamble to its Resolution,[290] and citing Chapter VII only specifically in the context of establishing an arms embargo.[291]

Indeed, these Resolutions are quite vague. De Wet argues that the language is broad and vague enough to apply only to those aspects of intervention that constituted classic peacekeeping.[292] Nevertheless, the persistent advocates of ex post facto authorisation argue that the Security Council's subsequent legal

[283] Abass (n 236) 189.

[284] TM Frank, *Recourse to Force: State Action Against Threats and Armed Attacks*, (Cambridge, Cambridge University Press, 2002) 156.

[285] Joint Declaration (n 268).

[286] ECOWAS, 'Final Communiqué of the First Session of the Community Standing Mediation Committee – Banjul, The Gambia, 6–7 August 1990' (7 August 1990) 21 *ECOWAS Official Journal* 41, [13].

[287] See, generally, Walter (n 277) 299; Frank (n 284) 155 and 162.

[288] See UNSC Res 788 (1992) (19 November 1992) UN Doc S/RES/788(1992) [1]; see also UNSC Res 813 (1993) (26 March 1993) UN Doc S/RES/813(1993) [2]; UNSC Res 856 (1993) (10 August 1993) UN Doc S/RES/856(1993) [6].

[289] UNSC Res 788 (1992) (n 288) preamble [8].

[290] ibid, preamble [6].

[291] ibid, operative [8] and [9].

[292] De Wet (n 97) 300–01; for similar criticisms, see Gray (n 264) 404–05, 418.

'sanitisation' of such interventions may well be implicit in their general approval or commendations of these missions.[293]

The ECOWAS mission in Sierra Leone is also cited in favour of such a practice. The crisis in Sierra Leone erupted in May 1997 when a coup d'état overthrew the established government. ECOMOG forces were already present in the country to monitor the overspill of the ongoing Liberian conflict, and Nigeria and Guinea sent further troops into Sierra Leonne in response to this coup – claiming to be acting as ECOMOG forces.[294]

In a Meeting of Foreign Ministers in June 1997,[295] ECOWAS ministers agreed that

> no country should grant recognition to the regime that emerged following the coup d'état of 25 May 1997, and to work towards the reinstatement of the legitimate government by a combination of three measures, namely, dialogue, imposition of sanctions and enforcement of an embargo *and the use of force*.[296]

In August 1997, ECOWAS formally extended the mandate of ECOMOG to Sierra Leone to monitor and supervise all ceasefire violations, and enforce a sanctions regime and embargo.[297] Abass again noted that ECOMOG's action in Sierra Leonne commenced undisguised as *enforcement* action rather than peacekeeping.[298]

Eventually, the UN Security Council adopted Resolution 1132 (1997)[299] in October 1997, which authorised the enforcement of an arms and oil embargo by ECOMOG, but did not explicitly authorise any other use for force or enforcement action.[300] De Wet notes that ECOMOG's enforcement action extended beyond its mandate, and was not authorised by the Security Council.[301]

On this point, Gray notes that in its reports to the Security Council, ECOMOG was careful to claim only to be acting in self-defence.[302] Most notably, when ECOMOG made its final military push to overthrow the junta,

[293] See Frank (n 284) 156; Walter (n 277) 180–85; see also a discussion of this issue by J Bröjmer and G Ress, 'Article 53' in Simma (n 27) 865–66.

[294] For details of this crisis, see Gray (n 264) 395ff; Frank (n 284) 155–62.

[295] Final Communiqué included in: Letter Dated 27 June 1997 From the Permanent Representative of Nigeria To the United Nations Addressed to the President of the Security Council (27 June 1997) UN Doc S/1997/499, Annex.

[296] S/1997/499 (n 295), Annex [9(iii)], emphasis added.

[297] ECOWAS Authority of Heads of State and Government, 'Decision A/DEC.7/8/97 Extending the Scope of Activity and Mandate of ECOMOG to Cover Sierra Leone' (29 August 1997) 33 *ECOWAS Official Journal* 13–14; for the sanctions regime, see ECOWAS Authority of Heads of State and Government, 'Decision A/Dec.8/8/97 on Sanctions Against the Illegal Regime in Sierra Leone' (29 August 1997) 33 *ECOWAS Official Journal* 14–15.

[298] Abass (n 236) 145.

[299] UNSC Res 1132 (1997) (8 October 1997) UN Doc S/RES/1132(1997).

[300] ibid, [8].

[301] De Wet (n 97) 303.

[302] Gray (n 264) 414.

ECOMOG claimed that this was as a direct result of unprovoked attacks against it,[303] and referred to 'international rules of engagement for peacekeeping operations'.[304]

Once again, some argue that ECOMOG was invited by the overthrown government to intervene in the State,[305] although this is also contested.[306] Therefore, it is difficult to determine without further investigation whether ECOMOG's action in Sierra Leonne was truly enforcement, or simply intervention by invitation.

Like the situation in Liberia, the Security Council did commend ECOMOG on its role 'in support of the objectives related to the restoration of peace and security'.[307] But these were similarly vague and not sufficiently precise enough to be convincing 'authorisations' of ECOMOG's earlier military actions, even if they can be interpreted to indicate support for them.[308]

Based on this analysis, it does not seem that ECOWAS's actions in Liberia and Sierra Leone provide sufficiently unambiguous evidence of a practice that indicates the interpretation of Article 53(1) of the Charter. Nevertheless, considering the issue more generally, there are a few conceptual arguments worth addressing.

For example, when addressing the possibility of regional organisations taking emergency action to implement the responsibility to protect, the ICISS noted that a strict interpretation of Article 53(1) requires enforcement by regional organisations *always* to be subject to *prior* Security Council authorisation.[309] On the other hand, Walter argues that the wording of Article 53(1) does not seem to exclude the possibility that an authorisation can be given after the fact.[310] Instead, the reasons against such an interpretation seem to be based upon concerns about the Security Council's control over such operations, fettering the discretion of the Council in this regard and the centralised use of force that is purportedly inherent in the Charter system.[311]

[303] See Letter Dated 13 February 1998 From the Permanent Representative of Nigeria to the United Nations Addressed to the President of the Security Council (13 February 1998) UN Doc S/1998/123, Annex, [2].

[304] See Letter Dated 27 February 1988 from the Permanent Representative of Nigeria to the United Nations Addressed to the President of the Security Council (27 February 1998) UN Doc S/1998/170, Annex, [7].

[305] De Wet (n 97) 303.

[306] Frank (n 284) 162.

[307] See eg UNSC Res 1162 (1998) (17 April 1998) UN Doc S/RES/1162(1998) at para [2].

[308] See De Wet (n 97) 303; see also on this point U Villani, 'The Security Council's Authorisation of Enforcement Action by Regional Organisations' (2002) 6 *Max Planck Yearbook of United Nations Law*, 535, 555.

[309] ICISS (n 73) [6.35]; the ICISS only considers the possibility of an interpretation allowing leeway for ex post facto authorisation in light of the ECOWAS actions in Liberia and Sierra Leonne.

[310] Walter (n 277) 177.

[311] De Wet (n 97) 295; see also M Akehurst, 'Enforcement Action by Regional Agencies, with Special Reference to the Organisation of American States' (1967) 42 *British Yearbook of International Law* 175, 214; these arguments were also acknowledged, but rejected, by Walter (n 277) 178–79.

Akehurst suggests that such a practice would encourage illegal acts.[312] Moreover, De We suggests that this interpretation would negate the fact that the Security Council may be deliberately refraining from action, arguing that this would turn the Charter system on its head and force the Security Council to explain why it was not adopting military measures.[313] This, she argues, is the opposite of what was envisaged for the Charter whereby the Council should have the freedom to 'opt-in' to its choice of enforcement measures rather than 'opt-out' of those already being taken.[314]

Of course, the Council does have the freedom to choose whether to employ enforcement measures. But, as addressed earlier in Chapter III, it does not have the freedom to *ignore* a situation altogether, and its lack of action in this regard may well be taken into account when determining whether it has failed in its responsibilities under the Charter, and its responsibility to protect.[315] Furthermore, should a regional organisation decide to take enforcement action that is deemed inappropriate, or is conducted with duplicitous intentions, the Security Council is well within its powers to either condemn such action, or to decide *not* to authorise it ex post facto.[316] This would simply mean that the regional action remains illegal as both a breach of Article 53(1) and Article 2(4).[317] In this situation, the risk is really on the regional organisation taking action without authorisation – if the Security Council does not authorise its intervention after the fact, its actions will remain illegal and it will still be liable in international law for this violation.[318]

Regarding the worries that such an emergency response could be abused by regional organisations, analogies may be drawn to the 'emergency response' permitted under self-defence in Article 51 of the Charter.[319] Indeed, concerns about the abuse of an emergency response by regional organisations (which is still to be authorised in any case) might be compared to the possibility of the right to self-defence itself being abused by States. Such abuses are the responsibility of the Security Council to monitor in any case, and arguments suggesting that these abuses might be used by Permanent Members of the Security Council to their political advantage[320] perhaps reveal more problems with the law of the Security Council itself rather than the dangers of allowing ex post facto

[312] ibid.
[313] De Wet (n 97) 295–96.
[314] ibid, 296.
[315] See Chapter III generally.
[316] De Wet addresses such a possibility (n 97) 296.
[317] Walter (n 277) 179.
[318] See also Villani (n 308) 556–57, who argues that those actions by ECOWAS in Liberia and Sierra Leone that were not explicitly authorised by the Security Council remained wrongful acts.
[319] For a similar discussion regarding a 'right of emergency', reflecting a 'collective humanitarian intervention of regional organisations', see Walter (n 277) 162–71; also addressed by De Wet (n 97) 295.
[320] See eg De Wet (n 97) 296–97.

authorisations. Indeed, some authors suggest that the risk of abuse by regional organisations is alleviated by their institutional and collective safeguards.[321]

Finally, commentators have also acknowledged the novel possibility of the Security Council adopting a *general* authorisation to regional organisations that might permit future emergency responses before the Council itself is able to take up the matter.[322] Such an authorisation could, for example, take the form of a carefully drafted Resolution which permits emergency action in very limited circumstances *until* the Security Council acts. This solution could prescribe safeguards and principles, and does seem to provide a suitable middle ground between relying on a regional organisations own safeguards and standards against the abuse of an ex post facto method, and harmonising international standards for emergency local responses to humanitarian crises.[323] Although such a solution might be unlikely in the current political climate, it would certainly offer a legal alternative to the status quo.

One final issue with Article 53(1) and the use of force is whether this provision means that enforcement action can be authorised via a recommendation of the General Assembly, rather than the Security Council. The problem here is that Article 53(1) only refers to the Security Council making the requisite authorisation. However, if one accepts the practice of States interpreting the General Assembly's powers as including the ability to recommend enforcement action, as established above, it is not too much of a stretch also to imply that this practice necessitates an interpretation of Article 53(1) that allows regional organisations to act upon such recommendations. The necessary implication here would be to interpret Article 53(1) as requiring authorisation by the Security Council, only where such authorisation is possible – ie when the Security Council has not failed in its responsibility for the maintenance of international peace and security, and the General Assembly has not assumed its residual responsibilities in this regard.

This would not mean that upon Security Council failure regional organisations no longer have to seek authorisation from the UN. For their actions to remain compatible with Article 2(4), and the requirement of action being consistent with the Purposes of the United Nations, such authorisation is still necessary to render any use of force consistent with these Purposes.[324] In other words, Article 52(1) may be interpreted to be contingent on the Security Council's ability to authorise action, and therefore its responsibilities under the Charter, but Article 2(4) is not.

[321] Nolte (n 276) 635; White and Ülgen (n 141) 388–89; also noted, and rejected, by De Wet (n 97) 295.

[322] See eg Bröjmer and Ress (n 293) 865, who view this as conceivable, but not very realistic; Walter (n 277) 186–88.

[323] Bröjmer and Ress (n 293) 865 note that a limited blanket authorisation would be necessary to avoid fostering regional hegemony, as the Charter was designed to counter.

[324] As explained above, Chapter IV, section 3.3.

2.2.4. *Conclusions on Forcible Measures by Regional Organisations*

Generally, any use of force by a regional organisation, without the authorisation of the Security Council, would fall foul of the prohibition of force in Article 2(4) and the separate requirement under Article 53(1) that no enforcement action shall be undertaken without such authorisation. Regional mechanisms that provide for 'rights' or 'powers' in treaty law for intervention are not necessarily void due to their potential derogation from the *jus cogens* prohibition of force, so long as they remain consistent with the Purposes of the UN by ensuring that any intervention undertaken in accordance with such provisions is authorised by a competent organ of the United Nations. Indeed, any treaty provision that sought to grant a power to forcibly change borders (in violation of territorial integrity) or remove and replace a head of State (in violation of political independence) would automatically fall foul of Article 2(4) in any case.

Arguments in favour of a 'right' to use force and then seek ex post facto authorisation currently do not have convincing State practice to support such an ability. However, it is certainly possible for the Security Council to do this. The only problem is that any regional enforcement action undertaken prior to such authorisation will remain illegal until the Council authorises such action, if it ever does.

Fitting this into the tertiary responsibility to protect, this issue would be rendered moot in any case. This is because the tertiary responsibility only applies when the Security Council is paralysed or deadlocked and has failed in its responsibilities under the Charter. The next stage in the responsibility is then to seek action through the General Assembly – and, as highlighted above, this itself may come with political inaction. Where both UN organs fail to act, the use of force by a regional organisation cannot be authorised and would therefore be illegal. Emergency action that is taken in this regard might well be seen as legitimate or necessary in some limited situations, but it will remain illegal, and it is a risk for the organisation in question to gamble on the hope that the Security Council might resume its responsibilities in response to the organisation's efforts to protect populations.

This author does not believe that any apparent legitimacy or necessity arising out of such emergency action can justify an illegal use of force. To implement the responsibility to protect with illegal action not only taints the credibility of the concept, but also provides fuel for those who are willing to turn a blind eye and maintain deadlock or paralysis to criticise necessary action as hypocritical or having hidden agendas. If the responsibility to protect is to be implemented beyond the Security Council, it must be done so in a way that does not fundamentally undermine the concept, and perhaps even the United Nations itself. If illegality implies inaction in such circumstances, one solution is to change the law itself. Given that this is a monumental task and unlikely in the foreseeable future, the alternative would be to consider another approach. Non-forcible measures may well provide such an avenue.

2.3. Non-Forcible Coercive Measures

2.3.1. Regional 'Sanctions' Regimes

The ability of regional organisations or arrangements to utilise non-forcible coercive measures and 'sanctions' falls largely into two categories. Firstly, there are regional organisations whose constitutive treaties allow the imposition of these measures against their Member States. The logic here is that the Member States consent, via the treaty, to the possibility that sanctions be imposed against them – just as would be the case with Article 41 of the UN Charter.

Article 22(d) of the ECOWAS 1999 Protocol,[325] for example, charges ECOMOG with the enforcement of sanctions and embargoes. Similarly, the AU Constitutive Act provides for the imposition of sanctions in Article 23, with Article 23(2) specifically providing that

> [A]ny Member State that fails to comply with the decisions and policies of the Union may be subjected to other sanctions, such as the denial of transport and communications links with other Member States, and other measures of a political and economic nature to be determined by the Assembly.

The main issue that may arise here is whether the imposition of such measures could be considered 'enforcement action' for the purpose of Article 53(1) of the Charter, thus requiring Security Council authorisation for them to be imposed legally. This will be addressed below.

The second category includes regional organisations where the founding treaty provides for the power to take economic or coercive measures against *non-Member States*. The European Union's powers to implement measures under the Common Foreign and Security Policy (CFSP)[326] is a very clear example of this. For example, Article 215 of the Treaty on the Functioning of the European Union (TFEU)[327] provides for the imposition of restrictive measures which include 'the interruption or reduction, in part or completely, of economic and financial relations with one or more third countries' following the adoption of a decision to take such measures under the provisions of the CFSP in Chapter 2 of Title V, TEU.

Such provisions are clearly designed to render the measures compatible with the internal rules of the organisation – for example, it would allow derogation from certain trade rules for the European Union, enabling certain goods to be subject to restriction where this might not otherwise be allowed.[328] The issue

[325] ECOWAS 1999 Protocol (n 247), Art 22(d).

[326] See Consolidated Version of the Treaty on European Union (TEU) [2012] OJ C326/13, Title V.

[327] Consolidated Version of the Treaty on the Functioning of the European Union (TFEU) [2012] OJ C326/47.

[328] See also Arts 347 and 348 TFEU in the context of measures taken for the maintenance of international peace and security.

here is that these treaties cannot logically bind external States, and so any incompatibility of these measures with either non-intervention or other obligations in international law must be based upon a principle of general international law. In this case, as addressed in Chapter V, this would be the doctrine of countermeasures.

2.3.2. Compatibility with Non-Intervention/Countermeasures

The adoption of coercive measures by regional organisations against *non-Member States* would require legal justification where these measures go beyond retorsion. For example, as addressed in Chapter V, this would be the case where trade restrictions or embargoes fall foul of WTO rules and cannot be justified under the security exceptions therein.[329]

Generally, the doctrine of countermeasures could provide a legal basis for such action, allowing States or regional organisations to disregard certain international obligations as a countermeasure against another prior breach of an international obligation by the target State. The requirements of the doctrine of countermeasures have been covered in some detail in Chapter V, and so will not be repeated in detail here, but we shall apply these requirements to this tertiary responsibility to protect by regional organisations.

In the context of the responsibility to protect, it was argued in Chapter V that the commission of atrocity crimes automatically reaches the threshold of a 'serious' violation of an *erga omnes* obligation for the purpose of non-injured party countermeasures.[330] In this regard, this author argued that non-injured party countermeasures are permissible where atrocity crimes are occurring, or where there are serious and widespread violations of human rights as a 'precursor' to such atrocities occurring. When it comes to the *prevention* of the atrocities associated with the responsibility to protect, because countermeasures are only available in response to a breach of an international obligation, utilising such measures to *prevent* atrocities would be restricted to proportionate measures in response to violations of *erga omnes* obligations that have not yet amounted to actual atrocity crimes – hence the association with serious human rights abuses.

Again, although this seems to provide a limited response when it comes to *prevention*, rather than suppression, in any event it would be less likely (although not impossible) that the Security Council had failed in its secondary responsibility to protect if atrocity crimes were not yet occurring. When assessing the implementation of the *tertiary* responsibility to protect, following failure and deadlock, the situation is likely to be much more imminent, and so regional organisations would likely be able to respond to violations of international law

[329] See GATT (n 188) Art XXI; see also Chapter V, section 1.2.3.
[330] See Chapter V, section 2.3.2.

and *erga omnes* that had not yet occurred when the Security Council was seized of the matter.

As noted with regard to the taking of these measures by the General Assembly, the taking of countermeasures by a regional organisation also comes with additional safeguards. Briefly, the ILC's Articles on the Responsibility of International Organisations for Internationally Wrongful Acts[331] require: (i) that the substantive and procedural conditions required by international law are adhered to;[332] (ii) that the countermeasures are not inconsistent with the rules of the organisation;[333] (iii) that no appropriate means are available for otherwise inducing compliance with the obligations breached;[334] and (iv) that countermeasures may not be taken by an international organisation in response to a breach of the rules of that organisation, unless so provided for by those rules.[335] Just as point (ii) essentially meant that the General Assembly may not use a breach of the UN Charter as a countermeasure, regional organisations are equally restricted as regards their founding treaties.

As will be recalled, the substantive and procedural conditions in point (i), as outlined above, include: proportionality, reversibility, compatibility with fundamental norms and *jus cogens*, and the opportunity of the target State to be notified of such measures and comply with its obligations.[336]

Finally, in terms of the risks of abuse surrounding non-injured party countermeasures, acting through regional organisations arguably also provides another institutional safeguard.[337] Although actions by individual regional organisations do not harmonise the actions of the international community as well as the General Assembly or the Security Council would, it would certainly add to the legitimacy of the action, especially if conducted by a regional organisation within its own region.

2.3.3. Compatibility with Article 53(1)

The only contentious issue left to be addressed in this regard is whether the taking of such countermeasures by a regional organisation could be considered 'enforcement action' for the purposes of Article 53(1) of the Charter, and therefore require authorisation by the Security Council. This issue was debated by States in the 1960s.

[331] ILC Articles on Responsibility of International Organisations (n 204).
[332] ibid, Art 22(1) and Art 22(2)(a).
[333] ibid, Art 22(2)(b).
[334] ibid, Art 22(2)(c).
[335] ibid, Art 22(3).
[336] For States, see ILC Articles on State Responsibility (n 213) Art 43, and 49–53 generally; for international organisations, see ILC Articles on Responsibility of International Organisations (n 204) Arts 51–56.
[337] See the debate outlined in Chapter V, section 2.2; see also Dawidowicz (n 187) 415–16, 418.

Firstly, the Organization of American States (OAS) imposed sanctions against the Dominican Republic in response to certain interventions and interferences within Venezuela.[338] Walter makes note of events in the Security Council at this time, whereby the Soviet Union put forward a draft resolution seeking to 'authorise' these sanctions under Article 53 ex post facto, apparently attempting to create a precedent requiring non-military measures by regional organisations to be authorised under Chapter VIII, thus defining them as 'enforcement action'.[339] Indeed, this did spark some debate in the Security Council on the scope of Article 53, with the Soviet Union making comparisons to the measures available to the Council itself under Article 41, and the US and other States rejecting such arguments.[340] The Soviet draft was ultimately rejected, and a US draft which simply 'took note' of the OAS measures was adopted instead.[341]

In October 1962, President John F Kennedy announced that he would impose a naval quarantine on Cuba to compel the removal of Soviet missiles from the country.[342] At the same time, the OAS issued a Resolution[343] recommending that members

> take all measures, individually and collectively including the use of armed force, which they may deem necessary to ensure that the Government of Cuba cannot continue to receive from the Sino-Soviet Powers military material and related supplies which may threaten the peace and security of the Continent and to prevent the missiles in Cuba with offensive capability from ever becoming an active threat to the peace and security of the Continent.[344]

This action seems much more robust than the Dominican Republic example, but nevertheless is considered by some as an instance of action that does not fall within the purview of 'enforcement action' under Article 53(1).[345] In fact, the OAS did take other economic measures against Cuba in January 1962, but this was based upon the State's communist ideology, which the OAS States viewed

[338] See Final Act of the Sixth Meeting of Consultation of Minister of Foreign Affairs (20 August 1960) Doc OEA/SER.C/II.6, annexed to: Letter Dated 26 August 1960 from the Secretary-General of the Organization of American Sates to the Secretary-General of the United Nations (1 September 1960) UN Doc S/4476, 5.

[339] Walter (n 277) 136–37, 177–78; see also Abass (n 236) 44, 49.

[340] UNSC Verbatim Record, 894th Meeting (9 September 1960) UN Doc S/PV.894, generally, and at [49]–[76] for USSR; see also the debates in UNSC Verbatim Record, 895th Meeting (9 September 1960) UN Doc S/PV.895; and UNSC Verbatim Record, 893rd Meeting (8 September 1960) UN Doc S/PV.893.

[341] UNSC Res 156 (1960) (9 September 1960) UN Doc S/RES/156(1960).

[342] Presidential Proclamation 3504 of 23 October 1962, 27 Fed Reg 10401 (1962), available in (1963) 57(2) *American Journal of International Law* 512.

[343] See Letter Dated 23 October 1962 from the Secretary-General of the Organisation of American States Addressed to the Acting Secretary-General of the United Nations (25 October 1962) UN Doc S/5193, Annex.

[344] ibid, Annex, 3.

[345] See, generally, L Meeker, 'Defensive Quarantine and the Law' (1963) 57(3) *American Journal of International Law* 515, 521–22.

as inconsistent with their principles, and its support for 'subversive activities' within Venezuela.[346]

Bröjmer and Ress suggest that these instances in the 1960s indicate a conclusive interpretation of Article 53 as *not* including sanctions as 'enforcement' measures.[347] While the Cuban missile crisis perhaps does not warrant such a clear conclusion,[348] the discussions in the Security Council following the OAS sanctions against the Dominican Republic are certainly more convincing.

In any case, since the OAS measures of the 1960s, as O'Connell notes, '[e]conomic sanctions have been imposed often enough by individual states and organizations without prior Security Council authorization to suggest that the term "enforcement" no longer encompasses these cases'.[349] This much is now clear, especially considering the numerous examples of measures adopted by States discussed in Chapter V. Therefore, given the vast evidence of non-forcible measures being taken by States and regional agencies *without* Security Council authorisations, this author submits that such coercive measures are not to be considered 'enforcement action' within the meaning of Article 53(1).

2.4. Unilateral Coercive Measures

It is left for us to assess briefly whether non-forcible coercive methods might be taken by States unilaterally, rather than through a regional organisation, to implement the tertiary responsibility to protect.

2.4.1. Countermeasures by States

Since the law of countermeasures is, at its most fundamental level, applicable directly to States, it is certainly possible based upon the analysis above that a State may take countermeasures where the requisite conditions are met. For example, if a neighbouring State is committing atrocity crimes related to the responsibility to protect, there is no reason why this State cannot take proportionate countermeasures – for example, relating to trade between the two States, or even perhaps related to bilateral agreements that might be logistically and tactically important to the target State's objectives.

The concern here would be that the State's measures alone would either not be enough to be effective, or may be inconsistent with any wider regional or international measures that might be taken by regional organisations or

[346] On these points, see Gray (n 264) 397; Abass (n 236) 49; Akehurst (n 311) 190–92.

[347] Bröjmer and Ress (n 293) 860.

[348] Akehurst, for example, discusses the Cuban Missile Crisis and the quarantine therein as a possible use of force: (n 311) 197–203.

[349] ME O'Connell, 'The UN, NATO, and International Law After Kosovo' (2000) 22 *Human Rights Quarterly* 57, 64.

the General Assembly. Therefore, coordination is important with the tertiary responsibility to protect, and it might therefore be preferable to implement the tertiary responsibility to protect through the relevant institutions rather than on a unilateral basis.

Finally, in theory such measures might become available to a State unilaterally before the tertiary responsibility to protect is 'activated' – ie before the Security Council is even considered to have failed in its responsibilities. Although measures may be legally available, the compartmentalisation of different responsibilities under the 'responsibility to protect' provides further safeguards to prevent their abuse by acting as a clear framework as to *when* these measures should be available. In other words, the tertiary responsibility to protect is the opening of another compartment of the overall responsibility to protect toolbox. The tertiary responsibility reveals the tools that are available and who should consider using them – it does not necessarily determine which tools would be most appropriate in any given situation.

2.4.2. *A Note on the Supply of Arms, Equipment and Assistance*

Finally, it is worth briefly addressing the possibility of States (or even regional organisations for that matter) supplying arms, or non-lethal equipment, to rebel groups or armed factions within a State. This may be provided as either a measure to help defend civilians against a government committing, or about to commit, atrocity crimes, or as a measure to aid non-State groups in the suppression of such atrocities. This method became a contentious issue during the Syrian crisis, where some States and regional organisations have supplied funding, arms and assistance to the Syrian opposition.[350] Although it is beyond the scope of this book to consider this issue in detail, it is worth highlighting briefly, especially given the growing use of this tactic in recent crises, to demonstrate some possible implications of a tertiary responsibility to protect, and indeed the indicate paths that may be taken for future research in this regard.[351]

In terms of the supply of arms to rebel groups or factions in a civil war, even where there may be atrocities underway or threatened by the controlling government, international law is very clear that such assistance is a violation of international law. Firstly, in the *Nicaragua* case[352] the ICJ made very clear that the arming and training of armed groups could amount to a threat or use of force, contrary to the prohibition of force in international law.[353] The court

[350] For a detailed overview of this practice, see T Ruys, 'Of Arms, Funding and "Non-Lethal Assistance" – Issues Surrounding Third-State Intervention in the Syrian Civil War' (2014) 13 *Chinese Journal of International Law* 13.

[351] Indeed, academic investigation of this issue seems to be very limited.

[352] *Case Concerning Military and Paramilitary Activities in and against Nicaragua (Nicaragua v USA)* (Merits), Judgment of 27 June 1986, [1986] ICJ Rep 14.

[353] ibid, [228].

cited the *Declaration on Friendly Relations*[354] in support of this conclusion – in particular the provisions that declare an illegal use of force to include 'organizing or encouraging the organization of irregular forces or armed bands … for incursion into the territory of another State' and 'participating in acts of civil strife … in another State'.[355]

The supply of funding to such groups, however, does not violate the prohibition of force.[356] This funding does, on the other hand, constitute an intervention into the internal affairs of the State concerned, and thus a violation of the principle of non-intervention.[357] Indeed, the *Declaration on the Inadmissibility of Intervention*[358] could not be clearer:

> [N]o State shall organise, assist, foment, finance, incite or tolerate subversive, terrorist or armed activities directed towards the violent overthrow of the regime of another State, or interfere in civil strife in another State.[359]

The question therefore is whether the breach of this obligation – the principle of non-intervention – is permissible under the law of countermeasures. In such circumstances, the same safeguards would apply as above, including the requirement of a prior breach, and the principle of proportionality. Unfortunately, even at this point it seems unlikely that aid to rebels could be compatible with the law of countermeasures for one fundamental reason – such measures are generally not by their nature reversible, and so they fall foul of one of the key requirements of the doctrine.[360] Even if it could be considered proportionate in response to the commission of mass atrocity crimes, the funding of groups that are fighting (perhaps rightfully so) for a permanent change in their country – a change that would be irreversible even if the breaches of *erga omnes* obligations ceased. Of course, funding could well be stopped, but those funds would no longer be in the control of the regional organisation or State that originally supplied them, and so the violation of the principle of non-intervention would not be remedied and reversed as a true countermeasure could be.

As Ruys rightly highlights,[361] the principle of non-intervention itself is still elusive as a concept, and much more investigation is needed on this matter to determine the legality of these measures of intervention. Even with this in mind,

[354] UNGA Res 2625(XXV), *Declaration on Principles of International Law Concerning Friendly Relations and Co-operation among States in Accordance with the Charter of the United Nations*, Annex.

[355] See also Ruys (n 350) [26].

[356] *Nicaragua* (n 352) [228].

[357] ibid, [228], [242].

[358] UNGA Res 2131(XX), *Declaration on the Inadmissibility of Intervention in the Domestic Affairs of States and the Protection of Their Independence and Sovereignty* (21 December 1965) UN Doc A/RES/2131(XX).

[359] ibid, [2].

[360] See ILC Articles on State Responsibility (n 213) Art 49; ILC Articles on Responsibility of International Organisations (n 204) Art 51.

[361] Ruys (n 350) [62], [69].

there is also a question as to whether there exists a standalone principle in international law prohibiting intervention in civil war – on both sides.[362]

Regardless of the legal hurdles still to be assessed, the fundamental problem with this type of measure is that it is perhaps not an implementation of the tertiary responsibility to protect, but rather a 'delegation' or a 'passing of the buck' of this responsibility to groups within the State in crisis. For the State providing such assistance, it does not implement their responsibility to protect, and it certainly does not absolve them of it either.

3. CONCLUSIONS

Having established the detailed legal competences and powers of the General Assembly, regional organisations and States acting unilaterally, it may be concluded that there is legal space for the tertiary responsibility to protect to be adopted and implemented by the relevant actors.

In the event of failure by the Security Council of its legal responsibility to maintain international peace and security, there are legal avenues for the General Assembly to utilise forcible measures, and to implement non-forcible measures in line with the doctrine of countermeasures, where the requisite legal criteria is met. Acting through the General Assembly provides the best institutional legitimacy for such action, but mobilising the Assembly into action comes with its inherent political difficulties.

Where the General Assembly cannot be mobilised, there is still a residual responsibility on the international community as a whole that can be assumed through the actions of regional organisations. Forcible action by regional organisations remains illegal without the authorisation of either the Security Council or the General Assembly, and although there is a legal possibility of ex post facto authorisation in the event of emergency responses, it is certainly a risk for such organisations to take and for their action not to be subsequently authorised. Non-forcible measures once again can only be taken based upon the customary international law doctrine of countermeasures, where the threat or commission of atrocities results in violations of *erga omnes* obligations.

Therefore, having established that those actors with a residual responsibility to maintain international peace and security, and thus a responsibility to protect in applicable situations, are capable of implementing their responsibilities, there is not only *room* for the tertiary responsibility to protect, but there are also a great number of tools available for its implementation.

[362] ibid, [39]–[51].

VII

General Conclusions

AT THE TIME of writing this book, almost 75 years after the United Nations was created following the atrocities of the Second World War to save succeeding generations from the scourge of war, it is nothing short of a disappointment that an extensive study on the legal alternatives to protecting populations from some of those very same atrocities is necessary because the body tasked with maintaining international peace and security too often fails to uphold its responsibilities. It is also disheartening that the responsibility to protect – a concept driven by the desire to unite the international community and move forward in collective action – has also reached a point where we need to find a way past deadlock, indifference and inaction just 15 years after its adoption.[1]

But this study has not sought to offer simple solutions to complex problems – the main motivation of this book has been to offer an insight into bypassing the deadlock, and finding a new starting point from which the international community can move past its failures and proceed to uphold the fundamental promises of peace, protection and security that States undertook to deliver in 1945, and again in 2005. That new starting point, beyond inaction and failure, is the tertiary responsibility to protect.

When the UN Security Council fails in its responsibility to protect, and does not step in to take timely and decisive action in response to a State's manifest failure to protect its populations from genocide, war crimes, crimes against humanity and ethnic cleansing, this study has demonstrated that there is room for a 'tertiary' responsibility to protect beyond the inaction of the Security Council. This study has sought to demonstrate from the outset that the Security Council's responsibility to protect is more than a moral commitment to do the right thing. When a situation involving mass atrocities can be objectively determined to constitute at least a threat to international peace, the responsibility to protect overlaps with the Security Council's primary responsibility for the maintenance of international peace and security. This responsibility to maintain international peace and security, unlike the responsibility to protect, is much more powerful. While the responsibility to protect is currently a political undertaking, still to develop into a legal doctrine, the responsibility to maintain peace

[1] Even then, some of this deadlock and inaction began to transpire just six years after the World Summit, when the crisis in Syria divided the UN Security Council.

and security is enshrined in international law – in the UN Charter – and brings with it the force of a *duty*, and not just an aspiration, to do something when international peace and security is threatened.

In such circumstances, where the Security Council fails to act, either paralysed by the abuse of the veto power, or failing to respond to a colossal situation like Rwanda in 1994 or Myanmar in 2017, its responsibility for the maintenance of international peace and security does not cease with this inaction. Instead, there is a continuum of responsibility, whereby the responsibility continues to be assumed by the actors with residual responsibility. When this happens, the responsibility to protect also continues with it.

However, in order to determine whether this responsibility is actionable, the study set out to demonstrate two things. First, that there was 'room' for this responsibility, in the sense that there was legal space for the responsibility to continue. In this regard, the study investigated the use of force and non-forcible coercive measures as methods of implementing this tertiary responsibility. Considering the fact that the responsibility to protect requires a 'timely and decisive response' where 'peaceful measures are inadequate', the only way in which the responsibility to protect could continue beyond the Security Council, in this form, is where there are legal avenues to either utilise non-forcible measures, or the use of force.

Secondly, even where such legal avenues might exist, the actors with residual responsibility must also be capable of implementing these measures. Therefore, the second part of the investigation sought to demonstrate whether the relevant actors in question have the necessary legal competences to act, and that they were not bound by any other restrictions in international law to utilise the proposed measures.

By conducting an in-depth assessment of the prohibition of force, it was established that the original intentions of the drafters of the Charter sought to create a carefully constructed prohibition in Article 2(4) that was *not* general and all-encompassing in nature, but *did* prohibit the unilateral use of force. This interpretation, it was argued, is consistent with the practice of States today, whereby the main methods of using force that are *consistent* with this prohibition are in self-defence, and under the powers of the Security Council. However, the interpretation does leave room for force to be utilised by the UN General Assembly, where it can be established that it has the competence to do so. Therefore, one legal avenue was found that met the first test for establishing the tertiary responsibility to protect. In this sense, the study did not argue in favour of what the law *should* be, instead it argued in favour of what the law was *supposed* to be.

In terms of non-forcible coercive measures, the study investigated the use of measures such as asset freezes, trade restrictions and travel bans as a method of implementing the tertiary responsibility to protect beyond the Security Council. By conducting an assessment of the principle of non-intervention, the general legal position is that unilateral economic coercion is unlawful in general international law without a legal basis to utilise such measures. Furthermore, some of the coercive measures in question, even if they do not infringe the principle of non-intervention, may be outlawed by other international agreements, including bilateral agreements or multilateral treaties such as GATT.[2]

However, the book argues that many of these coercive measures can find a legal basis under the doctrine of countermeasures, and that there are special circumstances where these measures may be utilised by actors beyond the Security Council. In particular, where there has been a serious violation of an obligation *erga omnes* – in this case, a gross and systematic violation of human rights that may lead to mass atrocities, or the commission of atrocity crimes themselves – recent State practice shows evidence that the doctrine of countermeasures allows proportionate measures to be taken that would normally violate an international obligation, even where the party taking such measures has not been directly injured by the *erga omnes* breach. It was argued therein that such a breach is very likely to 'injure' the international community in any case by virtue of the type and seriousness of such obligations.

The doctrine of countermeasures also provides for procedural and substantive safeguards to prevent the misuse or abuse of this legal avenue, including: that the measures recommended must above all be proportionate; their purpose must be to induce the wrongdoing State to comply with its obligations under international law, and in that sense be reversible; they must not involve the use of force, or affect obligations such as the protection of fundamental rights, and norms of *jus cogens*; and, finally, the target of the countermeasures must be given an opportunity to comply with its obligations, and be notified of the decision to take such measures. Even including these safeguards, it was also argued that the framework of the tertiary responsibility to protect could provide an additional safeguard itself too by offering a guiding framework detailing when responsibility to maintain peace and security is assumed by an actor beyond the Security Council, and what measures are available at that point.

Finally, when establishing the actors with the competence to implement these measures, the tertiary responsibility to protect moves to the actor with the most relevant residual responsibilities and competences. At first, the General Assembly's residual responsibility is engaged within the UN system of collective security, because it has a residual responsibility to maintain international peace and security under the UN Charter. It was argued that the competences of the General Assembly provided sufficient grounds to demonstrate that the Assembly itself could recommend both forcible and non-forcible measures to implement the tertiary responsibility to protect. Forcible measures by the

[2] General Agreement on Tariffs and Trade 1947 (GATT 1947) (adopted 30 October 1947, entered into force 1 January 1948), 55 UNTS 187, amended by the Marrakech Agreement Establishing the World Trade Organization (adopted 15 April 1994, entered into force 1 January 1995), 1867 UNTS 154, and the General Agreement on Tariffs and Trade 1994 (GATT 1994) (adopted 15 April 1994, entered into force 1 January 1995) 1867 UNTS 187.

General Assembly are compatible with the prohibition of force in Article 2(4) because: (i) the powers of the Assembly, as established by the subsequent agreement and practice of States, constitute an inherent limitation of the territorial integrity and political independence of a State in accordance with the first part of the prohibition; and (ii) such measures are consistent with the Purposes of the United Nations, being a collective measure within the UN framework and by harmonising the actions of States in this regard. Non-forcible measures by the Assembly, because of the nature of recommendations as non-binding acts, and the lack of evidence demonstrating the ability of the Assembly to disregard States' other international obligations, must still be recommended in accordance with the doctrine of countermeasures.

Where the General Assembly does not assume its residual responsibilities, the responsibility to protect and the responsibility for the maintenance of international peace and security revert back to the international community as a whole. To implement this responsibility *beyond* the UN, it was argued that regional organisations and arrangements are the next most suitable and competent actors to implement this. While the use of force by such organisations would still be unilateral, and therefore fall foul of the prohibition of force, there is a controversial possibility that these organisations might take action in an emergency and receive authorisation from the United Nations *after the fact*. This course of action runs the risk of remaining an illegal use of force should authorisation not be granted, and so this was not considered a suitable avenue for implementing the tertiary responsibility to protect. Finally, the use of non-forcible measures, in line with the doctrine of countermeasures, may be used by regional organisations. By utilising such institutions, a further 'institutional safeguard' against the abuse of this doctrine exists, increasing the legitimacy of these measures and adding a further layer of protection against the abuse of the doctrine of countermeasures.

In sum, this study has sought to demonstrate that inaction in the face of atrocities such as genocide, war crimes, crimes against humanity and ethnic cleansing does not have to be weighed down by the paralysis of the UN Security Council. Not only is there *room* for the tertiary responsibility to protect, but in situations where the responsibility to maintain international peace and security is engaged, the tertiary responsibility to protect is a legal necessity.

This is the new starting point beyond inaction and failure – that the responsibility to maintain international peace and security continues as a legal responsibility beyond the UN Security Council. The General Assembly, or failing that the international community, can and must step in to *do something* when the most harrowing atrocities are occurring. It is not enough to remain inactive or silent, and it is certainly not enough to simply condemn the Security Council's own failures without assuming its responsibilities. When the tertiary responsibility to protect is engaged, it has moved past the point of strongly worded statements and commitments to diplomacy – these tools are certainly necessary in the long-term resolution of a crisis, but they alone do not prevent or halt atrocities when peaceful means are inadequate and 'timely and decisive' action is required. This study does not attempt to stipulate what action should be taken – each crisis requires its own case-by-case response. The tertiary responsibility to protect does, however, require that something more is done.

Should the warnings to humanity fall on deaf ears, and should Auschwitz–Birkenau continue to cry out in despair, then perhaps it is *our* responsibility to demonstrate *our* revolt against this inaction and do whatever is in *our* own legal powers to encourage those with the responsibility to protect to step up and stick to their word. Responsibility is a continuum, and it does not cease to exist with failure.

Index

www.ingramcontent.com/pod-product-compliance
Ingram Content Group UK Ltd.
Pitfield, Milton Keynes, MK11 3LW, UK
UKHW021909150926
475560UK00003B/274

9 781509 930807